THE Location OF SODOM

Key Facts for Navigating the Maze of Arguments for the Location of the Cities of the Plain

Second Edition

DAVID E. GRAVES

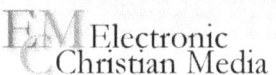
Electronic Christian Media
Toronto, Canada
2018

Unless otherwise indicated, all Scripture quotations are from the *ESV*® Bible (*The Holy Bible, English Standard Version*®), copyright © 2001 by Crossway Bibles, a publishing ministry of Good News Publishers. Used by permission. All rights reserved.

Italics within Scripture quotations indicate emphasis added.

The Location of Sodom: Key Facts for Navigating the Maze of Arguments for the Location of the Cities of the Plain. B&W
Includes bibliographic references and indexes.
Copyright © 2021 by David E. Graves
Hardcover Rev 1: Feb, 2021; Rev 2: Sept, 2021

Published by Electronic Christian Media, Moncton, NB, Canada

ISBN-13: 9780994806031
ISBN-10: 0994806035

1. Dead Sea (Israel and Jordan)-Antiquities 2. Sodom (Extinct city) 3. Bible-O. T. Genesis XVII-XIX-Criticism, interpretation, etc. 4. Bible. O.T. Antiquities. I. Graves, David E. II. Title
BISAC History/Expeditions and Discoveries Category HIS051000

All rights reserved. No portion of this publication may be reproduced, stored in a retrieval system, or transmitted in any form (i.e., electronic, scanning, photocopy, or recording) without the written permission of the publisher. The only exception is brief excerpts for reviews.

Printed in the United States of America.

Interior Book Design: David E. Graves
Cover Design: David E. Graves

Centre Front – Middle Bronze Tell el-Yahudieh ware juglet from Tall el-Ḥammâm (Area L). Photo by David E. Graves
Bottom Front – Madaba map mosaic indicating the possible site of Sodom. Photo by David E. Graves
Background Front Cover – Hebrew text of the Dead Sea Scroll Messianic Testimony (4Q175) located in the Amman Museum, Jordan. Photo by David E. Graves
Background Back Cover – Madaba map mosaic indicating the Byzantine location of Zoar. Photo by David E. Graves

Picture Acknowledgements
All photographs are by the author, unless otherwise indicated. For the credits of the photographs used in the charts see *Credits and Permissions.*

Charts
David E. Graves: all charts

Maps
All Maps are by the author, unless otherwise indicated.
Ritmeyer Archaeological Design: No. 65
Hugh Barnes, The Follow the Pots Project: No. 66

*To
Dr. Steven Collins
and
Dr. Bryant Wood*

*For modeling Christian scholarship
and
the privilege of their friendship.*

Intentionally Left Blank

Acknowlegements

This book owes a great debt of gratitude to many friends and family whose profession and passion for the Bible and archaeology have contributed to its completion. First among them is Bryant Wood, who long ago inspired my interest in the Cities of the Plain. Second, is Steven Collins, who has allowed me to have the privilege of working as a square and field supervisor at Tall el-Ḥammâm. Their dedication to biblical truth and archaeology has truly been inspiring.

Another individual not to be forgotten is Scott Stripling, a friend and colleague who dug with me at Tall el-Ḥammâm, Jordan for several seasons and is now the director of the excavation at Khirbet el-Maqatir, where Bryant Wood had been director for many years. His insights, over the years, have been greatly appreciated.

And thanks, are also due to Glen Ruffle who performed the bulk of the proof reading of the final manuscript. His eye to detail and prompt attention to minor issues is much appreciated.

I wish to thank Kimberly Day, the resource sharing librarian, at the Jerry Falwell Library for her help in locating journal articles and books for my research.

I also wish to express my gratitude to Leen Ritmeyer, Michael Luddeni, Morag M. Kersel, and Meredith S. Chesson for their advice and permission to use their fine work in photographs, illustrations, and images.

Lastly, I wish to express my thankfulness to my wife Irina for her helpful comments, deep love, care, and patience during the long hours of writing and editing this work.

Sola Deo Gloria

TABLE OF CONTENTS

ACKNOWLEDGEMENTS V
TABLE OF CONTENTS VI
INDEX OF IMAGES XIII
ABBREVIATIONS XVIII
    HEBREW BIBLE / OLD TESTAMENT XVIII
    NEW TESTAMENT XVIII
    ANCIENT SOURCES XVIII
    MODERN SOURCES XIX
PREFACE XXII
PREFACE TO SECOND EDITION XXIII
INTRODUCTION 25
    MAXIMALIST OR MINIMALIST VIEWPOINT 27
        Minimalist View 27
        Maximalist View 29
        Summary 30
CHAPTER ONE – PRIMARY SOURCES 31
    BIBLICAL REFERENCES TO SODOM 31
        Genesis 10:19 31
        Genesis 13:3, 10–12 32
        Genesis 14:1–12 33
        Genesis 19:24–28 35
        Deuteronomy 29:22–24 35
        Deuteronomy 34:1–3 35
        Isaiah 15:4–7; Jeremiah 48:4, 34 36
        Ezekiel 16:46 37
    ANCIENT TEXTUAL REFERENCES 37
        Ebla Tablets (ca. 2500–ca. 2250 BC) 37
        Ugaritic texts (ca. 1250 BC) 40
    TRADITIONAL REFERENCES 40
        Philo (ca. 20 BC–AD 50) 41
        Strabo (64/63 BC–ca. AD 24) 42
        Josephus (ca. AD 37–100) 42
        Tacitus (AD 56 – after 117) 43
        Tertullian (ca. AD 160–ca. 225) 44
        Pionius (AD ?–250) 44
        Gaius Julius Solinus (early 3rd cent. AD) 45
        Eusebius (AD 260/265–339/340) 46
        Severus, Bishop of Sodom (AD 325) 47

Egeria (late 4th century AD) *49*
Madaba Map (AD 542 and 570) *50*

CHAPTER TWO – A BRIEF HISTORY OF RESEARCH 53
SOUTHERN THEORY 54
NORTHERN THEORY 58

CHAPTER THREE – PRELIMINARY FACTS 61
FACT 1: SODOM IS NOT A FICTION FOR WOOD AND COLLINS 61
FACT 2: THE SST IS NOT A NEW VIEW 62
Thomas Fuller (1650) *63*
Peter Graham (1836) *63*
William Francis Lynch (1848) *63*
Louis Félix de Saulcy (1851) *64*
Samuel Wolcott (1868) *64*
Georg Heinrich Ewald (1883) *65*
Charles Simon Clermont-Ganneau (1886) *65*
Charles Warren (1899) *65*
William F. Albright (1924) *66*
James Penrose Harland (1943) *67*
David Noel Freedman (1978) *67*
William H. Shea (1983) *67*
Gordon J. Wenham (1998) *68*
FACT 3: THE NST IS NOT A NEW VIEW 68
Charles William Wilson (1869) *68*
Edward Henry Palmer (1871) *69*
Henry Baker Tristram (1873) *69*
Selah Merrill (1876, 1881) *69*
William F. Birch (1879) *71*
Claude Reignier Conder (1879–1883) *71*
William M. Thomson (1882–85) *72*
George Grove (1884) *73*
John Cunningham Geikie (1887) *73*
E. Power (1930) *74*
Père Alexis Mallon (1929–1934) *74*
FACT 4: WOOD BELIEVES THAT BED IS SODOM 75
FACT 5: ALBRIGHT DID NOT BELIEVE THAT BED WAS SODOM 75
FACT 6: RAST AND SCHAUB DID NOT BELIEVE THAT BED WAS SODOM 77
FACT 7: COLLINS BELIEVES THAT TEH IS SODOM 77
FACT 8: PUBLICATIONS PRIOR TO 2006 DO NOT INCLUDE COLLINS' TEH
RESEARCH 79

CHAPTER FOUR – METHODOLOGY FACTS (PROPER SCIENTIFIC
METHOD) 80
FACT 9: THE *A PRIORI* METHOD IS GOOD SCIENCE 80
FACT 10: THE SERIAL GEOGRAPHY OF THE BIBLE IS RELIABLE 81
FACT 11: FEW BIBLICAL SITES HAVE EVER BEEN IDENTIFIED USING AN
INSCRIPTION 82

FACT 12: WOOD HAS NEVER EXCAVATED BeD 83
FACT 13: THE EARLY READ OF THE TeH STRATIGRAPHY WAS DUE TO MODERN
  MILITARY ACTIVITY 83
FACT 14: A SURFACE SURVEY IS DIFFERENT TO AN EXCAVATION 85

CHAPTER FIVE – HERMENEUTIC FACTS (PROPER INTERPRETIVE METHOD) 86

FACT 15: THE KEY PASSAGE ON SODOM'S GEOGRAPHY IS GEN 13:1–12 86
FACT 16: GENESIS 14:10 IS REFERRING TO THE LOCATION FOR THE BATTLE OF
  THE MESOPOTAMIAN KINGS, NOT THE LOCATION OF THE CITIES OF
  THE PLAIN 87
FACT 17: ZEBOIIM IS PLURAL IN HEBREW 88
FACT 18: HEBREW DOES NOT HAVE THE WORDS NORTH, SOUTH, EAST OR
  WEST 89
FACT 19: EZEKIEL IS NOT BIBLICAL NARRATIVE 90
FACT 20: JEREMIAH 50:35–46 IS PROPHETIC LITERATURE 91
FACT 21: THERE IS A SALT CURSE MENTIONED IN THE BIBLE 92

CHAPTER SIX – GEOGRAPHY FACTS (THE LOCATION) 94

FACT 22: THE JORDAN VALLEY WAS VISIBLE FROM BETWEEN BETHEL AND AI 94
FACT 23: SODOM WAS LOCATED ON THE PLAIN (*KIKKĀR*) OF THE JORDAN................. 96
FACT 24: THE EXACT LOCATION OF THE VALLEY OF SIDDIM IS NOT KNOWN 98
FACT 25: BeD AND TeH ARE BOTH LOCATED IN THE GREAT RIFT VALLEY 99
FACT 26: SMOKE FROM BOTH TeH AND BeD WOULD HAVE BEEN VISIBLE FROM
  HEBRON 100
FACT 27: TeH IS ALSO ABEL-SHITTIM 100
FACT 28: TeH IS ALSO LIVIAS 101
FACT 29: ABRAHAM WAS GIVEN THE LAND OF CANAAN 102
FACT 30: FOR THE SST ADVOCATES, GEN 14:1–14 WOULD REQUIRE
  CHEDORLAOMER TO HAVE GONE BACK ON HIS TRACKS 102
FACT 31: THE SOUTHERN DEAD SEA REGION LOOKS CURSED 103
FACT 32: SHEA'S IDENTIFICATION OF CITIES BASED ON THE EBLAITE
  GEOGRAPHIC ATLAS IS SUSPECT 104
FACT 33: THERE ARE SEVERAL POSSIBLE LOCATIONS FOR ZOAR 105
  Southern Zoar – Ghor eṣ-Ṣafi *105*
  Northern Zoar 1 – Tall Iktanu *107*
  Northern Zoar 2 – Serâbît el-Mushaqqar *108*
  Northern Zoar 3 – On the Arnon River *109*
FACT 34: LOT'S CAVE IS LOCATED ON THE MADABA MAP 109

CHAPTER SEVEN – CHRONOLOGY FACTS (THE TIME PERIOD) 112

FACT 35: NOT ALL ARCHAEOLOGISTS APPROACH BIBLICAL NUMBERS IN THE
  SAME WAY 112
FACT 36: CONSERVATIVE SCHOLARS DEBATE THE DATE OF THE EXODUS 113
FACT 37: MOST MAXIMALISTS BELIEVE THAT THE PATRIARCHS LIVED IN THE
  MIDDLE BRONZE AGE 114
FACT 38: BeD WAS DESTROYED IN THE EB III BUT WAS REOCCUPIED IN EB IV 115
FACT 39: BeD AND NUMEIRA WERE DESTROYED AT DIFFERENT TIMES 118

Fact 40: TeH was destroyed in the MBA and lay unoccupied for over 500 years 120

CHAPTER EIGHT – ARCHAEOLOGY FACTS (MATERIAL EVIDENCE) 121

Fact 41: TeH is the largest EB site and third largest MB site in the southern Levant 121
Fact 42: BeD is the largest EB site in the Southern Dead Sea region 125
Fact 43: BeD and Numeira are the only inhabited towns in the southern Dead Sea region in the EBA 126
   1. Bâb edh-Dhrâ' (see Fig 11, 26) 126
   2. Numeira (see Fig. 30) 127
   3. eṣ-Ṣafi 127
   4. Feifa 128
   5. Khirbet al-Khanazir 129
Fact 44: There are four MB sites in the Jordan Valley with evidence of destruction 129
   1. Tall el-Ḥammâm (see Fig. 10, 12) 129
   2. Tall Nimrin (see Fig. 36) 130
   3. Tall al-Kafrayn (see Fig. 38) 130
   4. Tall Bleibel and Tall el-Musṭâḥ 131
Fact 45: There is no LBA architectural occupation in the Jordan Valley 131
   Tall el-Ḥammâm 132
   Tall Nimrin 132
   Tall al-Kafrayn 133
   Tall Iktanu 133
   Tell Al Sultan (Jericho) 133
   Tall Bleibel (Tall Bulaybil) 134
   Tall el-Musṭâḥ (Tall al-Musṭâḥ) 134
Fact 46: TeH is not MB Heshbon 135
Fact 47: The Pentapolis are not all mentioned together in the Ebla Tablets, and most doubt they are listed at all 136
Fact 48: There are reports of a Minoan connection at TeH 138

CHAPTER NINE – DESTRUCTION FACTS (MATERIAL EVIDENCE) 140

Fact 49: Both sites provide fiery destruction evidence 140
   Bâb edh-Dhrâ' 140
   Tall el-Ḥammâm 141
Fact 50: Both sites have a city gate complex that was destroyed 142
   Bâb edh-Dhrâ' 142
   Tall el-Ḥammâm 143
Fact 51: Human remains have been found at both sites 145
   Bâb edh-Dhrâ' 145
   Tall el-Ḥammâm 145
Fact 52: There are various theories for the destruction of the Pentapolis 146
   Destroyed by a volcano 146
   Destroyed by an earthquake 146

  Destroyed by liquefaction *147*
  Destruction by an air burst *147*
  Conclusion *148*
 FACT 53: THE CEMETERY AT BED WAS BURNED 148
 FACT 54: SHOOTING FLAMING ARROWS INTO THE AIR WAS COMMONLY USED BY
   ENEMIES IN THE ANE 150
 FACT 55: MYSTERIOUS CLINKERS, IDENTIFIED AS TRINITITE, WERE
   DISCOVERED AT TEH 151

CHAPTER TEN – GEOLOGY FACTS (MATERIAL EVIDENCE) 152

 FACT 56: THE DEAD SEA IS AT ITS LOWEST POINT IN HISTORY AND THERE ARE
   NO EXPOSED RUINS 152
 FACT 57: BITUMEN IS FOUND ALL AROUND THE DEAD SEA 154
  South *156*
  North *156*
  East *156*
  West *157*
  Location of bitumen pits *158*
 FACT 58: JEBEL USDUM IS NOT SODOM OR LOT'S WIFE 158
 FACT 59: TEH IS WELL WATERED 159
 FACT 60: THE SOUTHERN JORDAN VALLEY WAS WELL-WATERED IN ANCIENT
   TIMES 159
 FACT 61: THE DEAD SEA EXISTED PRIOR TO GENESIS 19 160
 FACT 62: THERE IS PALEO-BOTANICAL EVIDENCE AT BOTH SITES 160
 CONCLUSION 161

CHAPTER ELEVEN – TESTIMONY FACTS 162

 TESTIMONIES SUPPORTING BÂB EDH-DHRÂ' 162
  Todd Bolen *162*
  Clyde Billington *163*
  Eugene H. Merrill *163*
  J. Randall Price *163*
 TESTIMONIES NOT SUPPORTIVE OF BED 163
  Eric Cline *163*
 TESTIMONIES SUPPORTING TALL EL-ḤAMMÂM 164
  Norman L. Geisler and Joseph M. Holden (2013) *164*
  Robert A. Mullins *164*
  James D. Tabor *164*
  Anson F. Rainey *165*
  Hershel Shanks *165*
  Amahai Mazar *165*
  Leen Ritmeyer *165*
  William J. Fulco *166*

CHAPTER TWELVE – SUMMARY 167

 BACKGROUND 167
 NOT A DEBATE OVER MINIMALISM 167
 MOOT ARGUMENTS 168

TABLE OF CONTENTS

    Both were large cities *168*
    Both have a large cemetery *168*
    Both have evidence of a fiery destruction *168*
    Both were well-watered *169*
    Both are in the Great Rift Jordan Valley *170*
    Both are visible from the Hebron plateau *171*
    There are not two destructions of Sodom mentioned in the Bible. *171*
    Both were resettled *172*
    Both have possible locations for Zoar *172*
    The Ebla Tablets do not help *173*
  COMPELLING ARGUMENTS 174
    Serial Geography is Central in Determining the Location of the Pentapolis *174*
    The Chronology fits with the Date of the Patriarchs *176*
    Most maximalists believe that the Patriarchs lived in the Middle Bronze Age *179*
    Logical Conclusion *180*

CHAPTER THIRTEEN – CONCLUSION 183

MAPS 185

  MAP 1: PROPOSED SITES FOR THE CITIES OF THE PLAIN 185
  MAP 2: PROPOSED NORTHERN SITES FOR THE THE CITIES OF THE PLAIN 186
  MAP 3: PROPOSED SOUTHERN SITES FOR THE THE CITIES OF THE PLAIN 186
  MAP 4: DEAD SEA FAULT LINES AND CHEDORLAOMER'S CAMPAIGN OF THE
         REGION 188
  MAP 5: BORDERS OF THE PROMISED LAND 188
  MAP 6: BOUNDARIES OF PALESTINAE 190
  MAP 7: LOCATION OF THE TARPITS AROUND THE DEAD SEA 191
  MAP 8: *KIKKAR* REGION NORTH OF THE DEAD SEA 192
  MAP 9: AREA AROUND TALL EL-ḤAMMÂM 193
  MAP 10: AREA AROUND BÀB EDH-DHRÂʿ 193
  MAP 11: SITE PLAN OF TALL EL-ḤAMMÂM 194
  MAP 12: SITE PLAN OF FEIFA 195
  CHART 1: ARCHAEOLOGICAL PERIODS 197
  CHART 2: COMPARATIVE ARCHAEOLOGICAL DATING 199
  CHART 3: THE REGIONS FOR THE CHURCH COUNCIL REPRESENTATIVES 201
  CHART 4: PROPOSED DATING FOR THE PATRIARCHS 203
  CHART 5: NORTHERN LOCATION SITES 206
  CHART 6: SOUTHERN LOCATION SITES 210
  CHART 7: TIMELINE 214

GLOSSARY 216

BIBLIOGRAPHY 219

INDEX OF SUBJECTS 248

Index of Images

1. The Destruction of Sodom and Gomorrah, Oil on Canvas. John Martin, 1852. 25
2. Tall el-Ḥammâm and the area around the Tall which is believed, by the author, to be Livias. The white arrows indicate the location of two hot springs. Livias was famous for its hot springs. 26
3. Photographic reproduction of the Great Isaiah Scroll, the best preserved of the biblical scrolls found at Qumran. Isaish spoke of Sodom in 15:4–7. 31
4. View of the Dead Sea from Machaerus in Jordan looking over to En-Gendi, Israel. 33
5. One of 1800 clay Ebla tablets dating to between 2500 and 2250 BC discovered in 1974–75 during the excavations of the ancient city of *Tell Mardikh* (Ebla). Together with the Mari tablets they give a clearer picture of life in the ancient Near East. 37
6. The Sodom apple (*Calotropis procera* or *Asclepias gigantea*) is a flowering plant native to North Africa which produces a green pod that resembles an apple. However, when squeezed it pops and sends a bitter poisonous white powder into the air. Josephus has the apple "dissolve into smoke and ashes," since it is growing near the site of Sodom (Josephus *J.W.* 4.8.4; Tacitus *Hist.* 5.6; Bede *Loc. Sanct.* 11.317). 45
7. Close up view of Tall el-Ḥammâm (Sodom?, Abel Shittim, and Livias) from the top of Mt. Nebo. According to Egeria the land of the Sodomites and Segor was just to the left of Livias (see Fig. 10). 47
8. A section of the Madaba map marked as *Balak Zoora*, identified by the six palm trees, indicating the location of Byzantine Zoar (*Segor* or *eṣ-Ṣafi*) at the southern end of the Dead Sea. Lot's cave is also identified above Zoar. Notice that there is no Lisan (tongue) peninsula on the map as it had dried up in the Byzantine period much as it has today. 48
9. Segment of the Madaba Map found on the floor of St. George's church in Madaba, Jordan indicating the unidentified Site One and Two (see Fig. 13). 51
10. Jordan Valley (*Kikkar*) seen from the Jordanian side. Tall el-Hammam (Sodom?) is seen in the center, with Tall Kifrein (Gomorrah?) also visible on the plain. 53
11. Western fortifications of Bâb edh-Dhrâʿ overlooking the southern Jordan Valley. This is the southern candidate for the location of Sodom. 54
12. View from Tall Habbassa overlooking Tall el-Ḥammâm and the Middle Bronze age city-state area around the Tall. Jericho is directly across the Jordan Valley and Tell Kefrein is visible to the right below the arrow. 58
13. A cargo boat on the Dead Sea as seen on the Madaba Map, from the 6th cent. AD. The two unnamed sites in the upper left hand corner are possibly Sodom and Gomorrah (see Fig. 9). 61
14. View of Israel from Mt. Nebo. The plaque indicates the location of various sites on the opposite side of the Jordan. The southern Dead Sea area and Bâb edh-Dhrâʿ are not visible from this location on top of Mt. Nebo. 62

15. The Jordan Valley (*kikkār*). Several archaeological sites are identified which were cities on the plain in the Early and Middle Bronze Age. The NST places Sodom at Tall el-Hammam, Gomorrah at Tall Kefrein and Admah at Tall Nimrin. 70

16. Royal dedicatory inscription from the Philistine city of Ekron, discovered in 1996. This Philistine (Phonecian) script partially translates as: "The temple (which) he built, *'kyš* [Akhayus] son of Padi, son of *Ysd*, son of Ada, son of *Ya'ir*, ruler of Ekron, for *Ptgyh* his lady [Asherah?]" [Gitin, Dothan, and Naveh]. This is the only biblical city (Zeph 2:4) for which there is a primary inscription. Dan, Gezer, Gibeon, Hazor, Hebron, Shiloh, and Jerusalem only have a secondary inscription identifying their location. Rather than inscriptions, geographic indicators are more often used to locate biblical sites. 80

17. The author, standing in front of a cut-away section of the city wall at Tall el-Ḥammâm, in season 1 (2006). The military cut a road through the wall and exposed this cross section, which was later clarified. At my feet is the location of a 0.5 m thick MB burn layer in the mud brick section of the city wall, dated by a MB handle (inset photo) at the same location (see Fig. 40, 41). The IA stone wall was built over the earlier burned MB mud brick wall. 84

18. Torah displayed in the former Glockengasse Synagogue in Cologne. 86

19. One of many pillars of salt around the Dead Sea which have become known as Lot's wife (not actually his wife). This pillar is on the Jordanian side of the Dead Sea north of the Lisan. 93

20. Jordan valley visible from Mt. Nebo, Jordan. The north end of the Dead Sea is visible on the left. From this location Moses was given the view of the promised land and Egeria the land of the Sodomites around Livias. 94

21. The view of the well-watered plain (*kikkar*) in the distance as seen from between Bethel and Ai. The Cities of the Plain, proposed by the NST, are clearly visible from this location. However, the southern end of the Dead Sea is not visible. 95

22. Burnt gate at Khirbet el-Maqatir (Ai?) from the time of Joshua (Late Bronze 1400 BC). The Bible states that Joshua burned the gate. 96

23. Livia Drusilla, (58 BC-AD 29, Tiberius' mother). After her formal adoption into the Julian family in AD 14, she was deified by Claudius and became known as Julia Augusta. Livias (the city) was given her name by Herod Antipas in the 1st cent. AD. 101

24. Roman bath complex excavated in 2011–2012 from Tall el-Ḥammâm, Jordan. The site is believed to be Livias and may have originally been Herod Antipas' bath complex. The building this room was located in measures 35 x 40 metres. 102

25. The author standing beside the Roman mile marker indicating 6 Roman miles to Livias. Mt. Nebo museum, Jordan. 102

26. The cemetery at Bab edh-Dhra overlooking the Dead Sea below and the salt plains. Many of the shaft tombs have been robbed out by local looters. 103

27. Drawing of the Monastery of St. Lot at Deir 'Ain 'Abata, Jordan, on display in the Museum at the Lowest Place on Earth at es-Safi. 110

28. The restoration of the 7th cent. Byzantine church in front of Lot's Cave. 111

29. Early Bronze pottery identified by the characteristic ledge handles on their kraters and double handled cooking pots both display a puncture decoration around the rim. from 112

30. The site of Numeira looking west over the evaporation ponds of the Dead Sea and the Arab Potash Company (APC) on the shore. 118

Index of Images

31. Early Bronze age pottery displayed as it was discovered in the charnel house tombs at the Bâb edh-Dhrâʿ cemetery. Bones were placed in the centre of the room with the skulls lined around them and the various household pottery stacked around the perimiter of the room. The bedouin would drop off their decomposed deseased to be deposited at the Bâb edh-Dhrâʿ cemetery. 121

32. Chart showing the relative sizes of major cities in the Levant during the Late Chalcolithic through to the IB II periods, ca. 4000–2000 BC. Bâb edh-Dhrâʿ at this time would have been 9–10 acres, the size of Jerusalem and Jericho. 122

33. Chart showing relative sizes of major cities in the Levant during the MB1-2 (MB IIA-B-C), ca. 2000-1540 BC. During the MB Age Bâb edh-Dhrâʿ did not exist. 123

34. Hoard of pottery excavated in an undisturbed dolmen near Tall el-Ḥammâm in 2011. The vessels were identified as Early Bronze and Middle Bronze. 124

35. The author sitting in front of a dolmen by the blue mosque next to Tall el-Ḥammâm. 125

36. The fenced site of Tall Nimrin overlooking the local school. 130

37. Tall Bleibel is the small hill in the foreground. It is an archaeological site that has been identified with Zeboiim north. It is located on the north side of the road that descends to the Jordan Valley. Tall Mustah (not shown), the southern of the two Zeboiim sites, is located on the south side of the road that descends from the highland plateau. Today an army post is located at the site of Tall Mustah. 131

38. The site of Tall al-Kafrayn. 132

39. Early Bronze 3 bull's head motif with downturned hornes on a storages jar with a rope decoration on the neck. The horn orinentation is typically found in Minoean culture. 138

40. Wood char from a 0.5 m thick MB burn layer in the mud brick section of the city wall at Tall el-Ḥammâm, in season 1 (2006), dated by a MB handle (left of the dustpan) at the same location (see Fig. 17). The military cut a road through the wall and exposed this cross section, which was being clarified. 140

41. Wood char from a 0.5 m thick MB burn layer in the mud brick section of the city wall at Tall el-Ḥammâm, in season 1 (2006), dated by a MB handle (left of the dustpan) at the same location (see Figs. 17 and 40). The evidence of destruction is consistent through the tall in every square where there is an MB strata. 141

42. Drawing of the 10 acre site of Bâb edh-Dhrâʿ idenifying the gate, cemetery and terranced houses. 143

43. The city gate at Bab Edh-Dhra. 143

44. Reconstruction of the TeH MB gate complex discovered in 2012 and drawn by L. Ritmeyer from the archaeological data provided by archaeologists. Note the inside pillared room of the gate chamber. This was distictive Minoan cultural influence. 144

45. Human remains in the Middle Bronze Age destruction layer at TeH. 145

46. A burial installation called a "charnel house" located in the cemetery at Bâb edh-Dhrâʿ used during the urban occupation period (EB III). Dr. John Moore (foreground) and the author (background) are standing on the outside wall of the mudbrick house. It originally contained burned human remains and some 900 pottery vessels. 149

THE LOCATION OF SODOM

47. The 4.5-inch-long clinker of melted pottery (large piece to the left in the photo) that was discovered in the MB layer at TeH. To the right are two smaller pieces of trinitite from ground zero at Trinity New Mexico. 151

48. Southern end of the Dead Sea with visible salt deposits along the shore. This photo was taken in 2010. Today the Dead Sea is at its lowest point in history. There are no visible signs of EB or MB ruins comparable with Sodom along the shore. There Roman and Byzantine harbor ruins. 152

49. The Dead Sea elevations over an 8-year period. See Fig. 48 for 2010 levels. Today the Dead Sea is at its lowest point in history due to modern irrigation and industrial plants along the southern end of the Dead Sea. There are no visible signs of EB or MB ruins comparable with Sodom along the shore. 153

50. Natural formed ashphalt called Bitumen collected along the shore of the Dead Sea. 155

51. A sink hole on the eastern side of the Dead Sea during a visit in February 2014, although the majority of these are located on the western side. 157

52. Southern end of the Dead Sea seen from Numeira with white salt deposits visible along the shore. The Arab Potash Company (APC) is visible to the right and is primarily involved in harvesting minerals from the Dead Sea. It is the eighth largest potash producer worldwide by volume of production and the sole Arab producer of potash. The company also produces magnesium chloride, industrial salts, de-icers, bath salts, table salt, and raw materials for the cosmetic industry. Visible in the distance are the solar ponds where the water is evaporated to leave behind the raw materials. There are no visible signs of EB or MB ruins comperable with Sodom along the shore. 162

53. Tall el-Ḥammâm, Jordan, which is the likely location for Sodom (MBA). Later in the Late Bronze age it became Abel-shittim (the meadow of the acacias), a Solomonic administrative site in the Iron Age and in the Roman Period was part of the city of Livias. An important biblical site throughout history and one of the largest strategic sites in the Levant 167

54. The balk of a room in the monumental palace in the Upper Area of Tall el-Ḥammâm 2015 (season 10) with the stratigraphy marked for the various loci. The destruction layer (black line Locus 27) of the Middle Bronze age period is clearly visible in the middle of the balk with the Late Bronze occupation sitting above the Middle Bronze age walls. A distinctive palace ware type pottery was recovered from these rooms in subsequent seasons. If this is Sodom, this would be part of King Bara's palace (Gen 14:2) 183

55. **MAP 1:** Proposed sites for the northern and southern location of the Cities of the Plain. 185

56. **MAP 2:** The proposed northern locations for the Cities of the Plain. The *kikkār* is indicated by the circle in the centre. The altitude in the Jordan Valley is given in negative numbers. In the upper left hand corner, the several options for Bethel and Ai are indicated; though these do not affect the general location from where Lot looked East across the *kikkār* to see the city of Sodom. 186

57. **MAP 3:** Proposed southern locations for the Cities of the Plain. The southern basin of the Dead Sea was once covered by water but is now an artificial industrial pond filled with water from the northern basin and used to extract salts and minerals. 187

58. **MAP 4:** representing the fault lines and the level of the Dead Sea in the Middle Bronze Age (about 2000 BC; A. D. Riddle, and David Parker, "Interactive Dead Sea Map," The Dead Sea: A History of Change, December 2013. http://www.riddlemaps.com/deadSea/map.swf). This map also depicts the southern campaign (① – ⑧) of Chedorlaomer, the king of Elam described in Genesis 14:1–12. Following his attack on Ḥaṣaṣon-Tamar (En-Gedi) ⑥ he

encountered the confederation of the kings of the Cities of the Plain. Unfortunately the location of the Valley of Siddim is uncertain and bitumen deposits can be found in several locations around the Dead Sea (See Map 7 for the location of Sink holes). Chedorlaomer would have needed to have backtracked to encounter the Cities of the Plain in the south ⑦. Whereas traveling north ⑦ he would be traveling in the direction of Dan ⑧ where he was pursued by Abraham... 188

59. **MAP 5:** representing the outside borders of the Promised Land that God showed to Moses on Mount Nebo, described in Deuteronomy 34:1-3. It is unlikely that es-Safi (Byzantine Zoar) is the location of the eastern boundary of the Promised Land, as it would lay in Moabite territory, south of the Arnon River. It is more likely that Serâbît el-Mushaqqar, located on the ascent to Mount Nebo, or another site nearby, was the OT Zoar ⑨ and represents the eastern boundary of the Promised Land. 189

60. **MAP 6:** Historical boundaries of Roman / Byzantine / Islamic Palestine (sourced from Irfan Shahîd, Byzantium and the Arabs in the Sixth Century, 683, Bernard Lewis, Islam in History: Ideas, People, and Events in the Middle East, 155 and the borders of Mandate Palestine from multiple sources). CM 01 190

61. **MAP 7:** The location of sinkholes from recent surveys overlayed on the map of the Dead Sea as it would have appeared during the time of Chedorlaomer, in the Middle Bronze Age (2000-1550 BC). The slime pits or bitumen pits were probably these sinkholes. 191

62. **MAP 8:** The region of the *Kikkār* indicating the Roman road from Esbus to Livias and sites mentioned in this book. 192

63. **MAP 9:** Map close-up of the area around Tall el-Ḥammâm. Multi-period site plan showing the excavation fields of the upper and lower tall. The survey plot of Tall el-Ḥammâm was used with permission from Leen Ritmeyer, architect and Qutaiba Dasouqi, Surveyor. 193

64. **MAP 10:** Map close-up of the area around Bâb Edh-Dhrâʿ and Khirbet Qazone cemetery. 194

65. **MAP 11.** Multi-period site plan of Tall el-Ḥammâm showing excavation Fields. 195

66. **MAP 12.** Site plan for the EB and IAII remains at Feifa (or Fifa). 196

67. **Chart 7:** Timeline for the proposed location of the sites associated with the Northern and Southern Sodom theories. 214

68. **Timeline:** The period of the Patriarchs. 215

ABBREVIATIONS

This work will conform to the abbreviations and general format conventions set out by *The SBL Handbook of Style: for Ancient Near Eastern, Biblical and Early Christian Studies* by Patrick H. Alexander, et al. eds. second printing (Peabody, Mass.: Hendrickson, 2002) for general literary conventions, Bible translations, biblical books, Dead Sea scrolls, pseudepigraphical, early patristic books, targumic material, *Mishnah*, Talmud, other Rabbinic works, *Nag Hammadi* tractates, commonly used periodicals, reference works and serials. Unless otherwise indicated the references to the works of ancient sources reflect the Loeb Classical Library numbering system and Latin abbreviations. For simplicity the North Sodom Theory will be noted as NST and the Southern Sodom Theory will be noted as SST. Also, Bâb edh-Dhrâ' will be noted as BeD and Tall el-Ḥammâm as TeH. Note that there are several spelling variations for most sites especially as used by early explorers, since they spell the Arabic words as they sound.

HEBREW BIBLE / OLD TESTAMENT

Gen	Genesis
Exod	Exodus
Num	Numbers
Deut	Deuteronomy
Judg	Judges
Josh	Joshua
1–2 Sam	1–2 Samuel
1–2 Kgs	1–2 Kings
1–2 Chr	1–2 Chronicles
Neh	Nehemiah
Job	Job
Ps/Pss	Psalms
Prov	Proverbs
Eccl	Ecclesiastes
Isa	Isaiah
Jer	Jeremiah
Ezek	Ezekiel
Joel	Joel
Amos	Amos

NEW TESTAMENT

Matt	Matthew
Luke	Luke
Gal	Galatians
1–2 Pet	1–2 Peter

ANCIENT SOURCES

3Q15	The Copper Scroll
Abr.	Philo, *De Abrahamo, A Treatise on the Life of the Wise Man Made Perfect by Instruction or, On the Unwritten Law, That Is To Say, On Abraham* [1]
abbr.	abbreviation
Ant.	Josephus, *Antiquitates judaicae, Jewish Antiquities*, LCL 242, 489
Apol.	Tertullian, *Apologeticus, Apology*, ANF 3
Apol.	Justin Martyr, *Apologia, Apology*, ANF 1
Autol.	Theophilus of Antioch, *Ad Autolycum, To Autolycus*, ANF 1
b.	(before rabb. txt.) Babylonian Talmud
ca.	Lat. *circa* around, about, approximately
Cels.	Origen of Alexandria, *Contra*

---

[1] Philo, *The Works of Philo Judaeus: The Contemporary of Josephus*, trans. C. D. Yonge, 3 vols. (Whitefish, Mont.: Kessinger, 2007).

ABBREVIATIONS

	Celsum Against Celsus, ANF 9	*Pall.*	Tertullian, *De pallio* The Pallium or on the Mantle, Trans. Hunink
Dial.	Justin Martyr, *Dialogus cum Tryphone*, Dialogue with Trypho a Jew, ANF 1	*Prax.*	Tertullian, *Adversus Praxean* Against Praxeas, ANF 4
DSS	Dead Sea Scrolls	*Princ.*	Origen of Alexandria, *De principiis (Peri archǼn)*, First Principles, ANF 9
Eg.	The Pilgrimage of Etheria [2]		
Exh. cast.	Tertullian, *De exhortatione castitatis* Exhortation to Chastity, ANF 4	*Qu. hebr. Gen.*	Jerome, *Quaestionum hebraicarum liber in Genesim*, APNF[2] 3
Geogr.	Strabo, *Geographica*, Geography, LCL 211, 241	*Rab.*	*Rabbah*, rabbinic writing
Haer.	Irenaeus, *Adversus haereses*, Against Heresies, ANF 1	*Strom.*	Clement of Alexandria, *Stromata*, Miscellanies, ANF 1
Hist.	Tacitus, *Historiae*, Histories, trans. Church and Brodribb	*t.*	The *Talmudic* tractates of the Tosefta
Hist. Lib.	Diodorus Siculus, *Bibliotheca historica*, Historical Library, LCL 390	*Test.*	Cyprian, *Ad Quirinum testimonia adversus Judaeos* To Quirinius: Testomonies against the Jews, ANF 5
J.W.	Josephus, *Bellum judaicum*, Jewish War, LCL 203, 210, 487	*Top.*	Theodosius, *De Situ Terrae Sanctae or Topografia*, Topography of the Holy Land [3]
Jejun.	Tertullian, *De jejunio adversus psychicos* On Fasting, against the Psychics, ANF 4	*Ux.*	Tertullian, *Ad uxorem* To His Wife, ANF
m.	The Mishnah (ed. Eugene J. Lipman)	*Vita Per. Iber.*	*Vita Petri Iberi*, Life of Peter the Iberian [4]
m. Sanh.	Mishnah tractate *Sanhedrin*	Wis	Wisdom of Solomon
Marc.	Tertullian, *Adversus Marcionem*, Against Marcion, ANF 4		

MODERN SOURCES

Mart. Pionii	Martyrdom of Pionius
Mem.	Gaius Julius Solinus, *Collectanea rerum memorabilium*, Collection of Curiosities, Ed. Mommsen
Mos.	Philo, *De vita Mosis I, II*, On the Life of Moses 1, 2, Trans. Yonge, The Works of Philo Judaeus: The Contemporary of Josephus.
Mon.	Tertullian, *De monogamia* Monogamy, ANF 4
On.	Eusebius, *Onomasticon*, On the Place-Names in the Holy Scripture, Trans. Wolf
Paed.	Clement of Alexandria, *Paedagogus*, Christ the Educator, ANF 1

AASOR	The Annual of the American Schools of Oriental Research
ABD	The Anchor Yale Bible Dictionary [5]
ad loc.	*ad locum*, at the place discussed
ADAJ	Annual of the Department of Antiquities of Jordan
AEHL	The Archaeological Encyclopedia of the

---

[2] Egeria, *The Pilgrimage of Etheria*, trans. M. L. McClure and C. L. Feltoe (London, U.K.: Society for Promoting Christian Knowledge, 1919).

[3] Theodosius, "Topografia: The Topography of the Holy Land," in *Jerusalem Pilgrims Before the Crusades*, ed. John Wilkinson (Oxford, U.K.: Aris & Phillips, 2002), 103–16.

[4] Cornelia B. Horn and Robert R. Phenix Jr., *John Rufus: The Lives of Peter the Iberian, Theodosius of Jerusalem, and the Monk Romanus* (Atlanta, Ga.: SBL, 2008).

[5] David Noel Freedman et al., eds., *The Anchor Yale Bible Dictionary*, 6 vols. (New York, N.Y.: Doubleday, 1996).

	Holy Land [6]		Contents Including the Biblical Theology [11]
AJA	*American Journal of Archaeology*		
amsl	Height above mean sea level	DOA	Department of Antiquities
ANE	ancient Near East	e.g.	*exempli gratia*, for example
ANF	*The Ante-Nicene Fathers* [7]	EAEHL	*Encyclopedia of Archaeological Excavations in the Holy Land* [12]
ASOR	American Schools of Oriental Research		
		EB	Early Bronze
AUSS	*Andrews University Seminary Studies*	EBA	Early Bronze Age
Ayy.	Ayyubid Period	ed(s).	editor(s), edited by
BA	*The Biblical Archaeologist*	*EJ*	*Encyclopedia Judaica* [13]
BAR	*Biblical Archaeology Review*	ESV	English Standard Version
BASOR	*Bulletin of the American Schools of Oriental Research*	et al.	*et alii*, and others
		etc.	*et cetera*, and the rest
BDB	*A Hebrew and English Lexicon of the Old Testament* [8]	ft.	feet
		Ger.	German
BeD	Bâb edh-Dhrâʿ	Gr.	Greek
bmsl	below mean sea level	Heb.	Hebrew
BRB	*Biblical Research Bulletin*	Hell.	Hellenistic Period
BS	*Bible and Spade*	i.e.	*id est*, that is
BSac	*Bibliotheca sacra*	ICC	International Critical Commentary Series
Byz.	Byzantine Period		
ca.	*circa*	*IEJ*	*Israel Exploration Journal*
CE	*The Catholic Encyclopedia* [9]	ISBE1	*The International Standard Bible Encyclopedia* [14]
cent.	century		
ch.	chapter (s)	ISBE2	*The International Standard Bible Encyclopedia* [15]
DBib1	*Dictionary of the Bible, One Volume*[10]		
DBib5	*A Dictionary of the Bible: Dealing with Its Language, Literature and*	JETS	*Journal of the Evangelical Theological Society*
		JRA	Journal of Roman Archaeology
		JRS	*The Journal of Roman Studies*

---

[6] Avraham Negev, *The Archaeological Encyclopedia of the Holy Land*, 3rd ed. (New York: Prentice Hall Press, 1996).

[7] Alexander Roberts et al., eds., *Ante-Nicene Fathers*, New Ed, 10 vols. (Peabody, Mass.: Hendrickson, 1994).

[8] Charles A. Briggs, Samuel R. Driver, and Francis Brown, *The Brown-Driver-Briggs Hebrew and English Lexicon: With an Appendix Containing Biblical Aramaic* (Oxford, U.K.: Clarendon, 1907).

[9] Charles George Herbermann, Condé Bénoist Pallen, and Edward Aloysius Pace, eds., *The Catholic Encyclopedia; An International Work of Reference on the Constitution, Doctrine, Discipline, and History of the Catholic Church*, 16 vols. (New York, N.Y.: Appleton & Company, 1913).

[10] James Hastings and John A. Selbie, eds., *A Dictionary of the Bible*, Single Volume (New York, N.Y.: Scribner's Sons, 1909).

[11] James Hastings and John A. Selbie, eds., *A Dictionary of the Bible: Dealing with Its Language, Literature and Contents Including the Biblical Theology*, 5 vols. (New York, N.Y.: Scribner's Sons, 1911).

[12] Michael Avi-Yonah and Ephraim Stern, eds., *Encyclopedia of Archaeological Excavations in the Holy Land*, 3rd ed., 4 vols. (New York, N.Y.: Prentice Hall, 1996).

[13] Michael Berenbaum and Fred Skolnik, eds., *Encyclopedia Judaica*, 2nd ed., 22 vols. (New York, N.Y.: MacMillan, 2006).

[14] James Orr and Melvin Grove Kyle, eds., *The International Standard Bible Encyclopedia*, 5 vols. (Chicago, Ill.: Howard-Severance, 1915).

[15] Geoffrey W. Bromiley, ed., *The International Standard Bible Encyclopedia*, Revised, 4 vols. (Grand Rapids, Mich.: Eerdmans, 1995).

JSOT	*Journal for the Study of the Old Testament*	PEF	Palestine Exploration Fund
Kh.	Khirbet	*PEFSt.*	*Palestine Exploration Fund: Quarterly Statement*
km	kilometer	Pers.	Persian Period
LASBF	*Liber annuus Studii biblici franciscani*	pls.	plates
Lat.	Latin	*RB*	*Revue Biblique*
LB	Late Bronze	SHAJ	Studies in the History and Archaeology of Jordan
LBA	Late Bronze Age		
LXX	Septuagint (Greek Translation of the Old Testament)	*sic*	"so, thus, in this manner" meaning the error was in the original
m	meter		
Mam.	Mamluk Period	SST	southern Sodom theory
MB	Middle Bronze	*TDOT*	*Theological Dictionary of the Old Testament* [20]
MBA	Middle Bronze Age		
MT	Massoretic Text	TeH	Tall el-Ḥammâm or Tall al-Ḥammâm
NEA	*Near Eastern Archaeology*		
NEAEHL	*The New Encyclopedia of Archaeological Excavations in the Holy Land* [16]	TeHEP	Tall el-Ḥammâm Exploration Project
		TWOT	*Theological Wordbook of the Old Testament* [21]
NEASB	*Near East Archaeology Society Bulletin*	Umay.	Umayyad Period
NICOT	New International Commentary on the Old Testament	WBC	Word Biblical Commentary
		ZPEB	*Zondervan Pictorial Encyclopedia of the Bible* [22]
NIDBA	*The New International Dictionary of Biblical Archaeology* [17]		
NIV	New International Version		
NPNF	*Nicene and Post-Nicene Fathers, Series II* [18]		
NST	northern Sodom theory		
OEANE	*The Oxford Encyclopedia of Archaeology in the Near East* [19]		
op. cit.	*opere citato*, in the work cited		

---

[16] Ephraim Stern, Ayelet Levinson-Gilboa, and Joseph Aviram, eds., *The New Encyclopedia of Archaeological Excavations in the Holy Land*, 4 vols. (New York, N.Y.: MacMillan, 1993).

[17] Edward M. Blaiklock and R. K. Harrison, eds., *The New International Dictionary of Biblical Archaeology* (Grand Rapids, Mich.: Zondervan, 1983).

[18] Alexander Roberts et al., eds., *Nicene and Post-Nicene Fathers, Series II*, 14 vols. (Peabody, Mass.: Hendrickson, 1994).

[19] Eric M. Meyers, ed., *The Oxford Encyclopedia of Archaeology in the Near East*, 5 vols. (Oxford, U.K.: Oxford University Press, 1997).

[20] G. Johannes Botterweck, Helmer Ringgren, and Heinz-Josef Fabry, eds., *Theological Dictionary of the Old Testament*, trans. Douglas W. Stott, 15 vols. (Grand Rapids, Mich.: Eerdmans, 2003).

[21] R. Laird Harris, Gleason L. Archer, Jr., and Bruce K. Waltke, eds., *Theological Wordbook of the Old Testament*, 2 vols. (Chicago, Ill.: Moody, 1980).

[22] Merrill C. Tenney and Moises Silva, eds., *The Zondervan Encyclopedia of the Bible: Revised Full-Color Edition*, Revised, 5 vols. (Grand Rapids, Mich.: Zondervan, 2009).

Preface

*M*y interest in Sodom and Gomorrah goes back over 35 years to my first archaeology course and the choice of Sodom and Gomorrah for my first paper. I was a student at Ontario Bible College (now Tyndale University College and Seminary) at the time (1979), and my professor, Gordon Wright, said that I should meet an archaeologist who had claimed to have identified the location of Sodom. His name was Bryant Wood, and he was in Toronto at the time working on his PhD in Syro-Palestinian archaeology at the University of Toronto and guest lecturing at Toronto Baptist Seminary. I arranged an appointment and had a wonderful conversation and interaction with Bryant. Bryant provided copies of his magazine article from the *Bible and Spade* magazine, of which he later became the editor. After doing my research, I concluded that the best candidate for Sodom was Bâb edh-Dhrâ. The argument seemed compelling and since I did not doubt its historicity it was the best candidate at that time.

In 2006 I had plans to join the excavation at Khirbet al-Maqatir (Ai?) with Dr. Wood, but it was cancelled due to security reasons, so instead I joined the Tall el-Ḥammâm (TeH) excavation during the first season. I had no idea at the time that Dr. Steven Collins believed this site to be Sodom (Northern Sodom Theory NST), but soon came to hear him explain and appreciate his reasons for his hypothesis. It was during those nine seasons that Scott Stripling and I also identified the Roman/Byzantine remains at Tall el-Ḥammâm as part of Livias and located TeH on the Madaba Map.

This work arose out of my own frustration at marking papers on the location of Sodom and finding students continually mentioning the same fallacies about the location of Sodom. Prior to writing their papers they should have been able to get certain facts right. This motivated me to write *Key Facts for the Location of Sodom: Student Edition* to guide the students, while trying to maintain a natural perspective to allow students to come to their own conclusions in their assignments.

This volume is an updated version of the *Student Edition* that provides more primary source quotations and testimonial facts. It also includes an essay (Chapter Twelve) originally entitled "My Journey to Locate the Genesis Pentapolis North of the Dead Sea" and forthcoming in *Kikkar Dialogues*, edited by Steven Collins, 2nd ed., 100–128. It summarizes the facts laid out in the book and concludes that Tall el-Ḥammâm is presently the best option for the location of Sodom.

Numerous photographs, charts, timelines, maps, and a glossary that were available in the *Student Edition* have been included here as well. These will assist in navigating the unfamiliar terrain of the Dead Sea and Jordan Valley. This work is not designed to be exhaustive but provides sixty-two facts grouped together in methodological, hermeneutical, geographical, chronological, archaeological, cataclysmal, and geological chapters which set the stage for further research and consideration.

I am indebted to both Dr. Bryant Wood and Dr. Steven Collins for their dedication to archaeology and to the quest for Sodom. Both scholars have been role models for me and have contributed greatly to this area of research. Little did I know in 1979 that out of my research then, I would be writing a book some 35 years later!

David E. Graves
Toronto, Ont. 2016

Preface to Second Edition

While the Bible does not change, the same cannot be said for archaeological finds. There is a continual release of archaeological information each year that demands the need to update the discoveries for the public in a format that is both informative and understandable. Thus, this second edition was completed to provide the most up-to-date archaeological material for the sites proposed for Sodom and make the material available in both black and white and color. The layout has been refreshed with may new images being added. It is the hope and prayer of the author that those who read these discoveries would be blessed and encouraged in their faith and that know that the Bible is historically accurate, so they can better understand what is being said.

David E. Graves, PhD
Toronto, Canada
March 1, 2018

THE LOCATION OF SODOM

Introduction

1. The Destruction of Sodom and Gomorrah, Oil on Canvas. John Martin, 1852.
Wikimedia Commons

The biblical account of Sodom and Gomorrah is a well known yet frightening story in the Old Testament (OT; Gen 10–19). The biblical narrative described the nature of God, showing his mercy on Lot and his family, while not diminishing his holiness, in the annihilation by fire[1] of four[2] of the five, "Cities of the Plain" (Zoar was spared) or what some have called the *Pentapolis* (Gr. "five cities;" Wis 10:6).

Wolcott said of the site of Sodom: "there is no site, ancient or modern, which combines all the elements of interest that belong to the site of Sodom and the other 'cities of the plain' whose destruction is recorded in the book of Genesis."[3]

Howard went on to state that:

> perhaps because of their notoriety, perhaps because of the way in which they have resisted discovery, perhaps because of the bearing they have on the patriarchal narratives, and perhaps even because of the strangeness of the Dead Sea area, in which they were once located, the site of these cities of the plain. . . . has been a focus of interest for centuries.[4]

But apart from the moral notoriety of the story,[5] one of the most mysterious and most interesting aspects of the account concerns whereabouts exactly the cities were located. The city which appears most prominently in the biblical narrative is Sodom. It appears to have been the largest and most important city in the region, likely to have been in control of the surrounding area as a large city-state under the rule of King Bara (Gen 14:2). You would think that it would be easy to find such a large, ruined site, but mysteriously it has eluded archaeologists ever since it was destroyed by God (Gen 19:24). Some might suggest that Sodom was so utterly destroyed, that any archaeological trace of it was obliterated; yet surely there would be some remains left, even if only the ashes mentioned by Peter, who stated: "turning the cities of Sodom and Gomorrah to ashes he condemned them to extinction" (2 Pet 2:6).

Even after the destruction of Hiroshima and Nagasaki from the atomic blast that ended the Second World War, physical evidence was left that could be identified. There is no reason to believe that the site of Sodom and the other cities of the plain still had some visible remains following their

---

[1] Gen 19:24; Amos 4:11.

[2] The four cities destroyed include Sodom, Gomorrah, Admah, Zeboiim (Gen 13:12; 19:28, 29; Deut 3:10; Josh 13:21).

[3] Samuel Wolcott, "The Site of Sodom," *BSac* 25, no. 97 (1868): 112–51.

[4] David M. Howard, Jr., "Sodom and Gomorrah Revisited," *Journal of the Evangelical Theological Society* 27, no. 4 (1984): 385.

[5] David M. Howard, Jr., "Sodom," ed. Geoffrey W. Bromiley, *ISBE2* (Grand Rapids, Mich.: Eerdmans, 1995), 560–61.

2. Tall el-Ḥammâm and the area around the Tall which is believed, by the author, to be Livias. The white arrows indicate the location of two hot springs. Livias was famous for its hot springs.

destruction that can be excavated today. Merrill argues:

> There is no warrant in the Bible for supposing that the sites of these cities were destroyed when the cities themselves were, or that they were obliterated. . . . Indeed, there is a passage in Deuteronomy (xxxii, 32), where "the vine of Sodom and the fields of Gomorrah" are spoken of in such a way as to indicate that this was far from being a barren region.[6]

Due to its strong miraculous content and mysterious disappearance from the archaeological record, some scholars[7] question the validity and historicity of the account. But if one admits that the account found in the Bible is historical, which many scholars do (Collins and Wood), where does one begin to look for the sin cities of Sodom and Gomorrah? Perhaps the best place to start is the Bible itself.

Taking the details of the two accounts about Sodom from Genesis 13, 14, and 19, "biblical archaeologists"[8] have sought the location of the five "Cities of the Plain" around the area of the Dead Sea. While there have been proposals for their location in every direction around and under the Dead Sea,[9] and some as far away as Arabia or Iraq,[10] two predominant areas stand out: various locations around the southern end of the Dead Sea, and the northern end of the Dead Sea.[11] Within these general areas, two important Talls[12] have been excavated in recent years and proposed as candidates for Sodom: Bâb edh-Dhrâ' (BeD)[13] in the south

---

[6] Selah Merrill, "Modern Researches in Palestine," *Journal of the American Geographical Society of New York* 9 (1877): 118–19; "Modern Researches in Palestine," *PEFSt.* 11, no. 1 (1879): 146; *East of the Jordan: A Record of Travel and Observation in the Countries of Moab, Gilead, and Bashan* (London, U.K.: Darf, 1881), 234.

[7] Thomas L. Thompson, *The Historicity of the Patriarchal Narratives: The Quest for the Historical Abraham* (Valley Forge, PA: Trinity Press International, 2002), 328.

[8] Ziony Zevit, "The Biblical Archaeology versus Syro-Palestinian Archaeology Debate in Its American Institutional and Intellectual Contexts," in *The Future of Biblical Archaeology: Reassessing Methodologies and Assumptions*, ed. James Karl Hoffmeier and Alan R. Millard, The Proceedings of a Symposium, August 12-14, 2001 at Trinity International University (Grand Rapids, Mich.: Eerdmans, 2004), 3–19; Norman L. Geisler and Joseph M. Holden, *The Popular Handbook of Archaeology and the Bible* (Eugene, Oreg.: Harvest House, 2013), 183.

[9] William F. Albright, "The Archæological Results of an Expedition to Moab and the Dead Sea," *BASOR* 14 (1924): 7–9; G. Ernest Wright, *Biblical Archaeology*, Abridged (Philadelphia, Pa.: Westminster, 1960), 30.

[10] See Chapter Two - A Brief History of Research.

[11] M. J. Mulder, "Sodom; Gomorrah," in *Theological Dictionary of the Old Testament*, ed. G. Johannes Botterweck, Helmer Ringgren, and Heinz-Josef Fabry, trans. Douglas W. Stott, vol. 10 (Grand Rapids, Mich.: Eerdmans, 2003), 153.

[12] The spelling of Tel or Tall is determined by its location. Tall, which means "mound or hill," is Arabic and is the usual spelling in Arabic countries, like Jordan (i.e., Tall el-Hammam), while Tel means the same thing but is the Hebrew spelling used in Israel (i.e., Tel Dan).

[13] Bryant G. Wood, "The Discovery of the Sin Cities of Sodom and Gomorrah," *Bible and Spade* 12, no. 3 (1999): 67–80; "Sodom and Gomorrah: Is There Evidence for Their Destruction?" *Associates For Biblical Research*, May 6, 2008, 1–4.

(Southern Sodom Theory – SST) and Tall el-Ḥammâm (TeH)[14] in the north (Northern Sodom Theory – NST).[15]

The main proponent of the SST at Bâb edh-Dhrâʿ is Dr. Bryant G. Wood, a biblical archaeologist and research director with the Associates for Biblical Research, Akron, PA, and editor of their quarterly magazine, the *Bible and Spade* magazine. He holds a M.S. in Mechanical engineering from Rensselaer Polytechnic Institute in Troy, N.Y., an M.A. in Biblical History from the University of Michigan (1974) and a Ph.D. in Syro-Palestinian archaeology from the University of Toronto (1985). He has held several teaching positions at various Christian schools.[16]

The NST is proposed by Dr. Steven Collins, Consulting Research Professor, Trinity Southwest University, Director at Veritas International University School of Archaeology/PhD Program and Director of the Tall el-Ḥammâm Excavation Project. Collins has a Ph.D. in biblical history and religion from Trinity Theological Seminary (1983) along with post-doctoral studies in advanced archaeological methodologies from Southwest Biblical Seminary (1985) and in ancient Near Eastern archaeology and ceramic typology from Southwest Biblical Seminary (1988) and in Levantine ceramic typology from the Jerusalem Center for Biblical Studies (1989). Wood and Collins remain good friends and have dug together at the Khirbet el-Maqatir (proposed as biblical Ai) excavation in Israel/West Bank for six seasons (1995–2000).

They both share a desire to defend the historicity of the biblical text and passionately believe that their candidate for Sodom is the biblical site.

This work will not seek to resolve the debate but rather provide some of the essential facts that are often misrepresented in navigating the maze of arguments for locating Sodom and the Cities of the Plain. These facts are not exhaustive but represent the popular misconceptions put forth when arguing for the southern or northern locations.

Maximalist or Minimalist Viewpoint

Before proceeding we must differentiate between what is meant by a minimalist and a maximalist in the context of archaeology, as these terms are commonly used in both the debate over the historical reliability of the Bible and in the remaining chapters.

Minimalist View

In archaeology, a *minimalist* (The Copenhagen School) or revisionist[17], as they sometimes call themselves, is one who finds that the Bible contributes little or not at all to our understanding of the history of Palestine before about 500 BC (That is before Israel's return from exile). The leading spokespersons for this view are Finkelstein, Lemche, and

---

[14] Steven Collins, "If You Thought You Knew the Location of Sodom and Gomorrah… Think Again," *BRB* 7, no. 4 (2007): 1–6; "Tall El-Hammam: A Key Witness to the Archaeology and History of the Southern Jordan Valley—Summary, Conclusions, and Recommendations from the 2006/2007 Excavation Season," in *Annual Meeting of the ASOR: San Diego, CA* (Albuquerque, N.M.: TSU Press, 2007), 1–20; "Where Is Sodom? The Case for Tall El-Hammam," *BAR* 39, no. 2 (2013): 32–41, 70–71; Steven Collins and Latayne C. Scott, *Discovering the City of Sodom: The Fascinating, True Account of the Discovery of the Old Testament's Most Infamous City* (New York, N.Y.: Simon & Schuster, 2013).

[15] Early adopters (1930's) of the NST proposed Teleilat el-Ghassul but it was discovered to be too early for Sodom. Power, "The Site of the Pentapolis: Part 1," 23, 62.

[16] Bryant G. Wood, "Bryant G. Wood, PhD. Biography," *Detroit Baptist Theological Seminary*, 2013, http://dbts.edu/pdf/rls/WoodBio.pdf.

[17] William G. Dever, "The Current School of Revisionist and Their Nonhistories of Ancient Israel," in *What Did the Biblical Writers Know, and When Did They Know It?* (Grand Rapids, Mich.: Eerdmans, 2001), 23.

Thompson, among others.[18] They argue that the primary OT characters, like the patriarchs, Moses, David, and Solomon, did not exist except in the minds of the Israelites. Davies, a professed revisionist, explains it this way:

> There is no way in which history automatically reveals itself in a biblical text; there are no literary criteria for believing David to be more historical than Joshua, Joshua more historical than Abraham, and Abraham more historical than Adam. An additional problem, in fact, is that there is no non-literary way of making this judgment either, since none of these characters has left a trace outside the biblical text![19]

Dever, who does not consider himself to be a minimalist, summarizes their position in his work *What Did the Biblical Writers Know, and When Did They Know It?*:

> There was no "ancient" or "biblical" Israel. These are all late "intellectual constructs," forced back upon an imagined past by centuries of Jewish and Christian believers. The notion of "ancient Israel" stems ultimately from the Bible itself; but the Bible is "pious fiction," not historical fact. The Bible, too, is a late literary construct, written in and reflecting the realities of the Persian-Hellenistic era (*ca.* 5th–1st centuries), not the Iron Age of Palestine (*ca.* 12th–6th centuries) that purports to be its setting.[20]

Minimalists look to the date of the earliest discovered manuscripts of the Dead Sea Scrolls (DSS), written sometime after the second cent. BC to provide the date for the writing of the OT books. For the minimalist, the biblical books were originally composed just before the time of the DSS (4th-3rd cent. BC). Kenneth Kitchen reveals the implications of this view:

> With that late date they would couple an ultralow view of the reality of that history, dismissing virtually the whole of it as pure fiction, as an attempt by the puny Jewish community in Palestine to write themselves an imaginary past large, as a form of national propaganda.[21]

Others were already involved in this practice, setting the precedent for Israel. Both Manetho's (Egyptian priest, 3rd cent. BC) *Aegyptiaka*[22] and Berossus' (Babylonian priest of Marduk) *Chaldaika*[23] were written as political propaganda. However, the OT books were written in Hebrew for their own nation, not as political propaganda for others. The Greek translation of the OT (LXX) was produced years later and then only for their own community.

The minimalists have even gone so far as to campaign against the use of the term *biblical archaeology* and replace it with *Near-Eastern archaeology*. Holden and Geisler explain their motivation behind this change:

> Their [Minimalists] contempt for any title associated with the Bible appears to be driven by its perceived association to biased research, antiquated

---

[18] Thomas L. Thompson, *Early History of the Israelite People: From the Written & Archaeological Sources* (Leiden: Brill, 2000); Niels Peter Lemche, *The Israelites in History and Tradition*, Library of Ancient Israel (Louisville, Ky.: Westminster/Knox, 1998); Hershel Shanks et al., "Face to Face: Biblical Minimalists Meet Their Challenge," *BAR* 23, no. 4 (1997): 26–42, 66; Israel Finkelstein and Nadav Na'aman, eds., *From Nomadism to Monarchy: Archaeological and Historical Aspects of Early Israel* (Jerusalem: Israel Exploration Society, 1994); Israel Finkelstein and Neil Asher Silberman, *The Bible Unearthed: Archaeology's New Vision of Ancient Israel* (New York, N.Y.: Touchstone, 2002); Israel Finkelstein and Amihai Mazar, *The Quest for the Historical Israel*, ed. Brian B. Schmidt, Archaeology and Biblical Studies 17 (Atlanta, Ga.: SBL, 2007); Robert B. Coote and Keith W. Whitelam, *The Emergence of Early Israel in Historical Perspective*, Social World of Biblical Antiquity Series (Sheffield: Sheffield Phoenix, 2010).

[19] Philip R. Davies, *In Search of "Ancient Israel": A Study in Biblical Origins*, The Library of Hebrew Bible/OT Studies (London, U.K.: Continuum International, 2006), 12.

[20] William G. Dever, *What Did the Biblical Writers Know, and When Did They Know It?* (Grand Rapids, Mich.: Eerdmans, 2001), 4.

[21] Kenneth A. Kitchen, *On the Reliability of the Old Testament* (Grand Rapids, Mich.: Eerdmans, 2003), 2.

[22] Manetho, *History of Egypt and Other Works*, trans. W. G. Waddell, Loeb Classical Library 350 (Cambridge, Mass.: Harvard University Press, 1940).

[23] Stanley Mayer Burstein, *The Babyloniaca of Berossus*, 2nd ed., vol. 1, 5 vols., Sources from the Ancient Near East 1 (Malibu: Undena Publications, 1978).

methodology, rigid ideology, lack of objectivity, and contempt for the scientific method. (However, this notion seems to be shortsighted since it requires archaeologists to discriminate against the Bible as a valid primary-source document originating from the ancient Near-Eastern world.)²⁴

Kitchen asks several important questions which deserve answering:

> Were the Old Testament books all composed within circa 400–200 BC? And are they virtually pure fiction of that time, with few or no roots in the real history of the Near East during circa 2000–400 BC? . . . Are they purely fiction, containing nothing of historical value, or of major historical content and value, or a fictional matrix with a few historical nuggets embedded?
>
> Merely sitting back in a comfy armchair just wondering or speculating about the matter will achieve us nothing. Merely proclaiming one's personal convictions for any of the three options just mentioned (all, nothing, or something historical) simply out of personal belief or agenda, and not from firm evidence on the question, is also a total waste of time.²⁵

As such, before writing off stories such as the fate of Sodom and Gomorrah, it is important to first examine the evidence regarding their location, and to this end one requires accurate facts and clear evidence to make an educated decision. It is hoped that the subsequent chapters of this book will provide some of these facts and evidence.

Maximalist View

By contrast the *maximalists* are those who generally accept the biblical text as historically accurate and see a significant correspondence between the Bible and the archaeological data. They find that the Bible contributes significantly to our understanding of the history of Palestine and generally agree with the early dates for the authorship of the OT books. Kitchen lays out significant evidence for such an early date in his life's work entitled *On the Reliability of the Old Testament*.²⁶ There is not always agreement on the exact dates between these scholars, as dates can be very difficult to verify with pinpoint accuracy.

Leading maximalist scholars would include Kitchen, Hoerth, Hoffmeier, Millard, Ortiz, McRay, Yamauchi, and others.²⁷ While some would place William Dever in this camp, he would not consider himself either a maximalist or a minimalist but a middleist, placing himself somewhere in the middle. From his own statements, most evangelicals would not consider him to be a maximalist. Dever states:

> We cannot turn the clock back on the time when archaeology allegedly "proved the Bible." We must allow archaeology as it is practiced today to challenge, as well as to confirm, the Bible's stories. Some things described there really did happen, but *others did not*. The Biblical narratives about Abraham, Moses, Joshua and Solomon probably do reflect some historical memories of actual people and places, but the "larger-than-life" portraits of the Bible are *unrealistic* and are, in fact, *contradicted by the archaeological evidence*. Some of Israel's ancestors probably did come out of Egyptian slavery, but there was *no military conquest of Canaan*, and most early Israelites were displaced Canaanites (emphasis

---

²⁴ Geisler and Holden, *Popular Handbook of Archaeology and the Bible*, 183.

²⁵ Kitchen, *Reliability of the OT*, 2–3.

²⁶ Ibid., 283–99.

²⁷ Kitchen, *Reliability of the OT*; *Ancient Orient and Old Testament* (Wheaton, Ill.: Tyndale, 1966); Alfred Hoerth and John McRay, *Bible Archaeology: An Exploration of the History and Culture of Early Civilizations* (Grand Rapids: Baker, 2006); Alfred J. Hoerth, *Archaeology and the Old Testament* (Grand Rapids: Baker, 1999); James K. Hoffmeier, ed., *The Archaeology of the Bible: Reassessing Methodologies and Assumptions* (Oxford, U.K.: Lion Hudson, 2008); Edwin M. Yamauchi, "Homer and Archaeology: Minimalists and Maximalists in Classical Context," in *The Future of Biblical Archaeology: Reassessing Methodologies and Assumptions*, ed. James K. Hoffmeier and Alan R. Millard (Grand Rapids, Mich.: Eerdmans, 2008), 69–90; James Karl Hoffmeier and Alan R. Millard, eds., *The Future of Biblical Archaeology: Reassessing Methodologies and Assumptions*, The Proceedings of a Symposium, August 12-14, 2001 at Trinity International University (Grand Rapids, Mich.: Eerdmans, 2004); John McRay, *Archaeology and the New Testament* (Grand Rapids, Mich.: Baker, 1991).

added).²⁸

What the revisionists seem to mean by "biblical" Israel is the Israel of mythic proportions. This is the Israel reflected in numerous "stories" that are *embellished with exaggerations* and *fanciful features* such as miracles, compiled partly from sagas, legends, folktales, and outright inventions. Above all, it is the story of an Israel that is set in an over-arching theocratic framework whose intent is always didactic. It aims not at historical narrative per se, but at elucidating the hidden theological meaning of events and their moral significance. Of course this "Israel" is *not historical*, except for revealing something of the historical context of its writers and final editors. But then few modern readers except Fundamentalists ever thought that it was (emphasis added).²⁹

While he is often very critical of the minimalists, he himself clearly does not believe that the Bible is historical, and thus Dever is a minimalist. However, Dever has criticized scholars for holding the view that every historical event in the Bible should be "assumed to be false" unless supported by archaeological evidence. On this point maximalists would agree with Dever.

It is apparent that the distinction is not as simple as saying that Minimalists are theological liberals and Maximalists are theological conservatives. A person, like Dever, may deny the miracles of the OT, attributing such biblical accounts to the superstitious nature of people in biblical days, and still believe that the overall history of Israel is accurately portrayed in the Bible. Likewise, a person may not believe in the miracles of the Bible, such as the Resurrection, but may still be a maximalist and believe that most of the Bible's history is true.

Summary

The minimalist approaches the biblical text from the viewpoint that it contains a minimal amount of real history, as opposed to the maximalist viewpoint that holds to a more conservative position and embraces the maximum amount of history. While these are broad generalizations, most archaeologists would fall somewhere between these two approaches to biblical history.

Based on these definitions, both Bryant G. Wood and Steven Collins should be considered maximalists, and neither would deny the historical validity of the Sodom account as described in scripture. Both view the Bible as a reliable primary source that contains the historical accounts of the lives of the Patriarchs, including Abraham and Lot, along with accurate descriptions of the geography, culture and customs of the ancient Near East (ANE).

---

[28] William G. Dever, "The Western Cultural Tradition Is At Risk," *BAR* 32, no. 2 (2006): 76.

[29] Dever, *What Did the Biblical Writers Know, and When Did They Know It?*, 46.

Primary Sources

The first primary source for the location of the Cities of the Plain is the Bible, which will be treated as an historical document with reliable geography (adopting the maximalist, as opposed to the minimalist, approach; see the discussion in the *Introduction*).[1] In addition to this, the possible mention of the Cities of the Plain found in ancient tablets will also be considered. Other, less reliable and later sources, based largely on tradition, will also be assessed, including ancient writers, pilgrims, and the Byzantine Madaba map.

3. Photographic reproduction of the Great Isaiah Scroll, the best preserved of the biblical scrolls found at Qumran. Isaish spoke of Sodom in 15:4–7.

© Ardon Bar Hama / Wikimedia Commons

Biblical references to Sodom

Genesis 10:19

Sodom is mentioned as early as Genesis 10:19 in what is called the Table of Nations,[2] which is an early descriptive map listing four of the Cities of the Plain as a boundary for the territory of the Canaanites (See Map 5).

It would appear that the boundary of the Canaanite territory is identified by four geographical markers: Sidon in the north in Phoenicia, Gaza in the west in Philistia, Gerar (Tel Haror or Tel Abu Hureira in the Wadi Eš-Šari'ah)[3] in the south,[4] leaving the Cities of the Plain as far as Lasha, as the eastern boundary. Since the identification and location of Lasha is unknown and Zoar is not mentioned in the list of cities, some scholars have suggested that Lasha is Zoar.

Howard's explanation, based on prepositions (near or at, *b`kh . . . . ʿd*),[5] and which tried to find a parallelism between Gerar/Gaza and the Cities of the Plain/Lasha, in order to identify a southern location for the Cities of the Plain,[6] seems forced and unnatural to the clear eastern identification indicated by the geography.

Some scholars have suggested that Lasha is an emendation for Laish (later known as Dan,[7] identified by an inscription at Tel al-

---

[1] Geisler and Holden, *Popular Handbook of Archaeology and the Bible*, 186.

[2] Allen P. Ross, *The Table of Nations in Genesis* (Dallas, Tex.: Dallas Theological Seminary, 1976).

[3] T. C. Mitchell, "Gerar," ed. I. Howard Marshall et al., *NBD* (Downers Grove, Ill.: InterVarsity, 1996), 405; Yohanan Aharoni, "The Land of Gerar," *IEJ* 6, no. 1 (1956): 26–32.

[4] Aharoni points out that "there is no reason to assume from this passage that Gerar was situated near Gaza. It is clear only that Gerar, like Gaza, was situated on the border of the settled land of Canaan." Aharoni, "The Land of Gerar," 26 n. 3.

[5] H. L. Ginsberg, "A Preposition of Interest to Historical Geographers," *BASOR* 122 (1951): 12–14; Salomon Speier, "On Hebrew `Ad Meaning 'At, By, near,'" *BASOR* 126 (1952): 27.

[6] Howard, Jr., "Sodom and Gomorrah Revisited," 386.

[7] Efraim Orni and Shaked Gilboa, "Dan," ed. Fred Skolnik and Michael Berenbaum, *EJ* (New York, N.Y.: MacMillan, 2006), 5:404.

Qadi[8]),[9] however there is no textual evidence for this theory and Sidon is already indicated as the northern boundary. Harland has suggested that if the Cities of the Plain were located in the Jordan Valley, then perhaps a more suitable city marker would have been used, like Jerusalem or Hebron, but this argument is based purely on speculation.[10] Carl Rasmussen suggests that an even more suitable location would be Jericho, since it is down in the Jordan Valley.[11]

Power suggests that "Laša which should be read Bala'[12] = Ṣo'ar [Gen 14:2], is the city at the eastern limit of the South-eastern Pentapolis district."[13] According to the Jerusalem Targum (compiled *ca.* 370–420 AD) and Jerome (*ca.* 347–420 AD; *Qu. hebr. Gen.* ad loc. Pl, 23, 1004), *Laša* is identified as Callirhoe, famous for its hot springs (Josephus *J.W.* 1.33.5)[14] and called *Baarou* on the Madaba Map (*ca.* 542–570 AD),[15] but this is clearly a late Byzantine tradition. Also, as Power points out, "it is impossible to suppose that Canaanite territory included part of the east shore of the Dead Sea."[16] However, during this early period in the history of the Levant, it is more believable that the Canaanites occupied the north-eastern side of the Jordan River (NST), than the Moabite and Edomite territory south of the Arnon River (SST). It is possible that Laša, whether it is *Ṣo'ar* or not, resided in the northern end of the Dead Sea, providing the eastern boundary for the Cities of the Plain.

As Power points out:

> This passage does not determine of itself whether the Pentapolis district was to the north or to the south of the Dead Sea, but it shows a marked agreement with Deut 34:3 by placing the region of the Pentapolis on the south-eastern boundary of Canaan and thus identifying it with the Round of the valley of Jericho.[17]

The connection between the two passages (Gen 10 and Deut 34) is the eastern boundary assigned to *Ṣo'ar* and *Laša*.

Genesis 13:3, 10–12

The next mention of the Pentapolis is found in Gen 13:10–12. This passage is perhaps the key geographic passage for the identification of Sodom's location (see *Fact 15*). The location of the Jordan Valley (Heb. *kikkār hayyardēn*) or the plain of the Jordan is pivotal to the argument for identifying the possible location of the Cities of the Plain.

Abraham and Lot are, between Bethel and Ai (Gen 13:3; 12:8), on the western hills, 16 km north of Jerusalem, looking east toward (Heb. *b'kh*) Zoar, one of the Cities of the Plain (Gen 13:10), located in the well-watered *kikkār* of the Jordan (See Map 1). Note that Zoar is again used as an eastern geographical boundary. Merrill points out to his readers that:

---

[8] John Bright, *A History of Israel*, 4th ed. (Philadelphia, Pa.: Westminster/Knox, 2000), 54; Walter C. Kaiser, Jr. and Duane Garrett, eds., *NIV Archaeological Study Bible: An Illustrated Walk Through Biblical History and Culture* (Grand Rapids, Mich.: Zondervan, 2006), 378.

[9] Howard, Jr., "Sodom and Gomorrah Revisited," 387.

[10] James Penrose Harland, "Sodom and Gomorrah Part I: The Location of the Cities of the Plain," *BA* 5, no. 2 (1942): 20.

[11] Howard, Jr., "Sodom and Gomorrah Revisited," 387 n. 7.

[12] Rudolf Kittel, *Biblia Hebraica* (Leipzig: Hinrichs, 1906), passim.

[13] E. Power, "The Site of the Pentapolis: Part 1," *Biblica* 11 (1930): 43.

[14] Flavius Josephus, *The Jewish War: Volume I, Books 1-2*, trans. H. St. J. Thackeray, vol. 2, 13 vols., LCL 203 (Cambridge, Mass.: Harvard University Press, 1927).

[15] Christa Clamer, "The Hot Springs of Kallirrhoe and Baarou," in *The Madaba Map Centenary: Travelling Through the Byzantine Umayyad Period. Proceedings of the International Conference Held in Amman 7–9 April 1997*, ed. Michele Piccirillo and Eugenio Alliata, Studium Biblicum Franciscannum Collectio Maior 40 (Jerusalem: Studium Biblicum Franciscannum, 1999), 221–22.

[16] Power, "The Site of the Pentapolis: Part 1," 43 n. 3.

[17] Ibid., 44.

The middle portion of the verse is read as a parenthesis, as follows: "And Lot lifted up his eyes and beheld all the plain of Jordan (that it was well watered everywhere, before the Lord destroyed Sodom and Gomorrah, even as the garden of the Lord [Eden in Mesopotamia watered by the Euphrates and Tigris's rivers] like the land of Egypt [watered by the Nile River]), until thou comest to Zoar." The last clause qualifies the first. Lot saw the plain of Jordan as far as Zoar, or "until you come to Zoar." Zoar was both the limit of the plain and the limit of vision in that direction, so far as the land was concerned. How much of the Dead Sea he saw is not stated ; but no human vision, unless miraculously aided, could reach to the southern end and *distinguish anything*; while, from the point where he stood, the greenness and beauty of the great Shittim plain are distinctly seen. The phrase, "all the plain of the Jordan," cannot include the salt marsh at the southern end of the Dead Sea, since this marsh is fifty miles from the river, and belongs to a water system entirely distinct from that at the northern end of the sea.[18]

Power points out that there is a clear indication for the location of Sodom, Gomorrah and neighbouring Zoar in Gen 13. He states: "they are in the Round [*kikkār*] of the Jordan, east of Bethel, and visible from near Bethel. All three indications, collectively and individually, exclude the southern and impose the northern site."[19]

Even the strong SST advocate Samuel R. Driver admits that this passage suggests a northern site.[20] The *kikkār* is described as the "*kikkār* of the Jordan" (Gen 13:10) and "*kikkār* of Jericho" (Deut 34:3; see *Fact 23*) indicating that it is in the northern region of the Dead Sea, where the Jordan and Jericho are located.

Genesis 14:1–12

In this text, a confederate army of kings, representing the regions of Shinar (Babylonia,

4. View of the Dead Sea from Machaerus in Jordan looking over to En-Gendi, Israel.

Gen 10:11),[21] Elassar (eastern Asia Minor, i.e., Cappadocia or Hurrian)[22], Elamite (Sumerian, modern Iran), and Goiim (Hittites)[23] unite under Chedorlaomer (Kedorlaomer) to march south, no doubt on the King's Highway (Num 20:17–21), to make war (Heb. מלחמה Josh 11:18) against the tribes of the southern Levant (See Map 4). The list begins with the battle at ① Ashteroth-Karnaim (Tel Ash´-ari) in southern Syria where the Rephaim are defeated.[24] Next, the army travels to ② Ham (Zuzites) between Bashan and Moab, and then on to ③ Emim (Deut 2:10–11) in northern Moab (Shaveh-Kiriathaim [Shave-Qiryathaim]). The location of Emim is uncertain but may be near Madeba at Khirbet el-Qureiyeh, Qaryet el-Mekhairet[25] [Khirbet

---

[18] Merrill, *East of the Jordan*, 233–34.
[19] Power, "The Site of the Pentapolis: Part 1," 1:38.
[20] Samuel R. Driver, "Zoar," in *DBib5*, ed. James Hastings and John A. Selbie, vol. 4, 5 vols. (New York, N.Y.: Scribner's Sons, 1909), 986.

---

[21] Gordon J. Wenham, *Genesis 1-15*, ed. David Allan Hubbard and Glenn W. Barker, vol. 1, Word Biblical Commentary (Dallas, Tex.: Word Books, 1987), 308.
[22] Ibid.
[23] Ibid.
[24] S. Cohen, "Ashteroth-Karnaim," ed. G. A. Buttrick and Keith R. Crim, *IDB* (Nashville, Tenn.: Abingdon, 1962), 255; Trent C Butler, *Joshua*, vol. 7, WBC 7 (Waco, Tex.: Word Books, 1983), 136.
[25] Yohanan Aharoni, *The Land of the Bible: A Historical Geography*, trans. Anson F. Rainey, 2nd ed. (Louisville, Ky.: Westminster/Knox, 1981), 307; Wenham, *Genesis 1-15*, 1:309.

al-Mukhayyat] near Mt. Nebo [cf. Num 32:37; Josh 13:19; Jer 48:1]). Next Chedorlaomer enters the region of Seir to defeat the Horites (Deut 2:12–22) as far as ④ El-Paran (possibly Eilat; Deut 2:8; 1 Kgs 9:26) on the border of the wilderness of Zin. Turning back toward ⑤ En-Mishpat, which is identified as Kadesh-Barnea, they defeated the Amalekites (Exod 17:8, 14; Num 13:29; Deut 25:17, 19; 1 Sam 15:2–8). Next they defeated the Amorites, who were resident at ⑥ Hazazon-Tamar (also, Ḥaṣaṣon-Tamar), which is identified with En-Gedi (also Engedi or Ein-Gedi; 2 Chron 20:2).[26] Wenham points out that some scholars suggest that:

> Ḥaṣaṣon-Tamar should be identified with Tamar in southern Judah (1 Kgs 9:18; Ezek 47:18–19). Still other possible identifications include Kasr ejuniyeh or Ain Kusb (20 miles southwest of the Dead Sea).[27] Whichever is the correct location, it is clear that from Kadesh the kings turned northwest back toward the Dead Sea region and the cities of the plain.[28]

It is only then that Chedorlaomer encounters the kings of the Cities of the Plain[29] in the ⑦ Valley of Siddim which is full of bitumen pits (see *Fact 24* and *57* also consult Maps 4 and 7). Wood suggests that the presence of bitumen pits "tips the scales in favour of a southern location"[30] for the Cities of the Plain. However, two factors need to be resolved before this evidence may be admitted. First, where is the location for the battle in the Valley of Siddim (see *Fact 24*), and second, where is the location of the bitumen pits (see *Fact 57*)?

The first question which needs to be asked is: did the battle in the Valley of Siddim, near the bitumen pits, occur at the location of the Pentapolis or at another location, some distance away from the Cities of the Plain? And why would these ancient people build their cities near dangerous bitumen pits?

The second important factor in the debate is the location of the bitumen pits. Wood suggests that the bitumen pits are in the south,[31] while Collins points out that this would mean that Chedorlaomer had to backtrack to go south; while if he traveled north, this would correspond better with the direction in which he was already travelling to free Lot. Abraham was at Mamre (Hebron; Gen 14:13; see *Fact 26*) when he received word that Lot (Abraham's nephew) had been taken captive, and so he pursued Chedorlaomer to Dan (Laish, identified as Tel el-Qadi).[32] Since Chedorlaomer was travelling north to Dan, with Lot, it would make sense that Chedorlaomer would not have turned south with his armies to encounter the kings of the Pentapolis.[33] Since there are bitumen pits at both the north and south ends of the Dead Sea (see *Fact 57*), does this really help to indicate the location of the Valley of Siddim, which is associated with the Dead Sea? The heaviest concentration of sink holes (i.e., bitumen pits) are located along the western shore of the Dead Sea (see *Fact 57*; Maps 4 and 7).

---

[26] Power states: "this identification is confirmed by the preservation of the name Ḥaṣaṣon in the modern *Wady el-Ḥaṣaṣa* about ten kilometres to the north of Engaddi (*sic* En-Gedi)." Power, "The Site of the Pentapolis: Part 1," 44; J. Cunningham Geikie, *The Holy Land and the Bible: A Book of Scripture Illustrations Gathered in Palestine* (London, U.K.: Cassell & Company, 1887), 115; Wenham, *Genesis 1-15*, 1:312.

[27] Werner Schatz, *Genesis 14: Eine Untersuchung*, vol. 2, Europäische Hochschuleschriften 23 (Bern: Herbert Lang, 1972), 174–75; *Encyclopedia Miqra'it (Encyclopaedia Biblica)* (Jerusalem, 1976), 8:607–8.

[28] Wenham, *Genesis 1-15*, 1:312.

[29] This is the first time that the Cities of the Plain are listed in their standard order: Sodom, Gomorrah, Admah, Zeboiim and Bela/Zoar.

[30] Wood, "Discovery of the Sin Cities," 67; Howard, Jr., "Sodom and Gomorrah Revisited," 390.

[31] Wood, "Discovery of the Sin Cities," 67.

[32] Kaiser, Jr. and Garrett, *NIV Archaeological Study Bible*, 378.

[33] Steven Collins, "A Response to Bryant G. Wood's Critique of Collins' Northern Sodom Theory," *BRB* 7, no. 7 (2007): 8.

Genesis 19:24–28

This passage describes the overthrow (Heb. *hāpak*) of the Cities of the Plain, Lot's wife being turned into a "pillar of salt" (see *Fact 58*), the etymology of Zoar ("little one" [v. 20] which was not in the mountains), and that from where Abraham was standing, he could look down and see "all" the *kikkār* in smoke like a furnace. We know that Abraham's location was Mamre or Hebron, as he had earlier stood before the Lord there (Gen 14:13).

The question that requires attention from this passage is which site (BeD or TeH) would have been visible from where Abraham was standing (see *Fact 26*). If smoke was visible in both the northern and southern location, then this passage is not useful in determining the location of Sodom. However, if smoke could only have been visible from the north or south, this may assist in identifying the correct location.

Wenham suggests that the term "overthrow" (Heb. *hāpak*)[34] does not imply destruction by the turning over of an earthquake,[35] as has been suggested by some scholars (See FACT 52).

Deuteronomy 29:22–24

This passage is limited in its geographic clues but does connect Admah and Zeboiim with Sodom and Gomorrah (See also Gen 10:19; 14:2, 8). At the time of the writing of Deuteronomy (which scholars agree, Moses did at Abel-Shittim [meaning "Acacias of Mourning"] identified with Tall el-Ḥammâm;[36] see *Fact 26*) the evidence of the burned-out land was evident. Moses described Abel-Shittim as a wasteland or uninhabited (Num 21:20; 22:1). It also reinforces the use of brimstone and salt in the destruction, resulting in the inability of the ground to grow crops.

Deuteronomy 34:1–3

Moses' panorama of the wasteland of the *kikkār* (Num 21:20, 22:1) and the Promised Land begins at Mt. Pisgah, near Mt. Nebo in Moab, east of Jericho.[37] Then, facing the Mediterranean Sea, Moses begins on his right with ① Gilead (east of the Jordan. See the numbers on Map 5) traveling north as far as ② the city of Dan (N boundary, not to be confused with the tribe of Dan), where the Transjordan ends, then traveling from north to south along the Mediterranean Sea (W boundary) (③ Naphtali, ④ Manasseh, ⑤ Ephraim, and ⑥ Judah). Then in the south, the border is mentioned at ⑦ the Negev (S boundary), followed by ⑧ the *kikkār*, which he identified as the Valley of Jericho. This places the *kikkār* in the disk, north of the Dead Sea, connected with Jericho. Then having mentioned the northern (② Dan), western (③④⑤⑥ Mediterranean), and southern (⑦ Negev) borders, he identifies ⑨ Zoar as the Eastern boundary. Moses would have passed by the site of Serâbît el-Mushaqqar (OT Zoar?) on his climb up Mt. Nebo to view the Promised Land.

Power concludes that: "It is impossible to avoid the conclusion that Ṣo'ar is at the foot of Mount Nebo, where the vision began, and at the eastern limit of the Round of the valley of Jericho, where it ended."[38] Howard argues the same:

---

[34] Charles A. Briggs, Samuel R. Driver, and Francis Brown, eds., *A Hebrew and English Lexicon of the Old Testament with an Appendix Containing the Biblical Aramaic. Based on the Lexicon of William Gessenius as Translated by Edward Robinson* (Boston, Mass.: Houghton Milfflin, 1907), 245.

[35] Gordon J. Wenham, *Genesis 16-50*, ed. David Allan Hubbard and Glenn W. Barker, vol. 2, Word Biblical Commentary (Dallas, Tex.: Word Books, 1994), 59.

[36] Kaiser, Jr. and Garrett, *NIV Archaeological Study Bible*, 233.

[37] Joel F. Drinkard Jr., "'AL PÉNÊ as 'East of,'" *Journal of Biblical Literature* 98 (1978): 285–86.

[38] Power, "The Site of the Pentapolis: Part 1," 42.

> Since this scene begins with the most remote part of the *kikkār* it must end at the nearest, which places Zoar near the foot of Mount Nebo.[39] Furthermore, the point is often made that the Byzantine-Arabic site of Zoar and the southern end of the Dead Sea are not visible from the Mount Nebo vicinity, the view being obstructed by the mountains of Moab.[40]

Driver point out that "v. 3 implies naturally that Zoar was at some distance off, not a place at the foot of Nebo."[41] Although if Zoar is at es-Safi, as the SST advocates propose,[42] then the eastern border of the Promised Land is located in Moabite territory, south of the Arnon River, which never happened, as Reuben was north of the Arnon River. The Negev has already been identified as the southern boundary, so Zoar is not likely the southern boundary, but the eastern boundary. This passage would seem to favour the NST and place Zoar someplace near Mt. Nebo (see *Fact 33*).[43]

Isaiah 15:4–7; Jeremiah 48:4, 34

Isaiah and Jeremiah provide parallel passages which help us locate several biblical places, with bearings on where Sodom is situated. Power exegetes the passages of Isaiah 15 and Jeremiah 48 and argues for the NST based on the boundaries of Palestine with Moab[44] and locating Ṣo'ar at the north-east of the Dead Sea.

The identification of Luḥith is confirmed by a Nabatean inscription,[45] now in the Vatican Museum. It commemorates two military personnel from the military camp at Luḥitu, and this inscription was placed over their tomb. The inscription was reused to build a church in Madaba and according to Power "evidently belongs to that city or its immediate vicinity," placing Luḥitu near Madaba. There are several military posts near Mt. Nebo (i.e., el-Mḫeyyeṭ which may come from El-Uḫit, then el-Mḫeyyeṭ).[46]

Power points out that:

> The southern Luhith of the *Onomasticon* between Areopolis and Zoar, sixty to ninety kilometres south of Madaba and far away from all frontiers of the Nabataean kingdom, cannot possibly be the Luḥitu of CIS [*Corpus Inscriptionum Semiticarum*] 196.[47]

On the location of Ḥoronaim, Musil identifies it as Tell er-Rāme, which is well accepted as another form of Beth Ḥaran. Power agrees and bases his opinion on the Moabite Stone (Mesha Stele) inscription, which mentions Ḥoronaim as a significant city in the Jordan Valley at the north end of the Dead Sea.[48]

Some have tried to argue that Zoar and Ḥoronaim must be south of the Arnon because they are not mentioned among

---

[39] Jan Jozef Simons, *The Geographical and Topographical Texts of the Old Testament: A Concise Commentary in Xxxii Chapters* (Leiden: Brill, 1959), 406.

[40] Howard, Jr., "Sodom and Gomorrah Revisited," 390. Driver observes that there are many other locations mentioned here that were not visible from Mt. Nebo, including: Northern Gilead, Dan and, the Mediterranean Sea. Samuel R. Driver, *A Critical and Exegetical Commentary on Deuteronomy*, ICC 5 (Edinburgh: T. & T. Clark, 1978), 419–21; "Zoar," 986.

[41] Driver, "Zoar," 4:986.

[42] Konstantinos D. Politis, "Death at the Dead Sea," *BAR* 38, no. 2 (2013): 42.

[43] Howard argues for a southern location from this passage, based on a chiastic reading of the text but this chiastic layout seems unnatural and forced on the text which is otherwise a natural reading of a geographic map. Howard, Jr., "Sodom and Gomorrah Revisited," 391-92.

[44] Torrent or Brook of the Willows = Wadi el-Garaba, which is the north-western boundary of Moab in Isaiah 15:7 and the south-eastern boundary of Israel in Amos 6:14. Power, "The Site of the Pentapolis: Part 1," 33.

[45] *Corpus Inscriptionum Semiticarum: Ab Academia Inscriptionum et Litterarum Humaniorum Conditum Atque Digestum*, vol. 2 (Paris: Reipublicae Typographeo, 1881), 196.

[46] Power, "The Site of the Pentapolis: Part 1," 34 n. 2; Alois Musil, *Arabia Petraea: Moab*, vol. 1 (Wien: A. Hölder, 1907), 334–40.

[47] Power, "The Site of the Pentapolis: Part 1," 35.

[48] Ibid.

Israel's cities in the book of Joshua, but this is an argument from silence (*argumentum e silentio*). Nebo, or Elealeh, is also not mentioned in Joshua but is listed in Numbers 32 verses 3 and 37.

Howard uses these verses to locate Zoar in Moab and thus argue for a southern location for the Cities of the Plain.[49] However, even if Zoar is in Moab, this does not mean that the four destroyed Cities of the Plain were in the same location, since Zoar was spared.

Ezekiel 16:46

Howard believes that: "this is the one clear description of where Sodom was: It is pictured, along with its satellite villages ("daughters"), as south of Jerusalem and opposed to Samaria, which was north of it."[50]

Wood points out that: "Samaria is 55 km (34 miles) north of Jerusalem and Bab edh-Dhraʿ is 64 km (40 miles) southeast of Jerusalem but Tall el-Hammam is 42 km (26 miles) east-northeast of Jerusalem."[51]

However, the question must be asked: should poetic verse be treated the same as narrative literature (see *Fact 19*)? Power points out: "that it fails to distinguish between the absolute and the relative use of the expressions "on the right hand" and "on the left hand.". . . . for we must remember that the cities are here personified."[52]

It is also interesting to note that the same Hebrew words for left and right in Genesis 13:9 are translated "If you take the left hand, then I will go to the right, or if you take the right hand, then I will go to the left." (Gen 13:9). While Lot travels east to the *kikkār*, Abraham travels south to Hebron (Gen 14:13). Left and right here do not appear to

5. One of 1800 clay Ebla tablets dating to between 2500 and 2250 BC discovered in 1974–75 during the excavations of the ancient city of *Tell Mardikh* (Ebla). Together with the Mari tablets they give a clearer picture of life in the ancient Near East.

Photo by Clifford Wilson

be used in strict geographic sense of north and south (see *Fact 18)*. Abraham said he would go in another direction from Lot and if he went south, how could Lot also go in the same direction? If, in this narrative account in Genesis 13, the Hebrew terms, left (Heb. *śəmō'l*) and right (Heb. *yāmîn*) are not used as strict directional indicators, then it is likely that they are not used this way in a poetic passage like Ezekiel.

ANCIENT TEXTUAL REFERENCES

Ebla Tablets (*ca.* 2500–*ca.* 2250 BC)[53]

In 1974–75 some 1,757 clay tablets (with some 4,875 fragments) were discovered under the direction of Paolo Matthiae of the University of Rome, during the excavations of the ancient city of Tell Mardikh (Ebla, Syria), which contained about 1,000 place names

---

[49] Howard, "Sodom and Gomorah revisited", 392.
[50] Ibid.
[51] Bryant G. Wood, "Locating Sodom: A Critique of the Northern Proposal," *BS* 20, no. 3 (2007): 78.
[52] Power, "The Site of the Pentapolis: Part 1," 1:48.

[53] Michael R. T. Dumper and Bruce E. Stanley, *Cities of the Middle East and North Africa: A Historical Encyclopedia* (Santa Barbara, Calf.: ABC-CLIO, 2007), 141.

from the ancient Near East.⁵⁴ Giovanni Pettinato, the original epigrapher at Ebla,⁵⁵ announced in 1976 that he had identified the names of Sodom, Gomorrah, and Zoar/Bela in the Ebla tablets.⁵⁶ This announcement was picked up and reported by many non-specialists.⁵⁷ Matthiae dates the tablets to the Early Bronze III (2400 and 2250 BC)⁵⁸ which would be the earliest mention of the "Cities of the Plain" outside the biblical text and the time period would indicate that merchants from Ebla were trading with the Cities of the Plain prior to their destruction. If correct, this would certainly confirm the existence of the Cities of the Plain as early as Gen 10. G. Pettinato, M. Dahood, D. H. Freedman, and W. Shea have been the most outspoken proponents of this idea.⁵⁹

Eblaite has been identified as a Semitic language like ancient Hebrew, but "written in the cuneiform writing system of Sumer"⁶⁰ and related to Akkadian.⁶¹ Therefore, it should be closely identified with Hebrew, even though Eblaite is much earlier. Cyrus Gordon points out: "The earliest Hebrew records are about a thousand years later than the last texts in Eblaite. Pretending to know everything significant that happened in the interim may be an art, but it is not a science."⁶²

Wilson points out that: "The vocabularies at Ebla were distinctively Semitic: the word "to write" is *k-t-b* (as in Hebrew), while that for "king" is "malikum," [Heb. *melik*] and that for "man" is "adamu."

---

⁵⁴ Alfonso Archi, "The Epigraphic Evidence from Ebla and the Old Testament," *Biblica* 60, no. 4 (1979): 556–66; "The Archives of Ebla," in *Cuneiform Archives and Libraries*, ed. Klaas R. Veenhof, Papers Read at the 30e Rencontre Assyriologique Internationale, Leiden, 4-8 July 1983 (Leiden: Netherlands Institute for the Near East, 1986), 78.

⁵⁵ The epigrapher of the expedition was changed to Alfonso Archi, a non-Assyrian specialist, for political reasons. Biggs, "Ebla Texts", 264. None of Pettianto's publications are listed on the official Ebla website. http://www.ebla.it/epubblicazioni __bibliografia_scelta_su_ebla.html.

⁵⁶ Giovanni Pettinato, "Report on Ebla," in *Conference Paper* (Society of Biblical Literature, St. Louis, Miss., 1976); "Gli archivi reali di Tell Mardikh-Ebla: riflessioni e prospettive," *Rivista Biblica Italiana* 25, no. 1 (1977): 236; "Ebla and the Bible," *BA* 43 (1980): 203–16.

⁵⁷ David Noel Freedman, "The Real Story of the Ebla Tablets: Ebla and the Cities of the Plain," *BA* 41 (1978): 143–64; William H. Shea, "Two Palestinian Segments from the Eblaite Geographical Atlas," in *Word of the Lord Shall Go Forth: Essays in Honor of David Noel Freedman in Celebration of His Sixtieth Birthday*, ed. Carol L. Meyers and M. O'Connor, ASOR (Winona Lake, Ind.: Eisenbrauns, 1983), 589–612.

⁵⁸ Paolo Matthiae, "Ebla Recovered," in *Ebla to Damascus: Art and Archaeology of Ancient Syria: An Exhibition from the Directorate-General of Antiquities and Museums, Syrian Arab Republic*, ed. Harvey Weiss (Washington, D.C.: Smithsonian Institution Traveling Exhibition Service, 1985), 134–137.

⁵⁹ Pettinato, "Ebla and the Bible"; Mitchell J. Dahood, "Appendix," in *The Archives of Ebla: An Empire Inscribed in Clay*, ed. Giovanni Pettinato, Translation of Ebla: Un Impero Inciso Nell'Argilla (Garden City, N.Y.: Doubleday, 1981); "Ebla, Ugarit and the Old Testament," *BS* 8, no. 1–16 (1979); "Ebla, Ugarit and the Old Testament," in *Vetus Testamentum Supplements*, vol. 29 (Leiden: Brill, 1978), 81–112; Freedman, "The Real Story of the Ebla Tablets"; Clifford A. Wilson, *Ebla Tablets: Secrets of a Forgotten City: Revelations of Tell Mardikh*, Third, Enlarged and Updated (San Diego, CA: Creation-Life, 1981); Clifford A. Wilson, *The Impact of Ebla on Bible Records: The Sensational Tell Mardikh* (Word of Truth, 1977); Shea, "Two Palestinian Segments."

⁶⁰ Robert D. Biggs, "Ebla Texts," ed. David Noel Freedman et al., *ABD* (New York, N.Y.: Doubleday, 1996), 264.

⁶¹ Ignace J. Gelb, *Thoughts About Ibla: A Preliminary Evaluation*, Syro-Mesopotamian Studies 1 (Malibu, Calf.: Undena, 1980), 28; Edmond Sollberger, *Administrative Texts Chiefly Concerning Textiles (L. 2752)*, Archivi Reali de Ebla, Testi 8 (Rome: Missione Archaeologica Italiana in Siria, 1986), 1; Bruno W. W. Dombrowski, "'Eblaite': The Earliest Known Dialect of Akkadian," *Zeitschrift Der Deutschen Morgenländischen Gesellschaft* 138 (1988): 211–35.

⁶² Cyrus Herzl Gordon, Gary Rendsburg, and Nathan H. Winter, eds., *Eblaitica: Essays on the Ebla Archives and Eblaite Language* (Winona Lake, Ind.: Eisenbrauns, 1987), 2.

[Heb. *adama*]. The closeness to Hebrew is surprising."[63]

However, one of the difficulties in reading Eblaite is indicated by the fact that: "the handwriting of Ebla cuneiform texts demonstrates a distinctive regional style immediately recognizable as different from any cuneiform writing known from Mesopotamia."[64]

However, one does not need to be an expert Assyrian epigrapher to recognize the similarities between the transliteration of Hebrew and Eblaite.

The Cities of the Plain[65]		
Bible	Gen 14	Ebla Tablet
English	Hebrew	Eblaite
Sodom	sĕdōm	si-da-mu[66]
Gomorrah	'ămōrāh	e-ma-ra[67]
Admah	'admāh	ad-ma
Zeboiim	sĕbōyîm	si-ba-i-um
Bela	bela' [zoar][68]	be-la/ za-é-ar[69]

It needs to be remembered that these ancient languages were spoken dialects and written down phonetically,[70] which is further complicated in that "the Sumero-Eblaite writing system was polyphonic, i.e., one and the same sign could stand for more than one sound or value".[71] As Freedman points out:

> The names themselves are the same in the two sources, and there can be little doubt that the same cities are involved; the only differences in the names are in the vocalization, i.e., the vowels, and these reflect only the standard evolution in pronunciation that has been established on a broad scale as Canaanite evolved into Biblical Hebrew and ultimately the Masoretic vowels indications (the Masoretes between A.D. 500–950 preserved the oral tradition concerning the correct vowels and accents).[72]

However, the identification of all five Cities of the Plain in the Ebla tablets has been strongly criticized by most scholars,[73] and Pettinato has now denied that the names of all five cities are listed together in order in the tablets.[74] But, even if some of the cities are

---

[63] Clifford Wilson, "Ebla: Its Impact on Bible Records," *Institute for Creation Research: Acts & Facts.* 6 (4), 1977, 1, http://www.icr.org/article/92/; *Ebla Tablets*; Edward Ullendorff, *From the Bible to Enrico Cerulli: A Miscellany of Ethiopian and Semitic Papers* (Berlin: Franz Steiner, 1990), 178.

[64] Biggs, "Ebla Texts," 264; "On Regional Cuneiform Handwritings in Third Millennium Mesopotamia," *Orientalia (NS)* 42 (1973): 39–46.

[65] This chart is adapted from Freedman. Freedman, "The Real Story of the Ebla Tablets," 149. However, he does not provide any textual references for any of the Ebla words in the chart. The references for three of the cities have been provided from other sources.

[66] Giovanni Pettinato and A. Alberti, *Catalogo Dei Testi Cuneiformi Di Tell Mardikh-Ebla*, Materiali Epigrafici Di Ebla 1 (Naples: Istituto Universitario Orientale di Napoli, 1979), Catalog No. 6522; 76. G. 524; Catalog No. 75. G. 2377, obverse IV.8; Catalog No. 2379 reverse 1.5.

[67] Ibid., Catalog No. 1671; 75. G. 2233; Catalog No. 1008; 75. G. 1570 obverse 111.

[68] Genesis 14:2, 8. Freedman states that Zoar is found in another Ebla tablet as *za-è-ar*. Freedman, "The Real Story of the Ebla Tablets," 150; Hershel Shanks, "BAR Interviews Giovanni Pettinato: Original Ebla Epigrapher Attempts to Set the Record Straight," *BAR* 6, no. 5 (1980): 47.

[69] Pettinato and Alberti, *Catalogo Dei Testi Cuneiformi Di Tell Mardikh-Ebla*, Catalog No. 75. G. 1323, obverse IV.15–VII.3; Catalog No. 1024; 75. G. 1586 obverse IX.2–12; Catalog No. 75. G. 1527 reverse IV.6–11.

[70] For the factors which influence the transmission of texts in historical geography see Aharoni, *The Land of the Bible*, 100–112.

[71] Shea, "Two Palestinian Segments," 592.

[72] Freedman, "The Real Story of the Ebla Tablets," 149.

[73] Archi, "The Epigraphic Evidence from Ebla and the Old Testament," 563; Robert D. Biggs, "The Ebla Tablets: An Interim Perspective," *BA* 43, no. 2 (1980): 76–86; Alfonso Archi, "Further Concerning Ebla and the Bible," *BA* 44, no. 3 (1981): 145–54; "Are 'The Cities of the Plain' Mentioned in the Ebla Tablets?: Cities Identified by Pettinato Are Nowhere near the Dead Sea," *BAR* 7, no. 6 (1981): 54–55.

[74] Gary A. Rendsburg, "Ebla," in *Encyclopedia Judaica*, ed. Michael Berenbaum and Fred Skolnik, vol. 6, 2nd ed. (New York, N.Y.: MacMillan, 2007), 87.

mentioned in the Ebla tablets, this still does not help us provide a location for the Pentapolis (see *Fact 47*).

Concerning the EB date of the Ebla tablets, both Wood and Collins agree that Sodom existed in the Early Bronze Age, and both sites (BeD and TeH) were occupied in the EB age. The important question concerning the time of the destruction of the four Cities of the Plain is not answered by the Ebla tablets.

Ugaritic texts (*ca.* 1250 BC)

Mulder records that the name of Sodom has turned up in Ugaritic texts but is unwilling to admit that it is the Sodom of the OT. However, one wonders how many Sodoms there might have been in the ancient Near East at that time. Mulder states: "Evidence from Ugarit includes *šdmy*, [75] which one can probably view "according to form as a *gentilicium* of Sodom" without being able to identify it with the Sodom of the OT."[76]

Again, this identification does not help in the locating of the Cities of the Plain but only indicates that the city of Sodom existed or was known during this period of history.

TRADITIONAL REFERENCES

While several authors (Grove,[77] Conder,[78] Wilson,[79] Tristram,[80] Merrill,[81] Palmer,[82] Birth and others) wrote in support of the NST before 1930, Power, a NST advocate, is the first to mention it with a thorough treatment of the references within the writings of tradition, even though he argues that they strongly argue for the SST. He argues that this may be because the reliability of tradition is questionable.[83] Taylor points out the problems over the reliability of traditional information: "Apart from these snippets of historical information, pilgrims reported what guides told them and made personal observations, which generally resulted in a curious mix of erroneous and factual material."[84]

Freedman quotes from a letter he received from Dahood who was working with Pettinato that states: "the cities 3 and 4 of the Genesis 14 list do not occcur in the same tablet." David Noel Freedman, "The Real Story of the Ebla Tablets: Ebla and the Cities of the Plain," *Biblical Archaeologist* 41 (1978): 143.

[75] Charles Virolleaud, "Les Nouveaux Textes Alphabetiques de Ras-Shamra (XVIe Campagne, 1952)," *Syria* 30 (1953): 190; Cyrus H. Gordon, *Ugaritic Textbook: Grammar, Texts in Transliteration, Cuneiform Selections, Glossary, Indices*, Analecta Orientalia 38 (Rome: Pontifical Biblical Institute, 1998), no. 1742.

[76] Mulder, "Sodom; Gomorrah," 156.

[77] George Grove, "Sodom," ed. William Smith, *A Dictionary of the Bible* (Philadelphia, Pa.: Winston, 1884),

1338–42; "Zoar," ed. William Smith, *A Dictionary of the Bible* (Philadelphia, Pa.: Winston, 1884), 1856–58.

[78] Claude Reignier Conder, *Tent Work in Palestine: A Record of Discovery and Adventure* (London, U.K.: Bentley & Son, 1879), 2:13–17; Claude Reignier Conder and Horatio H. Kitchener, *The Survey of Eastern Palestine: The Adwan Country*, vol. 1 (London, U.K.: Palestine Exploration Fund, 1881), passim; Claude Reignier Conder, *Heth and Moab* (London, U.K.: Bentley & Son, 1883), 152–5.

[79] Charles W. Wilson, "On the Site of Ai and the Position of the Altar Which Abram Built Between Bethel and Ai," *PEFSt.* 1, no. 4 (1869): 125.

[80] Henry Baker Tristram, *The Land of Israel: A Journal of Travels in Palestine with Reference to Its Physical History* (London, U.K.: Society for the Promoting Christian Knowledge, 1865), 354; Henry Baker Tristram, *The Land of Moab: Travels and Discoveries on the East Side of the Dead Sea and the Jordan* (New York, N.Y.: Harper & Brothers, 1873), 334–47.

[81] Merrill, *East of the Jordan*, 232–39.

[82] Edward H. Palmer, *The Desert of the Exodus: Journeys on Foot in the Wilderness of the Forty Years' of Wanderings Undertaken in Connexion with the Ordance Survey of Sinai and the Palestine Exploration Fund*, vol. 1 (Cambridge, U.K.: Deighton, Bell & Co., 1871), 2:480–81.

[83] Power, "The Site of the Pentapolis: Part 1"; "The Site of the Pentapolis: Part 2," *Biblica* 12 (1930): 149–82.

[84] Joan E. Taylor, "The Dead Sea in Western Travellers' Accounts from the Byzantine to the Modern

Philo (*ca.* 20 BC–AD 50)

Philo (also Philo Judaeus of Alexandria) was a Hellenistic Jewish philosopher born in Alexandria during the reign of Herod the Great. His writing followed both Stoic philosophy and Jewish exegesis. Most of his works are only known through other writers like Eusebius of Caesarea (*ca.* AD 260–339).[85]

Quotes from Antiquity

Philo on the Pentapolis

(138) *The plain* too was consumed [by fire], and all the crop of wheat, and of everything else that was sown; and all the trees of *the mountain district* were burnt up . . . . And in one day these *populous cities* became the tomb of their inhabitants. . . . (140) And when *the flames had consumed everything that was visible* and that existed on the face of the earth, they proceeded to burn *even the earth itself*, penetrating into its lowest recesses, and destroying all the vivifying powers which existed within it so as to produce *a complete and everlasting barrenness, so that it should never again be able to bear fruit,* or to put forth any verdure; and *to this very day it is scorched up.* For the *fire of the lightning* is what is most *difficult to extinguish, and creeps on pervading everything, and smouldering.* (141) And a most evident proof of this is to be found in what is *seen to this day: for the smoke which is still emitted, and the sulphur which men dig up there, are a proof of the calamity which befell that country*; while a most *conspicuous proof of the ancient fertility of the land is left in one city,* and in the land around it. For the *city is very populous, and the land is fertile in grass and in corn, and in every kind of fruit,* as a constant evidence of the punishment which was inflicted by the divine will on the rest of the country. (*Abr.* 27.138–141 [Young])

(55) God determined to *destroy them* [the Cities of the Plain] *with fire*. (56) Therefore on this occasion, as the holy scriptures tell us, *thunderbolts* fell from heaven, and *burnt up those wicked men and their cities*; and *even to this day there are seen in Syria monuments of the unprecedented destruction* that fell upon them, in the *ruins, and ashes, and sulphur, and smoke, and dusky flame which still is sent up from the ground as of a fire smouldering beneath.* (*Mos.* 2.10.54–56 [Young] emphasis added)[86]

Power examines the late evidence of Philo from the first century tradition of the region and states:

> Philo gives us one indication of the site. . . . [and] cannot refer to the northern So'ar which was then in ruins, as we learn from Josephus (*J.W.* 4.8.4).[87] As to the Roman fort at Zoar at the south of the Dead Sea [Eusebius *On.* Section A Genesis 4], it can scarcely have been a populous city. Moreover Philo excludes the submission theory, peculiar to those who identify *So'ar* with Zoar in the south, and gives such existing signs of the catastrophe as are invariably located in the north. . . . Sulphur is found in various places on the shores of the lake, but the best known sulphur region, referred to in the northern tradition and by modern explorers, is three miles north of the Dead Sea and one mile west of the Jordan. There the air reeks with sulphur and there is no vegetation.[88]

But clearly, Philo is reporting the local tradition and describing what he saw in the first century in the region from its destruction by lightning, identified with sulphur, ash, smoke and fire. Although Power links Philo's comments to the NST, Philo's statements could easily describe any part of the Dead Sea area and are not helpful in identifying the location of the Pentapolis.

Period," *Bulletin of the Anglo-Israel Archaeological Society* 27 (2009): 13.

[85] David E. Graves, *Key Themes of the Old Testament: A Survey of Major Theological Themes* (Moncton, N.B.: Graves, 2013), 74.

[86] Philo, *Works of Philo*.

[87] Flavius Josephus, *The Jewish War: Volume II, Books 3-4*, trans. H. St. J. Thackeray, vol. 3, 13 vols., LCL 487 (Cambridge, Mass.: Harvard University Press, 1927).

[88] Power, "The Site of the Pentapolis: Part 2," 2:151; Max Blanckenhorn, *Entstehung und Geschichte des Toten Meeres: Beitraeg zur Geologie Palaestinas*, Zeitschrift des deutschen Palästina-Vereins 19 (Leipzig: Baedeker, 1896), 44–47.

The Location of Sodom

Strabo (64/63 BC–ca. AD 24)

Strabo, the Greek historian and geographer, identified Sodom on the western side of the Dead Sea at the Crusader / Muslim site of Jebel Usdum (Mount of Sodom), not far from the fortress of Masada (see *Fact 58*).

Quotes from Antiquity

Strabo on Sodom

Many other evidences are produced to show that the country is fiery; for *near Moasada [sic Masada modern es-Sebbbe]* are to be seen rugged rocks that have been scorched, as also, in many places, fissures and ashy soil, and drops of pitch that emit foul odours to a great distance, and ruined settlements here and there; and therefore people believe the oft-repeated assertions of the local inhabitants, that there were once *thirteen inhabited cities* in that region of which *Sodom was the metropolis*, but that a circuit of *about sixty stadia of that city escaped unharmed*; and that by reason of *earthquakes* and of eruptions of fire and of hot waters containing *asphalt [bitumen] and sulphur*, the lake burst its bounds, and rocks were enveloped with fire; and, as for *the cities, some were swallowed up and others were abandoned by such as were able to escape*. But Eratosthenes says, on the contrary, that the country was a lake, and that most of it was uncovered by outbreaks, as was the case with the sea. (Strabo *Geogr.* 16.2.44 [Jones])

It is obvious that Strabo was determining the location of the Pentapolis on the appearance of the destruction in the area around Masada, along with local tradition of an earthquake rather than on archaeological evidence. As Power points out:

> We should have an anticipation of the modern theory that the destruction of the cities was due to an earthquake which produced at the same time an extension of the lake by the subsidence and consequent submersion of the valley to the south of it. . . . Strabo attests that he got his information (mediately or immediately) from a Jewish source [*m. rab.* Job 28:9-10a], the natives of the place, whose views he records on the case of the disaster and the extent of the Pentapolis.[89]

Power points out that the submersion view (under the Dead Sea as one of the possible SST) is always connected to the activity of an earthquake in the south, a view thus identifying Strabo's testimony with the SST.[90]

Josephus (*ca.* AD 37–100)

Josephus was a first century Jewish historian, Roman general and apologist born and raised in Jerusalem.[91] He describes the location of destroyed Sodom as being near the Jordan River, as Lot also possessed the land of the plain. While the Jordan and the plain are located in the northern region of the Jordan Valley, SST proponents would argue that the southern region is near the Jordan River and part of the land of the plain. Josephus' comments could support either view.

Quotes from Antiquity

Josephus on Sodom

But Lot possessed the *land of the plain*, and the *river Jordan, not far from the city of Sodom*, which was then a fine city; but is *now destroyed*, by the will and wrath of God; the cause of which I shall show in its proper place hereafter. (*Ant.* 1:170 [Whiston])

Then, after describing the battle with the Elamite king, Chedorlaomer, Josephus indicates that following the destruction of Sodom, the bitumen (slime; see *Fact 57*) pits and the valley of Siddim became "the Dead Sea and places Ṣo'ar to the south of it".[92]

---

[89] Power, "The Site of the Pentapolis: Part 2," 2:155–56.
[90] Ibid., 2:156.
[91] Graves, *Key Themes of the OT*, 74.
[92] Power, "The Site of the Pentapolis: Part 2," 2:160; David Noel Freedman, Allen C. Myers, and Astrid B. Beck, eds., *Eerdmans Dictionary of the Bible* (Grand Rapids, Mich.: Eerdmans, 2000), 1218.

However, there is no geological evidence to suggest that the Dead Sea was created in the EB or MB periods (see *Fact 61*).

Quotes from Antiquity

> **Josephus on Sodom**
>
> These kings had laid waste all Syria, and overthrown the offspring of the giants; and when they were come *opposite Sodom*, they pitched their camp at *the vale called the Slime Pits*, for *at that time there were pits in that place*; but now, upon the destruction of the *city of Sodom*, that vale became the *Lake Asphaltites* [The Dead Sea], as it is called. (*Ant.* 1:174 [Whiston])

In this passage, Josephus additionally assumed that there was no longer in the first century any evidence of slime (bitumen) pits in the area, because the Dead Sea had swallowed them up and covered them over, making the vale the Lake *Asphaltites* [the Dead Sea].

Josephus then went on to describe the Dead Sea and the cities of Zoar and Sodom (*Ant.* 1.170f, 174, 179, 182, 198; 5:81; *J.W.* 4.453, 483, 485; 5.566)[93] as quoted below:

Quotes from Antiquity

> **Josephus on Sodom**
>
> The length of this lake [the Dead Sea] is about seventy-three miles, where it is *extended as far as Zoar in Arabia*; and its breadth is about nineteen miles. 483 The *country of Sodom borders it*. It was of old a most pleasant land, both for the fruits it bore and the riches of its cities, although it be now all burnt up. 484 It is related how, for the impiety of its inhabitants, it was *burnt by lightning*; in consequence of which there are still the remainders of that divine fire; and the traces [or shadows] of the five cities are still to be seen, as well as the ashes growing in their fruits, which fruits have a colour as if they were fit to be eaten, but if you pluck them with your hands, they dissolve into smoke and ashes. 485 And thus what is related of this *land of Sodom* has these marks of credibility which our very sight affords us. (Josephus *J.W.* 4:476–485 [Whiston])[94]

Tacitus (AD 56 – after 117)

Tacitus, the great Roman historian, wrote about the Dead Sea and highlighted the presence of bitumen in the lake (see *Fact 57*). He then dealt with the theory of destruction by lightning of the Cities of the Plain, which he claimed resulted in all the ash and the land being sterile. He also records how the plain was "once fertile, they say, and the site of great cities" (*Hist.* 5.7 [Church and Brodribb]).

Quotes from Antiquity

> **Tacitus on the Dead Sea and Pentapolis**
>
> At a certain season of the year the lake [Dead Sea] *throws up bitumen*, and the method of collecting it has been taught by that experience which teaches all other arts. It is naturally a fluid of dark colour; when vinegar is sprinkled upon it, it coagulates and floats upon the surface. Those whose business it is take it with the hand, and draw it on to the deck of the boat; it then continues of itself to flow in and lade the vessel till the stream is cut off. Nor can this be done by any instrument of brass or iron. It shrinks from blood or any cloth stained by the menstrua of women. Such is the account of old authors; but those who know the country say that the *bitumen moves in heaving masses on the water, that it is drawn by hand to the shore, and that there, when dried by the evaporation of the earth and the power of the sun,*

---

[93] Flavius Josephus, *Jewish Antiquities: Volume I, Book 1-3*, trans. H. St. J. Thackeray, vol. 5, 13 vols., LCL 242 (Cambridge, Mass.: Harvard University Press, 1930); *The Jewish War: Volume III, Books 5-7*, trans. H. St. J. Thackeray, vol. 4, 13 vols., LCL 210 (Cambridge, Mass.: Harvard University Press, 1928).

[94] Flavius Josephus, *The Works of Josephus: Complete and Unabridged*, trans. William Whiston, New Updated (Peabody, Mass.: Hendrickson, 1980).

The Location of Sodom

> *it is cut into pieces with axes and wedges just as timber or stone would be.*
>
> Not far from this lake lies *a plain, once fertile, they say, and the site of great cities*, but afterwards struck by *lightning and consumed*. Of this event, they declare, *traces still remain*, for the soil, which is *scorched in appearance*, has lost its productive power. Everything that grows spontaneously, as well as what is planted by hand, either when the leaf or flower have been developed, or after maturing in the usual form, *becomes black and rotten*, and *crumbles into a kind of dust* [likely the Sodom apple]. I am ready to allow, on the one hand, that cities, once famous, may have been *consumed by fire* from heaven, while, on the other, I imagine that the earth is infected by the exhalations of the lake, that the surrounding air is tainted, and that thus the growth of harvest and the fruits of autumn decay under the equally noxious influences of soil and climate. The river Belus also flows into the Jewish sea. About its mouth is a kind of sand which is collected, mixed with nitre, and fused into glass. This shore is of limited extent, but furnishes an inexhaustible supply to the exporter. (*Hist.* 5.6–7 [Church and Brodribb] emphasis added)

Tertullian (*ca.* AD 160–*ca.* 225)

While many of the Church Fathers make reference to Sodom and Gomorrah in their writings,[95] the Christian apologist Tertullian provides clues for the location of the Cities of the Plain. He states that they are in the region of the Jordan adjoining Palestine near the Dead Sea.

Quotes from Antiquity

Tertullian on Sodom

> Palestine had not yet received from Egypt its Jewish swarm (of emigrants), nor had the race from which Christians sprung yet settled down there, when its *neighbors Sodom and Gomorrah were consumed by fire from heaven*. (*Apol.* 40.1 [Lightfoot])
>
> Where the *river Jordan is the umpire of boundaries*, there is now an *immense wilderness*: the *country is deserted and the fields are barren*. But towns there used to be of old, and there was a large population there, and the soil tended to obey. Subsequently, now that God in censor and impiety has earned *rains of fire*, so much for *Sodom and there is no Gomorrha anymore*. All has turned into *ashes* and the *soil is living its death along with the nearby sea*. (*Pall.* 2.4 [Hunink] emphasis added)[96]

Pionius (AD ?–250)

Pionius was a disciple of the apostle John, and the bishop of Smyrna in Asia Minor (modern Turkey), who died as a martyr in 250 AD. Pionius places the land of the Sodomites opposite the Jordan River in the region of the Dead Sea.

Quotes from Antiquity

Pionius on the area of destruction

> I, myself, having gone abroad and traversed all Judaea and *crossed the Jordan* beheld a region still bearing witness to the wrath of God which came upon it owing to the sins of its inhabitants who slew their guests, refused them hospitality, offered violence to them. I saw the *smoke* still ascending from it and the region *burnt* into *ashes devoid of all produce and all moisture*. I saw also *the Dead Sea*, the water changed and unnaturally weakened by the fear of God, unable to nurture a living thing, casting up again whoever is thrown into it and incapable of retaining a man's body

---

[95] Justin Martyr *Apol.* 1.53; *Dial.* 19.2; 55.2; 56.1, 6, 12ff, 16; 60.2ff; 126.1; 127.1; 128.1; 129.1; 140.1; Irenaeus *Haer.* 3.6.1; 4.16.2; 4.28.1; 4.31.1; 4.36.3f; 4.41.3; 5.27.1; Theophilus of Antioch *Autol.* 2.31; Clement of Alexandria *Paed.* 1.8.11; 3.8.10; *Strom.* 2.20.1; 4.17.2; Tertullian *Marc.* 2.14.1; 2.25.1; 3.13.2; 4.23.1; 4.27.1; 4.29.1; *Prax.* 16.1; *Ux.* 1.5; *Exh. cast.* 9.1; *Mon.* 16.1; *Jejun.* 7.4; Origen of Alexandria, *Princ.* 2.5.1ff; *Cels.* 1.66; 2.66; 4.21, 45; Cyprian *Test.* 3.33.

[96] Tertullian, *De Pallio: A Commentary*, trans. Vincent Hunink (Amsterdam: Gieben, 2005).

> within it, for it is unwilling to admit man lest it should again be punished by reason of man. (*Mart. Pionii* 4.18–20 [Power] emphasis added)[97]

While this does not demand the NST, the Jordan River only flows in the northern region of the Dead Sea Jordan Valley. However, his description is not conclusive and his evidence of smoke, ash, and barrenness could refer to both the SST and the NST. Powers maintains that Pionius' Greek version had been mistranslated into Latin as "*divina formidine extra naturales terminos egredientem*" [the fear of God without natural borders] to "bring St. Pionius into agreement with the southern tradition, to which he is entirely opposed."[98] Whether this was accidental or on purpose, is difficult to determine.

Gaius Julius Solinus (early 3rd cent. AD)

Solinus was a third century Latin grammarian and historian, who wrote: *The Wonders of the World* (*De mirabilibus mundi;* also known as *Collectanea rerum memorabilium* and *Polyhistor*).

Quotes from Antiquity

Solinus on Sodom and Gomorrah

> Down from Jerusalem to the recesses of a long gloomy bay is spread out, the *soil is black and burned to ashes*, and it bears witness to being *touched from heaven*: there are two cities, one named *Sodom and the other mentioned Gomorrah*, among which grows an apple [Sodom Apple], which may have the appearance of being ripe but can not be eaten, for the dust on the inside is kept only by a delicate outer skin, which if even pressed evaporates into smoke and turns into dust. (Solinus *Mem.* 35.7–8 [Graves])[99]

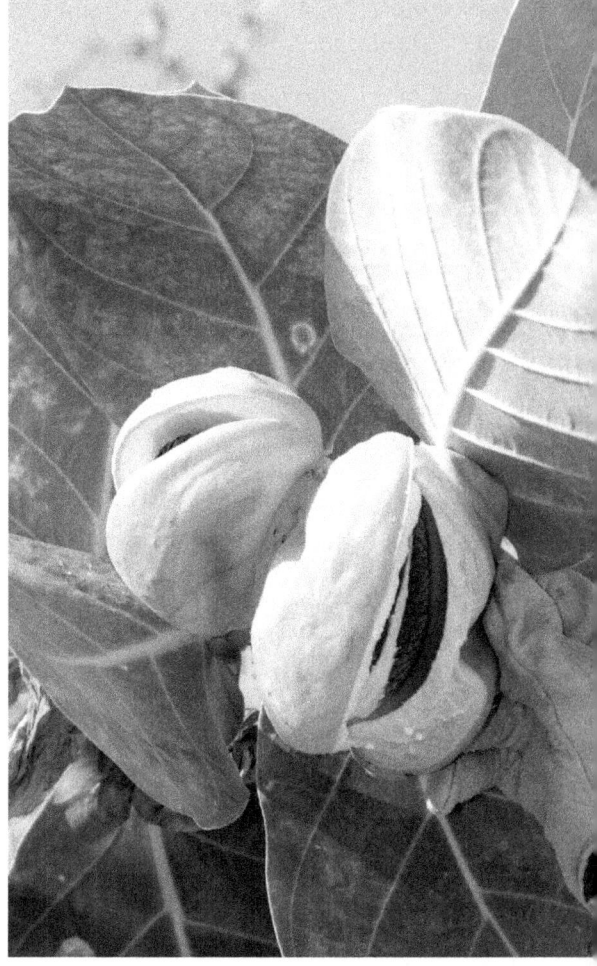

6. The Sodom apple (*Calotropis procera* or *Asclepias gigantea*) is a flowering plant native to North Africa which produces a green pod that resembles an apple. However, when squeezed it pops and sends a bitter poisonous white powder into the air. Josephus has the apple "dissolve into smoke and ashes," since it is growing near the site of Sodom (Josephus *J.W.* 4.8.4; Tacitus *Hist.* 5.6; Bede *Loc. Sanct.* 11.317).

Here the description is of a fiery catastrophe from heaven. The locations of the Sodom apples, as Power points out,

> are found also at the south of the Dead Sea but are always associated by early writers with its northern shore whenever a localisation is given. . . . After a

---

[97] Power, "The Site of the Pentapolis: Part 1," 1:53; R. Knopf, *Ausgewählte Märtyreracten: Martyrium Des Pionius*, ed. G. Krüger, Sammlung Ausgewählter Kirchen- Und Dogmengeschichtlicher Quellenschriften 3 (Tübingen: Mohr, 1913), 59.

[98] Power, "The Site of the Pentapolis: Part 1," 1:53.

[99] Gaius Julius Solinus, *Collectanea rerum memorabilium*, trans. Theodor Mommsen (Berlin: Weidmann, 1895), 118.

mention of Callirhoe and Jericho, Solinus speaks of the balm-trees of Judaea, which are particularly associated with Jericho (Jospehus *Ant.* 14.4.1). Then comes the passage cited above and immediately after it the region of the Essenes [Qumran] who are located north of Engaddi, Engaddi [*sic* En-Gedi] itself with its palm-groves and finally the fortress of Massada "terminus Iudaeae." Sodom and Gomorrha in the sinus between Jericho and the region north of Engaddi lie north of the Dead Sea on the eastern side of the Jordan.[100]

Eusebius (AD 260/265–339/340)

Eusebius was a church historian and the Bishop of Caesarea, who represented Palestine at the Council of Nicaea in 325 AD along with Severus, the Bishop of Sodom, who represented the province of Arabia (See Map 6[101] and *Chart 3: The Regions for the Church Council Representatives*).[102]

Quotes from Antiquity

Eusebius on the location of the Pentapolis

Astarōth Karnaein: Territory of the giants situated above (on the ridge). *Sodom* which Chodollagomor captured (destroyed). Today there are two towns (forts) of this name in Batabia or Beloloun the cities of Adara and Abila, about nine miles apart. (*On.* 4 [Wolf])

Adama: One of the five cities of Sodom which was destroyed with the others. (*On.* 7 [Wolf])

Bala: "That is *Sigor* (Heb. *Segor*). It is now called *Zoora* (Syriac *Zoara;* See Fig. 8), the only one [of the five cities] of the territory of *Sodom* which escaped [destruction]. It is now inhabited (remains still) in the *vicinity of the Dead Sea.* A garrison of (Roman) soldiers is (stationed) there (a peculiar people crowd in there.) The Balsam and the date palm in the land surrounding it proves the ancient fertility of the place." (*On.* 193 [Wolf])

Gomorra: One of the five cities of Sodom (which divine punishment) destroyed at the same time as the rest. (*On.* 293 [Wolf])

Zogera (Zogora): In Jeremia. City of Moab. It is now called *Zoora* or *Sigor* (Heb. *Segor*), one of the five cities of Sodom. (*On.* 467 [Wolf])

Lasan: *[Lisan]* Border of the Chanaanites [*sic* Canaanites] with the Sodomites. (*On.* 625 [Wolf])

Sodoma: City of wicked men which was completely destroyed (divine fire consumed) near the Dead Sea. (*On.* 809 [Wolf])

Sebōeim: City of the wicked near Sodom which was completely destroyed (disappeared in eternal ashes). (*On.* 810 [Wolf])

Sēgōr: [Which is also *Sala* and *Zoara*, one of the five cities of Sodom. By the prayer of Lot was saved from fire.] Up to now it is still pointed out, Isaia mentions it in the vision "Against the Moabites." (As we have spoken above). (*On.* 817 [Wolf])

In Eusebius' *Onomastican*,[103] a geographical work of place names around Palestine in the early fourth century; he describes the Lisan (Lasan *On.* 625) as the border between the Canaanites and the Sodomites.[104] He also places Zoora (Heb. *Segor;* See Fig. 8), known as *Bala,* in the region of Moab, south of the Arnon River. It becomes clear that in the fourth century the

---

[100] Power, "The Site of the Pentapolis: Part 1," 1:56.

[101] Irfan Shahîd, *Byzantium and the Arabs in the Sixth Century: Ecclesiastical History* (Washington, D.C.: Dumbarton Oaks, 1995), 683; Bernard Lewis, *Islam in History: Ideas, People, and Events in the Middle East* (Peru, Ill.: Open Court, 2013), 155.

[102] Michel Le Quien, *Oriens christianus in quatuor patriarchatus digestus, in quo exhibentur Ecclesiae patriarchae caeterique praesules totius Orientis* (Paris: Typographia Regia, 1740), 3:743.

[103] Pamphilus Eusebius, *The Onomasticon of Eusebius Pamphili: Compared with the Version of Jerome and Annotated*, ed. Noel C. Wolf, trans. C. Umhau Wolf (Washington, D.C.: Catholic University of America Press, 1971).

[104] It is well accepted that Eusebius' *Onomasticon* was heavily relied on for the creation of the Madaba Map.

PRIMARY SOURCES

7. Close up view of Tall el-Ḥammâm (Sodom?, Abel Shittim, and Livias) from the top of Mt. Nebo. According to Egeria the land of the Sodomites and Segor was just to the left of Livias (see Fig. 10).

area of Sodom was identified with the region south of the Lisan in the land of Moab.

Power points out that in his view, the origins of the SST can be found in the influence of Eusebius and Jerome, who were influenced by Jewish tradition:

> Eusebius and St. Jerome took over this [SST] tradition from the Jews and by their authority partially supplanted the ancient Christian tradition in favor of the northern site [NST], which survived however for a long period in the place of its origin as appears clearly from some of the narratives of the post-crusade pilgrims.[105]

Severus, Bishop of Sodom (AD 325)

It is known from Church records that Severus, the Bishop of Sodom (78 *Severus Sodomitanus*), attended the First Council of Nicaea in AD 325, as a representative of the ecclesiastical province of Arabia (Eusebius *On.* 26. See *Chart 3: The Regions for the Church Council Representatives*).[106] Eusebius, who was also present at the Council of Nicaea, states under Jordan (*Iordanēs*): "River dividing Judaea and Arabia and the Aulim next to the Dead Sea" (Eusebius *On.* 528 [Wolf]). At this period of its history the province of Arabia was on the eastern side of the Jordan River (modern day Jordan) but this would later change so that the Jordan Valley would become part of *Palæstina Prima* (I) which is evidenced in the travels and testimony of Egeria (AD 381–384. See below).

---

[105] Power, "The Site of the Pentapolis: Part 1," 30.

[106] Mounchy identified the Ecclesiastical province that the Bishop of Sodom represented as *Provincia Arabia*, while Le Quien identified the Bishop of Sodom in the section under *Ecclesia Zoarorum or Segor* in the *Provincia Palaestinae Tertiae* (III). Antoine de Mouchy, *Christianae religionis institutionisque Domini Nostri Jesu-Christi et apostolicae traditionis* (Paris: Macaeum, 1562), 85; Le Quien, *Oriens christianus*, 3:743; Peter Graham, *A Topographical Dictionary of Palestine, or the Holy Land* (London, U.K.: J. Davey, 1836), 242.

8. A section of the Madaba map marked as *Balak Zoora*, identified by the six palm trees, indicating the location of Byzantine Zoar (*Segor* or *eṣ-Ṣafi*) at the southern end of the Dead Sea. Lot's cave is also identified above Zoar. Notice that there is no Lisan (tongue) peninsula on the map as it had dried up in the Byzantine period much as it has today.

St. George Orthodox Church, Madaba Jordan

The ecclesiastical province of Arabia (See Map 6) was split into *Palæstina Prima* (I), *Palæstina Secunda* (II), *Palæstina Salutaris* (III later as *Tertia*) sometime between AD 357–358[107] and 409 (*Codex Theodosianus* 7.4.30).[108] It appears that it was a gradual process. In AD 357 Clematius was appointed governor of Palæstina and at that time it included Petra and Elusa, previously in Arabia.[109] According to the Verona List (*Laterculus Veronensis*),[110] in AD 358 the original Palaestina became *Palæstina Prima*, and a part of Arabia became *Palæstina Secunda*.[111]

Zoar (Lat. *Zoarorum*) was also in the ecclesiastical province of *Palæstina Tertiae* (III) after the division of *Palæstina*.[112] The first clear mention of the tripartite Palestine is in the *Codex Theodosianus* (7.4.30) which dates to 409. The ecclesiastical province of *Palæstina Prima* (I) included diocese[113] in the region of Judaea (Jericho Lat. *Hericho*[114]) and in the Transjordan (Livias Lat. *Libyadis*[115]), but did not include Madaba,[116] which remained in Arabia. The church records for the Council of Nicaea indicate that the Bishop of Sodom was representing Arabia.[117] However, Le Quien treated the reference to the Bishop of Sodom under VIII "The Church of Zoarorum or Segor" (Lat. *Ecclesia Zoarorum sive Segor*) in the Province of Palæstina III (*Provincia palaestinae Tertiae*)[118] since Sodom would later be associated with Palaestina III. However, Power concludes that:

> At the time of the Council of Nicaea a southern site of Sodom was entirely unknown to Christian tradition. There is therefore no doubt that Severus was a predecessor of the bishop of Segor. The conclusion that the bishop of Segor with whom Aetheria [Egeria; see article below] conversed occupied the same see as Severus bishop of Sodom implies that the early Christian tradition placed the

---

[107] Dan indicates that the division of Palestine into three sections is implied in the letters of Libanius: *Opera* (ed. R. Förster, X, Leipzig, 1921, epistles No. 334 to Clementius (p. 315) and No 686 to Cyrillus (p. 622) where "Libanius congratulates Cyrillus (in 361/2 C.E.) on his transfer from one 'Dominion' to another." However, this may be contradicted by Zosimus, who mentions that Hilarius is governor of all Palaestine at the beginning of the last decade of the fourth century. Yaron Dan, "Palaestina Salutaris (Tertia) and Its Capital," *IEJ* 32, no. 2/3 (1982): 134–35.

[108] Ibid., 135.

[109] J. B. Bury, "The Provincial List of Verona," *JRS* 13 (1923): 131.

[110] A seventh-century manuscript from Verona, which lists the earliest reorganization of Diocletian's late Roman provinces, at the end of the third century.

[111] John Wilkes, "Changes to Roman Provincial Organization," in *The Cambridge Ancient History: The Crisis of Empires AD 193-337*, ed. Alan K. Bowman, Averil Cameron, and Peter Garnsey, vol. 12 (Cambridge, U.K.: Cambridge University Press, 2007), 709; Bury, "The Provincial List of Verona," 131–32.

[112] Le Quien, *Oriens christianus*, 3:737–45.

[113] The district under a bishop's jurisdiction.

[114] Le Quien, *Oriens christianus*, 3:653.

[115] Ibid., 3:655–58.

[116] Alexander Kazhdan, ed., *The Oxford Dictionary of Byzantium* (Oxford, U.K.: Oxford University Press, 1991), 147.

[117] Mouchy, *Christianae religionis institutionisque*, 85.

[118] Le Quien, *Oriens christianus*, 3:743.

Sodomite region at the north of the Dead Sea.[119]

However, Power's assumption that the Bishop of Segor (Zoar) and the Bishop of Sodom occupied the same Ecclesiastical See, while likely, is not certain. Therefore, the identification of the Bishop of Sodom does not solve the mystery over the location of Sodom in the Byzantine era, although it does argue for the NST.

Egeria (late 4th century AD)

Egeria, a Spanish pilgrim, who visited the Holy Land in the Byzantine era (AD 381–384), stood at the door of the Christian church on the top of Mount Nebo (Jebel en-Neb) and identified the land of the Sodomites, and Segor, as being located just left of Livias (see map 6).

The region south of the Dead Sea is not visible from the top of Mt. Nebo, while Livias and the northern tip of the Dead Sea are clearly visible (see Fig. 7). This would indicate that Egeria saw the land of the Sodomites at the northern end of the Dead Sea, around the city of Livias, thus arguing for the NST.

Quotes from Antiquity

> **Egeria on the location of the Pentapolis**
>
> Crossing the river [Jordan] we came to a city called *Livias*,[120] which is in the plain where the children of Israel encamped at that time [Abel-Shittim]. . . . The plain is a very great one, lying under the *mountains of Arabia* above the Jordan. . . . After this, that the work begun should be accomplished, we began to hasten in order to reach mount Nebo. As we went, the *priest of the place, i.e., Livias*, whom we had prayed to accompany us from the station, because he knew the places well, advised us. . . .
>
> We arrived, then, at the summit of the mountain, where there is now a church of no great size, on the very top of mount Nebo. . . . From the door of the church we saw the place where the *Jordan runs into the Dead Sea,* which place appeared below us as we stood. On the opposite side we saw not only *Livias*, which was on the near side of Jordan, but also *Jericho*, which was beyond Jordan; to so great a height rose the lofty place where we stood, before the door of the church. The *greatest part of Palestine*, the land of promise, was in sight, together with the whole land of Jordan, as far as it could be seen with our eyes. On the left side we saw all the *lands of the Sodomites and Segor* which is the only one of the five cities that exists to-day. There is a memorial of it, but nothing appears of those other cities but a heap of ruins, just as they were turned into ashes. The place where was the inscription concerning Lot's wife was shown to us, which place is read of in the Scriptures. But believe me, reverend ladies, the pillar itself cannot be seen, only the place is shown, the pillar is said to have been covered by the Dead Sea. Certainly, when we saw the place we saw no pillar, I cannot therefore deceive you in this. The *bishop of the place*, that is of *Segor*, told us that it is now some years since the pillar could be seen. The spot where the pillar stood is about six miles from *Segor*, and the water now covers the whole of this space.[121]

At the Council of Alexandria in AD 362, Asterius, the bishop of Petra, is recorded as being in Arabia.[122] Dan points out that: "at the Council of Constantinople in 381 both "Provincia Arabia" and "Provincia Bostron" are mentioned; the former consisted of southern Arabia, while the later was certainly northern Arabia whose capital was Bostra."[123]

While the decision to split the Provinces took place around AD 357–58, the actual

---

[119] Power, "The Site of the Pentapolis: Part 1," 1:52.

[120] David E. Graves and D. Scott Stripling, "Re-Examination of the Location for the Ancient City of Livias," *Levant* 43, no. 2 (2011): 178–200.

[121] Egeria, *The Pilgrimage of Etheria*, 20, 23–24.

[122] Dan, "Palaestina Salutaris (Tertia) and Its Capital," 136.

[123] Ibid.

process happened gradually. After AD 390 the region of Arabia was identified as *Palaestina Prima* (I), *Palaestina Secundae* (II), and *Palaestina Salutaris* (III).[124] The Bishop of Livias (Palaestina I) and the Bishop of Zoar (Palaestina III) were present at the Council of Ephesus in AD 449,[125] but the earlier Bishop of Sodom represented Arabia at the Council of Nicaea in AD 325[126] before the region was split up into *Palaestina* I, II, and III.

During her travels, Egeria leaves Jerusalem and determines "to go as far as *Arabia*, to mount Nebo"[127] and speaks of the Jordan Valley under "the mountains of *Arabia* above the Jordan"[128] [emphasis added]. In addition, from Mt. Nebo Egeria states that "the greatest part of *Palestine*, the land of promise, was in sight" [emphasis added].[129] This indicates that in Egeria's day the boundary between *Arabia* and *Palaestina Prima* was up at sea level on the Jordanian side of the Jordan River. This is confirmed by Kazhdan, who states that:

> in the 4th C. [AD 390] its southern part (Negev) was separated from Arabia and named *Palaestina Salutaris* (Palaestina III); at the same time some northern regions were attached to the province of Arabia to create a barrier against independent Arab tribes. Arabia accepted the ecclesiastical jurisdiction of Antioch [on-the-Orontes], although from the 5th C. onward Jerusalem tried to absorb the region into its sphere of authority, but failed; by 518 only it's southern part (the bishopric of Areopolis) had changed its allegiance, but Madaba remained under Bostra [Arabia].[130]

Based on the above evidence it can be speculated that Egeria's Bishop of Sodom and Priest of Livias[131] were in *Palaestina Prima*. However, based on the statement of Eusebius, who was also present at the council of Nicaea, the region east of the Jordan River during this period was considered Arabia (Eusebius *On.* 528). The Bishop of Sodom does not show up in the church records after AD 384 but the Bishop of Zoar is identified as a representative at the council of Ephesus in AD 431. One could speculate that the diocese of Sodom was annexed by Zoar, but there is no definitive evidence of this.

Madaba Map (AD 542 and 570)

The next indication for the location of the Pentapolis is found on the famous 6th cent. AD Madaba mosaic map.[132] This Byzantine crusader map of the Holy Land displays the location of Byzantine holy sites. While the destroyed Cities of the Plain are not depicted on the Madaba Map, possibly due to the loss of part of the map tiles, it does depict the Byzantine location of the traditional site of Zoar often identified at eṣ-Ṣafi, Jordan (see *Fact 33*) and the location of the Byzantine church and monastery of St. Lot built over the traditional location of Lot's cave (see *Fact 34*).

However, there are two sites which may offer some clues. While most places portrayed on the Madaba Map are provided with names, Sites One and Two (see Fig. 9) are missing the tesserae (tiny mosaic tiles) depicting their names. Scholars have long speculated, based

---

[124] Alexander Kazhdan, "Arabia, Province of," in *The Oxford Dictionary of Byzantium*, ed. Alexander Kazhdan (Oxford, U.K.: Oxford University Press, 1991), 147.

[125] Le Quien, *Oriens christianus*, 3:655, 743.

[126] Mouchy, *Christianae religionis institutionisque*, 85 no. 78.

[127] Egeria, *The Pilgrimage of Etheria*, 19.

[128] Ibid., 20.

[129] Ibid., 24.

[130] Kazhdan, *The Oxford Dictionary of Byzantium*, 147.

---

[131] Egeria, *The Pilgrimage of Etheria*, 21, 24.

[132] Herbert Donner, *The Mosaic Map of Madaba. An Introductory Guide*, Palaestina Antiqua 7 (Kampen: Kok Pharos, 1992), 37–94; Eugenio Alliata and Michele Piccirillo, eds., *The Madaba Map Centenary: Travelling Through the Byzantine Umayyad Period. Proceedings of the International Conference Held in Amman 7–9 April 1997*, Studium Biblicum Franciscannum Collectio Maior 40 (Jerusalem: Studium Biblicum Franciscannum, 1999), 121–24.

on the tesserae depiction of the two cities and their general location on the map, about the identification of these sites.

Site 1 has been variously identified with Abila,[133] Livias-Bethramtha,[134] Bethnambris,[135] and Beth-Nimra.[136] Site 2 has equally variously been identified with Livias,[137] Suweimeh,[138] Betharam or Bethramphtha.[139]

Most scholars are divided as to which site on the Madaba Map is associated with Roman Livias. Avi-Yonah and Schick prefer Site One, while five scholars prefer Site Two. It is therefore a question open to debate as to

9. Segment of the Madaba Map found on the floor of St. George's church in Madaba, Jordan indicating the unidentified Site One and Two (see Fig. 13).

what the identification on the Madaba Map of the two towns is?[140]

However, it must be remembered that the Madaba Map was a sacred map used by religious pilgrims for traveling the Holy Land.[141] Since Byzantine Zoar is mentioned on the map, while none of the other Cities of

---

[133] Michael Avi-Yonah, *The Madaba Mosaic Map with Introduction and Commentary* (Jerusalem: Israel Exploration Society, 1954), 37; Nelson Glueck, "Some Ancient Towns in the Plains of Moab," *BASOR* 91 (1943): 15, 21; *Explorations in Eastern Palestine IV. Part 1*, AASOR 25-28 (New Haven, Conn.: ASOR, 1945), 377; David E. Graves and D. Scott Stripling, "Locating Tall El-Hammam on the Madaba Map," *BRB* 7, no. 6 (2007): 1–11; "Identification of Tall El-Hammam on the Madaba Map," *BS* 20, no. 2 (2007): 35–45; Robert Schick, "Northern Jordan: What Might Have Been in the Madaba Mosaic Map," in *The Madaba Map Centenary: Travelling Through the Byzantine Umayyad Period. Proceedings of the International Conference Held in Amman 7–9 April 1997*, ed. Michele Piccirillo and Eugenio Alliata, Studium Biblicum Franciscannum 40 (Jerusalem: Studium Biblicum Franciscannum, 1999), 228.

[134] Avi-Yonah, *Madaba Mosaic Map*, 37; Schick, "Northern Jordan," 228.

[135] Alliata and Piccirillo, *Madaba Map Centenary*, 54.

[136] Donner, *Mosaic Map of Madaba*, 39.

[137] Ibid.; Glueck, "Some Ancient Towns," 15, 21; *Explorations in Eastern Palestine*, 377; Graves and Stripling, "Identification of Tall El-Hammam," 35–45; "Locating Tall El-Hammam," 1–11; Kay Prag, "Tall El-Hammam as Livias, 8 Jan 2009," January 8, 2009, 1.

[138] Avi-Yonah, *Madaba Mosaic Map*, 37; Schick, "Northern Jordan," 228.

[139] Michele Piccirillo, "The Roman Esbus-Livias Road," in *Mount Nebo: New Archaeological Excavations 1967-1997*, ed. Michele Piccirillo and Eugenio Alliata, Studium Biblicum Franciscanum 27 (Jerusalem: Franciscan, 1998), 133–35.

[140] Graves and Stripling, "Re-Examination of the Location for the Ancient City of Livias," 182.

[141] "A comparison of the [Roman] Peutinger Table and the early fourth-century Onomasticon of Eusebius [on which the Madaba map was based] shows that the latter's interest is in a wide range of biblical and ecclesiastical sites." Burton MacDonald, "Review of John R. Bartlett, Mapping Jordan through Two Millennia. Palestine Exploration Fund Annual 10. Leeds: Maney, 2008," *BASOR* 358 (2010): 83.

The Location of Sodom

the Plain are identified, it may be possible that the two sites in the northern region missing their names are Sodom and Gomorrah.[142] The early pilgrims were interested in Sodom as is evident from Egeria's comments.[143] Livias would not be biblically important to early Christian Pilgrims, but Sodom and Gomorrah would be sites of interest. While a reasonable assumption the map is still not helpful in locating the biblical site of Sodom (see *Facts 32* and *33*).

---

[142] I was the first to make this deduction while doing research for Livias and shared with Dr. Collin who states in his book: "note that no cities are represented in the area south of the Dead Sea. Because this is primarily a map of famous biblical sites, the two city representations (1 and 2) northeast of the Dead Sea are, logically, Sodom and Gomorrah, although the captions are missing." Collins and Scott, *Discovering the City of Sodom*, 28.

[143] Egeria, *The Pilgrimage of Etheria*, 24.

A Brief History of Research

The search for the Cities of the Plain begins with some scholars saying they were non-existent, merely unhistorical legends[1] and "purely mythical tale[s]" from out of the past.[2] This will be dealt with in more detail in Fact 1. While some fringe scholars have argued, on the basis of volcanic activity (fire and brimstone), that Sodom should be sought in Arabia[3] or Iraq,[4] the biblical text clearly places it around the Dead Sea (Gen 13:11–12; 14:3).

During the 19th century, several explorers travelled through the strange and unique landscape of the Dead Sea region and spoke of the Cities of the Plain. At the southwestern end of the Dead Sea there is a salt formation (mountain), which the locals call Jebel Usdum (see *Fact 58*), which in Arabic means "Mount of Sodom" leading them to identify the mountain as Sodom. Zoar has traditionally been identified with eṣ-Ṣafi 24 km (15 miles) south of the Lisan. Local Byzantine tradition placed the Cities of the Plain in this southern region of the Dead Sea. Some placed the Pentapolis at and under the southern end of the Dead Sea (inundation theory)[5] and some, based on the geography of the biblical text, placed them at the northern end of the Dead Sea, in the *kikkār* (NST; see *Fact 3*). Prior to Albright in 1924, Bâb edh-Dhrâ' was unknown to these explorers but Tall el-Ḥammâm is mentioned by Selah Merrill in 1876 among the list of sites in the Jordan Valley that could be connected with the Pentapolis.[6]

10. Jordan Valley (*Kikkar*) seen from the Jordanian side. Tall el-Hammam (Sodom?) is seen in the center, with Tall Kifrein (Gomorrah?) also visible on the plain.

---

[1] Hermann Gunkel, *Das Marchen Im Alten Testament*, Fourth, Religionsgeschichtliche Volksbücher (Tübingen: Mohr, 1917), 80; Martin Noth, *The History of Israel* (New York, N.Y.: Harper, 1960), 121; *A History of Pentateuchal Traditions* (Upper Saddle River, N.J.: Prentice-Hall, 1972), 191; Dorothy Irwin, *Mytharion: The Comparison of Tales from the Old Testament and the Ancient Near East*, Alter Orient Und Altes Testament 32 (Neukirchen-Vluyn: Neukirchener Verlag, 1978), 23; James Maxwell Miller and John Haralson Hayes, *A History of Ancient Israel and Judah* (Louisville, Ky.: Westminster/Knox, 1986), 60; M. J. Mulder, "Sodom and Gomorrah," ed. David Noel Freedman et al., *ABD* (New York, N.Y.: Doubleday, 1996), 6:99, 102; Philip R. Davies, *Memories of Ancient Israel: An Introduction to Biblical History--Ancient and Modern* (Louisville, Ky.: Westminster/Knox, 2008), 64.

[2] Theodor Herzl Gaster and James G. Frazer, *Myth, Legend, and Custom in the Old Testament: A Comparative Study with Chapters from Sir James G. Frazer's Folklore in the Old Testament* (New York, N.Y.: Harper & Row, 1975), 157–58, 161.

[3] Eduard Meyer and Bernhard Luther, *Die Israeliten und ihre Nachbarstämme: Alttestamentliche Untersuchungen* (Halle: Max Niemeyer, 1906), 71.

[4] Charles R Pellegrino, *Return to Sodom and Gomorrah: Bible Stories from Archaeologists* (New York, N.Y.: Avon Books, 1995), 180.

[5] Georg Heinrich Ewald, *History of Israel: Introduction and Preliminary History*, ed. and trans. Russell Martineau, 2nd ed., vol. 1 (London, U.K.: Longmans, Green, & Company, 1869), 313–14; Blanckenhorn, *Entstehung und Geschichte des Toten Meeres*, 51–59; James Penrose Harland, "Sodom and Gomorrah Part II: The Destruction of the Cities of the Plain," *BA* 6, no. 3 (1943): 41–42; William Foxwell Albright, *The Archaeology of Palestine and the Bible*, The Richards Lectures Delivered at the University of Virginia (New York, N.Y.: Flavell, 1935), 135–36; David Neev and Kenneth O. Emery, *The Dead Sea: Depositional Processes and Environments of Evaporites*, Ministry of Development: Geological Survey 41 (Jerusalem: Geological Survey of Israel, 1967), 30.

[6] Merrill, *East of the Jordan*, 230–39.

11. Western fortifications of Bâb edh-Dhrâʿ overlooking the southern Jordan Valley. This is the southern candidate for the location of Sodom.

SOUTHERN THEORY

In February–March 1924, the prominent archaeologist, William F. Albright, led an archaeological expedition with the Reverend M. Kyle from Xenia Theological Seminary, to locate the Cities of the Plain. After an investigation of the area they could not locate any suitable sites, and not even the original site of Zoar prior to the Byzantine era fit. It was suggested that they were swallowed up by the Dead Sea and undiscoverable (inundation theory).[7] Albright published that "it seems perfectly rational to assume the correctness of the traditional view that the Cities of the Plain are now buried under the waters of the [southern end of the] Dead Sea"[8] of the Lisan peninsula. This theory was further corroborated by Ralph Baneyʿs discovery in 1960 of small trees in the upright growth position beneath the southern basin of the Dead Sea, although ancient structures were not found.[9] Also, in 2011, a Russian exploration group used submarines to explore and photograph the bottom of the Dead Sea, but found no evidence of ancient ruins.[10]

---

[7] William F. Albright, *The Archaeology of Palestine* (London, U.K.: Taylor & Francis, 1956), 135–36; Nelson Glueck, *Explorations in Eastern Palestine II*, AASOR 15 (New Haven, Conn.: ASOR, 1935), 8–9; Paul W. Lapp, "Bab Edh-Dhraʿ, Perizzites and Emim," in *Jerusalem Through the Ages: The Twenty-Fifth Archaeological Convention* (Jerusalem: Israel Exploration Society, 1968), 25; Joseph P. Free and Howard F. Vos, *Archaeology and Bible History* (Grand Rapids, Mich.: Zondervan, 1992), 57; David Neev and Kenneth O. Emery, *The Destruction of Sodom, Gomorrah and Jericho: Geological, Climatological and Archaeological Backgrounds* (Oxford, U.K.: Oxford University Press, 1995), 30.

[8] William F. Albright, "The Jordan Valley in the Bronze Age," *AASOR* 6 (1926): 57–58.

[9] Ralph E. Baney, *Search for Sodom and Gomorrah*, 2nd ed. (Kansas City, MO: CAM Press, 1962), 178.

[10] David Lev, "Russia Decides to Search for Sodom and Gomorrah-in Jordan," *Arutz Sheva 7: Israel National News*, December 14, 2010, http://www.israelnationalnews.com/News/News.aspx/141132; Collins and Scott, *Discovering the City of Sodom*, 101; Todd Bolen, "Search for Sodom under Dead Sea," *BiblePlaces*, December 14, 2010, http://blog.bibleplaces.com/2010/12/search-for-sodom-under-dead-sea.html.

Albright was willing to entertain the possibility of the NST but expressed two objections:

> It is possible that they [the Pentapolis] were actually situated farther north in the Plain of the Jordan (*kikkār hay-Yarden*), as the writer has suggested, but a serious argument against this view is the fact that Tell ed-Damieh (Adamah) is so small, while Seboyim [Zeboiim] is otherwise unrecorded in this region.[11]

Albright was also aware of the theory that the Cities of the Plain were proposed in the area around Tall er-Rameh, which is only 2.7 km (1.68 miles) from TeH. Albright writes off this theory of Merrill's[12] without explanation, other than, in his view, this is impossible.[13]

Albright did, however, find the ruins of a fortified site named Bâb edh-Dhrâʿ in the southern Dead Sea region, which he dated to the third millennium BC (EBA, 3150–2200 BC). The site overlooks the deep ravine of Wadi "Kerak, about five hundred feet above the Dead Sea."[14] Taking into consideration the lack of occupational debris and seven fallen limestone monoliths, found a short distance east of Bâb edh-Dhrâʿ,[15] Albright concluded that this was not one of the Cities of the Plain but a place of pilgrimage where annual cultic feasts were celebrated.

Between 1965 and 1967 Bâb edh-Dhrâʿ (See Map 3) was excavated under the direction of Paul Lapp. Extensive work was done at a large cemetery south of the city that contained a minimum of 20,000 EB I shaft tombs used by pastoral nomads from the region, estimating the number of dead at over half a million.[16] Unfortunately, Paul Lapp died unexpectedly in 1970, and so the task of further research fell to R. Thomas Schaub and Walter E. Rast (b. 1930–d. 2003[17]).[18] In late May, 1973, not far to the south of Bâb edh-Dhrâʿ, they discovered four other sites: Numeira (or Numayra),[19] eṣ-Ṣafi,[20] Feifa,[21] and Khirbet Khanazir; each, they claimed,

---

[11] Albright "The Jordan Valley in the Bronze Age," 58.

[12] Merrill, *East of the Jordan*, 222–239.

[13] Albright, "The Jordan Valley in the Bronze Age," 48 n. 121.

[14] William F. Albright, J. L. Kelso, and J. P. Thorley, "Early Bronze Age Pottery from Bab-Ed-Dra in Moab," *BASOR* 95 (1944): 1–13.

[15] Albright, "The Jordan Valley in the Bronze Age," 58.

[16] Paul W. Lapp, "Bab Edh-Dhraʿ (RB 1966)," *RB* 73 (1966): 556–61; "Bab Edh-Dhraʿ Tomb A 76 and Early Bronze I in Palestine," *BASOR* 189 (1968): 12–41; "Bab Edh-Dhraʿ (RB 1968)," *RB* 75 (1968): 86–93, pls. 3–6a; Donald J Ortner and Bruno Frohlich, *The Early Bronze Age I Tombs and Burials of Bâb Edh-Dhrâʾ, Jordan*, Reports of the Expedition to the Dead Sea Plain, Jordan 3 (Lanham, MD: AltaMira, 2008).

[17] R. Thomas Schaub, "In Memoriam: Walter Emil Rast 1930-2003," *BASOR* 332 (2003): 1–5.

[18] Walter E. Rast, "The Southeastern Dead Sea Valley Expedition, 1979," *BA* 43, no. 1 (1980): 60–61; Walter E. Rast and R. Thomas Schaub, "Expedition to the Southeastern Dead Sea Plain, Jordan, 1979," *American Schools of Oriental Research Newsletter*, no. 8 (1980): 12–17; *Bab Edh-Dhrâʿ: Excavations in the Cemetery Directed by Paul W Lapp, 1965-1967*, Reports of the Expedition to the Dead Sea Plain, Jordan 1 (Winona Lake, Ind.: Eisenbrauns, 1989).

[19] Walter E. Rast et al., "Preliminary Report of the 1979 Expedition to the Dead Sea Plain, Jordan," *BASOR* 240 (1980): 21–61; Walter E. Rast, "Settlement at Numeira," in *The Southeastern Dead Sea Plain Expedition: An Interim Report of the 1977 Season*, AASOR 46 (Cambridge: American Schools of Oriental Research, 1979), 35–44; Walter E. Rast and R. Thomas Schaub, "The Dead Sea Expedition: Bab Edh-Dhraʿ and Numeira, May 24-July 10, 1981," *American Schools of Oriental Research Newsletter*, no. 4 (1982): 4–12.

[20] Konstantinos D. Politis, "Biblical Zoar: The Looting of an Ancient Site," *Minerva* 5/6 (1994): 12–15; Konstantinos D. Politis, "Report to the Palestine Exploration Fund on the Surveys and Excavations at Zoara in the Ghor Es-Safi 2003-2004," *PEQ*, 2005; Konstantinos D. Politis et al., "Survey and Excavations in the Ghawr as-Safi 2004," *ADAJ* 49 (2005): 313–26.

[21] Walter E. Rast and R. Thomas Schaub, "Survey of the Southeastern Plain of the Dead Sea, 1973," *ADAJ* 19 (1974): 11–12.

with a similar footprint,[22] and including large cemeteries. While all the sites have been excavated to some extent only BeD and some of Numeira's dig reports have been published.[23] Feifa and Khanazir were excavated in 1989–1990 and both discovered to only have an Iron Age II (eighth century BC) fortress constructed over part of the early Bronze Age cemetery.[24] What were thought to be walls at Khanazir, identified by Rast and Schaub in 1973,[25] were later revealed to be Early Bronze IV (2300–2200 BC) shaft tombs.[26] Only BeD and Numeira have occupational structures dating to the Early Bronze Age. The other sites are only cemeteries (see *Fact 43*). As Chesson and Schaub report: "Unlike Bab adh-Dhra', Fifa is a one period cemetery from the EB IA; similarly, Khirbat al-Khanazir is a one period site with a cemetery from the EB IV."[27]

In 1974, Bryant G. Wood published an article titled "Have Sodom and Gomorrah Been Found?" in the *Bible and Spade* magazine, in which he identified Bâb edh-Dhrâ', Numeira, eṣ-Ṣafi, Feifa, and Khanazir as the five Cities of the Plain.[28] Originally, on his map, Wood identified Bâb edh-Dhrâ' with Zeboiim, Numeira with Admah, eṣ-Ṣafi with Zoar, Feifa with Gomorrah, and Khanazir with Sodom[29] but in his later article changed his opinion.[30]

In 1978, while David N. Freedman was the Professor of Biblical Studies at University of Michigan in Ann Arbor, he published an article on the Ebla tablets, which, he argued, gave evidence of the Cities of the Plain being in existence in the Early Bronze age. He argued that this matched the sites excavated by Lapp, Schaub, and Rast in the early 70's. While Freedman does not mention Wood's article, he states:

> In the light of the new information [Ebla tablets], we now propose that these are the cities of the plain (though which was which can be left for future investigation) and that we revise our views of their location and chronology accordingly.[31]

Based on additional research published in the following years, Wood reworked his previous 1974 material in his 1999 article "The Discovery of the Sin Cities of Sodom and Gomorrah.",[32] and incorporated the Ebla material published by Shea,[33] who cites Freedman,[34] to strengthen his argument for the SST. In his revised article Wood identified Bâb edh-Dhrâ' with Sodom, Numeira with Gomorrah, Feifa with Admah and Khanazir with Zeboiim.

---

[22] Rast, "Settlement at Numeira"; Rast and Schaub, "The Dead Sea Expedition."

[23] Walter E. Rast and R. Thomas Schaub, eds., *Bab Edh-Dhra': Excavations at the Town Site (1975-1981): Part 1: Text*, Reports of the Expedition to the Dead Sea Plain, Jordan 2 (Winona Lake, Ind.: Eisenbrauns, 2003); Rast and Schaub, *Bab Edh-Dhra': Excavations in the Cemetery*.

[24] Bert de Vries, ed., "Archaeology in Jordan, 1992," *AJA* 96, no. 3 (1992): 262; Burton MacDonald, "Southern Ghors and Northeast 'Arabah (OEANE)," in *OEANE*, ed. Eric M. Meyers, vol. 5 (Oxford, U.K.: Oxford University Press, 1997), 5:65.

[25] Rast and Schaub, "Survey of the Southeastern Plain of the Dead Sea, 1973," 12–14.

[26] Walter E. Rast, "Bab Edh-Dhra' (ABD)," ed. David Noel Freedman et al., *ABD* (New York, N.Y.: Doubleday, 1996), 560; R. Thomas Schaub, "Southeast Dead Sea Plain," in *OEANE*, ed. Eric M. Meyers, vol. 5 (Oxford, U.K.: Oxford University Press, 1997), 62.

[27] Meredith S. Chesson and R. Thomas Schaub, "Death and Dying on the Dead Sea Plain: Fifa, Al-Khanazir and Bab Adh-Dhra` Cemeteries," in *Crossing Jordan: North American Contributions to the Archaeology of Jordan*, ed. Thomas Evan Levy et al. (London, U.K.: Equinox, 2007), 253.

[28] Bryant G. Wood, "Have Sodom And Gomorrah Been Found?," *BS* 3, no. 3 (1974): 65–90.

[29] Ibid., 67.

[30] Wood, "Discovery of the Sin Cities," 67–80.

[31] Freedman, "The Real Story of the Ebla Tablets," 152–53.

[32] Wood, "Discovery of the Sin Cities," 67–80.

[33] Shea, "Two Palestinian Segments," 589–612.

[34] Freedman, "The Real Story of the Ebla Tablets," 143–64.

Following Steven Collins' publication claiming that TeH was Sodom,[35] Wood wrote an article (2007) titled "Locating Sodom: A Critique of the Northern Proposal."[36] Wood then posted a one page summary of his views in 2008 on the Associates for Biblical Research website[37] titled "Sodom and Gomorrah: Is There Evidence for Their Destruction?"[38]

Wood has a loyal following supporting the SST, including Bill Schlegel,[39] Clyde Billington,[40] Eugene Merrill,[41] Gordon Govier,[42] and Todd Bolen[43] to name but a few of the more vocal supporters. However, Lapp, Schaub, and Rast have never affirmed that Bâb edh-Dhrâʿ is Sodom in the same historical sense as Wood believes (see *Fact 6*).

Some SST supporters (Freedman and van Hattem) maintain an early date of 2650–2300 BC for the existence of the Patriarchs (including Abraham and Lot) which corresponds with the EB III destruction of Bâb edh-Dhrâʿ (see *Fact 37, 38* and Chart 4). However, Wood, who holds to BeD as Sodom that saw its major destruction in 2350 BC, argues that the Patriarchs lived around 2166–1991 BC (MB I or Intermediate Bronze). For those like Albright, Kitchen, and Collins who take a later Middle Bronze (MB 1950–1550 BC) Age date for the Patriarchs (see *Fact 38* and Chart 4) this rules out the southern location as a potential candidate for Sodom (see Chart 7). There seems little doubt that Sodom did exist as early as the EB Age, as it is mentioned in Genesis 10, but the important question is when was Sodom destroyed (see *Facts 37)*?

---

[35] Steven Collins, "Explorations on the Eastern Jordan Disk," *BRB* 2, no. 18 (2002): 1–28; Steven Collins, Gary A. Byers, and Michael C. Luddeni, "Tall El-Hammam Excavation Project, Season Activity Report, Season One: 2005/2006 Probe Excavation and Survey: Submitted to the Department of Antiquities of the Hashemite Kingdom of Jordan, Jan 22, 2006," *BRB* 6, no. 4 (2006): 1–13; Steven Collins et al., "Tall El-Hammam Excavation Project, Season Activity Report, Season Two: 2006/2007 Excavation and Survey: Submitted to the Department of Antiquities of the Hashemite Kingdom of Jordan, January 26, 2006," *BRB* 7, no. 9 (2007): 1–13; Steven Collins, Where is Biblical Sodom? An interview with Dr. Steven Collins, Director of the Tall el-Hammam Excavation project, Jordan, interview by Scott Stripling, 2006; Steven Collins, "Tall El-Hammam and Biblical Sodom: A Match," *Digging the Past: Voice of the Tall El-Hammam Excavation Project, Jordan*, 2006; "Rethinking the Location of Zoar: An Exercise in Biblical Geography," *BRB* 4, no. 1 (2006): 11–5; "Ten Reasons Why Sodom and Gomorrah Are Not Located in the Southeast Dead Sea Region," *BRB* 6, no. 1 (2006): 1–4; "Sodom: The Discovery of a Lost City," *BS* 20, no. 3 (2007): 70–77.

[36] Wood, "Locating Sodom: A Critique of the Northern Proposal," 78–84.

[37] Wood is the director and editor of the Associates for Biblical Research organization.

[38] Wood, "Sodom and Gomorrah: Is There Evidence for Their Destruction?"

[39] Bill Schlegel, "Biblical Problems with Locating Sodom at Tall El-Hammam," *BiblePlaces*, January 4, 2012, http://blog.bibleplaces.com/2012/01/biblical-problems-with-locating-sodom.html; Steven Collins, "The Geography of Sodom and Zoar: Reality Demolishes W. Schlegel's Attacks Against a Northern Sodom," *BRB* 13, no. 2 (2013): 1–14.

[40] Clyde E. Billington, "Tall El-Hammam Is Not Sodom," *Artifax*, Spring 2012, 1–3.

[41] Eugene H. Merrill, "Texts, Talls, and Old Testament Chronology: Tall El-Hammam as a Case Study," *Artifax* 27, no. 4 (2012): 20–21; Steven Collins, "Tall El-Hammam Is Still Sodom: Critical Data-Sets Cast Serious Doubt on E. H. Merrill's Chronological Analysis," *BRB* 13, no. 1 (2013): 1–31.

[42] Gordon Govier, "Looking Back: Claims to New Sodom Location Are Salted with Controversy," *Christianity Today* 52, no. 4 (2008): 15–16; "Searching for Sodom: Is It Time to Rewrite Old Testament Chronologies?," *ChristianityToday.com*, February 18, 2014, http://www.christianitytoday.com/ct/2014/february-web-only/searching-for-sodom.html.

[43] Todd Bolen, "Arguments Against Locating Sodom at Tall El-Hammam," *Biblical Archaeology Society*, February 27, 2013, http://www.biblicalarchaeology.org/daily/biblical-sites-places/biblical-archaeology-sites/arguments-against-locating-sodom-at-tall-el-hammam.

12. View from Tall Habbassa overlooking Tall el-Ḥammâm and the Middle Bronze age city-state area around the Tall. Jericho is directly across the Jordan Valley and Tell Kefrein is visible to the right below the arrow.

Northern Theory

The strength of the northern location is supported by the biblical description of the geography (*kikkār* Gen 13:3; see *Fact 23*) placing it in the eastern region of the Jordan Valley, as was argued by many archaeologists prior to Albright (see *Fact 3*).[44] The NST was suppressed by Albright and Wright's insistence that it was submerged under the Dead Sea.[45]

Interest in the NST was rekindled in 1996, following Steven Collins' re-evaluation of the evidence for BeD being Sodom,[46] as he discovered that BeD was destroyed "toward the end of the Early Bronze Age–Bâb edh-Dhrâʿ in 2350 BC. But Numeira was simply abandoned about 2600 BC."[47] Collins' quest for the real location of the Pentapolis continued in his research and he published four articles in the next six years in the *Biblical Research Bulletin* (2002)[48] where he analysed the previous research done by archaeologists and travellers.

---

[44] Wilson, "On the Site of Ai," 125; Tristram, *The Land of Moab*, 326–33; Merrill, *East of the Jordan*, 233–34; Conder, *Tent Work in Palestine*, 2:13–14; William M. Thomson, *The Land and the Book: Southern Palestine and Jerusalem*, vol. 1 (New York, N.Y.: Harper & Brothers, 1880), 371–76; *The Land and the Book: Lebanon, Damascus, and Beyond Jordan*, vol. 3 (New York, N.Y.: Harper & Brothers, 1886), 668–70; Grove, "Sodom," 976; Geikie, *Holy Land and the Bible*, 2:118; Power, "The Site of the Pentapolis: Part 1," 44. See *Fact 2*.

[45] Albright, "The Archæological Results of an Expedition to Moab and the Dead Sea," 7–9; George Frederick Wright, "Sodom," ed. James Orr and Melvin Grove Kyle, *ISBE1* (Grand Rapids, Mich.: Eerdmans, 1915), op. cit.; Wright, *Biblical Archaeology*, 30.

[46] Collins and Scott, *Discovering the City of Sodom*, 13–22; 87–99.

[47] Ibid., 90.

[48] Steven Collins, "The Geography of the Cities of the Plain," *BRB* 2, no. 1 (2002): 1–17; "A Chronology for the Cities of the Plain," *BRB* 2, no. 8 (2002): 1–9; "The Architecture of Sodom," *BRB* 2, no. 14 (2002): 1–9; "Explorations," 1–28.

The breakthrough came while Collins was in Jordan researching the sites in the Jordan Valley at the American Centre of Oriental Research (ACOR) in Amman. Khouri's book *The Antiquities of the Jordan Rift Valley* was brought to his attention, which contained a map which identified fourteen Talls.[49] Collins determined that of these fourteen sites only Tulaylat al-Ghassul [50] and Tall Iktanu[51] had been excavated and published.[52] Kay Prag, who had excavated Iktanu, had opened a probe square at TeH and published her findings[53] but was unable to do further work on the Tall because the upper Tall was unsafe due to the fact that it was mined during the 1967 war with Israel. This may be one of the reasons why this large[54] and important Tall had been passed over by archaeologists for so long.

Collins obtained dig permits in 2005[55] from the Department of Antiquities of the Hashemite Kingdom of Jordan and began excavations of the upper Tall in several locations that January. It was believed at the time that the MBA occupation was confined to the upper Tall, but in later seasons it was found to extend to a large walled area on the lower Tall. Evidence of the MBA presence on the site would eventually be found covering some 100 acres (See Map 9).[56]

The upper Tall had been badly damaged by the Ottoman's and Jordanians when their military put in a road through the centre of the Tall and then plowed several trenches to the edge of the Tall to put in gun placements.[57] At first this appeared to be a great tragedy, but since the road was cut through the ancient city wall, it acted as an x-ray, providing an early and easy read of the stratigraphy of the tall (see *Fact 13*).

---

[49] These include Tall Nimrin, Tall el-Musṭāḥ, Tall Bleibel, Tall Ghannam, Tall Ghrubba, Tall Kafrayn, Khirbet Kafrayn, Tall el-Hammam, Tall er-Rameh, Tall Iktanu, Tall eahl es-Sarabet, Tulaylat al-Ghassul, Khirbet Sweimeh, and Tall el-Azeimeh (See Map 2). Rami G. Khouri, *Antiquities of the Jordan Rift Valley* (Manchester, MI: Solipsist, 1988), 68–86.

[50] Père Alexis Mallon, Robert Koeppel, and René Neuville, *Teleilāt Ghassūl. I: Compte Rendu Des Fouilles de l'Institut Biblique Pontificale, 1929-1932* (Rome: Archaeological Institute of America, 1934); Robert Koeppel et al., *Teleilāt Ghassūl, II.: Compte Rendu Des Fouilles de l'Institut Biblique Pontifical, 1932-1936*, Scripta Pontificii Instituti Biblici 68 (Archaeological Institute of America, 1940); J. B. Hennessy, "Preliminary Report on a First Season of Excavations at Teleilat Ghassul," *Levant* 1, no. 1 (1969): 1–24; Stephen J. Bourke et al., "A First Season of Renewed Excavation by the University of Sydney at Tulaylat Al-Ghassul," *ADAJ* 39 (1995): 31–63; Stephen J. Bourke et al., "A Second and Third Season of Renewed Excavation by the University of Sydney at Tulaylat Al-Ghassul (1995-1997)," *ADAJ* 2000, no. 44 (2000): 37–90; Khouri, *Antiquities of the Jordan Rift Valley*, 81–85.

[51] Kay Prag, "The Intermediate Early-Middle Bronze Age Sequences at Jericho and Tell Iktanu Reviewed," *BASOR* 264 (1986): 61–72; Kay Prag, "Preliminary Report on the Excavations at Tell Iktanu, Jordan, 1987," *Levant* 21 (1989): 33–45; Kay Prag, "Preliminary Report on the Excavations at Tell Iktanu, Jordan, 1989," *ADAJ* 34 (1990): 119–30; Kay Prag, "The Excavations at Tell Iktanu 1989 and 1990," *Syria* 70 (1993): 269–73; Kay Prag, "Iktanu, Tell," in *OEANE*, ed. Eric M. Meyers, vol. 1, 5 vols. (Oxford, U.K.: Oxford University Press, 1997), 143–44; de Vries, "Archaeology in Jordan."

[52] Collins and Scott, *Discovering the City of Sodom*, 88–95.

[53] "Kay Prag Reports on Tall Iktanu and Tall El-Hammam 515-516," n.d.; Kay Prag, "The Excavations at Tell Al-Hammam," *Syria* 70, no. 1–2 (1990): 271–73; Kay Prag, "Tell Iktanu and Tell Al-Hammam. Excavations in Jordan," *Manchester Archaeological Bulletin* 7 (1992): 15–19.

[54] Tall el-Ḥammâm is the third largest MB Age site in the southern Levant (see *Fact 41*).

[55] Steven Collins, "2005-2006 Season Summary," *Digging the Past: Voice of the Tall El-Hammam Excavation Project, Jordan*, 2006.

[56] See *Fact 41*.

[57] Père Alexis Mallon, "Les Places Fortes Du Sud-Est de La Vallée Du Jourdain Au Temps d'Abraham," *Biblica* 13 (1932): 197–199; Kay Prag, "Preliminary Report on the Excavations at Tell Iktanu and Tall El-Hammam, Jordan 1990," *Levant* 23 (1991): 60.

Archaeological evidence indicates that TeH was occupied from the Chalcolithic period until the MB Age (2000–1550 BC), but based on the absence of LB Age (1550–1000 BC) pottery, it was not occupied for over five centuries until the Iron Age (1000–586 BC), following its MB Age destruction.[58]

This LB gap of 550 years is not unique to TeH but characteristic of all the sites in the entire *kikkār* region, including Tall Iktanu, Tall Kefrein (al-Kefrayn), Tall Nimrin, Tall el-Musṭāḥ, Tall Bleibel (Bulaybil), etc. (see *Fact 45*).[59]

Collins claims that TeH is in the right place (Eastern side of the *kikkār*),[60] at the right time (MB destruction),[61] with the right stuff (a large city-state[62] with human remains in the destruction layer[63] and evidence of trinitite unusually formed by high temperatures [see *Fact 55*]).[64]

While there is still debate over the Northern and Southern theories,[65] given the geographical characteristics of the northern end of the Dead Sea and recent discoveries at TeH, it would be foolish to ignore it as a possible candidate for one of the Cities of the Plain.

As Dr. William J. Fulco, the National Endowment of the Humanities Professor of Ancient Mediterranean Studies at Loyola Marymount University, states:

> Among the several sites or collection of sites that have been proposed for the notorious Cities of the Plain, which includes Sodom as its nucleus, Collins' proposal of Tall el-Hammam as this very place is convincing indeed. The evidence that the Tall al-Hammam Excavation Project (TeHEP) has brought to light and which Prof. Collins marshals to demonstrate the correlation between Tall Hammam and the biblical narrative must now enter the discussion as by far the strongest candidate for the site of Sodom.[66]

---

[58] Steven Collins, Carroll M. Kobs, and Michael C. Luddeni, *An Introduction to Tall Al-Hammam with Seven Seasons (2005-2011) of Ceramics and Eight Seasons (2005-2012) of Artifacts*, vol. 1 (Winona Lake, Ind.: Eisenbrauns, 2015), 10.

[59] Steven Collins, Khalil Hamdan, and Gary A. Byers, "Tall El-Hammam: Preliminary Report on Four Seasons of Excavation (2006–2009)," *ADAJ* 53 (2009): 385–414.

[60] Collins and Scott, *Discovering the City of Sodom*, 100–125.

[61] Ibid., 126–47.

[62] Ibid., 148–81.

[63] Ibid., 175.

[64] Ibid., 200–215.

[65] Wood, "Locating Sodom: A Critique of the Northern Proposal"; Collins, "A Response to Bryant G. Wood"; Billington, "Tall El-Hammam Is Not Sodom"; Steven Collins, "Tall El-Hammam Is Sodom: Billington's Heshbon Identification Suffers from Numerous Fatal Flaws," *Artifax* 27, no. 3 (Summer 2012): 16–18.

[66] Collins and Scott, *Discovering the City of Sodom*, Preface.

Preliminary Facts

The two preliminary facts that must be dealt with and which go to the heart of the topic of Sodom, concern its historicity and location.

FACT 1: SODOM IS NOT A FICTION FOR WOOD AND COLLINS

The search for the Cities of the Plain begins[1] here, with some minimalist scholars stating that these cities were non-existent, merely unhistorical legends[2] and "purely mythical tale[s]"[3] from out of the past. Rast, one of the excavators at Bâb edh-Dhrâ' believed that "Sodom was a fictional place . . . . [and] this name never existed."[4] M. J. Mulder in the *Anchor Bible Dictionary* article on Sodom concluded that they were, "Two legendary cities from prehistoric Israel in the neighborhood of the Dead Sea...it is highly uncertain, if not improbable, that the vanished cities of the Pentapolis will ever be recovered."[5]

13. A cargo boat on the Dead Sea as seen on the Madaba Map, from the 6th cent. AD. The two unnamed sites in the upper left hand corner are possibly Sodom and Gomorrah (see Fig. 9).

Photo by Berthold Werner

In their textbook *A History of Ancient Israel and Judah*, Miller and Hayes state:

> The Sodom and Gomorrah story reflects yet another motif pattern known from extrabiblical literature, that of divine beings who visit a city to test the hospitality of its people and eventually destroy the inhospitable city. One can compare in this regard the Greek myth of Baucis and Philemon. The presence of such traditional motifs in the Biblical narratives raises the possibility that at least some of these narratives are purely products of the storyteller's art, which of course raises serious questions about their usefulness for historical reconstruction.[6]

However, in the controversy over the Northern and Southern debate neither Wood nor Collins believe they are fictional. Collins argues that the historicity of the Cities of the Plain is not only verified by Jesus' treatment of the cities of Sodom and Gomorrah (Matt 10:1–15, 11:20–24; cf. Luke 10:1–12, 17:28–30) as historical, but also in their listing in Genesis 10 among other historically recognized cities such as:

> Babylon, Erech (Uruk), Akkad, Nineveh, Sidon, Gerar, Gaza—and regions—such as Shinar, Assyria, Mizraim (Egypt), Caphtor strongly suggests that Sodom, Gomorrah, Admah, and Zeboiim, in the same context, were also real cities in the true

---

[1] On the explorations of early travellers prior to the 1900's see Barbara Kreiger, *The Dead Sea: Myth, History, and Politics* (Hanover, N.H.: University Press of New England, 1988), 18–26; Barbara Wertheim Tuchman, *Bible and Sword: England and Palestine from the Bronze Age to Balfour* (London: Phoenix, 2001); Taylor, "The Dead Sea in Western Travellers' Accounts," 9–29; Astrid Swenson, "Sodom," in *Cities of God*, ed. David Gange and Michael Ledger-Lomas (Cambridge, U.K.: Cambridge University Press, 2013), 197–227.

[2] Noth, *A History of Pentateuchal Traditions*, 191; *The History of Israel*, 121; Miller and Hayes, *A History of Ancient Israel and Judah*, 60; Mulder, "Sodom and Gomorrah," 6:99, 102; Davies, *Memories of Ancient Israel*, 64.

[3] Gaster and Frazer, *Myth, Legend, and Custom in the Old Testament*, 161.

[4] Rast, "Bab Edh-Dhra' (ABD)," 1:561 (see *Fact 6: Rast and Schaub did not believe that Bâb edh-Dhrâ' was Sodom*.

---

[5] Mulder, "Sodom and Gomorrah," 99, 102.

[6] Miller and Hayes, *A History of Ancient Israel and Judah*, 60.

14. View of Israel from Mt. Nebo. The plaque indicates the location of various sites on the opposite side of the Jordan. The southern Dead Sea area and Bâb edh-Dhrâ' are not visible from this location on top of Mt. Nebo.

geographical sense.[7]

Wood takes the text at face value and states that "Sodom and Gomorrah were two of five cities referred to in Scripture as the Cities of the Plain."[8]

FACT 2: THE SST IS NOT A NEW VIEW

The view of ancient Byzantine tradition has tended to place the location of the Cities of the Plain in the south, primarily based on the tradition that Zoar is located at eṣ-Ṣafi in the south. As Power noted in 1930:

> At present however, scholars are practically unanimous in holding that the destroyed cities lay to the south of the Dead Sea. This conclusion is based, not on archaeological evidences, but on literary, especially traditional, data and a scientific theory of the cause of the disaster, which is supposed to have been a tectonic earthquake. Most of its supporters would readily admit that one or two Scripture passages, if interpreted according to their more obvious sense, favour the northern site where excavations [Teleilat el-Ghassûl][9] are now being made.[10]

The Greek geographer Strabo, along with historians such as Josephus and Tacitus, all point to a southern location for Sodom (Strabo Geogr. 16.2.42; Josephus J.W. 4.479–80; Tacitus Hist. 5.7[11]).[12] The medieval Arab geographers, Yakut, Mas'udi, Mukaddasi and Ibn 'Abbas, were also familiar with the Byzantine tradition of the south. The

---

[7] Steven Collins, "Forty Salient Points on the Geography of the Cities of the Kikkar," Brb 7, no. 1 (2007): 4.

[8] Wood, "Discovery of the Sin Cities," 67.

---

[9] It is now known that Teleilat el-Ghassûl is a Neolithic and Chalcolithic site that ceases to be occupied after this period and is too early to be Sodom or one of the Cities of the Plain. Tall el-Ḥammâm had not been excavated in the 1930's.

[10] Power, "The Site of the Pentapolis: Part 1," 1:23.

[11] Cornelius Tacitus, The Complete Works of Tacitus: The Annals. The History. The Life of Cnaeus Julius Agricola. Germany and Its Tribes. A Dialogue on Oratory, ed. Alfred John Church and William Jackson Brodribb (New York, N.Y.: Random House, 1942).

[12] Harland, "Sodom and Gomorrah Part I: Location," 22–23.

Preliminary Facts

following scholars and explorers will be examined to assess their support for either the southern or northern view, but their detailed arguments for either location will not be described here.[13]

Thomas Fuller (1650)

Thomas Fuller (1608–1661) was a minister and historian who wrote and published popular books of geography and history on the Holy Land.

He included a unique copper plated imaginary map, in his book, *A Pisgah-sight of Palestine and the Confines Thereof* titled "Iuda".[14] It was illustrated by T. F. John Goddard and depicts the four Cities of the Plain destroyed by God, drawn according to the standards of European architecture, in flames in the Dead Sea. The map is drawn north to south with Zeboim at the top, then Sodom, Gomorrah, followed by Admah at the bottom. Based on the testimony of travelers, Fuller placed the ruins of Zoar (Belah) above En-Gedi around Qumran on the north-western shore of the Dead Sea. He places the location of Lot's wife, who was turned into Salt and "the cave of Lot" close together on the map.

Peter Graham (1836)

One of the earliest SST proponents was Peter Graham, a Scottish author who stated:

> It is believed Sodom was one of the southern cities that was destroyed; because it was near Zoar, which was beyond the southern point of the Dead Sea. . . . Severus, a bishop of Sodom, is found among the bishops of Arabia, who had subscribed to the first council of Nice [*Sic* Nicaea]. M. Reland cannot persuade himself that Sodom was ever rebuilt; he believes the word Sodom, among the subscriptions to the council of Nice [*Sic* Nicaea], must be a fault of the copies; but we cannot be of his opinion.[15]

William Francis Lynch (1848)

William F. Lynch (1801–1865) was an American Naval officer who, with 16 colleagues, hauled a galvanized iron boat across Palestine overland by camels to survey the Jordan River and Dead Sea.[16] In 1847, William Lynch (1801–1865) published (republished as an enhanced version in 1849) his travels, *Narrative of the United States' Expedition to the River Jordan and the Dead Sea.* His entry for Tuesday, April 25, 1848 states:

> Notwithstanding the oppressive heat, there was a pleasure in our strange sensations, lying in the open air, upon the pebbly beach of this desolate and unknown sea [Dead Sea], *perhaps near the sites of Sodom and Gomorrah*; the salt mountains of Usdum [*Jebel Usdum*] in close proximity, and nothing but bright, familiar stars above us. . . . It was indeed a scene of unmitigated desolation. On one side, rugged and worn, was the salt mountain of Usdum, with its conspicuous pillar, which reminded us at least of the catastrophe of the plain; on the other were the lofty and barren cliffs of Moab, in one of the caves of which the fugitive Lot found shelter. To the south was an extensive flat intersected by sluggish drains, with the high hills of Edom semi-girding the salt plain where the Israelites repeatedly overthrew their enemies; and to the north was the calm and motionless sea, curtained with a purple mist, while many fathoms deep in the slimy mud beneath it lay embedded the *ruins of the ill-fated cities of Sodom and Gomorrah* [emphasis added].[17]
>
> *Wady Kerak is at the S. E.* extremity of the bay. Between it and us is the village of Mezra'a, and in

---

[13] All their works are in the public domain and available at the Internet Archive. https://archive.org/details/texts] and downloadable as a PDF file.

[14] Thomas Fuller, *A Pisgah-Sight of Palestine and the Confines Thereof: With the History of the Old and New Testament Acted Thereon* (London, U.K.: John Williams, 1650), 131.

[15] Graham, *A Topographical Dictionary of Palestine, or the Holy Land*, 242.

[16] Andrew C. A. Jampoler, *Sailors in the Holy Land: The 1848 American Expedition to the Dead Sea and the Search for Sodom and Gomorrah* (Annapolis, Md.: Naval Institute, 2005); David Haward Bain, *Bitter Waters: America's Forgotten Naval Mission to the Dead Sea* (New York: Overlook, 2011).

[17] William Francis Lynch, *Narrative of the United States Expedition to the River Jordan and the Dead Sea* (Philadelphia, Pa.: P. G. Collins, 1849), 201, 204.

the near vicinity of the latter are the supposed *ruins of Zoar* [emphasis added].[18]

Louis Félix de Saulcy (1851)

According to H. G. Cocks, the first claim of the discovery of Sodom came in 1851, during French *savant* Louis Félix de Saulcy's quest to "circumnavigate and map the Dead Sea."[19] He was accompanied by a Catholic priest and four young men. Religious tradition at that time held that "the Dead Sea stood for the fate of the Cities of the Plain, which had either been situated on its shores or consumed by its waters after an earthquake."[20]

During Saulcy's trip around the shores of the Dead Sea, he describes a "huge mass of disconnected ruins" on the southwestern side, at what he called Kharbet-Esdoum (the "Ruins of Sodom" i.e., Jebel Usdum; see *Fact 58*). He states:

> As it is unquestionable that, with the exception of Ayn-Djedy [En-Gedi], Masada, Thamara, and Zoar, there has not been since the catastrophe of the Pentapolis, any other town built on the western shores of the Dead Sea; it then necessarily follows, that we cannot help recognising Sodom in the Kharbet-Esdoum (ruins of Sodom) of the Arabs, and at the foot of the salt mountain [Jebel Usdum], which Galen expressly names *Sodoma*; and as a like consequence we are compelled also to recognize the other condemned cities in such ruins as we may happen to meet on the same shore.
>
> I cannot suppose that additional proof will be required of the fact—which may be questioned, but not invalidated—that the ruins which are known to the Arabs under the name of the Kharbet-Esdoum, are actually and really the ruins of the biblical Sodom.[21]

On the location of Zoar, Saulcy states: "We find still attached to the ruins in question the identical name of Zoar, are we not invincibly led to this conclusion that Kharbet-Zouera-et-Tahtah and the Zoar of the Bible are one and the same place?"[22]

Strangely Saulcy associates the location of Gomorrah with the ruins of Qumran on the north western side of the Dead Sea.[23] He states:

> From the head of Wadi-Goumran the extensive ruins that we have just met are called Kharbet-Goumran or Oumran [*Sic* Qumran]. We begin by pointing out a strange analogy, if it is not coincidental, that the name and that of Gomorrah destroyed by fire from heaven, with Sodom and the other guilty cities, I said, without any kind of hesitation, the ruins named by the Arabs Kharbet-ei-Yahud, Kharbet Feschkhah [Ein Feshkha] and Kharbet Goumran [*Sic* Qumran]; ruins which are but one and that extend over an area of more than six miles without interruption, in reality, for me, are the ruins of the biblical Gomorrah [translated from French by Graves and Ruffle].[24]

Samuel Wolcott (1868)

Samuel Wolcott (1813–1886) was a New England minister and hymn writer who served as a missionary in Syria for two years and wrote several archaeology articles on ancient

---

[18] Ibid., 223.

[19] Harry G. Cocks, "The Discovery of Sodom, 1851," *Representations* 112 (Fall 2010): 1.

[20] Ibid.

[21] Louis Félicien J. Caignart de Saulcy, *Narrative of a Journey Round the Dead Sea and in the Bible Lands in 1850 and 1851: Including an Account of the Discovery of the Sites of Sodom and Gomorrah*, ed. Edward de Warren (London, U.K.: R. Bentley, 1853), 1:452–53; Chevalier Van de Velde, "M. De Saulcy's Discoveries," *The Literary Gazette:* *A Weekly Journal of Literature, Science, and the Fine Art* 1944 (April 22, 1854): 377.

[22] Saulcy, *Narrative of a Journey Round the Dead Sea*, 1:459, 463.

[23] Jacques de Vitry's *Historia Orientalis seu Hierosolymitana* (1226); Burchard de Monte Sion, *Descriptio Terrae Sanctae* (1280) and Father Felix Fabri, a German Dominican friar, who made two trips to the Dead Sea region, in 1480 and another in 1483-4, all identify Zoar with Qumran. Taylor, "The Dead Sea in Western Travellers' Accounts," 15–18.

[24] Félix de Saulcy, "Lettre à M. Clermont-Ganneau Sur Les Ruines de Gomorrhe," *Revue Archéologique* 32 (1876): 307; Charles S. Clermont-Ganneau, "Gomorrah, Segor et Les Filles de Lot: Lettre à M. F. de Saulcy," *Revue Archéologique* 33 (1877): 193–98; de Velde, "M. De Saulcy's Discoveries," 377. Trelawney Saunders, *Map of Western Palestine* also shared this view.

biblical sites. He challenged George Grove's view, proposed in the *Smith Dictionary of the Bible*,[25] that Sodom and the Cities of the Plain, were in the northern region of the Jordan Valley. While Wolcott considered Grove's idea "a new theory"[26] he had also to deal with Tristram's northern views.[27] In an article in *Bibliotheca Sacra* Wolcott stated:

> We will now give in order the main reasons (some of them involved and implied in the preceding discussion) on which we ground our belief that Sodom lay south, and not north, of the Dead Sea. . . . If Zoar was in the district in which we have placed it, Sodom was south, and not north, of the sea.[28]

Georg Heinrich Ewald (1883)

Georg H. Ewald (1803–1875) was the professor of theology and oriental languages at the University of Gottingen in Germany (1827–1837). His work *Geschichte des Volkes Israel* was originally written and published in German in 1864[29] and later translated by Russell Martineau into English (1869) as *History of the People of Israel*. Ewald believes that the Cities of the Plain were located at the southern end of the Dead Sea and, based on the term "overthrow", believes that they were destroyed by an earthquake.

> *The engulfed cities must have been in the southern half of the Dead Sea.* This half has a strikingly shallow bottom, and undoubtedly only the larger northern part with its far greater depth existed before the last great change in the ground: oral tradition also places the ancient *Sodom on the south-west shore.* There, not far from the margin, still appears the strange cone of salt standing like a pillar, in which the ancient tradition so easily found a petrified human being (Lot's wife); and we see now that it was not without reason that Josephus testified that this pillar of salt existed to his day, and that he himself had seen it

(*Ant.* 1.11.4). And if the city of Zoar,[30] by itself, or even with its province, lay in the peninsula which cuts deeply into the *southern half of the Sea of Salt*, and looks like a portion of land that escaped the general overthrow, the tradition might easily take the form that it had belonged as a fifth to the four cities, and been spared by special grace (Gen 19:19–22) [emphasis added].[31]

Charles Simon Clermont-Ganneau (1886)

Charles Clermont-Ganneau (1846–1923) was the noted French orientalist and archaeologist teaching at the College of France. He suggests "that the name Gomorrah should perhaps be looked for in that of Wâdy Ghamr, 'Ain Ghamr, to the south of the Dead Sea."[32]

On the location of Sodom, Clermont-Ganneau states:

> Between this point [Wâdy N'meira] and Jebel Usdum, the uncontested representative of Sodom, in the region south-west of the lake, and nearly opposite there is a distance of about ten Roman miles. Now, the Talmud, in a passage which is not legendary, says that there are nine miles between Sodom and Segor [Zoar]. It is then about half-way that we must look for Segor in the Ghor es Safi, where in fact certain speculative maps have actually set is down. . . . In this case the cities would occupy the southern part of the basin of the Dead Sea— Sodom and Segor being to right and left the most northerly. This would very well conform with the Arabic tradition, which is not to be despised, and which places in this very region what it calls the "cities of the people of Lot." [see *Fact 58*][33]

Charles Warren (1899)

Sir Charles Warren (1840–1927) was an

---

[25] Grove, "Sodom"; Grove, "Zoar."
[26] Wolcott, "The Site of Sodom," 114.
[27] Ibid., 137–44; Tristram, *The Land of Israel*; Tristram, *The Land of Moab*.
[28] Wolcott, "The Site of Sodom," 130–31, 144.
[29] Georg Heinrich Ewald, *Geschichte Des Volkes Israel*, 2nd ed., vol. 1, 8 vols. (Göttingen: Dieterich, 1864).

[30] The LXX preserve the harder pronunciation Σηγώρ.
[31] Ewald, *History of Israel*, 1:314.
[32] Clermont-Ganneau, "Gomorrah, Segor et Les Filles de Lot: Lettre à M. F. de Saulcy," 193–98; Charles S. Clermont-Ganneau, "Segor, Gomorrah, and Sodom," *PEFSt.* 18, no. 2 (1886): 21; Charles S. Clermont-Ganneau, *Archaeological Researches in Palestine During the Years 1873 - 1874*, trans. John MacFarlane, vol. 2 (London, U.K.: Palestine Exploration Fund, 1896), 2:15.
[33] Clermont-Ganneau, "Segor, Gomorrah, and Sodom," 20–21.

officer in the British Royal Engineers who did extensive work on the Temple Mount in Jerusalem and discovered Warren's gate. Additionally, as head of the London Metropolitan Police, from 1886 to 1888, he worked on the Jack the Ripper crimes.[34] While Warren's article on "Jordan" in the Hasting's five-volume *Dictionary of the Bible* presents both views, he appears to favor the SST, stating:

> The Arab geographers, however, place these cities at the *southern end of the Salt Sea*. . . . The reference to the whole land which "is brimstone, and salt, and burning, that it is not sown, nor burneth, nor any grass groweth therein, like the overthrow of Sodom" (Deut 29:23), etc., would appear to apply more to *the southern end of the Salt Sea* than the generally accepted site on the northern end. . . . Assuming that the cities of the plain were situated at the N.E. end of the Salt Sea, it is suggested [by Merrill][35] that the following tells on the Abel-shittim plain were the five cities of the Plain: (1) Tell Kafrein (Abel or Abila), (2) Tell er-Rama (Beth-ramtha or Beth-haran, Julias or Livias), (3) Suweimeh (Beth-jesimoth or Besimoth), (4) Tell el-Hammam, (5) Tell Ektanu ("the little one," or Zoar). Ganneau, however, identifies Jebel Usdum as Sodom, and Gomorrah with 'Ain Ghamr, at the entrance of Wady Ghamr, about 20 leagues south of the Salt Sea, and Zoar in Wady es-Safi.[36] This would appear closely to agree with the traditional sites given by Josephus [emphasis added; see *Fact 58*].[37]

William F. Albright (1924)

The notable archaeologist, philologist, and biblical scholar, William F. Albright (1891–1971) hardly needs any introduction. He is considered the dean of the biblical archaeology movement[38] and has had a major influence on the search for Sodom by promoting the inundation theory.

> Most suggestive is the fact that the evidence of pottery sets the end of the settlement at Bâb ed-Drâ' at about the time when Biblical sources place the catastrophe of the Cities of the Plain. This coincidence can hardly be accidental. We therefore seem to be justified in supposing that Bâb ed-Drâ' was one of the sacred places of the inhabitants of Sodom and Gomorrah, to which they made annual pilgrimages, and where they may have practised nameless rites, the nature of which need not be surmised, in view of our other information about Canaanite religion.[39]
>
> In 1924 we obtained an entirely satisfactory solution of the problem of the situation of the five Cities of the Plain, Sodom, Gomorrah, Admah, Zeboim, and Zoar. . . . Even if the curious coincidence of the five Cities of the Plain with five modern oases in this region should be accidental, we are, therefore, quite justified in placing them here, and in supposing that their sites have long since been covered by the Dead Sea, though they may have been exposed to view until post-Biblical times. . . . Since the plain of Bâb ed-Drâ' [*sic*] is not suitable for cultivation, and is high above the gorge of the Seil ed-Drâ', it would in any case be a very unsatisfactory place for a town. As a festival site for the inhabitants of the oases below it is admirable, since it is situated on the first convenient rise of terrain above the central oasis of el-Mezra'ah, some five hundred feet above the level

---

[34] Brian Fagan, *Archaeologists: Explorers of the Human Past* (Oxford, U.K.: Oxford University Press, 2003), 61–63; Neil Asher Silberman, *Digging for God and Country: Exploration, Archaeology, and the Secret Struggle for the Holy Land, 1799-1917* (New York, N.Y.: Doubleday, 1990).

[35] Merrill, "Modern Researches in Palestine, PEFSt.," 144.

[36] Clermont-Ganneau, "Segor, Gomorrah, and Sodom," 20–21.

[37] Charles Warren, "Jordan," in *DBib5*, ed. James Hastings and John A. Selbie, vol. 2 (New York, N.Y.: Scribner's Sons, 1899), 2:764.

[38] David Noel Freedman, "William Foxwell Albright: In Memoriam," *BASOR* 205, no. 1 (February 1972): 1+3–13; Leona Glidden Running and David Noel Freedman, *William Foxwell Albright: A Twentieth-Century Genius: A Biography of the Acknowledged Dean of Biblical Archaeologists* (Berrien Springs, Mich.: Andrews University Press, 1975); Peter Douglas Feinman, *William Foxwell Albright and the Origins of Biblical Archaeology* (Berrien Springs, Mich.: Andrews University Press, 2004); "Methodism and the Origins of Biblical Archaeology: The William Foxwell Albright Story," *AUSS* 47, no. 1 (2009): 61–72; "Canaanites, Catholics, and Chosen Peoples: William Foxwell Albright's Biblical Archaeology," *NEA* 75, no. 3 (2012): 148–60.

[39] Melvin Grove Kyle and William F. Albright, "Results of the Archaeological Survey of the Ghor in Search for the Cities of the Plain," *BSac* 81 (1924): 281.

of the Dead Sea.[40]

For more on Albright see Fact 5.

James Penrose Harland (1943)

J. Penrose Harland (1891–1973) was a Princeton-educated classical archaeologist who taught at the University of North Carolina in the early 1900's. He excavated in Greece specializing in the Late Helladic period (15th cent. BC).[41] He wrote two articles on Sodom and Gomorrah in the *Biblical Archaeologist* which supported Albright's inundation theory. Many of the arguments were adopted by Bryant Wood to support BeD as Sodom and used in his articles on the SST. Harland reports:

> In summary, one may conclude that the evidence from the Bible and from the late Greek and Latin writers indicates a location around the southern end of the Sea.[42]

> In a previous article[43] it was shown that Sodom, Gomorrah, Admah, and Zeboiim were doubtless situated in the area now covered by the waters of the southern part of the Dead Sea, and that the site of the fifth City, Zoar, is probably to be sought near the southeast corner of the Sea. This conclusion was reached from a study of the evidence from the Bible (particularly Genesis), from certain Greek and Latin writers, from the study of geology, topography, and water-supply, and from both direct and indirect archaeological evidence.[44]

David Noel Freedman (1978)

David N. Freedman (1922–2008) was a Princeton-trained Presbyterian minister and archaeologist, who earned his doctorate in Semitic languages under W. F. Albright at Johns Hopkins University in 1948. He held teaching positions at various schools and was the director of the Albright Institute of Archaeological Research (American Schools of Oriental Research), Jerusalem (1969–1970, 1976–1977). He also authored and edited many books including the *Anchor Bible Series* (1956–2008), *Eerdmans Critical Commentaries* (2000–2008), and the *Eerdmans Dictionary of the Bible* (2000).[45] In his article on the Ebla tablets he states:

> All were occupied [Bâb edh-Dhrâ' and Numeira] during the Early Bronze Age for varying periods of time; the only period common to all is EB III, which is also the period of the Ebla tablets. The provisional conclusion to be drawn is that the cities of the plain have in fact been found, but until now they were not securely identified as such. In the light of the new information, we now propose that these are the cities of the plain (though which was which can be left for future investigation) and that we revise our views of their location and chronology accordingly.[46]

William H. Shea (1983)

Bill Shea is a retired professor of Hebrew and Old Testament at the Seventh Day-Adventist Seminary at Andrews University (14 years) and associate director of the Biblical Research Institute of the General Conference of the Seventh-day Adventists (13 years). In his article on the Ebla tablets Shea speculates that:

> With the evidence now available from the EGA [Eblaite Geographical Atlas] the locations [for the Pentapolis] proposed towards the north end of the Dead Sea may be discarded. The reason is that if those who travelled the route covered by the second segment of the EGA studied above had gone north from En Gedi (No. 207), they should have passed

---

[40] Albright, *The Archaeology of Palestine and the Bible*, 134, 136–37.

[41] James Penrose Harland, *Prehistoric Aigina. A History of the Island in the Bronze Age* (Paris: Librairie Ancienne Honore Champion, 1925).

[42] Harland, "Sodom and Gomorrah Part I: Location," 23.

[43] Ibid., 17–32.

[44] Harland, "Sodom and Gomorrah Part II: Destruction," 41–42.

[45] Barry Jagoda, "Leading Scholar of the Bible, David Noel Freedman, Dies at 85," *UCSanDiego News Center*, April 11, 2008, http://ucsdnews.ucsd.edu/archive/newsrel/general/04-08FreedmanObit.asp.

[46] Freedman, "The Real Story of the Ebla Tablets," 152–53.

by the forests and the river junction located at the southern end of the Jordan Valley by the first segment studied above from the EGA (cf. Nos. 123-127) *before* they came to Admah and Sodom. . . . If the correlations proposed above are correct, then Bâb edh-Dhrâ' could be identified with Sodom and Admah could be identified with es-Safi. . . . The site of Numeirah is located between Bâb edh-Dhrâ' and es-Safi, and thus it is a candidate for Gomorrah.[47]

For a refutation of this views see *Ancient Textual References: Ebla Tablets; Fact 32: Shea's Identification of the Cities based on the Eblaite Geographic Atlas is Suspect*; and *Fact 47: The Pentapolis are not all Mentioned Together in the Ebla Tablets, and Most Doubt they are Listed at all.*

Gordon J. Wenham (1998)

Gordon J. Wenham (b. 1943) is a prominent British OT scholar and currently lecturer at Trinity College, Bristol, U.K. In his commentary on Genesis he states:

> The location of the five towns (Zoar's king is not named) remains problematic. The next verse makes it clear that the towns were near the Dead Sea. Though it has been suggested that they lay at the northern end of the Dead Sea, it has usually been supposed that the cities lie under or near the shallow southern end where interesting salt formations and the reek of sulphur remind the visitor of Sodom's end (19:24–26).. . . . Recent explorations have noted five sites on the eastern shoreline of the Dead Sea, towns occupied in the Early Bronze Age ca. 3100–2350 B.C.. . . . Bab edh-Dhra (Sodom?) and Numeira were both destroyed about 2350 B.C. and then reoccupied for a short while. They were finally abandoned about 2200 or 2100 B.C. These dates are somewhat early for Abram, and the archeological evidence published to date suggests that a military attack rather than some (super)natural disaster led to the destruction of these sites.[48]

FACT 3: THE NST IS NOT A NEW VIEW

The northern location is not a new view and was argued by many archaeologists and Bible scholars in the nineteenth century prior to W. F. Albright and G. E. Wright, who argued it was under the Dead Sea. The archaeologists, interested in locating the lost Cities of the Plain, went to the only source they had at their disposal – the text of scripture (Gen 13:10–12) – and concluded that the Pentapolis were somewhere north of the Dead Sea on the eastern side of the Jordan Valley. Merrill even identified TeH as one of the Cities of the Plain prior to its excavation by Steven Collins.

Charles William Wilson (1869)

Charles W. Wilson (1836–1905) was a British military officer in the Royal Engineers and geographer with the Palestine Exploration Fund, who was involved in the Ordnance Survey of Jerusalem, where he discovered the Arch which now bears his name (Wilson's Arch).[49] He stated:

> It is hardly possible, I think, for anyone to read the account in Genesis xiii. 10, without feeling that Abram and Lot were actually looking down on Sodom and Gomorrah when "Lot lifted up his eyes, and beheld all the plain of Jordan, that it was well watered everywhere, before the Lord destroyed Sodom and Gomorrah," &c. If this be the case, thou the view from the hill fixes their position to have been on the plain at the northern end of the Dead Sea, not under the hills near Jericho, but out in mid-plain, possibly not far from the now barren tract which most travellers skirt on their way from the Dead Sea to the Jordan. That the greater portion of this tract was at one time cultivated, "well watered everywhere, even as a garden of the Lord," there is ample evidence in the numerous traces of former irrigation to be found on a careful examination of the ground. In support of this view may be cited the mention of the plain of Jordan in verse 10, which could not have extended below the point at which the river entered the Dead Sea, and the direct testimony in verse 11 that Lot journeyed east, a course which would lead him far away from the southern end of the Dead Sea where writers

---

[47] Shea, "Two Palestinian Segments," 609–10.
[48] Wenham, *Genesis 1-15*, 1:309.
[49] D. A. J., "Obituary: Major-General Sir Charles William Wilson, K. C. B., K. C. M. G., F. R. S., Etc.," *The Geographical Journal* 26, no. 6 (December 1905): 682–84.

from Josephus to the present day have placed the cities of the plain.⁵⁰

Edward Henry Palmer (1871)

Edward H. Palmer (1840–1882) was a Cambridge-educated orientalist specializing in Arabic and Persian who carried out some of his work with the Palestine Exploration Fund in the Middle East. In 1871 he became Lord Almoner's Professor of Arabic at Cambridge University.⁵¹ In volume two of his work, *The Desert of the Exodus,* Palmer writes:

> Writers on sacred topography, from Josephus downwards, have unanimously concurred in assuming the southern portion of the Dead Sea to have been the position of the "Vale of Siddim" and the "cities of the plain." Captain Wilson, in an able article upon the site of Ai,⁵² shows this view to be erroneous, and I entirely agree with him in placing the site of Sodom and Gomorrah at the northern extremity of the lake.⁵³

Henry Baker Tristram (1873)

Henry B. Tristram (1822–1906) was an English minister and scholar who travelled to Palestine four times in his career (1858, 1863, 1872, and 1881). He was also a Darwinian ornithologist.⁵⁴ According to Merrill,⁵⁵ Henry B. Tristram adopted Merrill's views for the northern location of the Cities of the Plain in his book, *The Land of Moab Travels and Discoveries on the East Side of the Dead Sea and the Jordan.* Tristram states:

> But for the northern site we have the argument from the simple statement of the inspired writer, who calls them "the cities of the plain," or circle, "ciccar," [*kikkār*] of [the] Jordan—an expression which can not possibly apply to any other than the *northern* end of the Dead Sea.⁵⁶

Selah Merrill (1876, 1881)

Selah Merrill (1837–1909) was an American Congregationalist clergyman who taught at Andover Theological Seminary in 1872 and again in 1879. Between 1874 and 1877 Merrill traveled to Palestine to work in Jerusalem as an archaeologist with the Palestine Exploration Fund. He served as the US Consul in Jerusalem in 1882–1885, 1891–1893, and 1898–1907.⁵⁷

In his book *East of the Jordan* Selah Merrill notes:

> My observations on the site of the Cities of the Plain, corresponding in the main to what I have stated in this chapter, were prepared by me early in the summer of 1876, and read to the Advisory Committee of the American Palestine Exploration Society, in Beirut. They were, in the course of that summer, published in the London "Athenæum," in the New York "Evangelist" and "Independent," also in the New York Daily "Times," and in other leading journals in Boston, Chicago, and San Francisco. They have been quoted also by various writers, among whom may be mentioned Rev. Wm. M. Thomson, D. D., who, in his new edition of "The Land and the Book," has adopted them almost entire.⁵⁸

Merrill published his findings again in 1877⁵⁹ in the *Journal of the American Geographical Society of New York* and then republished the

---

⁵⁰ Wilson, "On the Site of Ai," 125.
⁵¹ http://www.pef.org.uk/profiles/professor-edward-henry-palmer-1840-1882. Hugh Chisholm, ed., "E. H. Palmer," in *Encyclopædia Britannica Online*, 11th ed., 32 vols. (Cambridge, U.K.: Cambridge University Press, 1911), http://www.britannica.com/EBchecked/topic/440173/E-H-Palmer.
http://www.pef.org.uk/profiles/professor-edward-henry-palmer-1840-1882
⁵² Wilson, "On the Site of Ai," 123–26.
⁵³ Palmer, *The Desert of the Exodus*, 1:480.
⁵⁴ Patrick Armstrong, *The English Parson-Naturalist: A Companionship Between Science and Religion* (Leominster: Gracewing, 2000), 1–22.
⁵⁵ Merrill, *East of the Jordan*, 239.

⁵⁶ Tristram, *The Land of Moab*, 344.
⁵⁷ Shalom Goldman, "The Holy Land Appropriated: The Careers of Selah Merrill, Nineteenth Century Christian Hebraist, Palestine Explorer, and U.S. Consul in Jerusalem," *American Jewish History* 85, no. 2 (June 1997): 151–72.
⁵⁸ Merrill, *East of the Jordan*, 239.
⁵⁹ Merrill, "Modern Researches in Palestine, 1877," 109–25.

15. The Jordan Valley (*kikkār*). Several archaeological sites are identified which were cities on the plain in the Early and Middle Bronze Age. The NST places Sodom at Tall el-Hammam, Gomorrah at Tall Kefrein and Admah at Tall Nimrin.

same article in 1879 in the *Palestine Exploration Fund Quarterly Statement*.[60]

In his section on "The Site of Zoar" his number 10 argument states:

> Only five sites are required [for the Cities of the Plain], namely— Sodom, Gomorrah, Admah, Zeboim, and Zoar; and on the Shittim plain we have exactly five sites—Tel Kefrein or Abel Shittim, Tel er Rama or Beth Haram, Suweimeh or Beth Jeshimoth, Tel el Hammam and Tel Ektanu [emphasis added].[61]

In the section titled "Camp at Tell el Hammam, Saturday, April 8, 1876" in his book, *East of the Jordan* (1881), he argues strongly for the northern location of the "Cities of the Plain" and also identified a second Zoar in the north. He mentioned TeH as one of the Cities of the Plain but does not identify which site is which city. He wrote:

> I present here some considerations regarding the site of the "Cities of the Plain," one of the important Biblical questions connected with the topography of Eastern Palestine. Were they at the south end of the Dead Sea? Have they been submerged ? Or were they on the Shittim plain at the north end of the Dead Sea? . . . . there is a remarkable group of tells at the north end of the Dead Sea, which are covered with ruins, and some of which are the sites of cities that existed in the days of Joshua. . . . Only five sites are required, namely, Sodom, Gomorrah, Admah, Zeboim, and Zoar. . . .
>
> On the Shittim plain, at the north-east corner of the Dead Sea, there are five important ancient sites, namely, Tell Kefrein, Tell er Rama, Tell el Hammam, Tell Ektanu, and Suweimeh. Tell Ninirin, being some miles farther to the north, is not

---

[60] Merrill, "Modern Researches in Palestine, PEFSt.," 138–54.

[61] Merrill, "Modern Researches in Palestine, 1877," 119; "Modern Researches in Palestine, PEFSt.," 147.

reckoned in this list. To these should be added Tell esh Shaghûr....

On the other hand, the arguments for placing the Zoar of Lot at the north end of the Dead Sea [at Tell Ektanu] are to us convincing.[62]

William F. Birch (1879)

William F. Birch (1840–1916) was a minister who lived in Manchester, England and wrote numerous articles for the Palestine Exploration Fund (PEF). He wrote:

> As the southern end of the Dead Sea and the western side of the plain near Jericho are hidden from these heights by intervening mountains, we should be predisposed to think that Zoar near Sodom was at the *north* end of the Dead Sea and on the *eastern* side of the plain. The expression, "Lot journeyed east," also inclines us to infer the same... . we conclude that Zoar and the cities of the plain could not possibly have been at the southern but, of necessity, at the northern end of the Dead Sea.... Zoar of the Pentateuch was at the north end of the Dead Sea, and on the east side of the valley.... The LXX (with but one exception) render Zoar, by the word Σηγώρ (Segor), a still nearer approach to Shâghur. But the last shadow of doubt as to the fact that Tell esh-Shâghur[63] really means the "Hill of Zoar" seems to vanish, when we find that the Hebrew equivalent for Z becomes at times in Arabic Sh.[64]

In another article Birch identified the location of Sodom with Tall er-Rama, near TeH.

> After placing Zoar at Tell esh-Shâghur, I have no choice left but to identify Sodom with Tell er Rama, about a quarter of an hour's walk towards the south.[65]

Claude Reignier Conder (1879–1883)

Claude Reignier Conder (1848–1910)[66] was a British lieutenant in the Corps of Royal Engineers assigned to carry out survey work in Palestine from 1872 to 1874. Upon his return home, he became a member of the PEF. In 1881 he began to survey the region east of the Jordan.[67]

> The Moslems believe that the wicked cities lie beneath the Sea of Lot, as they call the Lake Asphaltites, but the geological evidence all goes to prove that the Dead Sea must have existed pretty much in [2:13] its present condition in the time of Abraham, and that such a convulsion as they suppose cannot have occurred within historical times. [2:14] Modern scholars, therefore, have sought anew for the sites of Sodom and Gomorrah, Zoar, Zeboim, and Admah. It seems almost certain that these cities should be placed towards the north end of the lake, because the term *Ciccar* [kikkār] applies properly to the Jordan valley and to the Jericho plain; our utmost efforts were therefore directed to the discovery of the sites of the Cities of the Plain (or *Ciccar*) in this direction. Over almost every acre of ground between Jericho and the Dead Sea, I rode day by day. The whole is a white desert, except near the hills, where rich herbage grows after the rains.[68]
>
> Thus the Vale of Siddim might well, so far as its name is concerned, have been situated in the vicinity of the northern shores of the Dead Sea.... Such are the only suggestions I am able to offer on this interesting question. To discover the sites of these cities, on the north shores of the Dead Sea, will, I

---

[62] Merrill, *East of the Jordan*, 232–37.

[63] Easton locates it as "a white rocky mound at the foot of the Moab Mountains, a mile East of Beth-haram (Tell er-Rameh), 7 miles northeast of the mouth of the Jordan" which Conder and Kitchen identify as Tall Ikatnu. Mathew George Easton, *Illustrated Bible Dictionary*, 3rd ed. (Nashville, Tenn.: Nelson, 1897), Zoar op. cit.; George Frederick Wright, "Zoar," ed. James Orr and Melvin Grove Kyle, *ISBE1* (Grand Rapids, Mich.: Eerdmans, 1915); Conder and Kitchener, *Survey of Eastern Palestine*, 1:230.

[64] William F. Birch, "Zoar," *PEFSt.* 11, no. 1 (1879): 15.

[65] William F. Birch, "Sodom," *PEFSt.* 13 (1881): 101.

[66] On a sidenote, Slemen and Andrews claim they have proof that Conder was the notorious "Jack the Ripper" and that Charles Warren, who investigated the crime, was his friend and concealed the truth. Tom Slemen and Keith Andrews, *Jack the Ripper: British Intelligence Officer?* (Liverpool: The Bluecoat Press, 2010).

[67] "Lt. Claude R. Conder, R.E., 1848-1910," *Palestine Exploration Fund*, January 16, 2014, http://www.pef.org.uk/profiles/lt-claude-r-conder-re-1848-1910.

[68] Conder, *Tent Work in Palestine*, 2:13–14.

The Location of Sodom

feel convinced, be impossible, unless springs of fresh water be also there discovered, which are not to be found on the Survey sheets.[69]

In his 1881 survey of the region east of the Jordan, Conder mentions TeH but only in conjunction with the dolmen fields (see Fig. 34, 35 and Map 9) and springs.[70]

> Near Nimrin it is partly cultivated with maize, but much of its soil lies fallow, with scattered groves of the sidr or lotus. Here grow the tall *'oshír* shrubs, with their dusty apples of Sodom, and here are mounds which mark the sites of Beth Haran, Beth Jeshimoth, Kefrein, Beth Nimrah, and in all probability of Zoar.... There is one more question which demands attention in concluding this sketch of the land of Sihon, for it is in this plain of the Seisebân that students have of late looked to find traces of the "Cities of the Ciccar," [*kikkār*] which were overthrown when Lot escaped to Zoar. It is probable that every important name has now been collected in the plains of Shittim, yet although Zoar may perhaps be considered as fixed, *no traces of Sodom or Gomorrah* were discovered by the surveyors.... Zoar, "the little" city, might in Arabic be recognised as Saghîr, "the little," and as first pointed out, I believe, by the Rev. W. F. Birch, there is a ruined mound, called Shaghûr in the Shittim plain, near the foot of the Moab range. The name is perhaps as nearly equivalent to the Hebrew as would be likely, and the site is certainly appropriate. Zoar formed the limit of Moab (Jer. xlviii. 34), and of the Jordan plain (Deut. xxxiv. 3). It was not in the mountains, but in the lowland (Gen. xix. 19), and the site of Tell Shaghûr answers all these requirements.... It is here, perhaps, that we may picture the trembling Lot looking on at the destruction of the Cities of the Plain, and from hence he fled to the cave in the mountains above, for he feared to dwell in Zoar.[71]

William M. Thomson (1882–85)

William M. Thomson (1806–1894) was educated at Princeton Theological Seminary and became a biblical scholar who spent over 40 years as a missionary in the Holy Land, often riding around on horseback to explore in detail the sites around him. He produced a three-volume work called *The Land and the Book*.[72]

> A better acquaintance with the topography and physical characteristics of this region had led many modern writers to reject this entire hypothesis [SST], and to locate those doomed cities at the north end of the sea instead of the south end, and the reasons for this change appear quite conclusive....
>
> Turning now to the Biblical narrative, let us examine some of the statements which seem to necessitate the transfer of the site of the destroyed cities to the north or north-east end of the Dead Sea. And first, it appears to be certain, from Genesis 13:1–13, that at the time of the separation between Abraham and Lot they were at or near Bethel, some twelve or fifteen miles north of Jerusalem, and sixty or seventy miles from the south end of the Dead Sea. Lot, therefore, without a miracle, could not have seen that region at all, however high he "lifted up his eyes." The distance is too great, there is a haze over the sea which obscures the view, and, finally, high mountains on the western shore entirely intercept the prospect. And, furthermore, it is evident that the region at the south end of the sea cannot be called the "plain of the Jordan" in any admissible sense; that plain stops at the north end. Moreover, Lot, when he separated from Abraham, is said to have "journeyed east"; whereas he must have gone to the south, if Sodom was at that end of the sea....
>
> Now, if Zoar was at the north end of the Dead Sea, it would be in the immediate vicinity of Jericho, almost at the foot of Pisgah, and superfluous to say that Moses saw it; but if it was at the other end of that sea, it would imply a large extension of the survey in that direction.[73]

In Thomson's book *The Land and the Book: Lebanon, Damascus, and Beyond Jordan* he describes the Shittim plain and lists the Talls that were visible in the 1800's. He recounts:

> The principal tells on the plain of Abel-shittim, commencing at the southern end and proceeding northward, are Tell es Suweimeh, ... Tell Ektanu, ..

---

[69] Ibid., 2:16–17.

[70] Conder and Kitchener, *Survey of Eastern Palestine*, 1:229–30.

[71] Conder, *Heth and Moab*, 151, 153–55.

[72] "About William M. Thomson," Logos Bible Software, January 16, 2014, https://www.logos.com/product/26753/the-land-and-the-book.

[73] Thomson, *Land and the Book: Southern Palestine and Jerusalem*, 1:371–76.

. Tell er Râmeh, . . . Tell esh Shaghûr, . . . Tell el Hammâm, . . . Tell Kefrein, . . . and Tell Nimrin. . . . . We have now reached Tell el Hammâm, the mound of the bath, at the foot of the mountain. I spent two nights near it, encamped on the west bank of this pretty little stream from Wady Kefrein, and I passed the intervening day wandering about this beautiful plain and exploring the surrounding hills. Tell el Hammâm is a high natural mound at the south-eastern end of the plain, and commands a wide view over it to the south and west, and the stream from Wady Kefrein flows past its north-western base. No part of the tall is artificial except the top, which is covered with the debris of ancient buildings which may be of any age [*Thompson was unaware of the occupational ruins around the lower tell that included a city wall*]. The summit appears to have been surrounded with a wall, and if it was well fortified it would command the entrance into the mountains up Wady Kefrein. . . . Tall el Hammâm is so called from some warm sulfur springs near the base of it on the south-west.[74]

George Grove (1884)

George Grove (1820–1900) was a founding member of the Palestine Exploration Fund and later founded the Royal College of Music. Wolcott spoke highly of Grove and, even though he disagreed with his view on Sodom's location, he praised his abilities.

> A gentleman who stands in the front rank of biblical scholars. Of the nearly seventy eminent writers and critics, whose multifarious learning has made the Dictionary [*Smith's Bible Dictionary*] such an invaluable Thesaurus of scriptural knowledge, there is probably no single contributor to whom it owes so much as to the one whom we have named [contributed over 1000 pages]. The wonderful versatility and competency which he has shown in the discussion of archaeological, exegetical, geographical, geological, historical, and topographical questions, pertaining to the sacred oracles, have given his name authority in biblical matters.[75]

> Of the situation of these cities [Cities of the Plain] we only know that, being in the "plain of the Jordan/ they must have been to the north of the lake"[76]

In his article on Sodom he states:

> In the subsequent account of their destruction, (Genesis 19:1) the topographical terms are employed with all the precision which is characteristic of such early times. The mention of the Jordan is conclusive as to the situation of the district, for *the Jordan ceases where it enters the Dead Sea, and can have no existence south of that point*. . . . That *Sodom and the rest of the cities of the plain of Jordan stood on the north of the Dead Sea* [emphasis added].[77]

In his article on Zoar, Grove once again reiterates the northern location and states:

> There can be little doubt that the plain of the Jordan was at the north side of the Dead Sea and that the cities of the plain must therefore have been situated there instead of at the southern end of the lake, as it is generally taken for granted they were.[78]

John Cunningham Geikie (1887)

J. Cunningham Geikie (1824–1906) was a Presbyterian minister educated in Edinburgh, UK and Toronto, Canada. He was considered by many to be one of the best religious authors of his day. He was impressed with Conder's work at the PEF and made several trips to the holy land, which provided the material for his book, *The Holy Land and the Bible*.

> The Cities of the Plain stood on some part of the plain of Jericho, which in Abraham's day was much the same as it is now. The shape of the basin of the sea, and its geological history, make it impossible that any towns could have existed except at its northern or southern end, but those which perished are expressly called the Cities of the *Plain*, or "Circle" [*kikkār*] of the Jordan; an expression used only of the slopes reaching, on both sides, from the hills to the river, immediately before it enters the lake. Abraham and Lot, moreover, could see the fertile region of Sodom and Gomorrah from the hill-top on which they stood, between Bethel and

---

[74] Thomson, *Land and the Book: Lebanon, Damascus, and Beyond Jordan*, 3:669.

[75] Wolcott, "The Site of Sodom," 113–14.

[76] George Grove, "The Salt Sea," ed. William Smith, *A Dictionary of the Bible* (Philadelphia, Pa.: Winston, 1884), 910.

[77] "Sodom," 976.

[78] Grove, "Zoar," 1153.

Ai, but intervening hills shut out the southern end of the sea, which is sixty miles off, from any point near that from which the patriarchs looked down into the great depression, while they could see the plain of Jericho and the rich green of the Sultan's Spring, as if at their feet. Nor could Abraham, as he stood at his tent door at Mamre, have seen, as he did, "the smoke of the country rising like the smoke of a furnace," as he looked "towards Sodom and Gomorrah," had they been at the south end of the lake; whereas the openings between the hills are such that, though the plain itself is not visible from near Hebron, the clouds of smoke ascending from the doomed cities must have been seen in all their grandeur. That Chedorlaomer, on his way north from Mount Seir, after smiting the Amorites at Engedi, should have fallen upon the kings of Sodom and Gomorrah in the plains of Siddim, continuing his march northwards towards home after defeating them, so that in his turn he was overcome by Abraham near the sources of the Jordan, further implies that the Cities of the Plain were north of the Dead Sea. Still more, the fact that Moses, from his lofty outlook on Mount Pisgah, "beheld the Negeb and the plain of the valley of Jericho, the city of palm-trees, unto Zoar," requires that this landscape should have been that of *the northern end of the sea* [emphasis added], for the other end cannot be seen from the neighbourhood from which Moses surveyed the landscape. Sodom and Gomorrah must therefore, apparently, have stood either on the eastern or western side of the Jordan, just above the lake; probably on the eastern. Both sides of the river are remarkable for the number of mounds which dot them—silent monuments of ancient towns or cities, for excavations in any of them bring to light fragments of pottery, and burnt or sun-dried bricks, and even fragments of pillars, and stones squared by the mason. In all probability, some of these indicate the true sites of the long-lost cities.[79]

E. Power (1930)

Power is one of the first to deal extensively with the tradition surrounding the Cities of the Plain in such individuals as Josephus, Eusebius, Jerome and others. He argues strongly for the NST. He concludes his section about the battle with Chedorlaomer, king of Elam, with this statement:

---

[79] Geikie, *Holy Land and the Bible*, 2: 118–19.

that neither the valley of Siddim nor the Pentapolis can have been at the south of the Dead Sea, and that Gen. c. 14 confirms the conclusion deduced from the other texts that the Pentapolis was in the valley to the north of the Dead Sea.[80]

Père Alexis Mallon (1929–1934)

Father Alexis Mallon (d. 1934), was a French Professor of Egyptology at the Pontifical Biblical Institute in Jerusalem and with Albright, led an expedition to the area NE of the Dead Sea in search of Sodom and Gomorrah. Mallon excavated Tulaylat al-Ghassul in the Transjordan from 1929–1938 with the anticipation of finding Gomorrah there, but was disappointed to discover that it was a Chalcolithic site and too early to be one of the Cities of the Plain.[81]

In his article "Palestinian Chronicle: Voyage of discovery southeast of the Dead Sea" he states:

> The main purpose of the expedition was to find some traces of the famous "Cities of the Plain", from the distant days of Abraham and Lot: Sodom, Gomorrah, Adama, Seboiim, Zoar, all royal towns, cities, and small principalities. Right now, from our point of view, our research south of *Lisān* was unsuccessful. . . .[82]

However, there are no tells throughout the eṣ-Ṣāfieh ghōr, nor on the east coast, south of the *Lisān*. Biblical Zoar, Sodom, and Gomorrah, are under the

---

[80] Power, "The Site of the Pentapolis: Part 1," 44.

[81] Mallon, Koeppel, and Neuville, *Teleilât Ghassûl. I: Compte Rendu Des Fouilles de l'Institut Biblique Pontificale, 1929-1932*; Robert North, *Les Fouilles Dans La Region de Jericho* (Rome: Pibia, 1967), 139–40.

[82] "Le but principal de notre expédition était de retrouver quelques traces des fameuses « cités de la plaine », si florissantes aux jours lointains d'Abraham et de Lot: Sodome, Gomorrhe, Adama, Seboiim, Zoar, toutes villes royales, métropoles de petites principautés. Disons, tout de suite, qu'à ce point de vue, nos recherches, au sud de la *Lisān*, ont été infructueuses." Père Alexis Mallon, "Chronique Palestinienne: Voyage D'exploration Au Sud-Est de La Mer Morte," *Biblica* 5, no. 3–4 (1924): 434.

waters of the Dead Sea [Graves].[83]

FACT 4: WOOD BELIEVES THAT BeD IS SODOM

Bryant G. Wood is one of the few working field archaeologists who believe that Bâb edh-Dhrâ' (Arabic "gate of the arm") is biblical Sodom, although he identified Sodom with Khanazir in 1974. In his 1974 article, Wood asks:

> Our suggested identification of the five EB sites then is: Khanazir = Sodom, Feifa = Gomorrah, Safi = Zoar, Numeira = Admah, and Bab edh-Dhra = Zeboiim. . . . We can say in summary that all of the evidence we have in hand at this time points to the identification of the EB sites discovered by Schaub and Rast as Sodom, Gomorrah and the Cities of the Plain.[84]

In his 1999 article, Wood states:

> Even though the locations of three of the Cities of the Plain remain elusive, evidence is strong that the two most important, Sodom and Gomorrah, have been found. Bab edh-Dhra and Numeira are the only known inhabited towns in the region of the Dead Sea between ca. 3300 and 900 BC. . . .[85]
>
> The site to the north of Numeira, Bab edh-Dhra, would then be Sodom. Since Bab edh-Dhra is the largest and Gomorrah ancient ruin in the region it stands to reason that it should be identified as Sodom, the most famous of the Cities of the Plain. . . .[86]
>
> When the archaeological, geographical, and epigraphic evidence is reviewed in detail, it is clear that the infamous cities of Sodom and Gomorrah have now been found.

For the list of *Excavation Reports* from Rast and Schab, who excavated the site of Bâb edh-Dhrâ', see the list on page 76.

FACT 5: ALBRIGHT DID NOT BELIEVE THAT BeD WAS SODOM

Albright stated that Bâb edh-Dhrâ' may be one of the "clues or links" which could help to identify the Cities of the Plain, but did not believe that it was Sodom. In Albright's own words he stated: "It therefore seems highly probable that Bâb edh-Dhrâ' is a link to the biblical Sodom and Gomorrah. . . ."[87] but this is not saying that BeD is Sodom. Albright believed that Sodom was in the southern region but now buried under the Dead Sea. Albright stated:

> one result of our expedition has been to demonstrate that the site of the Old Testament Zoar was submerged by the rise of the Sea, . . . There is, accordingly, little likelihood that the exact sites of the original Zoar, of Sodom, or of Gomorrah will ever be recovered, but we can probably locate these towns approximately. . . . Since Zoar controlled the Seil el-Qrahi, Sodom, which biblical tradition places next to Zoar, presumably lay on the Seil en-Nmeirah, while Gomorrah may have been in the oasis of the Seil 'Esal. There is no room here for Admah and Zeboim, which, though allied with Sodom and Gomorrah, were probably situated in the southern part of the Jordan Valley, east of the river, where an Adamah (so, with the same consonants), now Tell ed-Damieh.[88]

Albright believed that Bâb edh-Dhrâ' could not be Sodom because it was destroyed in the EBA. For more on Albright see Fact 2 *William F. Albright*.

---

[83] "Or, il n'y a actuellement pas de tell dans tout le *ghōr eṣ-Ṣāfieh*, non plus que sur la côte orientale, au sud de la *Lisān*. Zoar biblique, ainsi que Sodome et Gomorrhe, est donc sous les eaux de la Mer Mort." Ibid., 439.

[84] Wood, "Have Sodom And Gomorrah Been Found?," 84–85.

[85] Wood, "Discovery of the Sin Cities," 68.

[86] Ibid., 70.

[87] Running and Freedman, *William Foxwell Albright: A Twentieth-Century Genius: A Biography of the Acknowledged Dean of Biblical Archaeologists*, 119.

[88] Albright, "The Archæological Results of an Expedition to Moab and the Dead Sea," 8.

Excavation Reports

Lapp, Paul W. "Bâb edh-Dhrâʿ." *Revue Biblique* 73 (1966): 556–61.

———. "The Cemetery at Bâb edh-Dhrâʿ, Jordan." *Archaeology* 19, no. 2 (1966): 104–111.

———. "Bâb edh-Dhrâʿ." *Revue Biblique* 75 (1968): 86–93, pls. 3–6a.

———. "Bâb edh-Dhrâʿ Tomb A 76 and Early Bronze I in Palestine." *Bulletin of the American Schools of Oriental Research* 189 (1968): 12–41.

———. "Bâb edh-Dhrâʿ, Perizzites and Emim." In *Jerusalem Through the Ages: The Twenty-Fifth Archaeological Convention*, 1–25. Jerusalem: Israel Exploration Society, 1968.

Rast, Walter E. "Bâb edh-Dhrâʿ and the Origin of the Sodom Saga." In *Archaeology and Biblical Interpretation: Essays in Memory of D. Glenn Rose*, edited by Leo G. Perdue, Lawrence E. Toombs, and Gary L. Johnson, 185–201. Atlanta, Ga.: John Knox, 1987.

———. "Bâb edh-Dhrâʿ." Edited by David Noel Freedman, Gary A. Herion, David F. Graf, and John David Pleins. *ABD*. New York, N.Y.: Doubleday, 1996.

———. "Sodom and Its Environs: Can Recent Archaeology Offer a Perspective?" *NEASB* 51 (2006): 19–26.

———. "The Southeastern Dead Sea Valley Expedition, 1979." *Biblical Archaeologist* 43, no. 1 (1980): 60–61.

———. "The Late Bronze Age and Early Iron Ages of Central Transjordan: The Baq'ah Valley Project, 1977–1981." *Bulletin of the American Schools of Oriental Research* no. 280 (1990): 93–94.

Rast, Walter E., and R. Thomas Schaub. "Survey of the Southeastern Plain of the Dead Sea." *Annual of the Department of Antiquities of Jordan* 19 (1973): 5–53.

———. "Expedition to the Southeastern Dead Sea Plain, Jordan, 1979." *American Schools of Oriental Research Newsletter* no. 8 (1980): 12–17.

———. *The Southeastern Dead Sea Plain Expedition: An Interim Report of the 1977 Season*. Annual of the American Schools of Oriental Research 46. Boston, Mass.: American Schools of Oriental Research, 1979.

———. "The Dead Sea Expedition: Bâb edh-Dhrâʿ and Numeira, May 24–July 10, 1981." *American Schools of Oriental Research Newsletter* no. 4 (1982): 4–12.

———. "Preliminary Report of the 1981 Expedition to the Dead Sea Plain, Jordan." *Bulletin of the American Schools of Oriental Research* no. 254 (1984): 35–60.

———, eds. *Bâb edh-Dhrâʿ: Excavations in the Cemetery Directed by Paul W. Lapp, 1965–1967*. Reports of the Expedition to the Dead Sea Plain, Jordan 1. Winona Lake, Ind.: Eisenbrauns, 1989.

———. eds. *Bâb edh-Dhrâʿ: Excavations at the Town Site (1975–1981): Part 1: Text*. Reports of the Expedition to the Dead Sea Plain, Jordan 2. Winona Lake, Ind.: Eisenbrauns, 2003.

Rast, Walter E., R. Thomas Schaub, David W. McCreery, Jack Donahue, and Mark A. McConaughy. "Preliminary Report of the 1979 Expedition to the Dead Sea Plain, Jordan." *Bulletin of the American Schools of Oriental Research* 240 (1980): 21–61.

Schaub, Marilyn M. "Lot and the Cities of the Plain: A Little about a Lot." In *Proceedings, Eastern Great Lakes Biblical Society, Vol 2, 1982*, 1–21. Grand Rapids, Mich.: Eastern Great Lakes Biblical Society, 1982.

FACT 6: RAST AND SCHAUB DID NOT BELIEVE THAT BeD WAS SODOM

Paul W. Lapp, Walter E. Rast, and R. Thomas Schaub, who all have excavated Bâb edh-Dhrâʿ, never affirmed that it was Sodom in the same historical sense as Wood claimed; with Rast, who excavated BeD, in fact believing that:

> Sodom was *a fictional place name* to begin with, that a city by this name *never existed*, and that the name came into being as an element in *a local story or tale* stressing a destruction severe enough to account for the startling physiography of the Dead Sea region.[emphasis added][1]

Rast states in his article, "Bâb edh-Dhrâʿ and the origin of the Sodom Saga" that:

> What was represented was often *not historical* but rather theological or social in its intent. On the other hand, it will be proposed below that *encapsulated in the formula of two cities* ["Bâb edh-Dhrâʿ and Numeira] experiencing memorable destruction was *a fragment of local recollection* of great importance for the history of the occupation of the Dead Sea region. . . . In sum, then, the parallel sets of texts and site-based remains which have been considered here are enough to suggest that *the Sodom tradition* may well be a *palimpsest*[2] through which is refracted a remnant of experience from the latter part of the Early Bronze Age.[3]

Schaub maintained that "The two related Early Bronze towns of Bâb edh-Dhrâʿ and Numeira may thus have *generated* the popular biblical tradition."[4]

FACT 7: COLLINS BELIEVES THAT TeH IS SODOM

The first connection Collins made with Tall el-Ḥammâm was following his 2002 trip to Jordan and his research using Khouri's map of fourteen sites in the Jordan Valley (See Chapter Two).[5] The first article published by Collins to connect TeH with Sodom was "Explorations on the Eastern Jordan Disk."[6] This was Collins' account of his research following his Jordan trip. He states:

> But a piece of Khouri's description of Tall el-Hammam really caught my eye: "the 1975/76 valley survey team gathered much Iron Age I and II pottery from Tall el-Hammam, along with smaller quantities of pottery from the Early Bronze Age, the Middle Bronze Age and the Roman/Byzantine periods."[7] Tall el-Hammam had at least some indication of Middle Bronze Age occupation.[8]

> What we know about the archaeology of the eastern *Kikkar*, particularly from excavations at Tall Nimrin and Tall el-Hammam, is well enough to put an end to both the Albrightian legend of the southern Dead Sea location (SST), and the Finkelsteinian legend about aetiological legends.[9]

Collins published many articles and two books on his belief that TeH is Sodom: *The Search for Sodom and Gomorrah* (2008) and co-published with Latayne C. Scott *Discovering the City of Sodom: The Fascinating, True Account of the Discovery of the Old Testament's Most Infamous City* (2013). In addition, numerous excavation

---

[1] Rast, "Bab Edh-Dhraʿ (ABD)," 1:561.

[2] "A parchment, tablet, etc. that has been written upon or inscribed two or three times, the previous text or texts having been imperfectly erased and remaining, therefore, still partly visible." Michael E. Agnes, *Webster's New World College Dictionary*, 4th ed. (Cleveland, Ohio: Webster's New World, 1999).

[3] Walter E. Rast, "Bab Edh-Dhraʿ and the Origin of the Sodom Saga," in *Archaeology and Biblical Interpretation: Essays in Memory of D. Glenn Rose*, ed. Leo G. Perdue, Lawrence E. Toombs, and Gary L. Johnson (Atlanta, Ga.: Knox, 1987), 185, 197.

[4] R. Thomas Schaub, "Bab Edh-Dhraʿ (NEAEHL)," in *NEAEHL*, ed. Ephraim Stern, Ayelet Levinson-Gilboa, and Joseph Aviram, vol. 1 (Jerusalem: The Israel Exploration Society, 1993), 130.

[5] Collins and Scott, *Discovering the City of Sodom*, 93–96.

[6] Collins, "Explorations," 1–28.

[7] Khouri, *Antiquities of the Jordan Rift Valley*, 75–76.

[8] Collins, "Explorations," 14–15.

[9] Collins, "If You Thought You Knew the Location of Sodom and Gomorrah," 6.

reports are now available for TeH (see *Excavation Reports*).

Excavation Reports

Collins, Steven, Hussein Aljarrah, Gary A. Byers, Carroll M. Kobs, John Leslie, Adeib abu-Shmais, Jehad Haroun, et al. "Tall Al-Hammam Season Six, 2011: Excavation, Survey, Interpretations and Insights." *Annual of the Department of Antiquities of Jordan* 55 (2011): 581–607.

Collins, Steven, and Hussein Aljarrah. "The Tall El-Hammam Excavation Project Season Activity Report: Season Six: 2011 Excavation, Exploration, & Survey." *Biblical Research Bulletin* 11, no. 1 (2011): 1–31.

Collins, Steven, Gary A. Byers, Carroll M. Kobs, David Graves, Phillip Silvia, Khalid Tarawneh, and Khaled al Hawaw. "Tall El-Hammam Season Ten, 2015: Excavation, Survey, Interpretations and Insights" *Biblical Research Bulletin* 15, no. 1 (2015): 1–37.

Collins, Steven, Gary A. Byers, and Michael C. Luddeni. "Tall el-Ḥammâm Excavation Project, Season Activity Report, Season One: 2005/2006 Probe Excavation and Survey: Submitted to the Department of Antiquities of the Hashemite Kingdom of Jordan, Jan 22, 2006." *Biblical Research Bulletin* 6, no. 4 (2006): 1–13.

Collins, Steven, Gary A. Byers, Carroll M. Kobs, and Phillip Sylvia "Tall El -Hammam Season Nine, 2014: Excavation, Survey, Interpretations and Insights" *Biblical Research Bulletin* 14, no. 1 (2014): 1–33.

Collins, Steven, Gary A. Byers, Michael C. Luddeni, and John W. Moore. "Tall el-Ḥammâm Excavation Project, Season Activity Report, Season Two: 2006/2007 Excavation and Survey: Submitted to the Department of Antiquities of the Hashemite Kingdom of Jordan, January 26, 2006." *Biblical Research Bulletin* 7, no. 9 (2007): 1–13.

Collins, Steven, Gary A. Byers, Michael C. Luddeni, John W. Moore, Abdelsamee' Abu Dayyeh, Adeib abu-Shmais, Khalil Hamdan, Hussein Aljarrah, Jehad Haroun, and Steve McAllister. "Tall el-Ḥammâm Excavation Project, Season Activity Report, Season Three: 2008 Excavation, Exploration, and Survey: Submitted to the Department of Antiquities of the Hashemite Kingdom of Jordan, February 13, 2008." *Biblical Research Bulletin* 8, no. 2 (2008): 1–13.

Collins, Steven, Khalid Tarawneh, Gary A. Byers, and Carroll M. Kobs. "Tall el-Ḥammâm Season Eight, 2013: Excavation, Survey, Interpretations and Insights." *Biblical Research Bulletin* (2013): 1–20.

Collins, Steven, Khalil Hamdan, and Gary A. Byers. "Tall el-Ḥammâm: Preliminary Report on Four Seasons of Excavation (2006–2009)." *Annual of the Department of Antiquities of Jordan* 53 (2009): 385–414.

Collins, Steven, Khalil Hamdan, Gary A. Byers, Jehad Haroun, Hussein Aljarrah. "The Tall El-Hammam Excavation Project Season Activity Report Season Five: 2010 Excavation, Exploration, And Survey." *Biblical Research Bulletin* 10, no. 1 (2010): 1–27.

Collins, Steven, Khalil Hamdan, Gary A. Byers, Jehad Haroun, Hussein Aljarrah, Michael C. Luddeni, Steve McAllister, Qutaiba Dasouqi, and David E. Graves. "Tall el-Ḥammâm Excavation Project, Season Activity Report, Season Four: 2009 Excavation, Exploration, and Survey: Submitted to the Department of Antiquities of the Hashemite Kingdom of Jordan, February 29, 2009." *Biblical Research Bulletin* 9, no. 1 (2009): 1–30.

Collins, Steven. "Tall el-Ḥammâm, Season Four: Data, Interpretations, and Insights From the 2009 Excavations." In *Annual Meeting of the American Schools of Oriental Research: New Orleans, LA*, 1–31. Albuquerque, N.M.: TSU Press, 2009.

Collins, Steven. "Tall el-Ḥammâm: A Key Witness to the Archaeology and History of the Southern Jordan Valley—Summary, Conclusions, and Recommendations from the 2006/2007 Excavation Season." In

> *Annual Meeting of the American Schools of Oriental Research: San Diego, CA*, 1–20. Albuquerque, N.M.: TSU Press, 2007.
>
> Schath, Kenneth, Steven Collins, and Hussein Aljarrah. "Excavation of an Undisturbed Demi-Dolmen and Insights from the Al-Hammam Megalithic Field, 2011 Season." *Annual of the Department of Antiquities of Jordan* 55 (2011): 329–50.

Fact 8: Publications Prior to 2006 do not include Collins' TeH Research

Stratification is very important in archaeology. The sequence of history works from the top down starting with the later periods and then going down to the earlier occupations. So, also with the chronology of research.

Occasionally criticism is made of Collins' work at TeH, using articles that were published prior to the TeH excavation in 2006 (Dec 26, 2005–Jan 8, 2006). Normally they start with a quote from a work prior to 2006 that states something like: "so and so believes that the best option for the location of Sodom is in the south." The statement is taken out of context, and they are stating this without the added benefit of the new research being done at TeH. While the northern location is not a new idea (see Fact 3), excavations were carried out starting in 2005 at TeH and connecting TeH with Sodom is also a current idea (with the exception of Geikie, Conder, and Thomson who located Sodom around TeH).[1]

Conversely, sometimes the opposite criticism of Collins' research is made, that there is not enough evidence for the destruction, citing references from the excavation reports from the first season. As of the writing of this book, there are thirteen seasons of dig reports (See excavation reports above), which can be consulted for the evidence of destruction and a complete picture of the excavation.

---

[1] Conder, *Heth and Moab*, 151, 153–55; Thomson, *Land and the Book: Lebanon, Damascus, and Beyond Jordan*, 3:669.

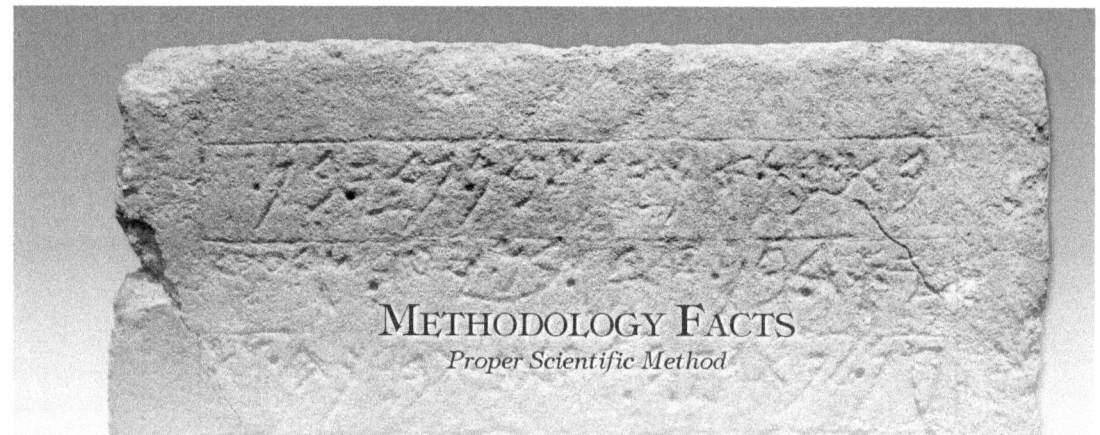

Methodology Facts
Proper Scientific Method

The methods employed by both Wood and Collins have been criticized. Doing good archaeology and following standard archaeological practice is essential for gathering and preserving reliable information, as archaeology is a destructive science.

16. Royal dedicatory inscription from the Philistine city of Ekron, discovered in 1996. This Philistine (Phonecian) script partially translates as: "The temple (which) he built, *'kyš* [Akhayus] son of Padi, son of *Ysd*, son of Ada, son of *Ya'ir*, ruler of Ekron, for *Ptgyh* his lady [Asherah?]" [Gitin, Dothan, and Naveh]. This is the only biblical city (Zeph 2:4) for which there is a primary inscription. Dan, Gezer, Gibeon, Hazor, Hebron, Shiloh, and Jerusalem only have a secondary inscription identifying their location. Rather than inscriptions, geographic indicators are more often used to locate biblical sites.

Israel Museum, Jerusalem (IAA 1997-2912) © Oren Rozen / Wikimedia Commons

Fact 9: The *A Priori* Method is Good Science

Sometimes Collins is criticized for his *a priori* approach and accused of reaching early conclusions in claiming that TeH was Sodom. Govier, interviewing archaeologist Eric Cline, stated that Collins:

> might be on to something but that he "has not yet produced any compelling archaeological evidence." Furthermore, Cline said, Collins's research was "putting the proverbial cart before the horse and excavating with an *a priori* bias." Cline said all Collins had so far was a hypothesis.[1]

The *Webster's New World College Dictionary* defined *a priori* as a theory which is determined "before examination or analysis."[2] However, the *a priori* approach is a standard method used by archaeologists for all locations. All good archaeologists begin with a working hypothesis and then excavate to test their hypothesis against the data collected. For example, James K. Hoffmeier, the Egyptologist and professor of Old Testament and Ancient Near Eastern History at Trinity Evangelical Divinity School, uses this same method for his research on Migdol. He argues: "We believe that Gardiner's proposed association of Migdol of Egyptian texts with Migdol of the Exodus narratives is a reasonable one, and thus accept it as our working hypothesis."[3]

Davis lists this principle as number four in his article on archaeological methods. He proposes:

> 4. *An excavation is a dialogue, not a monologue.* One of the basic aspects of an archaeological endeavor is a research design [hypothesis]. No excavation will enter the field without one. We all agree that data speak only in response to a question and that the question we seek to answer shapes our field methods. . . . An archaeologist must approach a site

---

[1] Govier, "Looking Back: Claims to New Sodom Location Are Salted with Controversy," 15–16.

[2] Agnes, *Webster's New World College Dictionary*, op. cit.

[3] James K. Hoffmeier, "The North Sinai Archaeological Project's Excavations at Tell El-Borg (Sinai): An Example of the 'New' Biblical Archaeology?," in *The Future of Biblical Archaeology: Reassessing Methodologies and Assumptions*, ed. James K. Hoffmeier and Alan R. Millard (Grand Rapids, Mich.: Eerdmans, 2004), 61.

with a question but should not seek a specific answer. The danger comes when we try to dictate what the answer should be. We need to remain flexible and respond to the site formation processes and to the material recovered from the site.[4]

The TeHEP not only proposes the hypothesis of TeH being Sodom in the EB and MB Age but also uses industry standard practices and procedures. The *Field Manual* [5] provided to all staff and used to govern the gathering of all data is an adaptation of the Madaba Plains Project.[6] In fact, Collins is using a triple blind pottery reading procedure; something which is unique in the Middle East. Three independent sets of experts from America and Jordan read the same pottery in three separate readings.

Collins describes the process as:

> We use a triple-blind system of analyzing all of our pottery at Tall el-Hammam—the only excavation to use this rigorous approach as far as I know. The first read is done by me and my senior staff (the field read each afternoon during the dig season). The second one is done by Jordan's top ceramicists without reference or knowledge of the first read. The third read is performed by yet another set of expert eyes State-side, without reference or knowledge of reads one or two.[7]

This pain staking process has analyzed "pottery sherds representing all or part of more than forty thousand separate vessels"[8] based on reading their rims, handles and bases. In some cases, there have been wonderful examples of decorative body sherds.

Collins' hypothesis is that the ruins of Tall el-Ḥammâm in the EB and MB Age are biblical Sodom. The question which demands answering is: what will the evidence from the ground reveal?

FACT 10: THE SERIAL GEOGRAPHY OF THE BIBLE IS RELIABLE

Sometimes I hear similar sentiments to those posted below in a *Christianity Today* article by someone going by the name of Pilgrim Progress, who criticized biblical archaeology, stating:

> Remember, please, that the Sodom Story, like the Noah's Ark Story, is a [*sic* an] ancient, plagiarized, purloined, Cultural Myth from dozens of prior cultures and religious traditions. There are NO original scenarios, doctrines or story lines in our Bible. None. All are simply Morality Plays, passed down from religion to religion. . . . Remember, first and foremost, that these are highly edited, plagiarized, Cultural Myths. Like Cinderella, The Three Bears, and Paul Bunyan, these are Morality Plays. Don't look for "facts" where there are only Traditions.[9]

But as William Dever has pointed out

> A generation ago, even a decade ago, Classicists and ancient historians would have dismissed Homer as a mythical figure and would have argued that the tales of the Trojan Wars were mainly "invented" by much later Greek writers.[10]

But Yamauchi has marshaled compelling evidence that demonstrates that although Homer's *Iliad* and *Odyssey* are literary creations, they "nonetheless preserve accurate historical memories."[11]

---

[4] Thomas W. Davis, "Theory and Method in Biblical Archaeology," in *The Future of Biblical Archaeology: Reassessing Methodologies and Assumptions*, ed. James K. Hoffmeier and Alan R. Millard (Grand Rapids, Mich.: Eerdmans, 2008), 27.

[5] Steven Collins, Carroll Kobs, and Phillip J. Silvia, *Tall El-Hammam Excavation Project Field Manual* (Albuquerque, N.M.: TSU Press, 2013).

[6] http://www.madabaplains.org/

[7] Collins, "Tall El-Hammam Is Sodom," 6; Collins and Scott, *Discovering the City of Sodom*, 128.

[8] Collins and Scott, *Discovering the City of Sodom*, 33.

[9] http://www.christianitytoday.com/ct/2014/february-web-only/searching-for-sodom.html.

[10] Dever, *What Did the Biblical Writers Know, and When Did They Know It?*, 279.

[11] Edwin M. Yamauchi, "Historic Homer: Did It Happen?," *BAR* 33, no. 2 (2007): 37; "Homer and Archaeology: Minimalists and Maximalists in Classical Context," 69–90; John K. Davies, "The Reliability of the Oral Tradition," in *The Trojan War: Its Historicity and Context*, ed. Lin Foxhall and John Kenyon Davies,

As Yamauchi concluded: "This raises an intriguing possibility: If the Hellenic world could have kept alive accurate historical details in an oral tradition lasting many centuries, couldn't the Biblical world have done so too?"[12]

As Dever concludes: "If Homer can in a sense be 'historical,' why not the Hebrew Bible?"[13]

Since Homer has been shown to be a historical figure, how much more should the Bible be given consideration as a historically accurate document? If Heinrich Schliemann could use the *Iliad* and *Odyssey*, which was considered a myth, to locate Troy, why can we not use the Bible, even if it is considered a myth by some, to locate cities mentioned in this ancient text? What is clear is that the serial geography used by these ancient writers was accurate.

FACT 11: FEW BIBLICAL SITES HAVE EVER BEEN IDENTIFIED USING AN INSCRIPTION

Occasionally critics state: "there is no inscriptional evidence to support the case"[14] for TeH being Sodom. However, only Ekron mentioned in Zephaniah 2:4, has a primary (i.e., in situ, in-period) inscription that mentions the name of the biblical city.[15] Of all the biblical cities on our Bible maps only Dan, Gezer, Gibeon, Hazor, Hebron, Shiloh, and Jerusalem have a secondary inscription identifying their location.[16] The *Biblical Archaeology Review* notes that the city of

> Gezer was the first biblical city to be identified by an [secondary] inscription found at the site. . . . In 1873, the great French scholar Clermont-Ganneau found a boundary inscription dating from the Herodian period which reads in Hebrew script, "boundary of Gezer."[17]

Collins further identify what he means by a primary inscription:

> For Old Testament sites, a primary inscription is one found *in situ* in a sealed archaeological context [locus], specifically providing the name of the site in question. Further, the inscription must date from the Old Testament period, i.e., either the Bronze Age or Iron Age. It must also be unquestionable as to translation.[18]

Not even Jerusalem has a primary inscription, and yet we obviously do not dispute its location. The accepted method used by scholars to identify the location of biblical cities are geographic indicators (i.e., by the Jordan River, below Mt. Nebo, near Jerusalem, etc.).[19] Collins is quoted stating:

> Well, to start with, the Tall el-Hammam site has 25 geographical indicators that align it with the description in Genesis. Compare this with something well known—like Jerusalem—that has only 16. Other sites have only 5 or 6. So, this site has many times more indicators than any other Old Testament site.[20]

Papers of the First Greenbank Colloquium, Liverpool, 1981 (Bristol: Bristol Classical, 1984), 101.

[12] Yamauchi, "Historic Homer: Did It Happen?," 29.

[13] Dever, *What Did the Biblical Writers Know, and When Did They Know It?*, 279.

[14] D. Gnanaraj, "Fire from Heaven? Archeological Light on the Destruction of Sodom and Gomorrah (Genesis 19:23-28)," *New Life Review* 1 (2012): 9.

[15] Ibid., 142.

[16] Collins and Scott, *Discovering the City of Sodom*, 273–96.

[17] Hershel Shanks, "The Sad Case of Tell Gezer," *BAR* 9, no. 4 (1983): 30–42.

[18] Ibid., 277.

[19] Anson F. Rainey, "Historical Geography," in *Benchmarks in Time and Culture: An Introduction to Palestinian Archaeology*, ed. Joel F Drinkard, Gerald L Mattingly, and J. Maxwell Callaway, Joseph A Miller, ASOR/SBL Archaeology And Biblical Studies (Atlanta, Ga.: Scholars Press, 1988), 353–68.

[20] Brian Nixon, "Sodom Found? The Quest For The Lost City Of Destruction -- Part 3," *ASSIST News Service*, June 16, 2009, http://www.assistnews.net/Stories/2009/s09060102.htm; Collins and Scott, *Discovering the City of Sodom*, 278–96.

Collins further describes his methodology:

> One chronological criterion is always included based on a face-value assessment of the biblical chronology. One criterion is assigned for each general archaeological period during which a city/town is said to have been occupied according to the biblical text. For example, if a site is included in the Joshua narrative (Late Bronze Age), one geo-criterion is assigned. If the same site is mentioned during the reign of Solomon (Iron 2), another geo-criterion is assigned. Further, if it is specifically stated or implied that a site was unoccupied during a given archaeological period, another geo-criterion is assigned.[21]

Thus, proper use of geographical indicators rather than waiting for an inscription to appear is the common approach for identifying biblical sites. The odds of an inscription appearing which will absolutely identify a site are like winning the lottery. The method relied on by all scholars is to use the geography of ancient texts to locate the site, unless they are fortunate enough to locate an inscription. For example, Heinrich Schliemann used the text of Homer's *Illiad* to locate ancient Troy.[22] Surely we can use the text of the Bible with its geographical markers to locate biblical sites such as Sodom.

Fact 12: Wood Has Never Excavated BeD

The excavations at Bâb edh-Dhrâ' were conducted in 1965 and 1967 by the late Paul W. Lapp, sponsored by the American Schools of Oriental Research. Then, following Lapp's death, Walter E. Rast and R. Thomas Schaub continued his work with four excavations in 1978, 1980, 1981, and 1983.[23] Bryant G. Wood has visited BeD on several occasions but has never excavated the site, basing his conclusions on a careful analysis of the excavation reports produced by Lapp, Rast, and Schaub, along with his surface surveys of the site. While this is a common method for "armchair" archaeologists, Wood is no armchair archaeologist. As his biography states, his:

> extensive archaeological field work includes serving as co-director of a survey of three reservoir areas in northern Jordan, 1978; area supervisor for the Wadi Tumilat Project excavation at Tell el-Maskhuta, Egypt, 1979, 1981, and 1983; volunteer at the Ben Gurion University of the Negev excavation at Haruvit in the northern Sinai, 1981; member of the Wadi Tumilat Project survey of the Wadi Tumilat, Egypt, 1983; field archaeologist for the Associates for Biblical Research excavation at Khirbet Nisya, Israel, 1985, 1987, 1990, 1991, 1993 and 1994; and Director of the Kh. el-Maqatir excavation, Israel, 1995–present.[24]

Wood has dug with Collins, for several seasons, at Khirbet el-Maqatir in Israel, which ironically is one of the proposed locations for the biblical city of Ai (see *Fact 22)*. Both scholars are very aware of the geographic location of Bethel and Ai and what can and cannot be seen from that location.

Fact 13: The early read of the TeH stratigraphy was due to modern military activity

Sometimes it is claimed that calling Tall el-Hammam Sodom so early was premature and that it was called only after a few seasons of excavation, and Collins made certain hasty assumptions about the periods of inhabitation. They claim that he read too much into the evidence. Gnanaraj claims:

> As for today [2012], this theory remains a minority opinion, vocally defended by Collins himself. In other words, the expedition is in its early stages to yield any conclusive evidence on the identification of the Cities of the Plain, including Sodom and Gomorrah.[25]

---

[21] Collins and Scott, *Discovering the City of Sodom*, 296.

[22] Susan Heuck Allen, *Finding the Walls of Troy: Frank Calvert and Heinrich Schliemann at Hisarlik* (Berkeley, Calf.: University of California Press, 1999), 1.

[23] Schaub, "Bab Edh-Dhra' (NEAEHL)," 130–31.

[24] Wood, "Bryant G. Wood, PhD. Biography," 2.
[25] Gnanaraj, "Fire from Heaven," 9.

17. The author, standing in front of a cut-away section of the city wall at Tall el-Ḥammâm, in season 1 (2006). The military cut a road through the wall and exposed this cross section, which was later clarified. At my feet is the location of a 0.5 m thick MB burn layer in the mud brick section of the city wall, dated by a MB handle (inset photo) at the same location (see Fig. 40, 41). The IA stone wall was built over the earlier burned MB mud brick wall.

However, what is often not known, is that the Ottoman and Jordanian military cut trenches into the inside of the upper tall to provide gun emplacements for military purposes.[26] This created an instant picture of the stratigraphy of the site and acted like an x-ray for the team to read the various layers of inhabitation. Collins states in 2002: "but they [military] had unwittingly opened up to us (and possibly the 1975/76 sherders, depending on when the trench was dug) much more than would normally have been exposed on the surface."[27]

It became instantly evident that there was not only no Late Bronze age occupation but also a massive destruction in the Middle

---

[26] Collins and Scott, *Discovering the City of Sodom*, 97.

[27] Collins, "Explorations," 20–21.

Bronze age period and later IA occupation. This was the main reason for the unusually early reading of the tall. The early conclusions were based on the archaeological evidence from reading the exposed balk and not on mere speculation of a surface survey.

In Season One (December 2005–January 2006) the author personally clarified the NE city wall along the military road to expose the MB Age level, with about .5 m (1.6 ft) of burn layer. This MB level was verified with diagnostic pottery, a MB handle (see Figs. 17, 40, and 41).

FACT 14: A SURFACE SURVEY IS DIFFERENT TO AN EXCAVATION

This may seem obvious, but an archaeological surface survey consists of walking across a Tell and identifying the various pottery sherds. This can give archaeologists an idea of what lies beneath the surface but is quite different from the archaeological excavation itself.

For example: *The East Jordan Valley Survey* conducted in 1995–1996 reported that there were few EB–MB sherds at Tall el-Ḥammâm (site 190).[28] They did however identify Iron I–III sherds.

However, the excavation reports from 2005–2014 clearly show that there are many EB and MB sherds and also architectural walls and structures.[29] Out of the 1,951 diagnostic pottery sherds read up to the fourth season in 2009, 8% were EB, 38% were MB, and 32% were IA II.[30]

The Iron Age ruins were lying on the surface of the upper Tell and visible to those conducting the surface survey, while the EB and MB structures and sherds were buried underground.

This distinction becomes very important when attempting to identify a LBA presence in the Jordan Valley (see *Fact 45*). One must not rely on a surface survey as the definitive word on the presence or absence of an archaeological period. LB pottery lying on the ground does not mean that there are archaeological structures below; while the absence of EB/MB sherds does not mean that there are no EB/MB structures lying under the ground.

Surface surveys are an important guide for initial identification but are always trumped by excavations with excavation reports.

---

[28] Khair Yassine, Moawiyah M. Ibrahim, and James A. Sauer, "The East Jordan Valley Survey 1975 (Part Two)," in *The Archaeology of Jordan: Essays and Reports*, ed. Khair Yassine (Amman: Department of Archaeology, University of Jordan, 1988), 192.

[29] Steven Collins et al., "Tall El-Hammam Season Eight, 2013: Excavation, Survey, Interpretations and Insights," *BRB* 13, no. 2 (2013): 13–14.

[30] Collins, Hamdan, and Byers, "Tall El-Hammam: Preliminary Report, Season Four, 2009," 406; Collins, Kobs, and Luddeni, *Introduction to Tall Al-Hammam with Seven Seasons of Ceramics*, 41–229.

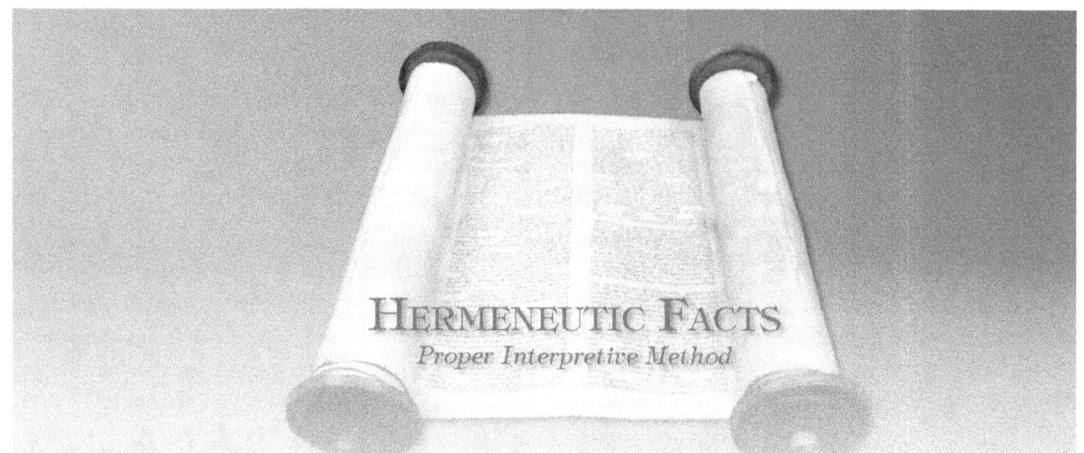

Hermeneutic Facts
Proper Interpretive Method

Archaeological methods are important; but equally so is the correct application of the methods we use to handle and interpret the text. Failure in this area can seriously affect the meaning of the text. This chapter will deal with several hermeneutic facts which deal with common misconceptions.

Fact 15: The key passage on Sodom's geography is Gen 13:1–12

While several passages in the Bible mention geographic indicators for the location of Sodom (Gen 13:10; 14:3; 19:28), there is debate as to which is more helpful. Wood claims that "the reference to 'bitumen pits' [see *Fact 57*] in Genesis 14:10, however, tips the scale in favor of a southern location."[1] However as Fact 16 points out, the bitumen pits (Gen 14:10) are referring to the battle of the Mesopotamian kings not the location of the Cities of the Plain. The context is very important. Poetic and prophetic passages are often also referenced for Sodom's location, but these must not be treated as narrative texts.[2]

Thus, Collins asserts, on good grounds, in his reply to Wood's criticism, that: "the

18. Torah displayed in the former Glockengasse Synagogue in Cologne.
Photo by Willy Horsch/ Wikimedia Commons

only *definitive* biblical text on the geography of the Cities of the Plain: [is] Genesis 13:1–12."[3] And again he reiterates his point: "Hermeneutically speaking, there is only one section of biblical text written specifically for the purpose of providing, by authorial intent, geographical directions to Sodom and the Cities of the Plain: Genesis 13:1–12."[4]

Wood does challenge Collins' use of Genesis 13, by quoting from Rast, who excavated BeD.[5] Rast states:

> One can safely say that the directions and locations in Genesis 13 are the most general and obscure of all the texts about Sodom. It is surprising that some scholars could put so much weight on the indistinct locations given there [for a northern location], while rejecting the more compelling references in other texts [for a southern location].[6]

However, as Collins points out, Rast does not believe in the historical reliability of the Genesis text,[7] and never exegeted the passage.[8]

---

[1] Wood, "Discovery of the Sin Cities," 67; Wood, "Locating Sodom: A Critique of the Northern Proposal," 78–79.

[2] See *Fact 17: Jeremiah 50:35-46 is prophetic literature*; Fact 18: *Ezekiel is poetry and not narrative*.

[3] Collins, "A Response to Bryant G. Wood," 5.

[4] Ibid., 7.

[5] Wood, "Locating Sodom: A Critique of the Northern Proposal," 81–82.

[6] Walter E. Rast, "Sodom and Its Environs: Can Recent Archaeology Offer a Perspective?," *NEASB* 51 (2006): 21.

[7] See *Fact 6: Rast and Schaub did not believe that Bâb edh-Dhrâ' was Sodom*.

[8] Collins, "A Response to Bryant G. Wood," 5–6.

Collins, whose "first doctorate was in the field of biblical hermeneutics" and who "still teach[es] biblical hermeneutics and exegesis at the graduate and doctoral levels,"[9] explains:

> When one speaks of a "definitive" biblical passage regarding an issue, the focus is on any given passage specifically written (or spoken) with the authorial intent to communicate information on said issue.[10] Additionally, secondary (non-definitive) passages must be interpreted in the light of a definitive passage, never the reverse. On the subject of biblical geography, a definitive passage is one that is specifically written to answer a question like "Where did so-and-so go, and by what route did he get there?" These kinds of passages occur when the travels/movements of a person or a group of people are being described, such as the routes the Israelites traveled from Egypt at the time of the Exodus. In these expressly geographical passages, it is often stated that a person/group went "here to there," then "there to there," and then "there to there." These statements are usually geographically sequential and chronologically serial.[11]

Collins points out that Wood ignored exegeting this passage in his attempt to locate Sodom south of the Dead Sea.[12] For Collins' exegesis of Genesis 13:1–12 and other passages, see his article on the "Geography of the Cities of the Plain."[13]

FACT 16: GENESIS 14:10 IS REFERRING TO THE LOCATION FOR THE BATTLE OF THE MESOPOTAMIAN KINGS, NOT THE LOCATION OF THE CITIES OF THE PLAIN

Gen 14:10 mentions bitumen/tar (literally slime or clay; see *Fact 57)* pits (i.e., sink holes; see Maps 4 and 7) near the Cities of the Plain. Mulder and Wenham believe that the bitumen pits located in the "Valley of Siddim"[14] point to the southern area of the Dead Sea. Mulder states: that "the 'bitumen pits' in 'the valley of Siddim' (Gen 14:10) have been localized in the shallow S part of the Dead Sea."[15] Wenham states: "The reference to bitumen pits (v 10) makes the area just to the south of the sea the most likely area."[16] But while there are a few sink holes (bitumen pits) in the Lisan near the southern end of the Dead Sea, the majority of them are along the western shore (See Maps 4 and 7). However, the real question that needs to be asked is: were the Cities of the Plain located near the bitumen pits?

A careful examination of Genesis 14:10 reveal that the battle, between the Elamite king (Chedorlaomer or Kedorlaomer, king of Elam) and the kings of the Cities of the Plain, took place in a different location from where they lived. The passage states that the kings of the Cities of the Plain "joined forces in the Valley of Siddim (that is, the Salt Sea)" (Gen 14:3 ESV) and that "the *Valley of Siddim* was *full of bitumen* (Heb. *ḥēmār;* see *Fact 57)*[17] *pits,*

---

[9] Ibid., 6n.20.
[10] See any good textbook on hermeneutics such as: A. Berkeley Mickelsen, *Interpreting the Bible* (Grand Rapids, Mich.: Eerdmans, 1963); Bernard Ramm, *Protestant Biblical Interpretation: A Textbook of Hermeneutics,* 3rd ed. (Grand Rapids, Mich.: Baker Academic & Brazos, 1980).
[11] Collins, "A Response to Bryant G. Wood," 6–7.
[12] Ibid., 5.
[13] Collins, "Geography of the Cities of the Plain," 1–17.

[14] Astour argues that the term Siddim (Akkadian *ikû;* Ugaritic *šiddu*) has Babylonian roots and the story is borrowed from the Babylonian story of the flood. He points out:"The author of Genesis 14, using the West Semitic equivalent of *ikû,* transferred the astral name of Babylon to the region of Sodom and Gomorrah, just as he did with the invasions of the four kings in the same 'Chedorlaomer texts.'" Michael C. Astour, "Siddim, Valley of (Place)," ed. David Noel Freedman et al., *ABD* (New York, N.Y.: Doubleday, 1996), 16; Michael C. Astour, "Political and Cosmic Symbolism in Genesis 14 and in Its Babylonian Sources," in *Biblical Motifs: Origins and Transformations,* ed. Alexander Altmann, Philip W. Lown Institute of Advanced Judaic Studies, Brandeis University, Studies and Texts 3 (Cambridge, Mass.: Harvard University Press, 1966), 65–112.
[15] Mulder, "Sodom and Gomorrah," 101.
[16] Wenham, *Genesis 1-15,* 1:310.
[17] BDB states that bitumen was "used for cement in building Babel (Gen 11:3)". . . and "used in coating

The Location of Sodom

and as the kings of Sodom and Gomorrah fled, some fell into them, and the rest fled to the hill country" (Gen 14:10).

Notice that this does not say that this was the location of the Cities of the Plain, but only that this is where the battle took place. The text states that, from their cities, the kings "marched out (Heb. *yatsa* Gen 14:8) to the valley of Siddim" and "went out, came out" (Heb. *yatsa* Gen 14:17) to meet him in the Valley of Siddim,[18] which has been identified as the Salt Sea (Gen 14:3).[19] This indicates that where they now were doing battle was a different place from where they lived. Collins rightfully points out that "battles were typically fought at a distance from home cities. So we wouldn't expect these particular 'pits' to be close to Sodom."[20] They did not fight in their front yard but came together in this location to fight Chedorlaomer.

Howard made this same argument in 1984: "that the kings (or at least some of them) did not live in the place where they joined forces and prepared for war but rather that this was a rendezvous point and that they lived nearby."[21]

Also, as there were bitumen pits (sink holes) in the area, one could ask, would ancient people build their cities in such a dangerous location? One would assume that they would have built their homes some distance from these dangerous pits.

All we can logically derive from the text is that the location of the battle was close to the area of the cities, but that this is all relative. "Close" could just as easily mean the northern Jordan Valley, as it could mean the southern Lisan.

The fact remains that the battle between the kings of Elam and the Cities of the Plain took place in a different vicinity from where the people of Sodom lived.

Fact 17: Zeboiim is plural in Hebrew

In Hebrew Zeboiim is given in the plural form as "*iim*," possibly indicating that there were twin sites.[22] It is likely derived from the Hebrew word *Tzebi* (*Tabitha*) meaning "gazelle."[23]

Birch, in dealing with the location of Zeboiim, states that it is connected with Tall esh Sha'ib. Birch bases this on the fact that Z becomes Sh in the name. Merrill states that "an older name for Tell Kefrein is Tall es Sharab ("Tall of drinking", or the place where good water is abundant)."[24] Initially in 1974 Wood proposed that "our suggested identification of the five EB sites then is: Khanazir = Sodom, Feifa = Gomorrah, eṣ-

---

Moses' 'ark' of bulrushes (Exod 2:3)." Francis Brown, Samuel R. Driver, and Charles A. Briggs, eds., *A Hebrew and English Lexicon of the Old Testament with an Appendix Containing the Biblical Aramaic. Based on the Lexicon of William Gessenius as Translated by Edward Robinson* (Boston, Mass.: Houghton Milfflin, 1907), 330.

[18] For a detailed analysis of the identification of the Valley of Siddim see: Collins, "The Geography of Sodom and Zoar," 5–6.

[19] The Valley of Siddim is likely identified with the Salt Sea due to the falling sea levels which were lower during the Bronze Age exposing the sinkholes.

[20] Collins and Scott, *Discovering the City of Sodom*, 150.

[21] Howard, Jr., "Sodom and Gomorrah Revisited," 389.

[22] Collins, "Geography of the Cities of the Plain," 2.

[23] William F. Birch, "Zeboim," *PEFSt.* 11, no. 1 (1879): 101; J. I. Packer, Merrill C. Tenney, and William White, eds., *Illustrated Manners and Customs of the Bible* (Nashville, Tenn.: Nelson, 1997), 745; Lidwig Koehler et al., eds., *The Hebrew and Aramaic Lexicon of the Old Testament*, trans. M. E. J. Richardson, 3rd ed. (Leiden: Brill, 1994), 791; William L. Holladay, *A Concise Hebrew and Aramaic Lexicon of the Old Testament,* Based upon the Lexical Work of Ludwig Koehler and Walter Baumgartner (Leiden: Brill, 2000), 302; Willem A. VanGemeren, ed., *New International Dictionary of Old Testament Theology and Exegesis* (Grand Rapids, Mich.: Zondervan, 1997), 3: 739–740.

[24] Birch, "Zeboim," 102.

Ṣafi = Zoar, Numeira = Admah, and Bâb edh-Dhrâʿ = Zeboiim."[25] In his later article Wood acknowledges that the evidence at Khanazir and Feifa (excavated between 16 December 1989 and 13 January 1990) revealed no identifiable settlements, with only cemeteries evident. Wood states "At Khanazir, walls observed by Rast and Schaub[26] in 1973 were in reality rectangular structures marking Early Bronze IV shaft tombs.[27]"[28] Wood changed his opinion on Khanazir to connect it with either Zeboiim or Admah, and identified Bâb edh-Dhrâʿ and Numeira as Sodom and Gomorrah (See Map 1 and 3).

By contrast Collins identified two small sites in the north end of the Dead Sea, Tall Bleibel and Tall el-Muṣṭāḥ (see Map 2), as possible members of the Cities of the Plain that were only separated by a small stream (Wadi Nimrin). Glueck stated that "The three sites of Tell el-Mustah, Tell Bleibil, Tell Nimrin, in that order of historical occupancy, can for all practical purposes be considered as one historical site."[29]

Collins commented that:

A cursory reading of the sherds at both sites confirmed what I already knew from previous sherding and survey activity. However, there was more surface pottery evidence of a Bronze Age presence at Tall Mustah and Tall Bleibel than pre-excavation analysis had revealed for Tall Nimrin and Tall Nimrin turned out to contain the ruins of a major MB fortified city.[30]

For Collins, the sites of Tall el-Muṣṭāḥ and Tall Bleibel fit the description of the plural Zeboiim. What is clear is that the biblical Zeboiim has not been archaeologically identified with certainty.

Fact 18: Hebrew does not have the words North, South, East or West

Similar to other Semitic languages, Hebrew does not use the words north, south, east or west to speak of direction. Direction is oriented against the rising of the sun (Gen 13:9; 14:15; Josh 17:7), so east is the Hebrew term "forward" (Heb. *qēdem*), and west is "behind" (Heb. *yām*). Thus, south is indicated "on the right hand" (Heb. *yāmǎn*) while north is indicated "on the left hand" (Heb. *śemāʾlî*).[31]

However, this is not always the case as is evident from Genesis 13:9. Abraham tells Lot "If you take the left hand, then I will go to the right, or if you take the right hand, then I will go to the left" (Gen 13:9 ESV). Lot takes the left hand and goes eastward to Sodom while Abraham takes the right hand but does not go westward towards the Philistine Plain or northward towards Samaria, but goes southward towards Hebron.

---

[25] Wood, "Have Sodom And Gomorrah Been Found?," 84.

[26] Rast and Schaub, "Survey of the Southeastern Plain of the Dead Sea, 1973," 12–14.

[27] Bert de Vries, ed., "Archaeology in Jordan, 1991," *AJA* 95, no. 2 (1991): 262; Rast, "Bab Edh-Dhraʿ (ABD)," 560; MacDonald, "Southern Ghors and Northeast ʾArabah (OEANE)," 65; Schaub, "Southeast Dead Sea Plain," 62.

[28] Wood, "Discovery of the Sin Cities," 69.

[29] Glueck, *Explorations in Eastern Palestine*, 371.

[30] Steven Collins, *The Search for Sodom and Gomorrah*, Research & Discovery Series 2 (Albuquerque, N.M.: TSU Press, 2008), 74.

[31] Harris, Archer, Jr., and Waltke, *Theological Wordbook of the Old Testament*, 2: op. cit. no. 2267b, 872; James Swanson, *A Dictionary of Biblical Languages with Semantic Domains: Hebrew Old Testament*, Electronic Edition (Oak Harbor: Logos Research Systems, 1997), op cit. nos. 8520, 3554; Leland Ryken et al., eds., *Dictionary of Biblical Imagery* (Downers Grove, Ill.: InterVarsity, 1998), 500, 727; Louis Isaac Rabinowitz and Stephen G. Wald, "Right and Left," *Jewish Virtual Library*, accessed March 14, 2014, http://www.jewishvirtuallibrary .org/jsource/judaica/ejud_0002_0017_0_16755.html.

Sometimes left and right directions are used in a relative sense,[32] especially in a prophetic text such as Ezekiel 16:46. Ezekiel identifies Samaria and her daughters on the left hand, and Sodom and her daughters on the right hand of their sister, Jerusalem. Some have assumed that Sodom must therefore be to the south of Jerusalem at the southern end of the Dead Sea.

However, as Power points out: "The fallacy in this argument is that it fails to distinguish between the absolute and the relative use of the expressions "on the right hand" and "on the left hand.". . . . we must remember that the cities are here personified."[33] Collins suggests: "He [Ezekiel] may simply be communicating that wicked Jerusalem was accompanied (metaphorically!) by her "sisters" in crime: Samaria at her left hand, and Sodom at her right hand."[34]

FACT 19: EZEKIEL IS NOT BIBLICAL NARRATIVE

In dealing with biblical literature one must pay special attention to the genre of the text. One does not approach allegorical, metaphorical, symbolical, prophetic or poetic passages the same way one approaches historical narrative.[35] The commentary on the *Chicago Statement on Biblical Inerrancy* (1978) states:

> Article XVIII: Interpretation: The second principle of the affirmation is that we are to take account of the literary forms and devices that are found within the Scriptures themselves. . . . A verb is to be interpreted as a verb; a noun as a noun, a parable as a parable, didactic literature as didactic literature, narrative history as narrative history, poetry as poetry, and the like. To turn narrative history into poetry, or poetry into narrative history would be to violate the intended meaning of the text. . . . .[36] In inspiration, God utilized the culture and conventions of the penman's milieu, a milieu that God controls in His sovereign providence; it is misinterpretation to imagine otherwise. . . . So history must be treated as history, poetry as poetry, hyperbole and metaphor as hyperbole and metaphor, generalization and approximation as what they are, and so forth.[37]

The *Chicago Statement on Biblical Hermeneutics* (1982) affirms:

> Article XIII: WE AFFIRM that awareness of the literary categories, formal and stylistic, of the various parts of Scripture is essential for proper exegesis, and hence we value genre criticism as one of the many disciplines of biblical study. [Commentary]: The awareness of what kind of literature one is interpreting is essential to a correct understanding of the text. A correct genre judgment should be made to ensure correct understanding. A parable, for example, should not be treated like a chronicle, nor should poetry be interpreted as though it were a straightforward narrative. Each passage has its own genre, and the interpreter should be cognizant of the specific kind of literature it is as he attempts to interpret it. Without genre recognition an interpreter can be misled in his understanding of the passage.[38]

Some have looked to Ezekiel for an indication of the location of Sodom and have treated the text as a narrative, while others treat the geography of the Mosaic writings as suspect because of the dating.

Schaub, one of the principal excavators of BeD, commented to Collins in personal correspondence:

---

[32] Power, "The Site of the Pentapolis: Part 1," 48–49.

[33] Ibid., 48.

[34] Collins, "A Response to Bryant G. Wood," 9.

[35] For a good summary of the principles for interpreting different kinds of literature see the standard works of Mickelsen and Ramm. Mickelsen, *Interpreting the Bible*, 323–37; Ramm, *Protestant Biblical Interpretation*.

[36] R. C. Sproul, *Explaining Inerrancy: A Commentary* (Oakland, CA: International Council on Biblical Inerrancy, 1980), 25; R. C. Sproul and Norman L. Geisler, *Explaining Biblical Inerrancy: Official Commentary on the ICBI Statements*, ed. Christopher T. Haun and Norman L. Geisler (Matthew, N.C.: Bastion, 2013), 59.

[37] Sproul, *Explaining Inerrancy*, 34.

[38] Norman L. Geisler, *Explaining Hermeneutics: A Commentary on the Chicago Statement on Biblical Hermeneutics*, ICBI Foundation Series (Oakland, Calf.: International Council on Biblical Inerrancy, 1983), Article 13; Sproul and Geisler, *Explaining Biblical Inerrancy*, 74.

I am wary of using the "geographical" references in stories about Moses and Lot—given the nature of the stories and the difficulty in dating them. It seems to me the best approach is to use the references in the Prophets which are more reliable for dating. Here we seem to have two separate traditions, one about Admah and Zeboiim for the northern prophets and another about Sodom and Gomorrah for the southern prophets. Perhaps there were two traditions about destroyed cities? Another approach would be to seek the locale which was involved in the passing on of the traditions. I have always thought Hebron could be a likely place for the southern traditions. All very difficult to prove.[39]

Collins replied:

Why would the "Yahwist's" geography necessarily be suspect, regardless of the time of writing? Finkelstein and Na'aman admit that the geographies of Hexateuchal stories probably accommodate real, known geography from the writers' experiences. Isn't it reasonable that the stories of Abram and Lot are "wrapped around" a real-world geography? Linguistically, geographical referents form powerful mental frameworks, and are some of the most tenacious elements of historical narrative and myth.[40]

In the course of Ezekiel's chastening of Jerusalem for her wickedness, he says to them:

Quotes from Antiquity

Ezekiel 16:46

And your elder sister is Samaria, who lived with her daughters to the north of you; and your younger sister, who lived to the south of you, is Sodom with her daughters.

Taylor treats Ezekiel 16:46 as an allegory.[41] Sometimes the left side and right side are used figuratively to represent evil and good (Eccl 10:2; Matt 25:33; see *Fact 19*).

Collins argues:

One must further note that Ezekiel calls Samaria the "older sister," while Sodom is the "younger sister." If one wants to get historically technical, then this Scripture passage is all wrong. Both Jerusalem and Sodom were millennia older than Samaria, which was not founded until after the division of the Israelite monarchy.[42] Biblically, Sodom dates to a time well before Abram (Gen 10). Additionally, Sodom did not even exist at the time this passage was written. Thus, historically and geographically, Samaria is not the "older" sister of Jerusalem any more than Sodom is a "southern" sister in any literal sense. The entire passage is metaphorical and poetic, and hermeneutically off-limits to geographical researchers. . . . Bad hermeneutics can lead to bad geography.[43]

Collins' point is well taken and illustrates the fact that Ezekiel must be treated differently than narrative.

FACT 20: JEREMIAH 50:35–46 IS PROPHETIC LITERATURE

Some people have argued that Jeremiah 50:39–40 indicates that Sodom will be abandoned forever; therefore, the archaeological site identified as the location of Sodom must be a site of destruction without any signs of later resettlement. According to this interpretation of Jeremiah, TeH is ruled out as a candidate for Sodom because it was resettled in the Iron Age and Roman, Byzantine and Umayyad periods. If this is the case, then BeD must also be ruled out, as it was also reoccupied after the major destruction of 2350 BC which some claim was the Sodom destruction (see *Fact 38).*

---

[39] Collins, "Rethinking the Location of Zoar," 1 no. 3.

[40] Ibid.

[41] John B. Taylor, *Ezekiel: An Introduction and Commentary*, Tyndale Old Testament Commentaries (Downers Grove, Ill.: InterVarsity Press, 2009), 140.

[42] The city of Samaria was founded during the reign of Omri. See Nachman Avigad, "Samaria (City)," in *The New Encyclopedia of Archaeological Excavations in the Holy Land*, ed. Ephraim Stern, Ayelet Levinson-Gilboa, and Joseph Aviram (New York, N.Y.: MacMillan, 1993), 1300–1310.

[43] Collins, "A Response to Bryant G. Wood," 9–10.

Quotes from Antiquity

Jeremiah 50:39–40

Therefore, wild beasts shall dwell with hyenas in Babylon, and ostriches shall dwell in her. She shall never again have people, nor be inhabited for all generations. As when God overthrew Sodom and Gomorrah and their neighboring cities, declares the LORD, so no man shall dwell there, and no son of man shall sojourn in her.

However, Jeremiah is prophetic literature and it is using a comparison with Sodom to make a point about Babylon. This passage does not say "forever" but for "all generations" (Heb. *dōr' wā dōr'* דור). According to Freedman and Lundbom:

like other ancient peoples, the early Hebrew dated long periods by lifetimes.... [furthermore there are] two different ideas concerning the length of a *dor*: a longer period of 100 years, and a shorter period of 30.... [One should also note] that the Hebrews began with the son and not the father in counting generations. The sons (*banim*) are the first generation; the grandsons (*bene bhanim*) the second, followed by the third (*shilleshim*) and fourth (*ribbe'im*) generation (Ex. 34:7).[44]

Jeremiah seems to indicate that Babylon will be destroyed to such an extent that one generation after another will not dwell in it (i.e., "generation to generation"). Although this is sometimes understood as "forever" (Heb. *olam* i.e., Joel 3:20), the area was resettled. Currently the fact there is a large international military force residing in Babylon which has become a Division headquarters[45] does not violate the meaning of the text.

Collins replies that:

this same poetic language of annihilation is used routinely against Israel's enemies in the prophetic literature. But the fact of the matter is that the Bronze Age Cities of the Kikkar were utterly destroyed at the same time, and were never inhabited again. Building on a relatively small part of the ancient ruins of Sodom seven centuries later does not constitute the rebuilding of Sodom!"[46]

The ca. 550 year "Late Bronze gap," when no one is living in most of the Jordan Valley,[47] including TeH, fulfills the prophecy of Jeremiah 50:35-46. But Ezekiel also promises that Sodom will be rebuilt along with Jerusalem (Ezekiel 16:53–55), so either way, placing Sodom near TeH would not violate the prophetic passages of Jeremiah or Ezekiel.

Quotes from Antiquity

Ezekiel 16:53–55

I will restore their fortunes, both the fortunes of Sodom and her daughters, and the fortunes of Samaria and her daughters, and I will restore your own fortunes in their midst, that you may bear your disgrace and be ashamed of all that you have done, becoming a consolation to them. As for your sisters, Sodom and her daughters shall return to their former state, and Samaria and her daughters shall return to their former state, and you and your daughters shall return to your former state.

The city of Sodom no longer existed but there is nothing to say that people did not rebuild a different city under a different name that was not called Sodom in the general vicinity which would not contradict the prophecies of Jeremiah or Ezekiel.

FACT 21: THERE IS A SALT CURSE MENTIONED IN THE BIBLE

The mention of Lot's wife being turned into a

---

[44] David Noel Freedman and J. Lundbom, "דור," in *TDOT*, ed. G. Johannes Botterweck, Helmer Ringgren, and Heinz-Josef Fabry, trans. Douglas W. Stott et al., vol. 3 (Grand Rapids, Mich.: Eerdmans, 2003), 3:174.

[45] Ibrahim Al-Marashi and Sammy Salama, *Iraq's Armed Forces: An Analytical History*, Middle Eastern Military Studies (London; New York: Routledge, 2009), 199–224.

[46] Collins, "The Geography of Sodom and Zoar," 3.

[47] There is some LB surface pottery at Tall Iktanu but as yet no LB structural remains (see *Fact 45*).

pillar of salt has led 19th century travellers to claim they have seen her along their route south of the Dead Sea. Condor in 1885 reported: "It is a crag somewhat like a human figure, jutting out of the cliffs near Kuiurdn, not far from the Hajr el Asbah."[48] These sightings are clearly just natural salt formations with no archaeological evidence connected to Lot's wife and are little help in locating Sodom (see *Fact 58*).

However, the mention of Lot's wife being turned into a pillar of salt (Gen 19:26) may be an ANE allusion to the salt curse and the destruction of a city and its vegetation (Deut 29:21–23; Judg 9:45).[49] When a city was cursed, salt was thrown on it to indicate it had been cursed. Ancient people would recognize the mention of salt as God speaking in ancient Near Eastern terms of the curse.[50] The fact that no one is living in the Jordan Valley for over 500 years known as the "Late Bronze gap" (see *Fact 45)* may be evidence of salt affecting the land so nothing could grow for such a long time.[51] Silvia and Collins call this catastrophe the 3.7KYrBP Kikkar Event.[52] Superstition of a cursed land would only keep shepherds, with hungry flocks of

19. One of many pillars of salt around the Dead Sea which have become known as Lot's wife (not actually his wife). This pillar is on the Jordanian side of the Dead Sea north of the Lisan.

Photo by Dan Galissini

sheep and goats, off the land for perhaps one generation. Recent research has documented that the soil in the region north of the Dead Sea reveals evidence of saline levels that are above normal following the MB destruction.[53] Geochemical analysis conducted by Allen West at the Activation Laboratories Ltd. in Ancaster, Ontario, Canada of the salt and sulphate content of the soil samples collected by Phillip J. Silvia at various levels at Tall el-Hammam indicated that the soil above the MB destruction layer had an abnormal rise in the level of salt and sulphates.[54] The salt was typical of Dead Sea salt in composition, and at these levels (above 300 ppm) would have made the soil toxic and unable to support the growth of vegetation or been conducive for agriculture. The soil would require a lengthy washing (i.e., 500 years) with water to purge the salt from the soil. Salt and the salt curse played an important role in the ancient Near Eastern mind and culture.

---

[48] Claude Reignier Conder, "Lot's Wife," *PEQ* 17–18 (1885): 20.

[49] David E. Graves, "Sodom And Salt in Their Ancient Near Eastern Cultural Context," *Near East Archaeological Society Bulletin* 61 (2016): 15–32.

[50] F. Charles Fensham, "Salt as a Curse in the Old Testament and the Ancient Near East," *BA* 25, no. 1 (February 1962): 48–50; James E. Latham, *The Religious Symbolism of Salt*, Theologie Historique 64 (Paris: Beauchesne, 1982), 81–82.

[51] Bunch et al., "A Tunguska Sized Airburst Destroyed Tall El-Hammam" 1.

[52] Phil Silvia and Steven Collins, "The Civilization-Ending 3.7KYrBP Kikkar Event: Archaeological Data, Sample Analyses, and Biblical Implications," in *Annual Meeting of the Near East Archaeological Society: Atlanta, Ga.* (Albuquerque, N.M.: TSU Press, 2015), 1–6; Phil Silvia, *The Destruction of Sodom: What We Have Learned from Tall El-Hammam and Its Neighbors* (Albuquerque, N.M.: Trinity Southwest University Press, 2016).

[53] Phillip J. Silvia, "The Middle Bronze Age Civilization-Ending Destruction of the Middle Ghor" (Trinity Southwest University, 2015), 111–13.

[54] Ibid.

GEOGRAPHY FACTS
The Location

Geography plays an important role in the identification of ancient sites and, contrary to popular belief, most ancient cities are located using geographical indicators found in the text rather than an inscription (see *Fact 11*). This chapter will address several important facts about the geography of the Holy Land connected with the location of Sodom.

20. Jordan valley visible from Mt. Nebo, Jordan. The north end of the Dead Sea is visible on the left. From this location Moses was given the view of the promised land and Egeria the land of the Sodomites around Livias.

FACT 22: THE JORDAN VALLEY WAS VISIBLE FROM BETWEEN BETHEL AND AI

The Bible states that the Jordan Valley (*kikkār*) was visible from between Bethel and Ai (Gen 13:3–4; 10–11) and that Lot travelled east and settled among the Cities of the valley, moving his tent to Sodom.

Quotes from Antiquity

Genesis 13:3–4; 10–12

And he [Abram] journeyed on from the Negeb as far as Bethel to the place where his tent had been at the beginning, *between Bethel and Ai,* 4 to the place where he had made an altar at the first. . . . .And Lot lifted up his eyes and saw that *the Jordan Valley* [Heb. *kikkār*] was well watered everywhere like the garden of the LORD, like the land of Egypt, in the *direction of Zoar.* (This was before the LORD destroyed *Sodom and Gomorrah.*) 11 So Lot chose for himself all *the Jordan Valley,* and Lot *journeyed east.* Thus they separated from each other. 12 Abram settled in the land of Canaan, while Lot settled among *the cities of the valley* and moved his tent as far as [Heb. *'ād*] *Sodom* (emphasis added).

First one needs to identify the location of Bethel and Ai.

While the exact location of Bethel (modern Beitin[1] or El-Bireh[2]) and Ai (modern et-Tell,[3] Khirbet Nisya[4] or Khirbet el-Maqatir[5]) are debated, they are roughly 11–12

---

[1] William F. Albright, "The Site of Bethel and Its Identification," in *The Excavation of Bethel (1934-1960),* ed. James Leon Kelso and William F. Albright, AASOR 39 (Cambridge, Mass.: American Schools of Oriental Research, 1968), 1–3; Michael Avi-Yonah and Ephraim Stern, eds., "Beth-El," in *EAEHL,* 4 vols. (Upper Saddle River, N.J.: Prentice Hall, 1978); Nadav Na'aman, "Bethel and Beth-Aven: The Location of the Early Israelite Sanctuaries," *Zion* 50 (1985): 25–25; Harold Brodsky, "Bethel (Place)," ed. David Noel Freedman et al., *ABD* (New York, N.Y.: Doubleday, 1996), 1:710–12; Robert T. Anderson, "Bethel (Place)," in *EDB,* ed. David Noel Freedman, Allen C. Myers, and Astrid B. Beck (Grand Rapids, Mich.: Eerdmans, 2000), 170.

[2] David P. Livingston, "The Location of Biblical Bethel and Ai Reconsidered," *Westminster Theological Journal* 33, no. 1 (1970): 20–44; "One Last Word on Bethel and Ai," *BAR* 15, no. 1 (1989): 11.

[3] Wilson, "On the Site of Ai"; Michael Avi-Yonah and Ephraim Stern, eds., "Ai; Hai," in *EAEHL,* 4 vols. (Upper Saddle River, N.J.: Prentice Hall, 1978); Joseph A. Callaway, "Ai," in *NEAEHL,* ed. Ephraim Stern, Ayelet Levinson-Gilboa, and Joseph Aviram, vol. 1, 4 vols. (New York, N.Y.: MacMillan, 1993), 39–45; "Ai (Place)," ed. David Noel Freedman et al., *ABD* (New York, N.Y.: Doubleday, 1996), 1:125–30.

[4] David P. Livingston, "Excavation Report for Khirbet Nisya," *BS* 12, no. 3 (1999): 95–96; "The Location of Biblical Bethel and Ai Reconsidered," 20–44; "Locating Biblical Ai Correctly," *Ancient Days,* 2003, http://davelivingston .com/ai15.htm.

[5] Khirbet el-Maqatir lies fifteen km north of Jerusalem, on the east side of Highway 60, and 3.7 km east of El-Bireh, 1.6 km southeast of Beitin and *ca.* 1 km

21. The view of the well-watered plain (*kikkar*) in the distance as seen from between Bethel and Ai. The Cities of the Plain, proposed by the NST, are clearly visible from this location. However, the southern end of the Dead Sea is not visible.

Photo courtesy of Michael Luddeni. Labels by David E. Graves

miles (19.31 km) north of Jerusalem on the other side of the Central Benjamin plateau, some 2,788 ft. (890 m) above sea level. The debated sites are so close to one another that their disputed location does not affect the location from where Abraham and Lot were standing (see Map 2 or the Hebrew map in Wood's article[6]).

However, regardless of which sites are biblical Bethel and Ai, the general location is still 2,788 ft. above sea level and granted a clear line of sight to the Jordan Valley (see Fig. 21). However, the southern region of the Dead Sea is blocked from sight by the hills of Hebron[7] which are 3,094 ft (943 m) above sea level.

Scott D. Stripling, the current director of excavations at Khirbet el-Maqatir (Ai?), stated:

---

west of et-Tell. Bryant G. Wood, "The Search for Joshua's Ai: Excavations at Kh. El-Maqatir," *BS* 12, no. 1 (1999): 21–32; "The Search for Joshua's Ai," in *Critical Issues in Early Israelite History*, ed. Richard S. Hess, Gerald A. Klingbeil, and Paul J. Ray Jr., Bulletin for Biblical Research Supplement 3 (Winona Lake, Ind.: Eisenbrauns, 2008), 205–40; "Excavations at Kh. El-Maqatir 1995–2000, 2009–2013: A Border Fortress in the Highlands of Canaan and a Proposed New Location for the Ai of Joshua 7-8," *The Bible and Interpretation*, 2014, 1–16; "Khirbet El-Maqatir, 1995-1998," *IEJ* 50, no. 1–2 (2000): 123–30; "Khirbet El-Maqatir, 1999," *IEJ* 50, no. 3–4 (2000): 249–54; "Khirbet El-Maqatir, 2000," *IEJ* 51, no. 2 (2001): 246–52; D. Scott Stripling et al., "Renewed Excavations at Khirbet El-Maqatir: Highlights of the 2009–2011 Seasons," in *Collected Studies of the Staff Office of Archaeology of Judea and Samaria*, Judea and Samaria Publication 13 (Jerusalem: Israel Antiquities Authority, 2014), Forthcoming; Bryant G. Wood and D. Scott Stripling, *Joshua's Ai at Khirbet El-Maqatir: History of a Biblical Site* (Houston, Tex.: Houston Baptist University Press, 2014).

---

[6] Wood, "The Search for Joshua's Ai," 1999, 21.
[7] Howard, Jr., "Sodom and Gomorrah Revisited," 387.

22. Burnt gate at Khirbet el-Maqatir (Ai?) from the time of Joshua (Late Bronze 1400 BC). The Bible states that Joshua burned the gate.

"I have been between Bethel and Ai at last 100 times. About 10% of the time there is good visibility of the *kikkar*."[8] This is also confirmed by Geikie who states:

> Abraham and Lot, moreover, could see the fertile region of Sodom and Gomorrah from the hill top on which they stood, between Bethel and Ai, but intervening hills shut out the southern end of the sea, which is sixty miles off, from any point near that from which the patriarchs looked down into the great depression, while they could see the plain of Jericho and the rich green of the Sultan's Spring, as if at their feet.[9]

The fact remains that the Jordan Valley plain (*kikkār*) was clearly visible from between Bethel and Ai (see Fig. 21) and this is important because the Cities of the Plain (*kikkār*) were located there.

FACT 23: SODOM WAS LOCATED ON THE PLAIN (*KIKKĀR*) OF THE JORDAN

The destroyed cities of the Pentapolis are repeatedly mentioned located in "the plain" or "valley" (Gen 13:12; Heb. *kikkār*), also called "the land of the valley" (Gen 19:28) and "Jordan Valley" (Gen 13:10f). This distinctive Hebrew term (*kikkār*) is central to the arguments around the location of the city of Sodom.

The etymology of the root word indicates that *kikkār* refers to something round, as in a "round loaf of bread" (1 Sam 2:36; Prov 6:26; Exod 29:23; Jer 37:21; 1 Chr 16:3; 1 Sam 10:3, Jud 8:5) or a "circular disk for payment" (2 Sam 12:30, 1 Kgs 20:39, 2 Kgs 5:5; 1 Chr 29:7; 2 Kgs 9:14).[10]

---

[8] Stripling, Scott. "Personal Correspondence," September 14, 2013.

[9] Geikie, *Holy Land and the Bible*, 118.

[10] George L. Robinson, "Jordan," in *Dictionary of the Bible, One Vol.*, ed. James Hastings and John A. Selbie (New York, N.Y.: Scribner's Sons, 1909), 761; R. Laird Harris, Gleason L. Archer, Jr., and Bruce K. Waltke,

Other references to the *kikkār* place it between Zarethan (*Tell es-Saidiyeh*;[11] Josh 3:16; 1 Kgs 7:46; 2 Chron 4:17) and Succoth (*Tall Deir 'Allā*,[12] Josh 13:27) in the Jordan Valley near the Jabbok River, east of the Jordan River (1 Kgs 7:46; 2 Chron 4:17; 2 Sam 18:23. See Map 4). This would place the *kikkār* in the northern region between the Sea of Galilee and the Dead Sea.

Later, during Nehemiah's time, the term *kikkār* was used to refer to an area surrounding (Heb. *sbybwt*) Jerusalem (Heb. *hakkikkār*; Neh 3:22; 12:28).[13] It would appear that *kikkār* was adopted as a technical geographical term due to the round appearance of the Jordan Valley when viewed from the surrounding hills. The term *kikkār* is still used in Israel for a traffic circle or roundabout.

The late Anson Rainey, Professor Emeritus of Ancient Near Eastern Cultures and Semitic Linguistics at Tel Aviv University, had suggested that the term *kikkār* should be turned into a technical geography term like Sea of Galilee. In an email correspondence with Collins, Rainey commented: "Your [Collins'] arguments about the *kikkār* are the most cogent. . . . As I said earlier, the references to the *kikkār* fit better with the area N. of the Dead Sea."[14]

Amihi Mazar, the Eleazer Sukenik Chair in the Archaeology of Israel and Professor at the Institute of Archaeology of the Hebrew University of Jerusalem, states in correspondence with Collins that:

> I also agree with you [Collins] that a straightforward reading of Gen 13:1–12 would call for the conclusion that when the author wrote *Kikkar Hayarden* he meant the southern Jordan Valley north of the Dead Sea.[15]

However, some arguing for the SST, have suggested that the roundness of the term *kikkār* must not be pressed too hard, as the Jordan Valley has an oval or rectangular shape, since it extends to Zarethan and Succoth,[16] and they include the entire southern region of the Dead Sea into the *kikkār*.[17] Also, the idea that Lot saw "all" the Plain from between Bethel and Ai must be figurative, since as Driver points out, "not even the entire valley north of the Dead Sea is visible from near Bethel."[18] This view is further explained by Howard that:

> most proponents of a southern hypothesis here postulate that the "*kikkār* of the Jordan" included not only the Jordan valley proper but also the Dead Sea itself and the area south of it. It is not a "circle" per se, then, but a region.[19]

This was challenged by Merrill in the 1800's, who protested the extension of the meaning of the word *kikkār* to include the entire Dead Sea valley.

> But I think it is to do violence to the language and to the facts of the case to attempt to make the phrase "all the plain of the Jordan" include the salt

---

eds., "כִּכָּר," in *TWOT* (Chicago, Ill.: Moody, 1980), 503, no. 4673; Charles A. Briggs, Samuel R. Driver, and Francis Brown, "כִּכָּר," in *BDB* (Oxford, U.K.: Clarendon, 1997), no. 1046c.

[11] Jonathan N. Tubb, "Sa'idryeh. Tell Es-," in *OEANE*, ed. Eric M. Meyers, vol. 4 (Oxford, U.K.: Oxford University Press, 1997), 452.

[12] Hendricus J. Franken, "Deir 'Alla, Tell," in *OEANE*, ed. Eric M. Meyers, vol. 2 (Oxford, U.K.: Oxford University Press, 1997), 138.

[13] Steven Collins, "Reassessing the Term Hakikkar in Nehemiah as Bearing on the Location of the Cities of the Plain," *BRB* 7, no. 3 (2007): 1–4.

[14] Collins, "A Response to Bryant G. Wood," 17.

[15] Ibid.

[16] Simons, *The Geographical and Topographical Texts of the Old Testament*, 407; Wood, "Locating Sodom: A Critique of the Northern Proposal," 81.

[17] Harland, "Sodom and Gomorrah Part I: Location," 20; Peter C. Craigie, *The Book of Deuteronomy*, ed. R. K. Harrison, NICOT 5 (Grand Rapids, Mich.: Eerdmans, 1976), 405; Menashe Har-El, "The Pride of the Jordan–The Jungle of the Jordan," *BA* 41 (1978): 66–67.

[18] Howard, Jr., "Sodom and Gomorrah Revisited," 388; Driver, "Zoar," 4:986.

[19] Howard, Jr., "Sodom and Gomorrah Revisited," 388.

marsh at the southern end of the Dead Sea, which is fifty miles from that river, and has nothing to do with it. Indeed, the region there belongs to another water-system altogether-entirely distinct from that at the northern end of the Dead Sea, with which the Jordan is connected.[20]

And Sarna agrees, stating several arguments in support of the northern location for the *kikkār*:

> The statement that King Solomon cast the bronze vessels for the Temple "in the plain of the Jordan [*kikkār*] between Succoth and Zerethan" (2 Chron 4:17), referring to the middle section of the Jordan Valley, between the Sea of Galilee and the Dead Sea, seems to imply that the northern shore of the Dead Sea is the southern extremity of the *Kikkār*. This conclusion is supported by the report that from the summit of Mount Nebo in Transjordan "facing Jericho" (Deut 32:49), Moses was able to see . . . "the Negeb, and the Plain, that is, the Valley of Jericho the city of palm trees, as far as Zoar" (Deut 34:3). Finally, as we noted above, Lot is said to have been able to view the entire Jordan Plain from a location between Bethel and Ai (Gen 13:3, 10), which would have been impossible if the cities were south of the Dead Sea.[21]

FACT 24: THE EXACT LOCATION OF THE VALLEY OF SIDDIM IS NOT KNOWN

The Valley of Siddim is mentioned in Genesis 14:3, 8, 10 as the location where the kings of the Pentapolis were defeated by Chedorlaomer and his three confederates.

The exact location of this valley is not known and the etymology of the Hebrew word *śdd* (Ugaritic *śd(d)*; Akkadian *šadādu*) meaning "to draw, drag, or plow (a furrow)"[22]

does not help in its location. However, as Howard points out:

> Regardless of etymology the implication in v 3 (and also in v 8) is that the kings (or at least some of them) did not live in the place where they joined forces and prepared for war but rather that this was a rendezvous point and that they lived nearby.[23]

Thus, even if the location of the Valley of Siddim could be verified, it still does not assist in locating the Cities of the Plain, since it was only a rendezvous point (see *Fact 16*). However, SST proponents argue that this is the location of the Cities of the Plain and that the Valley of Siddim is now under the southern end of the Dead Sea (See Ancient Textual References: Genesis 14:1–12).[24]

The text does state that the valley was filled with bitumen pits (Gen 14:10) and some argue that this is the region at the southern end of the Dead Sea.[25] For example, based on geotechnical speculation, Harris and Beardow suggest that: "the legendary Vale of Siddim was located to the northeast of the Lisan Peninsula at the southern extremity of the present-day North Basin of the Dead Sea."[26]

For them the Cities of the Plain have slid into the Dead Sea due to liquification of the ground following an earthquake. However, there is no physical evidence for this

---

[20] Merrill, "Modern Researches in Palestine, 1877," 117; Merrill, "Modern Researches in Palestine, PEFSt.," 145; Collins, "Forty Salient Points," 3.

[21] Nahum M Sarna, *Genesis: The Traditional Hebrew Text with the New JPS Translation*, JPS Torah Commentary (Philadelphia: Jewish Publication Society, 1989), 387; Weston W. Fields, *Sodom and Gomorrah: History and Motif in Biblical Narrative* (New York, N.Y.: Continuum International, 1997), 36 n. 28.

[22] Briggs, Driver, and Brown, *A Hebrew and English Lexicon of the Old Testament with an Appendix Containing the Biblical Aramaic. Based on the Lexicon of William Gessenius as Translated by Edward Robinson*, 961.

[23] Howard, Jr., "Sodom and Gomorrah Revisited," 389.

[24] Wood, "Have Sodom And Gomorrah Been Found?," 79; Graham M. Harris and Anthony P. Beardow, "The Destruction of Sodom and Gomorrah: A Geotechnical Perspective," *Quarterly Journal of Engineering Geology* 28 (1995): 349–62.

[25] G. W. Wade, "Siddim, Vale of," in *DBib1*, ed. James Hastings and John A. Selbie (New York, N.Y.: Scribner's Sons, 1909), 853; Samuel R. Driver, "Siddim, Vale of," in *DBib5*, ed. James Hastings and John A. Selbie, vol. 4 (New York, N.Y.: Scribner's Sons, 1911), 4:512; Astour, "Siddim," 6:15–16.

[26] Harris and Beardow, "The Destruction of Sodom and Gomorrah: A Geotechnical Perspective," 349.

hypothesis (see *Fact 52*).

Howard explains that:

> The valley of Siddim, . . . is explained in a gloss as being the Salt Sea. The likelihood is that the valley was in what is today the shallow end of the Dead Sea, south of the Lisān peninsula. The Sea's water level has varied dramatically over the centuries: It was c. 130 feet higher in the early 1970's than it was in Biblical times. Since the average depth today [1984] of the southern basin is no more than twenty feet, it is a most likely candidate for this valley.[27]

The low levels of the Dead Sea may explain the appearance of the bitumen (slime) pits although they are concentrated along the western shore of the Dead Sea (see *Fact 57* and Maps 4 and 7).[28] As Albright points out:

> The only possible location for the Vale of Siddim, with its asphalt wells (rendered "slime-pits" in the AV) is in the southwestern part of the Dead Sea, west of the course of the three streams just mentioned and their oases.[29]

The Valley of Siddim is likely the valley on the southwestern side of the Dead Sea, but regardless of its location, this does not help in locating the Cities of the Plain since the kings of the Pentapolis came out to do battle in this plain from their cities that were probably located elsewhere.

FACT 25: BeD AND TeH ARE BOTH LOCATED IN THE GREAT RIFT VALLEY

Both BeD and TeH are located in the Great Rift Jordan Valley along two fault lines which are known to have bitumen/asphalt, sulphur, tar, and natural gas in this region (see Map 4 and *Fact 57*).[30] Ben-Avraham and Niemi point out that the Dead Sea:

> occupies part of a long and narrow continental trough—the Dead Sea basin [Dead Sea-Jordan Transform]—located in the Dead Sea rift. Tectonically, the Dead Sea rift is a transform fault system that separates the Arabian plate on the east from the African plate on the west, connecting the spreading zone of the Red Sea in the south to the Taurus collision zone in the north.[31]

Nissenbaum and Goldberg provide additional details stating:

> The Syrian-African rift extends from the Taurus Mountains to the Dead Sea, a distance of over 1000 km. The Dead Sea Basin is located in the deepest part of this rift, with its lowermost point 401 m below mean sea level.[32]

This valley is the lowest point on earth and with mountains rising 1300 ft above sea level on all sides it appears very deep when standing on the mountains looking down. Lyakhovsky, Ben-Avraham, and Achmon describe that "the southern and central portions of the Dead Sea rift trend north to north-northeast and approximately follow a small circle [*kikkār*]."[33]

Some have tried to speculate that Sodom was destroyed by an earthquake, (see *Fact 52*)

---

[27] Howard, Jr., "Sodom and Gomorrah Revisited," 389.

[28] Albright, "The Archæological Results of an Expedition to Moab and the Dead Sea," 9.

[29] Albright, "The Archæological Results of an Expedition to Moab and the Dead Sea," 9.

[30] Tina M. Niemi and Zvi Ben-Avraham, "Active Tectonics in the Dead Sea Basin," in *The Dead Sea: The Lake and Its Setting*, ed. Zvi Ben-Avraham, Tina M. Niemi, and Joel R. Gat, Oxford Monographs on Geology and Geophysics 36 (New York, N.Y.: Oxford University Press, USA, 1997), 73–81; Ora Amit and Amos Bein, "The Genesis of the Asphalt in the Dead Sea Area," *Journal of Geochemical Exploration* 11, no. 3 (1979): 211–25.

[31] Michael Gardosh et al., "Hydrocarbon Exploration in the Southern Dead Sea Area," in *The Dead Sea: The Lake and Its Setting*, ed. Zvi Ben-Avraham, Tina M. Niemi, and Joel R. Gat, Oxford Monographs on Geology and Geophysics 36 (New York, N.Y.: Oxford University Press, USA, 1997), 58; Zvi Garfunkel, "Internal Structure of the Dead Sea Leaky Transform (Rift) in Relation to Plate Kinematics," *Tectonophysics* 80, no. 1–4 (1981): 81–108; Neev and Emery, *The Destruction of Sodom, Gomorrah and Jericho*.

[32] Arie Nissenbaum and M. Goldberg, "Asphalts, Heavy Oils, Ozocerite and Gases in the Dead Sea Basin," *Organic Geochemistry* 2, no. 3 (1975): 167–77.

[33] Vladimir Lyakhovsky, Zvi Ben-Avraham, and Moshe Achmon, "The Origin of the Dead Sea Rift," *Tectonophysics* 240 (1994): 29.

and that since BeD is located on a known fault line, this proves that Sodom is in the south.[34] However, because fault lines ran through the entire Jordan Valley, if an earthquake took out BeD, it would have also taken out TeH. A hypothetical geological description of the destruction of Sodom is no indication to its location.

FACT 26: SMOKE FROM BOTH TeH AND BeD WOULD HAVE BEEN VISIBLE FROM HEBRON

When Abraham and lot separated, Lot chose the Plain of Jordan while Abraham "settled by the oaks of Mamre, which are at Hebron, and there he built an altar to the LORD." (Gen 13:18). After the destruction of Sodom and Gomorrah, Abraham witnessed the smoke from the destruction of the Cities of the Plain (Heb. *kikkār*) from the door of his tent.

Quotes from Antiquity

Genesis 19:28
And he [Abraham] looked down [elevation and not direction provided by translators] toward [direction below Heb. *'al-*] Sodom and Gomorrah and toward [direction below Heb. *'al-*] all the land of the valley (Heb. *kikkār*), and he looked and, behold, the smoke of the land went up like the smoke of a furnace.

Geikie suggests that only the smoke would be visible from cities destroyed in the northern region in the Jordan Valley, stating:

Nor could Abraham, as he stood at his tent door at Mamre, have seen, as he did, "the smoke of the country rising like the smoke of a furnace," as he looked "towards Sodom and Gomorrah," had they been at the south end of the lake; whereas the openings between the hills are such that, though the plain itself is not visible from near Hebron, the clouds of smoke ascending from the doomed cities must have been seen in all their grandeur.[35]

Howard, quoting Harland[36] and Simons[37], states that "smoke is more easily seen at a southern site than at a northern one from Hebron."[38]

While there are reports from both the NST and the SST proponents claiming that only smoke from their site could be visible from Hebron, the fact is that thick smoke rising from either the northern Jordan Valley or southern Ghor would be visible from the Hebron plateau, which rises 3,094 ft. (943 m) above sea level and is halfway between BeD and TeH. Again, what is central to the argument is the location of the *kikkār* (see Fact 23) since this was where Abraham was looking.

FACT 27: TeH IS ALSO ABEL-SHITTIM

The area around TeH, in the Late Bronze Age, is identified by most scholars as Abel Shittim (Heb. meaning "Acacias of Mourning"),[39] which is the location of Israel's encampment prior to entering the Promised Land (Num 25:1, Deut 34:9; Josh 2:1; 3:1). In Merrill's article under the section titled "The Shittim Plain," he states:

---

[34] Frederick G. Clapp, "The Site of Sodom and Gomorrah: A Diversity of Views," *AJA* 40, no. 3 (1936): 326; Wood, "Have Sodom And Gomorrah Been Found?," 80.

[35] Geikie, *Holy Land and the Bible*, 118–119.

[36] Harland, "Sodom and Gomorrah Part I: Location," 22.

[37] Simons, *The Geographical and Topographical Texts of the Old Testament*, 409.

[38] Howard, Jr., "Sodom and Gomorrah Revisited," 390; Wood, "Discovery of the Sin Cities," 67.

[39] Thomson, *Land and the Book: Lebanon, Damascus, and Beyond Jordan*, 3:3:669; Glueck, *Explorations in Eastern Palestine*, 378; "Some Ancient Towns," 15; J. Maxwell Miller and Gene M. Tucker, *The Book of Joshua*, The Cambridge Bible Commentary of the English Bible (Cambridge, Mass.: Cambridge University Press, 1974), 199; R. K. Harrison, "Shittim," ed. Edward M. Blaiklock, *NIDBA* (Grand Rapids, Mich.: Zondervan, 1983), 413; Khouri, *Antiquities of the Jordan Rift Valley*, 76; Burton MacDonald, *East of the Jordan: Territories and Sites of the Hebrew Scriptures*, ed. Victor H. Matthews, ASOR Books 6 (Boston, Mass.: American Schools of Oriental Research, 2000), 90.

When the Hebrews came down from the mountains of Moab, they pitched from Beth Jeshimoth on the south, to *Abel Shittim on the north*, and their tents must have covered the whole plain. . . . between Tel Kefrein and Tel er Eama on the west, and the mountains on the east, there are two important tels which remain to be noticed. *These are Tel el Hammam in the north, where there are extensive ruins and a hot spring; and Tel Ektanu in the south* [emphasis added].[40]

The *Archaeological Study Bible* identifies TeH as Abel-Shittim, however it gives no archaeological evidence for this identification,[41] perhaps because its identification is based on geographic location instead of physical discoveries. In Moses day (LB) the region of Abel-Shittim, below Mt. Pisgah (beside Mt. Nebo), was described as a "desert" ("wasteland below Pisgah" Num 21:20 NIV). Collins reports that after eight seasons of excavation at TeH and thousands of shards: "Late Bronze Age sherds are extremely rare in the area, and there is no discernable LBA architecture thus far (the only LBA sherds from around the site were found in a tomb)."[42]

While Moses and Joshua were camped out around TeH they did not build any structures nor leave behind much in the way of discernable artifacts.

FACT 28: TeH IS ALSO LIVIAS

TeH, during the Roman, Byzantine and Umayyad period, was Livias. Scott D. Stripling and David E. Graves have published their finding and arguments from TeH for being Livias in an article in *Levant* Journal.[43] The fact that the property around TeH was

23. Livia Drusilla, (58 BC-AD 29, Tiberius' mother). After her formal adoption into the Julian family in AD 14, she was deified by Claudius and became known as Julia Augusta. Livias (the city) was given her name by Herod Antipas in the 1st cent. AD.

Selçuk Archaeological Museum, Turkey.

resettled in later periods (Iron Age, Roman, Byzantine, and Umayyad; see *Fact 27* and *28*) does not do violence to the idea of Sodom being cursed and then generations later, resettled (see *Fact 20*). The pilgrim Egeria (late 4th cent AD) also identified the city of Livias with the land of the Sodomites (See *Primary Sources*).

---

[40] Merrill, "Modern Researches in Palestine, 1877," 117; Merrill, "Modern Researches in Palestine, PEFSt.," 144.

[41] Kaiser, Jr. and Garrett, *NIV Archaeological Study Bible*, 233.

[42] Collins et al., "Tall El-Hammam, Season Eight, 2013," 4.

[43] Graves and Stripling, "Re-Examination of the Location for the Ancient City of Livias," 178–200.

The Location of Sodom

24. Roman bath complex excavated in 2011–2012 from Tall el-Ḥammâm, Jordan. The site is believed to be Livias and may have originally been Herod Antipas' bath complex. The building this room was located in measures 35 x 40 metres.

25. The author standing beside the Roman mile marker indicating 6 Roman miles to Livias. Mt. Nebo museum, Jordan.

Fact 29: Abraham was given the land of Canaan

In the covenant with Abraham, God gave him the land of Canaan (Gen 12:4a, 12:5d). The Bible defines Canaan's southern border as "the river of Egypt." This is NOT the Nile River, but the Wadi el Arish, located in Egypt's northeastern region. The northern border of Canaan is defined as the River Euphrates (Gen 15:18). The southern border of the Promised Land (Canaan) runs from the southern end of the Dead Sea (Salt Sea), to approximately the middle of the Negev desert. From there, it turns northward toward Wadi el Arish (brook of Egypt) and ends at the Mediterranean Sea (Num 34:3–9).

Both TeH and BeD would have been in Canaan as defined by Scripture. The dispute that arose between Abraham and Lot (who were relatives) had nothing to do with the covenant or the location of Canaan. They parted company and traveled within Canaan as they knew it. Lot traveled east as far as Sodom.

Fact 30: For the SST advocates, Gen 14:1–14 would require Chedorlaomer to have gone back on his tracks

The SST proponents must have Chedorlaomer backtracking with his army to

26. The cemetery at Bab edh-Dhra overlooking the Dead Sea below and the salt plains. Many of the shaft tombs have been robbed out by local looters.

encounter the kings from the Cities of the Plain, following their defeat of the Amorites dwelling in Ḥaṣaṣon-Tamar or En-Gedi, on the western shore of the Dead Sea. Chedorlaomer has been traveling north from Kadesh in the south, likely early in the seventeenth century BC.[44] It is not unreasonable for him to turn around after defeating his enemies at Ḥaṣaṣon-Tamar, but it does seem rather unnatural.

Geikie reads the details of this passage as an argument for the NST when he explains:

> That Chedorlaomer, on his way north from Mount Seir, after smiting the Amorites at Engedi, should have fallen upon the kings of Sodom and Gomorrah in the plains of Siddim, continuing his march northwards towards home after defeating them, so that in his turn he was overcome by Abraham near the sources of the Jordan, further implies that the Cities of the Plain were north of the Dead Sea.[45]

Power, arguing for the NST on the basis of the direction of the attacking army of Chedorlaomer, states:

It is difficult to imagine what circumstances could have made the invaders impose on themselves unnecessary marches through the difficult desert country which lies south of Engaddi [*sic* En-Gedi]. It seems absurd to suppose that the Amorrhaeans of Engaddi, separated by the desert from the Pentapolis in the south, were of such importance that they had to be reduced before the Pentapolis could be attacked.[46]

While this argument can be explained as backtracking to meet the Kings of the Cities of the Plain, the text does make more sense if the Cities of the Plain are located in the Jordan Valley north of the Dead Sea. Following the battle at En-Gedi, Chedorlaomer keeps moving north to return home with a weary army.

FACT 31: THE SOUTHERN DEAD SEA REGION LOOKS CURSED

Today while visiting the southern Dead Sea region it is easy to believe that the story of Sodom originated there. It looks and feels like a cursed land. For example, one can see salt pillars[47] that remind them of Lot's wife being turned into a pillar of salt, (see *Fact 58*), a

---

[44] Albright, "The Archæological Results of an Expedition to Moab and the Dead Sea," 7; "A Revision of Early Hebrew Chronology," *Journal of the Palestine Oriental Society* 1 (1921): 68–76; "Shinar–Sangar and Its Monarch Amraphel," *The American Journal of Semitic Languages and Literatures* 40, no. 2 (1924): 125–33.

[45] Geikie, *Holy Land and the Bible*, 119.

[46] Power, "The Site of the Pentapolis: Part 1," 45 n. 1.

[47] Harland, "Sodom and Gomorrah Part I: Location," 12.

mountain called "Mount Sodom" (Jebel Usdum; see *Fact 58*), Lot's cave (see *Fact 34*), Byzantine Zoar (see *Fact 33*), bits of asphalt lying around (see Fig. 50), sulphur balls, see what looks like the structures of buildings, and believe that it looks cursed, therefore it must be the land of the Sodomites. Wyatt and Fisher who are not archaeologists have come to this conclusion.[48] But this is nothing more than pseudo-archaeology and pure nonsense.

Certainly, the southern region of the Dead Sea looks cursed by God (see Fig. 26). However, looking cursed is different from being cursed and there is no empirical evidence that either location have been cursed by God. This does not mean that it never happened, just that there is no evidence for it. As Kitchen points out the "absence of evidence is not evidence of absence."[49] Certainly both BeD and TeH were both destroyed in a fiery destruction, but this was common for most ancient sites which were burned during sieges. The fact of the destruction of the cities by fire does not indicate that they were cursed by God.

Just because it looks cursed does not mean it is the location for the destroyed cities of the Pentapolis.

FACT 32: SHEA'S IDENTIFICATION OF CITIES BASED ON THE EBLAITE GEOGRAPHIC ATLAS IS SUSPECT

William H. Shea in his article, "Two Palestinian Segments from the Eblaite Geographic Atlas," argues that the place names from the Ebla tablets are places visited by merchants from Ebla and "listed in geographical order."[50] Wood picks up on Shea's theory to argue for the SST. Wood states that:

> One of the tablets is a geographic atlas listing 289 place names. An analysis of two segments of the list by William Shea indicates that they are sites located in Palestine, possibly places visited by merchants from Ebla.[51] The second segment, sites 188–219, traces a route from Syria south through the central hill country of Cisjordan, along the western shore of the Dead Sea, south of the Dead Sea Plain and then north along the east side of the Plain and Dead Sea. In the area corresponding to the east side of the Dead Sea Plain there are two places named— Number 210, Admah, and Number 211, Sodom. If Shea's readings are correct, this would be the only confirmed mention of the Cities of the Plain outside the Bible.[52]

Shea's designation of sites around the Dead Sea, based on the order they were visited by merchants, is very subjective and arbitrary. For example, Shea provided the place names on the Ebla tablets followed by his proposed identification, from what he believes is the SW end of the Dead Sea, beginning with site 208.[53]

- 208 *ḫul-gal-ga-a*^{ki} = SW Dead Sea Shore Circuit
- 209 *da-me-GU*^{ki} = Dead Sea Shore at Admah
- 210 *ad-mu-ut*^{ki} = (Town of) Admah
- 211 *sa-dam*^{ki} = Sodom
- 212 *ar-me*^{ki} = Arnon River
- 213 *la-ti-a*^{ki} = Kiriathaim[54]

The only two sites that are even remotely recognizable are Admah and Sodom, which could easily be in the northern region of the Jordan Valley since the other sites are

---

[48] Kevin Fisher and William F. Wyatt, "Sodom and Gomorrah: The Cities of the Plain: Ash and Brimstone Remain," *Ark Discovery: Revealing God's Treasure*, 2013, http://www.arkdiscovery.com/sodom_&_gomorrah.htm.

[49] Kenneth A. Kitchen, "The Patriarchal Age: Myth or History?," *BAR* 21, no. 2 (1995): 48.

[50] Shea, "Two Palestinian Segments," 591.

[51] Ibid., 589–612.

[52] Wood, "Discovery of the Sin Cities," 13.

[53] Note that KI, at the end of the name, is the Eblaite determinative for place. Shea, "Two Palestinian Segments," 589.

[54] Ibid., 601.

Geography Facts

impossible to identify with any degree of certainty. All other place names could be anywhere in the region.

According to Alfonso Archi, the new epigrapher for the Ebla excavation, based on the surrounding city names in the cuneiform tablets, *si-da-mu* is located in northern Syria and not around the Dead Sea.[55] Also, *ì-ma-ar*[ki] is not Gomorrah but a variant of *ì-mar*, closely identified with the city of Emar near Ebla. It is also listed in a series of names with *Ḫa-ra-an*, suggesting to Archi, that: "the mention of Ḫaran shows that the cities are to be placed in the northern end and eastern regions, not on the shore of the Dead Sea"[56] (See Chapter One under "Ancient Textual References"). It must also be pointed out that neither Shea nor Archi are Sumerologists. Shea is a biblical scholar and Archi is a Hittitologist.

The two radically different locations for these cuneiform place names demonstrate the difficulty in identifying the location with any degree of accuracy, leaving most proposals as educated guesses at best.

FACT 33: THERE ARE SEVERAL POSSIBLE LOCATIONS FOR ZOAR

Merrill points out that "Zoar formed one of the group that were to be destroyed,"[57] so the question needs to be asked: does Zoar help identify Sodom? Isaiah (15:5) and Jeremiah (48:34) locate Zoar in Moabite territory, as the prophets deliver a judgment against Moab and include Zoar, which would suggest Zoar is in the south in Moab territory.

Other clues are given in the text, which suggests a northern location, as Merrill points out:

> Since Zoar was one of the "cities of the plain," a hint as to their situation may be derived from Gen. xiii., 10, where Lot and Abraham are represented as standing on a hill near Bethel, and looking down the Jordan valley towards the Dead Sea. As this verse is rendered in our English Bible, the meaning is not clear; but it will become so when all the middle portion of the verse is read as a parenthesis, as follows: "And Lot lifted up his eyes and beheld all the plain of Jordan (that it was well watered everywhere, before the Lord destroyed Sodom and Gomorrah, even as the garden of the Lord like the land of Egypt), until thou comest to Zoar." The last clause qualifies the first. Lot saw all the plain of Jordan as far as Zoar, or "until you come to Zoar." Zoar was both the limit of the plain and the limit of vision in that direction, so far as the land was concerned. How much of the Dead Sea he saw is not stated; but no human vision, unless miraculously aided, could reach to the southern end and *distinguish anything*, while, from the point where he stood, the greenness and beauty of the great Shittim plain are distinctly seen. The phrase, "all the plain of the Jordan," cannot include the salt marsh at the southern end of the Dead Sea, since this marsh is fifty miles from the river, and belongs to a water system entirely distinct from that at the northern end of the sea.[58]

The difficulty in answering the question "does Zoar help?" is that no one really knows for sure where Zoar is located. No archaeological evidence has been unearthed to positively identify it. Over the years scholars have proposed several locations.

Southern Zoar – *Ghor eṣ-Ṣafi*

Albright believed that Zoar was buried under the Dead Sea with the rest of the Cities of the Plain. He reported:

> one result of our expedition has been to demonstrate that the site of the Old Testament Zoar was submerged by the rise of the Sea, . . . There is, accordingly, little likelihood that the exact sites of the original Zoar, of Sodom, or of Gomorrah will ever be recovered, but we can probably locate these towns approximately. . . . Since Zoar controlled the Seil el-Qurâhi, Sodom, which biblical tradition places next to Zoar, presumably lay on the Seil en-

---

[55] Archi, "Are 'The Cities of the Plain' Mentioned in the Ebla Tablets?," 54.
[56] Ibid.
[57] Merrill, "Modern Researches in Palestine, PEFSt.," 147.

[58] Merrill, *East of the Jordan*, 233–34.

Nmeirah.[59] He concludes: "The Old Testament Zoar would then have been situated on the Seil 'El-Qurâhi below the Byzantine site [of Lot's cave]"[60] and identified with Ghor eṣ-Ṣafi on the Wadi Hesa "some 5 mi. S of the Dead Sea."[61] This site has traditionally retained the name of Zoar since Roman and Byzantine times.[62] Politis states that: "According to the [Roman document] *Notitia Dignitatum* (73, 26), a garrison with a local cavalry unit (*Equites sagittarii indigenae*) was stationed at Zoar during the early fourth century."[63] In a cave near En-Gedi, on the western shore of the Dead Sea, a bundle of 35 Aramaic and Greek papyri were found called the Babatha Archives "containing a number of Babatha's legal documents—showing that she came from Zoara!"[64] This is the location preserved in Greek on the Madaba Map in the Greek Orthodox Parish Church of St. George in Madaba, Jordan, as "Balak, also Segor [Rom. Seghor], now Zoora [Byz. Zoara]" (See Chapter One under "Traditional References: Madaba Map" and Fig. 6).[65] This beautiful mosaic depicts the region of the Holy Land during the 6th cent. AD and places Zoar (then Zoora) at the southern end of the Dead Sea.

Early surveys of the area reported no archaeological evidence uncovered at this site earlier than the Hellenistic Period.[66] Albright reported in 1942 that "the pottery is all Byzantine and Early Arabic, mostly the latter, since Zughar was a most flourishing town in the early Middle Ages, thanks to its sugar and indigo industries."[67] Sarna points out "remains of Roman and Nabatean settlements have been found here, but none from biblical times. The later Zoar is hardly likely to have been the city to which Lot fled."[68] Schaub, who excavated BeD, states that the 6th cent. Zoar on the Madaba map is not the same as the Middle Bronze age Zoar as listed in Genesis.[69] He reports:

> Although some have identified the Byzantine Zoara with the mound of Sheikh Issa, recent surveys have interpreted this site as dominantly Mamluk. It seems likely that Zoar was located in different areas of the Safi region throughout its history, with placement probably influenced by the changing shoreline of the Dead Sea and erosional patterns in Wadi el-Hasa. Umm et-Tawabin is the most likely identification for Zoar of the Nabatean-Roman period, and Qasr et-Tuba may offer a remnant of the Byzantine Zoar.[70]

Politis, a Greek archaeologist, reports that:

> A large settlement with substantial buildings adorned with mosaic floor pavements and enclosed by fortification walls reflecting those depicted on the Madaba map has been located in an area known as Khirbet Sheik 'Isa. Recent excavations here suggest

---

[59] Albright, "The Archæological Results of an Expedition to Moab and the Dead Sea," 8.

[60] Albright, "The Jordan Valley in the Bronze Age," 58.

[61] Michael C. Astour, "Zoar (Place)," ed. David Noel Freedman et al., *ABD* (New York, N.Y.: Doubleday, 1996), 6:1107.

[62] Avraham Negev, "Zoar," in *AEHL*, 3rd ed. (New York: Prentice Hall Press, 1996), op. cit.

[63] Politis, "Death at the Dead Sea," 45.

[64] Ibid.; Anthony D. Saldarini, "Babatha's Story," *BAR* 24, no. 2 (1998): 29; Naphtali Lewis, Jonas C. Greenfield, and Yigael Yadin, eds., *The Documents from the Bar Kokhba Period in the Cave of Letters, Greek Papyri*, Judaean Desert Series 2 (Jerusalem: Israel Exploration Society, 1989); Ada Yardeni et al., eds., *The Documents from the Bar Kokhba Period in the Cave of Letters: Hebrew, Aramaic and Nabatean-Aramaic Papyri*, (Jerusalem: Israel Exploration Society, 2002), 1–4, 6–10.

[65] Donner, *Mosaic Map of Madaba*, op. cit.; Avi-Yonah, *Madaba Mosaic Map*, 42–43 pl. 4.

[66] Palmer, *The Desert of the Exodus*, 1:1:29; Alexis Mallon, "Biblica" 10 (1929): 438; Albright, "The Jordan Valley in the Bronze Age," 57; Sue Rollin and Jane Streetly, *Jordan*, 3rd ed., Blue Guide (London, U.K.: A & C Black, 2001), 164–65.

[67] Albright, "The Archæological Results of an Expedition to Moab and the Dead Sea," 4.

[68] Sarna, *Genesis*, 388–89.

[69] Schaub, "Southeast Dead Sea Plain," 5:64.

[70] Walter E. Rast and R. Thomas Schaub, "Expedition to the Dead Sea Plain," 5:64, accessed December 4, 2008, http://www.nd.edu/~edsp/.

this was the urban center of Byzantine Zoara.[71]

Again Politis states:

> Although the exact date of this Old Testament story is contested, it is placed some time in the Bronze Age, 2300–1700 BC. The Ghor es-Safi has a plethora of archaeological remains from this period which seem strangely to attest to the Biblical episode. . . . Specifically, in the vicinity of Khirbet Sheik 'Issa where the ancient city of Zoar once stood, and at Al Naqe its adjacent cemetery.[72]

However, Politis goes on to state that as of 1994 "no official archaeological excavations have ever taken place in Safi."[73] Following his excavations, Politis' early optimism about eṣ-Ṣafi being biblical Zoar changed as it has not produced the evidence he had predicted. Politis' own archaeological work (1998–2005) revealed that the ancient site of Khirbet ash-Shaykh 'Īsā is about 0.5 km from the modern village of eṣ-Ṣafi and the cemetery at An-Naqʿ, and has only evidence of settlements from the Iron Age II settlement,[74] Byzantine,[75] and Islamic periods (Islamic ceramic evidence from the Umayyad, Abbasid (8th cent. AD), and Mamluk (*ca.* 15th cent. AD) periods).[76]

Politis does identify Khirbat ash-Shaykh 'Īsā with Byzantine Zoar, and there is no question that Zoar was commemorated south of the Dead Sea in the Byzantine period, with the placing of it on the Madaba Map; however, how does this help in locating the ancient site of Sodom? Even though Bishop Severos of Sodom, who attended the Nicaean Council, was known in Byzantine times, there is no identification of Sodom on the Madaba Map, unless it is site 2 in Figure 5, which is unnamed.

Schaub who has spent years excavating the southern Dead Sea Plain lists some of the options:

> Although some have identified the Byzantine Zoara with the mound of Sheikh Issa, recent surveys have interpreted this site as dominantly Mamluk. It seems likely that Zoar was located in different areas of the Safi region throughout its history, with placement probably influenced by the changing shoreline of the Dead Sea and erosional patterns in Wadi el-Hasa. Umm et-Tawabin is the most likely identification for Zoar of the Nabatean-Roman period, and Qasr et-Tuba may offer a remnant of the Byzantine Zoar. The monastic complex at ʿAin Abata with the Lot inscription may be identified with the building on the Madaba map with the notation "Agios L(ot)." Tawahin es-Sukkar, and perhaps the mound of Sheikh Issa, represents the flourishing Zughar of the Mamluk period.[77]

And even if the identification of Zoar is eṣ-Ṣafi in the southern region, it could have been reached from both TeH and BeD, so it does not help in locating Sodom.

Northern Zoar 1 – *Tall Iktanu*

Merrill proposes Tall Iktanu (also Ektanu) for the location of Zoar, which is located on highway 80 in the northern Jordan Valley (see Map 8). He associated the Arabic name with the Hebrew name *katan* meaning "little."[78] Merrill states based on the direction and distance from his other northern sites that:

> I think there are unanswerable arguments in favour of the opinion that the "cities of the plain" were situated at the north end of the Dead Sea, and upon

---

[71] Konstantinos D. Politis, "The Monastery of Aghios Lot at Deir 'Ain 'Abata in Jordan," in *Byzanz – Das Römerreich Im Mittelalter*, ed. Falko Daim and Jörg Drauschke, 3 (Mainz: Römisch-Germanischen Zentralmuseums, 2010), 1.

[72] Politis, "Biblical Zoar: The Looting of an Ancient Site," 12.

[73] Ibid., 13.

[74] Politis et al., "Survey and Excavations in the Ghawr as-Safi 2004," 314.

[75] David F. Graf, "Zoora Rises from the Grave: New Funerary Stelae from Palaestina Tertia," *JRA* 22 (2009): 752–58.

[76] Politis et al., "Survey and Excavations in the Ghawr as-Safi 2004," 318; Konstantinos D. Politis et al., "Survey and Excavations in the Ghawr as-Safi 2006-07," *ADAJ* 51 (2007): 199–210; Konstantinos D. Politis, Adamantios Sampson, and Margaret O'Hea, "Ghawr As-Safi Survey and Excavations 2008-2009," *ADAJ* 53 (2009): 303–304.

[77] Schaub, "Southeast Dead Sea Plain," 64.

[78] Merrill, *East of the Jordan*, 236–39.

the mounds whose names [Tel Kefrein, Tel er Rama, Suweimeh, Tall el Hammam] I have given, and that Tel Ektanu is identical with the site of ancient Zoar.[79]

Excavated by Kay Prag between 1987 and 1990, Early Bronze I and II (ca. 3200–2800 BC) and Intermediate EB–MB (=EB IV) occupations were identified.[80]

Northern Zoar 2 – Serâbît el-Mushaqqar

Culver argues on the basis of the textual evidence and "against ancient traditions and current scholarship, the present writer [Culver] prefers this northern area as the location of Zoar and the rest of the Pentapolis."[81]

Taylor documents that *Ṣo'ar* (Gr. Σηγώρ *Segor*) is identified as the Arabic *Siyagha*, and the modern village of el-Makhayyat (or el-Mushaqqar). He recounts how the Piacenza Pilgrim writes:

> From the Jordan it is eight miles to the place where Moses departed from this life, and a little further on is Segor . . . . and we saw too the tomb of Absalom" (Piacenza Pilgrim *Itin.* 10:166). This may relate to one of the few identifiable places in the Copper Scroll (3Q15: 12–13). The place where Moses died is identified at Ras el-Siyagha, ancient Mount Nebo (Eg. 12: 1; Theodosius *Top.* 19:145; John Rufus *Vita Per. Iber.* 85–9),[82] which means the tomb of Absalom was located somewhere nearby. Segor here appears to relate to the Arabic name "Siyagha", which may then preserve an ancient name. Ruins from the Early Bronze Age and Iron Age have been found around the Hellenistic-Byzantine settlement at *modern el-Makhayyat, which were perhaps identified with Segor of old*, and it is interesting to note the presence of a number of Iron Age tombs[83] [emphasis added].[84]

Birch was the first to identify *Tell eš-Šāġūr* (Hill of Zoar) with Σηγώρ (Gr. *Segor* or *Ṣo'ar*) since, as he argues, the Hebrew "Z" sometimes becomes "Sh" in Arabic.[85] The American Expedition Society map, published in 1875, places *Tell eš-Šāġūr* (*Tell esh Shaghur; Um Sheggar;* or *M'Shuggar*) "as a hill just on the south bank of Wady Hesban near the foot of the mountains, a mile east of Tell er-Rameh."[86] They may be referring to Merrill's Tall Iktanu[87] as it is also about one and a half miles east of Tell er-Rameh and there are no other significant tells between them, except TeH.

However, from Birch's description of the etymology of the name, he concludes that

> it seems, then to me that in *Tell esh Shâghur*, happily marked on the American map, we have the very site and name of ancient Zoar. The native name clings to the neighbourhood. Mr. Finn speaks of *Um Sheggar*; Dr. Tristram of *M'Shuggar*; the American map also gives *Mushâqqâr*.[88]

There is a site called *Serâbît el-Mushaqqar* (See Maps 2, 4, 5, and 7)[89] 3 km from the

---

[79] Merrill, "Modern Researches in Palestine, PEFSt.," 149.

[80] Prag, "Excavations at Tell Iktanu, 1987," 33–45; "Excavations at Tell Iktanu, 1989," 119–30; "Tell Iktanu and Tall El-Hammam 1990," 55–57; "Tell Iktanu and Tell Al-Hammam. Excavations in Jordan," 15–19; "The Excavations at Tell Iktanu 1989 and 1990," 269–73; de Vries, "Archaeology in Jordan," 515.

[81] Robert D. Culver, "Zoar," in *ZPEB*, ed. Merrill C. Tenney and Moisés Silva, Revised, Full-Color Edition, vol. 5 (Grand Rapids, Mich.: Zondervan, 2009), 5:1240.

[82] Theodosius, "Topografia: The Topography of the Holy Land," 103–16; Horn and Phenix Jr., *John Rufus*.

[83] Sylvester J. Saller and Bellarmino Bagatti, *The Town of Nebo (Khirbet El-Mekhayyat): With a Brief Survey of Other Ancient Christian Monuments in Transjordan*, Publications of the Studium Biblicum Franciscanum 7 (Jerusalem: Franciscan, 1949); Sylvester J. Saller, "Iron Age Tombs at Nebo, Jordan," *LASBF* 16 (1966): 165–298.

[84] Taylor, "The Dead Sea in Western Travellers' Accounts," 11–12.

[85] Birch, "Zoar," 17.

[86] Ibid., 18; Power, "The Site of the Pentapolis: Part 1," 32 n. 2.

[87] Merrill, *East of the Jordan*, 236–39.

[88] Birch, "Zoar," 17.

[89] Sylvester J. Saller, *The Memorial of Moses on Mount Nebo I: The Text; II: The Plates*, Studium Biblicum Franciscanum Collection 1 (Jerusalem: Studium Biblicum Franciscanum, 1941), 1:6–7, 2:Plate 6, 1.

modern village by the name of *el-Mushaqqar*.[90] During the 1973 survey "13 fragments of 12 milestones [Roman mile markers]"[91] which bore Latin inscriptions that stated it was 5 Roman miles to Livias (TeH which is -160 meters below sea level) were located here.[92] This is located 360 meters above sea level, on the Roman road going up Mt. Nebo to Esbus (*Essebōn*, Tall Hesban, or Heshbon; Eusebius *On.* 12. 18; 48; 136). As Birch states "At *Tell esh Shâghur* begins the ascent of the pass to Hesbon [*sic* Heshbon]."[93] There is only early IA pottery at the site, but a significant MB site at *Khirbet Qarn al Qubish (Kh. Qurn el-Kibsh)* is only 3 km east of *Serâbît el-Mushaqqar* and 1 km south of *el-Mushaqqar* (See Map 7, 8).[94]

It certainly would meet the biblical requirements; in that it is small. However, Schumacher rejects this location for Zoar, based on the testimony of Arab geographers Yakut and Mokaddasi, who place Zoar in the south at Segor (Sughar or Zughar).[95]

Northern Zoar 3 – On the Arnon River

Collins proposes that Zoar is a "port" on the Arnon River moved to the Bay of Mazra'a, since it was the southern border for the land of Israel promised to Moses (Deut 2:4–5, 9; 34:1–4; Josh 13:9–10).[96] Also, *eṣ-Ṣafi* is located well inside the territories of Moab and Edom which "were off-limits to the Israelites" (Deut 2:4–5, 9).[97] Neev and Emery also support his view:

> As Zoar of the first century A.D. was a seaport, it had to be on the shore and must have been north of [the paved Roman road traversing the Lisan] or near the head of the Bay of Mazra'a [at the south end of the north basin]. The absence of any geographic indication for the [Lisan] peninsula's existence on the Madaba Map leads to a similar conclusion. Such an outstanding and picturesque tongue-like shore would not have been overlooked by the artist-cartographer of that map. . . . [They further state that] postures of two cargo vessels portrayed on the Madaba Map imply that the main traffic was between Zoar, port at the southeast corner of the north basin, and the north coast as close as possible to Jericho, the gate to Judea. The Bay of Mazra'a was always the main, if not the only, natural deepwater haven . . . . If Zoar were at Es-Safi, it never could have functioned as an efficient harbor.[98]

The difficulty with this location is the absence of any ruins apart from a Roman port at this location. Collins responds that the name Zoar means "small, insignificant." Collins argues: "On this basis I have always suggested that it probably had little or no permanent architecture in the Bronze Age and was substantially a "tent city" near a perennial water source such as a spring or surface flow."[99]

While this theory is plausible it is certainly difficult to prove or support. But with four, possibly more, locations for Zoar and none proven, the question whether Zoar can help in the location of Sodom is still open. There are various potential northern and southern locations for Zoar.

FACT 34: LOT'S CAVE IS LOCATED ON THE MADABA MAP

In 1983, Lot's cave at Deir Ain Abata, near eṣ-Ṣafi, Jordan, was discovered by H. Donner

---

[90] Saller and Bagatti, *Town of Nebo (Khirbet El-Mekhayyat)*.

[91] Another milestone was located at the VIIIth mile during the 2010 survey by Graves and another milestone in 2011.

[92] S. D. Waterhouse and R. Ibach, "Heshbon 1973: The Topographical Survey," *AUSS* 13 (1975): 221.

[93] Birch, "Zoar," 17.

[94] Glueck, *Explorations in Eastern Palestine II*, 111.

[95] Gottlieb Schumacher, *Across the Jordan: Being an Exploration and Survey of Part of Hauran and Jaulan* (London, U.K.: Watt, 1889), 317–21.

[96] Collins, "Rethinking the Location of Zoar," 1–5; "The Geography of Sodom and Zoar," 1–14.

[97] Collins, "Rethinking the Location of Zoar," 2.

[98] Neev and Emery, *The Destruction of Sodom, Gomorrah and Jericho*, 131–38.

[99] Collins, "Rethinking the Location of Zoar," 3; Collins, *The Search for Sodom and Gomorrah*, 15.

THE LOCATION OF SODOM

27. Drawing of the Monastery of St. Lot at Deir 'Ain 'Abata, Jordan, on display in the Museum at the Lowest Place on Earth at es-Safi.

Illustration by James M. Farrant

and E. A. Knauf. Between 1988 and 1996, Greek archaeologist Konstantinos D. Politis and staff from the British Museum excavated the proposed venerated site of Lot's cave. The site is identified on the Madaba Map above Zoora (Zoar; see Fig. 8). During the Byzantine period a Church was built over the cave and a monastery was established to venerate the location of Lot's cave.[100]

The display text in the Museum of the Lowest Point on Earth at eṣ-Ṣafi, under the direction of Politis, states:

> Three architectural fragments with Greek inscriptions alluding to Lot were also found on the site [of the church]. Literary and archaeological evidence suggests that it was a pilgrimage site, based around a natural cave that was believed to have been where Lot took refuge with his daughters after the destruction of Sodom and Gomorrah (Gen 19). The excavations revealed an Early Byzantine monastery complex, with a church built over the cave. The church was adorned with six mosaic pavements, dated by inscriptions to 572–3, 605–7 and 692 respectively—the latest dating from after the Islamic conquest of the area.[101]

The 7th cent. Byzantine church built in front of the cave had a mosaic with a dedication to "St Lot". Politis also reports that:

> Roman-period finds suggest an earlier veneration of the site. The additional discovery of substantial Early and Middle Bronze Age remains indicates that the cave was occupied during the period when, it is thought, the Genesis story occurred.[102]

While the cave did have EB[103] and MB[104] pottery (along with Hellenistic, Roman, Byzantine, Umayyad, and 'Abbasid[105]), there was no archaeological evidence which directly linked the cave to Lot. As there are many caves in the side of the mountains all along the Dead Sea (i.e., Qumran), and many people lived in the area during the EB and MB periods (i.e., the large cemeteries at BeD, Numeira, eṣ-Ṣafi, Feifeh, and Khanazir; see *Fact 43*), there was nothing special about this cave which connected it to Lot, other than Roman/Byzantine tradition that people used it during antiquity. The early Byzantine Christians often venerated sites to draw pilgrims and thus the inscriptions placed on the floor of the church were commemorating

---

[100] Konstantinos D. Politis, "Where Lot's Daughters Seduced Their Father Excavations Reveal Commemorative Monastery," *BAR* 30, no. 1 (2004): 20–31, 64; "The Monastery of Aghios Lot at Deir 'Ain 'Abata in Jordan"; *Sanctuary of Lot at Deir 'Ain 'Abata in Jordan Excavations 1988–2003* (Amman: Jordan Distribution Agency, 2012).

[101] Text displayed in the "Museum at the Lowest Place on Earth," Jordan.

[102] Konstantinos D. Politis, "The Lost Cities of Sodom and Gomorrah," in *The Seventy Great Mysteries of the Ancient World: Unlocking the Secrets of Past Civilizations*, ed. Brian M Fagan (New York: Thames & Hudson, 2001), 37.

[103] Politis, *Sanctuary of Lot at Deir 'Ain 'Abata in Jordan Excavations 1988–2003*, 31–36.

[104] Ibid., 57–78; Michele Piccirillo, ed., "Ricerca Storico-Archeologica In Giordania 16 - 1996," *LASBF* 46 (1996): 413–14.

[105] Politis, *Sanctuary of Lot at Deir 'Ain 'Abata in Jordan Excavations 1988–2003*, 108–114, 179–366.

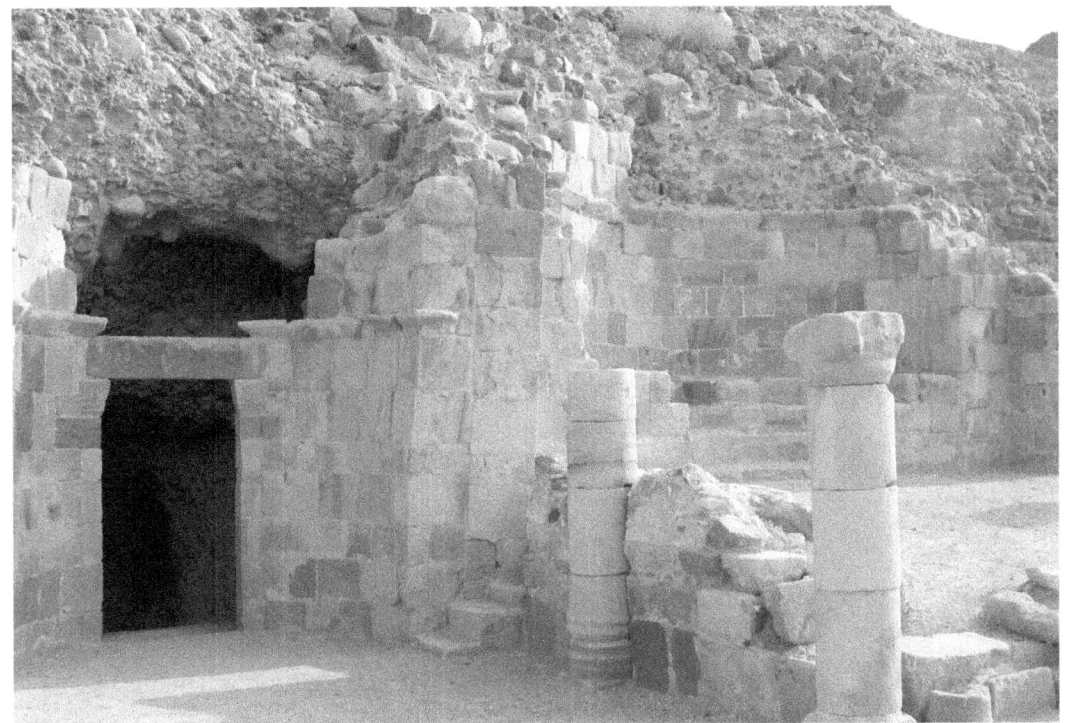

28. The restoration of the 7th cent. Byzantine church in front of Lot's Cave.

this as a holy site in typical Byzantine tradition.

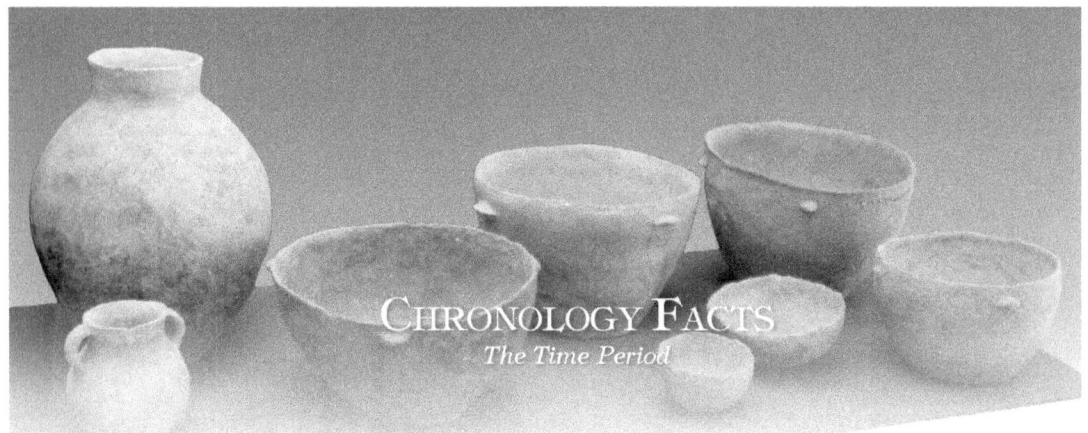

CHRONOLOGY FACTS
The Time Period

Chronology and dating is the Gordian Knot of archaeology and is always a difficult, complex maze to unravel. The chronological facts in this chapter will be useful in helping to untangle the dates of the events surrounding the location of Sodom. As will become apparent, this is the crux of the issue and the most important area of disagreement in the controversy between the SST and the NST.

FACT 35: NOT ALL ARCHAEOLOGISTS APPROACH BIBLICAL NUMBERS IN THE SAME WAY

An issue which affects chronology is the different methods of handling biblical numbers. Wood proposes a literal chronology using base-10 hard numbers.[1] Wood states that he bases his dating scheme on "a straightforward reading of the chronological data in the Old Testament."[2]

29. Early Bronze pottery identified by the characteristic ledge handles on their kraters and double handled cooking pots both display a puncture decoration around the rim. from Tomb G2 at Bab Edh-Dhra now displayed in The British Museum

By contrast, Collins uses a different method of accounting for numbers, also employed by other conservative evangelical scholars,[3] where he treats the years as "formulaic/honorific" or authentic.[4] He states: "I do take the number [440] as formulaic and not literal in the arithmetic sense, and I rely on historical synchronisms to link the Exodus to Egyptian history."[5]

Collins goes on to explain "in terms of its original cultural context.... Authentic may equate to literal if that's what the writer intended."[6]

This explains why two otherwise conservative scholars both arrive at conclusions with such a large spread between the dates of the Patriarchs.

---

[1] Wood, "Locating Sodom: A Critique of the Northern Proposal," 81; Eugene H. Merrill, *Kingdom of Priests: A History of Old Testament Israel*, 2nd ed. (Grand Rapids, Mich.: Baker Academic, 2008), 83–96; "Fixed Dates in Patriarchal Chronology," *BSac* 137, no. 547 (1980): 241–51; "Texts, Tells, and Old Testament Chronology," 20–21; Edwin Richard Thiele, *The Mysterious Numbers of the Hebrew Kings: A Reconstruction of the Chronology of the Kingdoms of Israel and Judah*, revised (Grand Rapids, Mich.: Kregel Academic & Professional, 1994).

[2] Wood, "Locating Sodom: A Critique of the Northern Proposal," 81.

[3] David Mark Fouts, "A Defense of the Hyperbolic Interpretation of Large Numbers in the Old Testament," *JETS* 40 (1997): 377–87; "The Demographics of Ancient Israel," *BRB* 7, no. 2 (2007): 1–10; Carol A. Hill, "Making Sense of the Numbers of Genesis," *Perspectives on Science and Christian Faith* 55, no. 4 (2003): 239–51; Andrew E. Steinmann, "The Mysterious Numbers Of the Book of Judges," *JETS* 48 (2005): 491–500.

[4] Collins, "Tall El-Hammam Is Still Sodom," 4; "Tall El-Hammam Is Sodom," 6.

[5] Collins, "Tall El-Hammam Is Still Sodom," 8.

[6] Collins and Scott, *Discovering the City of Sodom*, 138.

FACT 36: CONSERVATIVE SCHOLARS DEBATE THE DATE OF THE EXODUS

The date of the Patriarchs is determined in large part by the date of the Exodus and then worked backwards. The generally accepted dates for the Exodus among conservative scholars fall into two camps: the early dates (1491[7], 1461[8], 1447[9], 1446[10], 1445,[11] 1430[12] BC LBIIA) and the late dates (1300,[13] 1290[14], 1270–1230,[15] 1260[16] BC LBIIB).[17] Collins argues for what he calls "a middle date" between 1416–1386 BC, in the eighteenth Dynasty and during the reign of Pharaoh Tutmoses IV.[18]

What is clear in this brief, and certainly not exhaustive, sampling of dates is that there is no consensus even within each camp as to the exact date of the Exodus.[19] The conservative scholar, Charles Pfeiffer, commented four decades ago with a statement, which is still relevant, that: "the evidence for the historicity of the Exodus account is decisive, but the evidence for the specific date is still inconclusive."[20]

To further complicate the matter, conservative scholars hold to both early and late dates for the Exodus. While the early date is often categorized as the view of conservative theologians, the late date is also held by many eminent conservative biblical scholars and archaeologists[21] (see dates

---

[7] Floyd Nolen Jones, *Chronology of the Old Testament: A Return to the Basics* (Green Forest, Ark.: Master Books, 2004), 53.

[8] E. W Faulstich, *History, Harmony and the Hebrew Kings* (Spencer, Iowa: Chronology Books, 1986), 196–200.

[9] Tutmose III would be the Pharaoh of the oppression and Amenhoptep II would be the Pharaoh of the Exodus. Hoerth and McRay, *Bible Archaeology*, 82; J. Randall Price, *The Stones Cry Out: What Archaeology Reveals About the Truth of the Bible* (Eugene, Oreg.: Harvest House, 1997), 129.

[10] Bryant G. Wood, "The Rise and Fall of the 13th-Century Exodus-Conquest Theory," *JETS* 48, no. 3 (2005): 488; James K. Hoffmeier, "What Is the Biblical Date for the Exodus? A Response to Bryant Wood," *JETS* 50, no. 2 (2007): 225–47; Bryant G. Wood, "The Biblical Date for the Exodus Is 1446 BC: A Response to James Hoffmeier," *JETS* 50, no. 2 (2007): 249–58.

[11] Charles H. Dyer, "The Date of the Exodus Reexamined," *BSac* 140, no. 559 (1983): 225–43.

[12] John J. Bimson, *Redating the Exodus and Conquest*, 2nd ed., JSOT Supplement Series 5 (Sheffield, U.K.: Almond, 1981), Part 2; John Van Seters, "Review of John J. Bimson, Redating the Exodus and Conquest," *The Journal of Egyptian Archaeology* 70 (1984): 180–82.

[13] Brad C. Sparks, "Egyptian Text Parallels to the Exodus: The Egyptology Literature," in *Out of Egypt: Israel's Exodus Between Text and Memory, History and Imagination Conference*, ed. Thomas E. Levy (Qualcomm Institute, University of California, San Diego, 2013), https://www.youtube.com/watch?v=F-Aomm4O794.

[14] Hoerth and McRay, *Bible Archaeology*, 83; Price, *The Stones Cry Out*, 130; Charles F. Aling, "Historical Synchronisms and the Date of the Exodus," *Artifax* 17, no. 2 (n.d.): 19.

[15] Kenneth A. Kitchen and T. C. Mitchell, "Chronology of the Old Testament," ed. I. Howard Marshall et al., *NBD* (Downers Grove, Ill.: InterVarsity, 1996), 191; Kitchen, *Reliability of the OT*, 307–311.

[16] Kitchen, *Reliability of the OT*, 159, 307, 359.

[17] Rameses II (1279-1213 BC) would be the Pharaoh of both the oppression and the Exodus. Lawrence T. Geraty, "Dates for the Exodus I Have Known," in *Out of Egypt: Israel's Exodus Between Text and Memory, History and Imagination Conference* (Qualcomm Institute, University of California, San Diego, 2013), https://www.youtube.com/watch?v=6MM2ao1euTU.

[18] Collins and Scott, *Discovering the City of Sodom*, 140; Steven Collins, *Let My People Go!: Using Historical Synchronisms to Identify the Pharaoh of the Exodus* (Albuquerque, N.M.: TSU Press, 2012); "Using Historical Synchronisms to Identify the Pharaoh of the Exodus," *BRB* 5, no. 7 (2005): 1–70.

[19] Omar Zuhdi, "Dating the Exodus: A Study in Egyptian Chronology," *KMT: A Modern Journal of Ancient Egypt* 4, no. 2 (1993): 15–27.

[20] Charles F. Pfeiffer, "Exodus," in *The New International Dictionary of the Bible*, ed. Merrill C. Tenney and James D. Douglas (Grand Rapids: Zondervan, 1987), 333.

[21] R. K Harrison, *Introduction to the Old Testament* (Grand Rapids: Eerdmans, 1969), 115–16; Donald J. Wiseman, *1 and 2 Kings: An Introduction and Commentary*, Tyndale Old Testament Commentaries (Downers

above).²² James K. Hoffmeier, Professor of Near Eastern Archaeology and Old Testament at Trinity Evangelical Divinity School, states:

> many conservative scholars are adherents of the so-called "early" date [1446 BC]. Unfortunately for some, this date has become a sort of litmus test for one's evangelical orthodoxy. This is lamentable, because I believe that the 13th-century date [late date] is equally based on biblical evidence.²³

Steven M. Ortiz, the Professor of Archaeology and Biblical Backgrounds and Director of the Charles D. Tandy Institute for Archaeology at Southwestern Baptist Theological Seminary, also maintains a late date for the Exodus, placing it in the 13th cent. BC.²⁴

The dates for the Exodus are calculated based on the statement in Exodus 12:40 about the 430 years of travel.²⁵ But when does this period begin and end? Wood follows the Masoretic text (MT),²⁶ while Collins follows the Septuagint (LXX) reading, which is supported by the MT patriarchal chronologies, the Samaritan Pentateuch (SP), the apostle Paul (Gal 3:16–17), and Josephus who claimed that the sojourn was 215 years in Canaan and 215 years in Egypt (*Ant.* 2.15.2).²⁷

Depending on when one places the date of the Exodus, the date of the Patriarchs also moves to arrive in different periods.

FACT 37: MOST MAXIMALISTS BELIEVE THAT THE PATRIARCHS LIVED IN THE MIDDLE BRONZE AGE

Most conservative evangelical scholars and maximalists (see Introduction) would place the period of the Patriarchs (including Abraham and Lot) in the Middle Bronze Age (See Charts 2, 4, 5 and 6). This is based not so much on archaeological finds as on correlating characteristics in the biblical text with the cultural markers of the MB periods. Scholars who hold to a MB I period for the Patriarchs base their position on the literal biblical chronology based on a mid–15th cent. BC date for the Exodus, the antiquity of the biblical accounts (Gen 14), the geopolitical conditions and climate of the regions in the MB I period, nomadism and migration exemplified in the domestication of camels, and personal names and places identified in MB texts from Egypt, Ur, Mari, Ebla, Nuzi and Anatolia (20th–18th cent. BC).²⁸ Those who support a MB IIA/B date for the Patriarchs rely on the 13th cent. BC date for the Exodus, the presence of the Hyksos in

---

Grove, Ill.: IVP Academic, 2008), 104; Caroline Masom, Pat Alexander, and Alan R. Millard, eds., *Picture Archive of the Bible* (Tring, Herts, UK: Lion, 1987), 22; R. Alan Cole, *Exodus*, Tyndale Old Testament Commentaries 2 (Downers Grove, Ill.: IVP Academic, 2008), 40–43; John D Currid, *A Study Commentary on Exodus*, An Evangelical Press Study Commentary (Auburn, Mass.: Evangelical, 2000), 27–29; Richard S Hess, *Joshua: An Introduction and Commentary*, Tyndale Old Testament Commentaries (Downers Grove, Ill.: InterVarsity, 1996), 139–43; Kitchen, *Ancient Orient*, 57–69; *The Bible in Its World* (Exeter, U.K.: Paternoster, 1977), 75–79; *Reliability of the OT*, 307–9.

²² Ralph K. Hawkins, "Propositions for Evangelical Acceptance of a Late-Date Exodus-Conquest: Biblical Data and the Royal Scarabs from Mt. Ebal," *JETS* 50, no. 1 (2007): 31–46.

²³ Hoffmeier, "What Is the Biblical Date for the Exodus?," 225.

²⁴ Steven M. Ortiz, "Hermeneutical and Methodological Comments on the History of the Conquest and Settlement: The Archaeological and Biblical Support for the 13th Century," in *Southwest Regional ETS Meetings* (Fort Worth, TX, 2006), 1.

²⁵ Paul J. Ray Jr., "The Duration of the Israelite Sojourn In Egypt," *BS* 17, no. 2 (2004): 33–45; Collins and Scott, *Discovering the City of Sodom*, 134–36, 139; Kitchen, *Reliability of the OT*, 307–308.

²⁶ Wood, "The Biblical Date for the Exodus Is 1446 BC," 249.

²⁷ Collins and Scott, *Discovering the City of Sodom*, 134–41; Collins, *Let My People Go!*

²⁸ John J. Bimson, "Archaeological Data and the Dating of the Patriarchs," in *Essays on the Patriarchal Narratives*, ed. Alan R. Millard and Donald J. Wiseman (Downers Grove, Ill.: InterVarsity, 1980), 59–92; Merrill, *Kingdom of Priests*, 47–48; "Texts, Talls, and Old Testament Chronology," 20–21.

Egypt, pottery in Negev, the Beni-Hasan mural (1890 BC), Middle kingdom Egyptian chronology, the geopolitical conditions (Gen 14), parallels with the MB culture and the price of slaves, and the structure of covenants.[29]

Collins explains some of the issues surrounding the question of chronology when he states:

> While high, middle, and low ANE chronologies exist—tied principally to the chronology(ies) of Egypt—the differences between them consist of one or two decades, not centuries [See Chart 2]. (I am talking about the well-worked-out chronologies of mainline scholars like W. F. Albright, K. Kenyon, A. Ben-Tor, B. Mazar, A. Mazar, K. A. Kitchen, D. Redford, Wente and Van Siclen, J. Hoffmeier, J. Currid, and W. Dever; not the fringe, radical revisions of ANE chronology suggested by D. Rohl, G. Aardsma, and a few others.).[30]

Based on Chart 4 below, almost all evangelical scholars place the Patriarchs in the Middle Bronze Age, including Wood (2166–1991 BC MB I) and Collins (2000–1600 MB IIA/B). Freedman and van Hattem place the Patriarchs in the EB age, to support a SST.[31]

The proponents who place them in the LB, Iron, and Persian/Greek periods are in the minority. Even Wood, who supports the idea of the EB destruction of BeD as supporting its claim on being Sodom, places the Patriarchs in the Middle Bronze I along with other scholars.[32] Wood acknowledges the discrepancy and explains:

> If we assume a mid–15th century BC date for the Exodus, the date for the destruction [of Sodom] would then be *ca.* 2070 BC. The archeological date for the destruction of Bab eh-Dhra and Numeira, however, is considerably earlier than this. . . . This leaves a discrepancy between the Biblical date and the archaeological date of 230–280 years.[33]

The fact remains that most evangelical scholars believe that the Patriarchs live in the MB period (2nd millennium BC).

FACT 38: BeD WAS DESTROYED IN THE EB III BUT WAS REOCCUPIED IN EB IV

The final excavation reports for Bâb edh-Dhrâ' have been published by Eisenbrauns, who specialize in publishing ANE material, and indicate at least five periods of occupation between *ca.* 3150 and 2200 BC.[34] The site was excavated between 1965 and 1967 by Paul Lapp prior to his early death.[35] Work was continued at the site by Walter E. Rast and R. Thomas Schaub, who excavated the site between 1975 and 1981[36] and they have published extensively on their finds. While they identified some Paleolithic and

---

[29] Kitchen, *Reliability of the OT*, 352–53; John E. Goldingay, "The Patriarchs in Scripture and History," in *Essays on the Patriarchal Narratives*, ed. Donald J. Wiseman and Alan R. Millard (Winona Lake, Ind.: Eisenbrauns, 1983), 11–42; Alan R. Millard, "Methods of Studying the Patriarchal Narratives as Ancient Texts," in *Essays on the Patriarchal Narratives*, ed. Donald J. Wiseman and Alan R. Millard (Winona Lake, Ind.: Eisenbrauns, 1983), 43–58; Nahum M Sarna, "The Patriarchs Genesis 12-36," in *Genesis: World of Myths and Patriarchs*, ed. Ada Feyerick, Cyrus Herzl Gordon, and Nahum M Sarna (New York, N.Y.: New York University Press, 1996), 117–66.

[30] Collins, "Tall El-Hammam Is Still Sodom," 10.

[31] Recently Kris Udd wrote his dissertation on the subject and states in his abstract "Combining the new lower archaeological chronologies and the higher dates for the patriarchs indicates the possibility that Bâb edh-Dhrâ'' and Numeira could be two of the biblical cities of the plain." Udd applies two extreme views to propose this speculative hypothesis. Kris J. Udd, "Bab Edh-Dhra', Numeira, and the Biblical Patriarchs: A Chronological Study" (Ph.D. diss., Andrews University, 2011).

[32] Wood, "Discovery of the Sin Cities," 78.

[33] Ibid.

[34] The dates and periods are according to Rast and Schaub.

[35] Rast and Schaub, *Bab Edh-Dhra': Excavations in the Cemetery*; Lapp, "Bab Edh-Dhra' (RB 1966)"; "Bab Edh-Dhra' Tomb A 76"; "Bab Edh-Dhra' (RB 1968)"; R. Thomas Schaub, "Bab Edh-Dhra' (OEANE)," in *OEANE*, ed. Eric M. Meyers, vol. 1 (Oxford, U.K.: Oxford University Press, 1997), 249.

[36] Rast and Schaub, *Bab Edh-Dhra': Excavations at the Town Site (1975-1981)*; Schaub, "Bab Edh-Dhra' (OEANE)," 1: 249.

pre-pottery Neolithic presence, the real history begins with a transient population of "pastoral nomads," evident mostly from tombs from the Chalcolithic, EB I (3200 BC), and EB IA (3250–3100 BC) periods.[37]

The permanent occupation dates to the EB IB (3150–3000), EB II and III (3000–2300).[38] Rast points out that:

> Although it is difficult to determine the exact time span of Early Bronze III Bab edh-Dhra, the fact that it had five major building phases would suggest that it lasted over a period of between 300 and 400 years, from *ca.* 2750 to 2350 B.C.[39]

Albright also correlated the dates of the tombs with the occupation of the city. He observed: "The burials [at Bâb edh-Dhrâ'] have been opened in several cases by Arabs and prove to date from the same period as the settlement."[40]

A massive EB III destruction took place around 2350 BC[41] or 2300 BC[42] for the fortified town and about 2250 BC for the unwalled rebuilt town. Additionally in this period the ANE suffered an unidentified regional catastrophe which affected life in Egypt and Mesopotamia.[43] It is speculative whether the two catastrophes of BeD and the rest of the ANE are connected.

Initially, in 1981, Rast and Schaub thought that "the EB IV peoples chose areas away from the town for settlement"[44] following the destruction of BeD at the end of the EBIII period. But new evidence, reported in their 1981 excavation reports, overturned this belief:

> A number of pits cut in the area also belonged to the EBIV settlement. This is the first clear evidence within the city of an EBIV usage following the destruction in EBIII necessitating a change in the previous view.[45] Several excellent groups of EBIV pottery came from these loci.[46]

Rast and Schaub, following their excavations of BeD and Numeira in 1981 state:

> What the double destruction with its human victims suggests to us is that about 2400 BC, or shortly before, the political situation in the Dead Sea valley had become unstable. Perhaps some limited assault was attempted against the two cities, as suggested by the first destruction with its human victim at Numeira, as well as by the decision to block the big western gate at Bâb edh-Dhrâ' and construct the two-tower gate at the less accessible northeastern end of the site. In not more than fifty years both sites experienced an apparent destruction, after which Numeira was abandoned altogether and Bâb edh-Dhrâ' resettled by people employing a different plan. It still remains unknown how to account for the termination of the two sites around 2350 BC. It is always possible that some natural phenomenon such as earthquake occurred, but destruction by

---

[37] Walter E. Rast, "Bronze Age Cities along the Dead Sea," *Archaeology* 40, no. 1 (1987): 44; "Patterns of Settlement at Bab Edh-Dhra'," in *The Southeastern Dead Sea Plain Expedition: An Interim Report of the 1977 Season*, ed. R. Thomas Schaub and Walter E. Rast, AASOR 46 (Boston, Mass.: American Schools of Oriental Research, 1979), 7–9; Schaub, "Bab Edh-Dhra' (NEAEHL)," 1:131–32.

[38] Rast, "Patterns of Settlement at Bab Edh-Dhra'," 9–31; Rast, "Bronze Age Cities along the Dead Sea," 46–47; Schaub, "Bab Edh-Dhra' (NEAEHL)," 1: 132–35.

[39] Rast, "Bronze Age Cities along the Dead Sea," 47.

[40] Albright, "The Jordan Valley in the Bronze Age," 59.

[41] Rast, "Bronze Age Cities along the Dead Sea," 47; "Bab Edh-Dhra' (ABD)," 1:560; "Bab Edh-Dhra' and the Origin of the Sodom Saga," 194.

[42] Schaub, "Bab Edh-Dhra' (OEANE)," 1:249.

[43] Nicolas Grimal, *A History of Ancient Egypt* (Oxford, U.K.: Wiley-Blackwell, 1994), 137ff; Donald B. Redford, *Egypt, Canaan, and Israel in Ancient Times* (Princeton, N.J.: Princeton University Press, 1993), 63–64; Susan Pollock, *Ancient Mesopotamia: The Eden That Never Was* (Cambridge, Mass.: Cambridge University Press, 1999), 117–48.

[44] Walter E. Rast and R. Thomas Schaub, "A Preliminary Report of Excavations at Bab Edh-Dhra', 1975," in *Preliminary Excavation Reports: Bab Edh-Dhrac, Sardis, Meiron, Tell El-Hesi, Carthage (Punic)*, ed. David Noel Freedman, AASOR 43 (Chicago, Ill.: American Schools of Oriental Research, 1978), 14.

[45] Ibid.

[46] Rast, "Patterns of Settlement at Bab Edh-Dhra'," 17.

human force cannot be ruled out.⁴⁷

Rast, in 1987, continued to theorize about the resettlement of BeD following its destruction, highlighting that this is one of the major differences with Numeira:

> Obviously the town [Numeira] suffered a severe fire and it was forever abandoned. But Bab edh-Dhra shows a different picture following its destruction. Here a population living during what is called the Early Bronze IV period (2350 BC–2100 BC) settled at the site, in several cases above the burned ruins of the former city, but mostly in the flatter areas to the north, east and south of the ruined city.⁴⁸

In 2003, Rast and Schaub postulated that the destruction in EB IV [2350–2100 BC] was due to lack of water:

> Preliminary environmental survey had indicated that conditions, including favorable water supplies (chapter 2) were at their prime during EB III, while in EB IV deflation of resources led to the long-term abandonment of the southern Ghor.⁴⁹

BeD was not permanently abandoned but resettled for about 100 years until the water dried up.

Chesson describes the transition between the EB III and EB IV occupation:

> Following a short period of abandonment, Stratum I (EB IV) people resettled here in an unwalled village. Structures associated with this period included a sanctuary along the northern ridge of the town and houses and courtyards to the east and south of the town.⁵⁰

Chesson observes that the change from the urban settlement of EB III is reflected in the change in burial practices, which return to the use of shaft tombs in EB IV, which were also used by the pastoral nomads of EBII, instead of the earlier EB III charnel houses. She explains that:

> the character of the EB IV settlement at Bab edh-Dhra' changes, and people are no longer living within a physically bounded community. In fact, some EB IV structures at the site were built on top of the ruined EB III fortifications walls, while the majority of the posturban structures were located outside the urban settlement.⁵¹ For these reasons, I suggest that we see a return to the primacy of the household, with the extended family, as one of the basic structuring forces in this post-urban society. The primacy of the corporate House has eroded with the abandonment of the urban lifestyle, and the shift back to shaft tombs and away from urban living reflects the changes in peoples' fundamental ideological and social structures.⁵²

Rast and Schaub agree and explain:

> A comparative study of all of the basic tomb forms throughout the Early Bronze Age suggests that the "new" EB IV [2350–2100 BC] forms are similar to the basic forms of EB IB and may reflect a return to a simpler life pattern following the breakup of the town and its trading networks. A series of calibrated C-14 dates from Field X suggest a date of 2200 BC for the latest EB IVA phases of occupation.⁵³

---

⁴⁷ Rast and Schaub, "The Dead Sea Expedition," 10–11.

⁴⁸ Rast, "Bronze Age Cities along the Dead Sea," 48.

⁴⁹ Rast and Schaub, *Bab Edh-Dhra': Excavations at the Town Site (1975-1981)*, 7–8.

⁵⁰ Meredith S. Chesson and R. Thomas Schaub, "Life in the Earliest Walled Towns on the Dead Sea Plain: Numayra and Bab Edh-Dhra'," in *Crossing Jordan: North American Contributions to the Archaeology of Jordan*, ed. Thomas Evan Levy et al. (London, U.K.: Equinox, 2007), 247; Schaub, "Bab Edh-Dhra' (OEANE)," 1:249; Rast, "Bronze Age Cities along the Dead Sea," 48; "Patterns of Settlement at Bab Edh-Dhra'," 17, 31–34.

⁵¹ R. Thomas Schaub and Walter E. Rast, *The Southeastern Dead Sea Plain Expedition: An Interim Report of the 1977 Season*, AASOR 46 (Boston, Mass.: American Schools of Oriental Research, 1979), 31–34.

⁵² Meredith S. Chesson, "Libraries of the Dead: Early Bronze Age Charnel Houses and Social Identity at Urban Bab Edh-Dhra', Jordan," *Journal of Anthropological Archaeology* 18 (1999): 161; Rast, "Bronze Age Cities along the Dead Sea," 48.

⁵³ Schaub, "Bab Edh-Dhra' (NEAEHL)," 1:136; Rast and Schaub, *Bab Edh-Dhra': Excavations in the Cemetery*; James M. Weinstein, "A New Set of Radiocarbon Dates from the Town Site," in *Bab Edh-Dhra': Excavations at the Town Site: 1975-1981: Part 1 Text*, ed. Walter E. Rast and R. Thomas Schaub, vol. 1, Reports of the Expedition to the Dead Sea Plain, Jordan 2 (Winona Lake, Ind.: Eisenbrauns, 2003), 648.

30. The site of Numeira looking west over the evaporation ponds of the Dead Sea and the Arab Potash Company (APC) on the shore.

The site was finally destroyed and abandoned after 2200[54]–2250 BC (EB IV).[55] Although Rast and Schaub question the reliability of some of their C-14 dates,[56] the evidence is clear that there was a reoccupation at BeD following the EB III destruction and hiatus with structural resettlement in the EB IV period.

FACT 39: BeD AND NUMEIRA WERE DESTROYED AT DIFFERENT TIMES

The destruction at Numeira is well documented. Rast and Schaub reported in 1977: "It [Numeira] was destroyed by fire toward the latter part of EB III and was not settled thereafter. Given the destruction debris, which sometimes reached a depth of 1.5 m the remains were unusually well preserved."[57]

The question is: Were BeD and Numeira destroyed at the same time? Initially in 1977 Jack Harlan, one of the BeD team members, reported: "Our present [1977] evidence suggests that Bâb edh-Dhrâʿ and Numeira were destroyed *ca.* 2350 BC, with only Bâb edh-Dhrâʿ being occupied during EB IV."[58]

The evidence at first suggested that the destruction occurred simultaneously. There was initial difficulty with the C-14 samples and the calibrated dates. But as apprehensive as Rast and Schaub were about the C-14 dates, they pointed out in 1980 that: "On the positive side, as a whole these dates tend to reinforce the ceramic evidence that EB III occupation at Bab edh-Dhraʿ and Numeira

---

[54] 2200 may be too early for the EBIV period based on suspicious C-14 dating. Schaub, "Bab Edh-Dhraʿ (NEAEHL)," 136.

[55] Rast and Schaub, *Bab Edh-Dhraʿ: Excavations in the Cemetery*.

[56] Rast et al., "Preliminary Report of the 1979 Expedition," 46–47.

[57] Rast, "Settlement at Numeira," 36.

[58] Jack R. Harlan, "Natural Resources of the Southern Ghor," in *The Southeastern Dead Sea Plain Expedition: An Interim Report of the 1977 Season*, ed. R. Thomas Schaub and Walter E. Rast, AASOR 46 (Boston, Mass.: American Schools of Oriental Research, 1979), 160.

came to an end probably within the same century."⁵⁹

Rast and Schaub were willing to isolate the destruction which occurred at the two sites to within 100 years of each other. However, as research progressed, and the C-14 dating was improved using better samples, the team began to re-examine the evidence and in 1981 acknowledged the implication of this issue and the need for further examination:

> Further study of the pottery from 1977 and future excavation of more of the site will be necessary to establish the relation between the destruction of Numeira in EB III and that at Bab edh-Dhra during the same period. It will be important to determine whether these two sites came to an end simultaneously and, thus, in connection with similar events, or whether their destruction took place at different times within EB III.⁶⁰

But in the same article Rast hints at the conclusion that BeD and Numeira may very well have met their ends at different times: "The possibility that Numeira lasted somewhat longer than the EB III city at Bâb edh-Dhrâʿ also cannot be ruled out."⁶¹

In 1987 Rast described the destruction of the two cities:

> These two towns [BeD and Numeira] also seem to have participated in a common fate, since ceramic evidence from carbon-14 tests have shown that they were *terminated at approximately the same time toward the end of EB III*.⁶² At Numeira the evidence is extensive that the town was burned during its last major phase, while the destruction of the EB III walled town at Bab edh-Dhra is attested by ruined and abandoned structures and by the demolished upper part of the town wall, the superstructure of which, made of mudbrick in some cases, had suffered exposure to fire [emphasis added].⁶³

Notice that Rast is careful not to say they were destroyed at *exactly* the same time but *approximately* the same time at the end of the EB III period.

Unlike BeD, Numeira was only occupied in the EB IB and EB III periods. The first occupation occurred in EB IB (3150–3000 BC) and was isolated to Ras an-Numayra. Several hundred years later the main settlement occurred in the EB III, identified as the pre-fortification phase, followed by another subphase that only lasted about 200 years, concluding in a final destruction in around 2600 BC.⁶⁴ In 2007, Schaub and Chesson speculated that it was an earthquake⁶⁵ that brought the final destruction in 2600 BC. They reported:

> The main occupational layers at an-Numayra were sealed by a major destruction with timber ash and debris in all areas. At the east end, at least two separate instances of collapses of the tower structure trapped several individuals whose articulated skeletons were found under the stone fall. It is possible that an earthquake⁶⁶ and later after-shocks may have brought about the demise of the town around 2600 BCE.⁶⁷

Wenham suggests that the destruction was not natural or supernatural but brought about through military means:

> Bab ed-Dhra (Sodom?) and Numeira were both destroyed about 2350 B.C. and then reoccupied for a short while. They were finally abandoned about 2200 or 2100 B.C. These dates are somewhat early for Abram, and the archeological evidence

---

⁵⁹ Rast et al., "Preliminary Report of the 1979 Expedition," 47.

⁶⁰ Rast, "Settlement at Numeira," 41.

⁶¹ Rast et al., "Preliminary Report of the 1979 Expedition," 46.

⁶² Ibid., 46–47.

⁶³ Rast, "Bab Edh-Dhraʿ and the Origin of the Sodom Saga," 194; Schaub and Rast, *The Southeastern Dead Sea Plain Expedition: 1977 Season*, 16–18.

⁶⁴ Chesson and Schaub, "Life in the Earliest Walled Towns," 247.

⁶⁵ See also Jack Donahue, "Geologic Reconstruction of Numeira," *BASOR* 255 (Summer 1984): 87.

⁶⁶ Michael David Coogan, "Numeira 1981," *BASOR* 255 (Summer 1984): 81.

⁶⁷ Chesson and Schaub, "Life in the Earliest Walled Towns," 247.

published to date suggests that a military attack rather than some (super)natural disaster led to the destruction of these sites.[68]

Another unusual feature of the final destruction of Numeira is that, as Coogan reports: "No human skeletal remains were found in the ashy debris of the final destruction in the center of town."[69] There were two skeletons in the east tower area. He speculates that the inhabitants left the city when the initial tremors were felt and were not in the city when the final quake took it out. Guards in the tower stayed behind to protect the city from looters.

While the early conclusions of Rast and Schaub, that BeD and Numeira were both destroyed at approximately the same time (i.e., 2350–2067 BC), are often reported, it is now held that their individual destructions were separated by approximately two and a half centuries, with the destruction of BeD at *ca.* 2350 BC and Numeira at *ca.* 2600 BC.

Fact 40: TeH was destroyed in the MBA and lay unoccupied for over 500 years

Preliminary reports, even as late as 2013, identified the terminal destruction of TeH in the MBA at *ca.* 1600 BC.[70] However later in 2013, following eight seasons of excavations and reading over 40,000 separate vessels,[71] Collins published that "our refined date-range for Tall el-Ḥammâm's destruction is 1750–1650 BCE, [MB IIB] not 1600."[72]

---

[68] Wenham, *Genesis 1-15*, 1:309.
[69] Coogan, "Numeira 1981," 81.
[70] Collins, "Where Is Sodom?," 70; Merrill, "Texts, Talls, and Old Testament Chronology," 1.
[71] Collins and Scott, *Discovering the City of Sodom*, 33.
[72] Collins, "Tall El-Hammam Is Still Sodom," 9; "Tall El-Hammam Is Sodom," 8; John Moore, "Dr. John Moore and Dr. Steven Collins Reflect on TeHEP's First Nine Years," *Update: Tall El-Hammam Excavation Project, The Official Newsletter of TeHEP*, April 11, 2014, 1; Collins and Scott, *Discovering the City of Sodom*, 226. This

In the 2015 report, after ten seasons Collins reports:

> The data through ten seasons of excavation support the existence of a general LBA occupational gap at TeH, with the exception of a modest, short-lived, singular LB2a structure excavated in 2015, likely a "waystation", "inn", or "tariff-house". Whatever caused the absence of settlements on the eastern Jordan Disk during the LBA/IA1 timeframe did, in fact, not continue, as most sites were resettled toward the end of Iron Age 1 into Iron Age 2. . . . Material from LB1 is systematically absent across the site. LB2a is missing in all sectors except for a short-lived, freestanding LB2a structure (tariff house?) in Field UA on the upper tall. (LB2a pottery vessels were found in a nearby tomb also containing forms dating from the Chalcolithic Period through the Iron Age.) No LB2b ceramics or structures have been identified at Tall el-Hammam.[73]

Since TeH is considered Abel-Shittim (see *Fact 27),* and Moses camped here with the Israelites for a few years, it is not surprising to find some LB pottery lying around, with no architecture dating[74] to the LB period.

TeH was reoccupied in the IA period. Collins reports:

> The Iron Age city is quite extensive on the upper tall, but at this point periodization/phasing is not entirely clear. Iron I pottery is infrequent at this point, but present (such as the IA1b pilgrim flask found in Field UB). The IA2b–c monumental gateway in Field UB has an earlier phase dating to IA2a (perhaps late IA1b), with the terminal phase dating to IA2c, perhaps IA3. The principal Iron Age city at Tall el-Hammam seems to have been built during IA2a–b. IA3 (Persian Period) sherds are present-but-infrequent at this point.[75]

Following the destruction of TeH in the MBA, it lay unoccupied for over 500 years only to be resettled in the IAII, about five centuries later.

---

has recently been confirmed by C-14 dating of organic material from the MB destruction strata.

[73] Steven Collins et al., "Tall El-Hammam Season Ten, 2015: Excavation, Survey, Interpretations and Insights," *BRB* 15, no. 1 (2015): 5, 29.

[74] Moses and the Israelites were camped in tents.
[75] Ibid., 13.

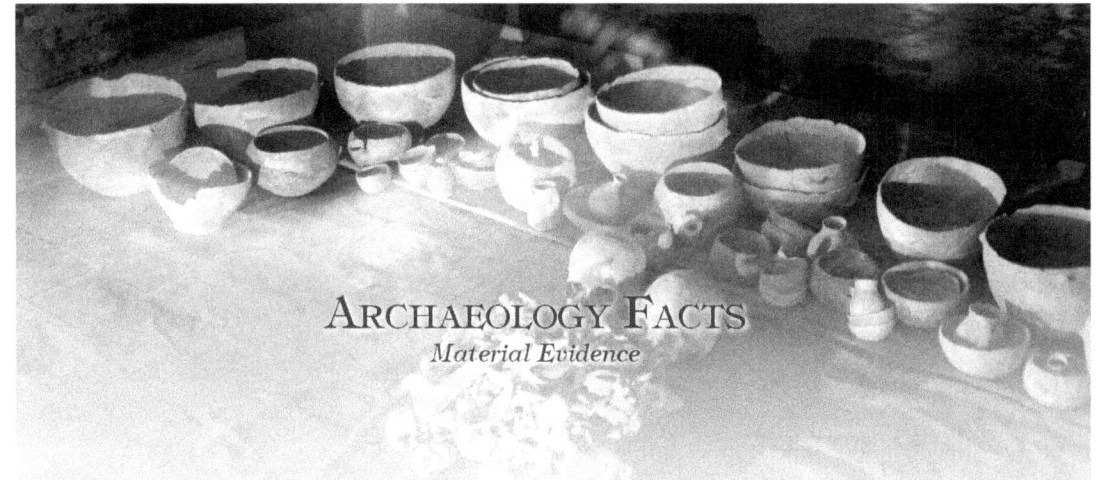

Archaeology Facts
Material Evidence

For identifying the city of Sodom, the material evidence found in the archaeological record is second in importance only to the geographic indicators. The evidence must correlate with what is known about the history of the cities from the biblical text. They must have existed during the time of the Patriarchs (Abraham and Lot; see *Fact 37*) and been destroyed by a catastrophic fire (fire and brimstone; Gen 19:24–25). This chapter will present the archaeological facts that are known about the two regions that have been proposed for the location of the Pentapolis.

Fact 41: TeH is the largest EB site and third largest MB site in the Southern Levant

Sometimes the claim is made that Bâb edh-Dhrâʿ is the largest EB site in the region, as it covers 10 acres. Certainly, this is true if one is talking about the southern end of the Dead Sea (see *Fact 42*). However, after eight seasons of excavations at TeH, Collins reports on it's enormous size. He states:

> Tall el-Hammam is the largest of the Jordan Disk sites. It is certainly one of the largest, if not the largest, Bronze Age site in Jordan. The tall proper spreads over approximately 36 ha[1] (360 dunams)[2]

31. Early Bronze age pottery displayed as it was discovered in the charnel house tombs at the Bâb edh-Dhrâʿ cemetery. Bones were placed in the centre of the room with the skulls lined around them and the various household pottery stacked around the perimeter of the room. The bedouin would drop off their decomposed deseased to be deposited at the Bâb edh-Dhrâʿ cemetery.

Museum at the Lowest Place on Earth, Jordan

> [89 acres] . . . . The site footprint for general settlement is well over 400 dunams (100+ acres).[3] These dimensions approximate the areas of the site occupied in more remote antiquity, from at least the Chalcolithic Period through the late Iron Age.[4]

Collins reports that the upper tall was enormous and explains that:

> Tall el-Hammam's massive city walls-twelve feet thick and higher than a three-story building-sat atop excavation squares, but only about eighty of those squares have been opened, and most are still in progress. It's hardly a raw, virgin tall after seven seasons of excavation….Pottery sherds representing all or part of more than forty thousand separate vessels have been brought out of the soil." Collins and Scott, *Discovering the City of Sodom*, 33.

---

[1] One hectare is equal to 10,000 square metres and contains about 2.47 acres.

[2] After seven seasons of excavation, Collins reports that the Jordanian TeHEP surveyors have "marked off more than thirteen thousand six-meter-by-six-meter

[3] A dunam (Arabic *dönüm*), was used in the Ottoman Empire for a unit of land area and represented the amount of land that could be plowed in a day. The legal definition was "forty standard paces in length and breadth." V. L. Ménage, "Review of Speros Vryonis, Jr., The Decline of Medieval Hellenism in Asia Minor and the Process of Islamization from the Eleventh through the Fifteenth Century, Berkeley, 1971," *Bulletin of the School of Oriental and African Studies* 36, no. 3 (1973): 659–661.

[4] Collins, Hamdan, and Byers, "Tall El-Hammam: Preliminary Report, Season Four, 2009," 386; Collins et al., "Tall El-Hammam, Season Eight, 2013," 4.

The Location of Sodom

Tall el-Hammam
(CL, EB1-2-3, IB1-2)
62 acres

Hazor
(EB1-2-3, IB1)
26 acres

Ashkelon (EB1-2-3)
16 acres

Laish (Tel Dan)
43 acres

Gezer
40 acres

Jerusalem
10 acres

Jericho
10 acres

Lachish
22 acres

Megiddo
20 acres

Chart showing relative sizes of major cities in the Levant during the late Chalcolithis through IB2, ca. 4000-2000 BCE

32. Chart showing the relative sizes of major cities in the Levant during the Late Chalcolithic through to the IB II periods, ca. 4000–2000 BC. Bâb edh-Dhrâʿ at this time would have been 9–10 acres, the size of Jerusalem and Jericho.

ARCHAEOLOGY FACTS

33. Chart showing relative sizes of major cities in the Levant during the MB1-2 (MB IIA-B-C), ca. 2000-1540 BC. During the MB Age Bâb edh-Dhrâ' did not exist.

The Location of Sodom

34. Hoard of pottery excavated in an undisturbed dolmen near Tall el-Ḥammâm in 2011. The vessels were identified as Early Bronze and Middle Bronze.

a huge mudbrick rampart[5] sloping outward 100 to 150 feet at an angle of 35 degrees. It was a sight to behold, and there wasn't anything to rival it between Syria and Egypt.[6]

The area of TeH not only comprises the 150–foot upper tall, but also the large circular area of the lower tall to the west, which was also walled and part of the city. Collins explains:

> Khouri[7] had indicated that the summit of the tall was about 25 x 140 meters, but that turned out to be inaccurate. In fact, the upper (eastern) tall is much bigger—on the order of 80–100 x 350 meters—with a lower tall extending to the west as a circular area 500+ meters in diameter.[8]

Collins put the size of TeH into perspective when he explains:

> With over 100 acres of Bronze Age occupational footprint and over 60 acres of that situated behind

---

[5] The fortification rampart is estimate to be built with 150-200 million mud bricks. Collins and Scott, *Discovering the City of Sodom*, 36.
[6] Collins and Scott, *Discovering the City of Sodom*, 47.
[7] Khouri, *Antiquities of the Jordan Rift Valley*, 76.
[8] Collins, "Explorations," 26.

an enormous defensive system, Tall el-Hammam was—on average over its 3,000-year history prior to its destruction toward the end of the Middle Bronze Age—the largest continuously-occupied city in the southern Levant.[9]

Leen Ritmeyer, the archaeological architect for TeH, graphically compares the walled city areas for the major cities of the Levant in the EB and MB periods (See Fig. 32 and 33). In Fig. 32, Ritmeyer compares the sizes of the cities in the late Chalcolithic through IB II periods (*ca.* 4000–2000 BC). TeH is the largest of all the cities, while BeD is only 10 acres, which is the size of Jerusalem and Jericho, six times smaller than TeH. According to Rast, Numeira was even smaller than BeD "having encompassed little more than 1 Hectare"[10] (see *Fact 42*).

In Fig. 33, Ritmeyer shows the relative sizes of major cities in the Levant during the MBI–II (MB IIA–B–C, *ca.* 2000–1540 BC). TeH is the third largest of all the cities during that period, while BeD did not exist at that time.

If one includes the area outside the walls of TeH, the area swells to over 100 acres, and in the MBA is in the same league with Hazor (200 acres) and Ashkelon (150 acres). It is certainly justified to speak of TeH as a city-state,[11] as all the surrounding sites are dwarfed by TeH and it would have acted as the controlling centre for the region.

There is also a large cemetery outside TeH that contains some 1,500 dolmens over a 17 km² area, known as the al-Hammam

---

[9] Collins, "Tall El-Hammam Is Still Sodom," 6.
[10] Rast, "Settlement at Numeira," 35.
[11] Beth-Shean is a mere 10 ha but considered by Mazar as a city state. Amihai Mazar, "Tel Beth-Shean: History and Archaeology," in *One God - One Cult - One Nation Archaeological and Biblical Perspectives*, ed. Reinhard Gregor Kratz and Hermann Spieckermann, Beihefte Zur Zeitschrift Fur Die Alttestamentliche Wissenschaft 405 (Berlin: De Gruyter, 2010), 241.

Megalithic Field (see Fig. 34, 35 and Map 9).¹² While many of these dolmens were created during the Chalcolithic periods they continued to be used into the EB and MBA, evident from the pottery excavated in the dolmens by the TeH team in 2011 (see Fig. 34).¹³ The northern region of the Dead Sea certainly contained a large population in the MBA.

There is no doubt that TeH is the largest EBA site and third largest MBA site in the southern Levant, almost six times larger than Jerusalem or Jericho at the time.

Fact 42: BeD is the largest EB site in the Southern Dead Sea region

Considering the southern end of the Dead Sea, compared with other cities the fortified area of Bâb edh-Dhrâ' was the largest EB site in this region. Rast calculated the fortified area of BeD at 10 acres [4 ha],¹⁴ Schaub at 12 acres,¹⁵ while Chesson and Schaub (who excavated the site) report that BeD was approximately 9 acres. They state:

> At Bab adh-Dhra' [sic], the northwest interior of the town has been deeply eroded. . . . Thus, large sections of the interior slopes of the town have been lost. The extent of the EB II–III walled town, however (approximately 9 acres), can be still gauged by the surviving areas of the northern ridge of the site. Based on this size, a population of 1,500–2,000

35. The author sitting in front of a dolmen by the blue mosque next to Tall el-Ḥammâm.

may have lived within the walled town area but there is also evidence of many houses and work areas to the east and south of the walled town. . . . The town of an-Numayra was approximately 1.5 acres.¹⁶

BeD also has a large cemetery (Khirbet Qazone), with possibly half a million people buried there from various periods, which is enormous by ancient standards. In describing the multiple period cemeteries at BeD, which contained tumuli (Chal. tombs), shaft tombs (EB IA, B), surface burials (EB IB), round buildings (EB IB, II), charnel houses (EB II, III), and tombs with stone-lined shafts (EB III–IV),¹⁷ Wood writes:

> The total size of the cemetery [BeD] is mind-boggling, archaeologically speaking. In overall extent it is more than five-eighths of a mile in length and at least half that wide [50 ha or 124 acres]. Lapp believed that the cemetery extended even farther, but he was limited in the area he could investigate because of military restrictions. . . . The archaeologist estimated that if the rest of the cemetery is like the area excavated, it contains a minimum of 20,000 shaft tombs. Conservative

---

¹² Kenneth Schath, Steven Collins, and Hussein Aljarrah, "Excavation of an Undisturbed Demi-Dolmen and Insights from the Al-Hammam Megalithic Field, 2011 Season," *ADAJ* 55 (2011): 329–50.

¹³ In season six (2011), the author was present during the extraction of fifteen whole, mendable vessels, from an undisturbed dolmen.

¹⁴ Rast, "Bab Edh-Dhra' (ABD)," 1:560; Meredith S. Chesson, "Remembering and Forgetting in Early Bronze Age Mortuary Practices on the Southeastern Dead Sea Plain, Jordan," in *Performing Death: Social Analyses of Funerary Traditions in the Ancient Near East and Mediterranean*, ed. Nicola Laneri, Oriental Institute Seminars 3 (Chicago: The Oriental Institute of the University of Chicago, 2007), 112.

¹⁵ Schaub, "Bab Edh-Dhra' (OEANE)," 1:249.

---

¹⁶ Chesson and Schaub, "Life in the Earliest Walled Towns," 249.

¹⁷ Schaub, "Bab Edh-Dhra' (NEAEHL)," 1:131.

estimates place the number of dead in these tombs at over half a million and the number of pottery vessels at two million! . . . From the size of the three cemeteries [Numeira and Feifa] found, the area of the southern Ghor supported an enormous population in the EB period.[18]

Although the cemetery outside the city at BeD is large, the EB I shaft tombs, which make up the bulk of the graves, predate the EB II and III occupation of the city of BeD. Lapp who excavated the cemetery at BeD states:

> These [late fourth and the early third millennium BC pots] belonged to people who camped at the site before the fortified city was built. For how long is difficult to say, but certainly the creation of a cemetery of twenty thousand tombs took considerable time.[19]

The size of the sites in the southern Dead Seas region is as follows:

Bâb edh-Dhrâ' – 9–12 acres (4 ha)[20] + cemetery at 124 acres (50 ha).

Numeira – 1.5 acres (.6 ha) + cemetery.

eṣ-Ṣafi – a large cemetery "on a par with those at Bab edh-Dhra and Feifa."[21]

Feifa – 15.8 acres (6.4 ha) cemetery.[22] There is an estimated 10,000–plus EBA I cist tombs.[23]

Khirbet al-Khanazir – Rast and Schaub report that the Khanazir cemetery was "smaller than the other sites discussed."[24] MacDonald reports that "it [Khanazir] consists of at least 50 structures [charnel houses] spread over an area of *ca.* 2 kilometres."[25]

FACT 43: BeD AND NUMEIRA ARE THE ONLY INHABITED TOWNS IN THE SOUTHERN DEAD SEA REGION IN THE EBA

There are five sites listed in the southern region of the Dead Sea that date to the EBA. While all five have a large cemetery, only two of them, Bâb edh-Dhrâ' and Numeira, are known to be inhabited with EBA occupational architecture in the southern region of the Dead Sea, between *ca.* 3300 and 900 BC. However, Bâb edh-Dhrâ' and Numeira were destroyed ca. 250 years apart.

1. Bâb edh-Dhrâ' (see Fig 11, 26)

Bâb edh-Dhrâ' was excavated between 1965 and 1967, under the direction of Paul Lapp (See Chapter Two; Fig. 11, 26). Unfortunately, Lapp died unexpectedly in 1970 and the task of further research fell to R. Thomas Schaub and Walter E. Rast.[26] Rast reports that following the 1979 season: "it seems that the most impressive urban period at Bab edh-Dhra' was EB III."[27] The evidence for this period at BeD is described by Schaub, who reported that:

> Evidence of the thriving EB II–III (3000–2300 BCE) urban culture of Bab edh-Dhra' is provided by a massive 7–meter-wide stone wall, built on the site's natural marl ridges; a sanctuary area with a

---

[18] Wood, "Have Sodom And Gomorrah Been Found?," 71–72, 75.

[19] Paul W. Lapp, "The Cemetery at Bab Edh-Dhra', Jordan," *Archaeology* 19, no. 2 (1966): 111.

[20] By comparison (see Fig. 32) EB Jerusalem and Jericho were also about the same size, at 10 acres.

[21] Wood, "Have Sodom And Gomorrah Been Found?," 73.

[22] Meredith S. Chesson and Morag M. Kersel, "Tomato Season In The Ghor Es-Safi: A Lesson in Community Archaeology," *NEA* 76, no. 3 (2013): 164.

[23] Ibid., 161.

[24] Rast and Schaub, "Survey of the Southeastern Plain of the Dead Sea, 1973," 12.

[25] Burton MacDonald et al., "Southern Ghors and Northeast `Arabah Archaeological Survey 1986, Jordan: A Preliminary Report," *ADAJ* 31 (1987): 406.

[26] Rast, "The Southeastern Dead Sea Valley Expedition, 1979," 60–61; Rast and Schaub, *Bab Edh-Dhra': Excavations in the Cemetery*; "Expedition to the Southeastern Dead Sea Plain, Jordan, 1979," 12–17.

[27] Rast, "The Southeastern Dead Sea Valley Expedition, 1979," 60; "Bronze Age Cities along the Dead Sea," 46; Schaub, "Bab Edh-Dhra' (NEAEHL)," 1:134; R. Thomas Schaub and Walter E. Rast, "Preliminary Report of the 1981 Expedition to the Dead Sea Plain, Jordan," *BASOR*, no. 254 (1984): 36, 43–55.

broadroom building; a courtyard with a circular stone altar; and [mudbrick] domestic and industrial areas within the walls.[28]

Rast pointed out that this urbanization was a slow process and reported that:

> Urbanization thus did not occur at once at Bab edh-Dhra', but was a gradual development from the EB IB village settlement to the walled city of EB III.... The charnel houses of the EB II and EB III phases continued in use until they became overloaded, at which time they were permanently closed.[29]

Following its destruction in the latter part of EB III (*ca.* 2350 BC), BeD was reoccupied in EB IV after a brief hiatus.[30] Rast and Schaub, who excavated it, explained that:

> It appears, however, that the EB IV horizon is not a simple extension of the preceding phase of EB II-III. There is an occupational break between the two cultures as indicated by the location of the later settlements outside the previous city, and sometimes over them as in the case of Field XVI. This evidence coincides with that from the cemetery, where a different burial tradition corresponding to this phase is found.[31]

Chesson provided the dates used by the archaeologists for the various periods. She stated: "The Early Bronze Age chronology at Bab edh-Dhra' is EB IA: c. 3150 B.C.–3050 B.C. [period may begin earlier than 3150 B.C.]; EB IB: 3050–2950 B.C.; EB II–III: 2950–2300 B.C.; EB IV: 2300–2150 B.C."[32]

2. Numeira (see Fig. 30)

In 1981, Rast described the 1977 discoveries at the site of Numeira (or Numayra; see Fig. 30) and reported:

> that Numeira was indeed an EB III site.... It does not appear that the occupation at Numeira extended over a lengthy period of time.... There are no indications of occupation earlier than EB III. Even with the prospect of an earlier phase of construction at the site, the time span during which the city was in existence seems not to have covered more than a century.[33]

While the exact terminal date of its destruction was questioned (see *Fact 39*), its EB III occupation was never disputed.[34] In 1979 Rast stated:

> Several phases were isolated, but it seems that the Numeira site was occupied for a relatively short period of time during EB III no doubt being related to the larger site of Bab edh-Dhra during this period.[35]

By 1983, four seasons of excavations had been completed and Rast stated:

> Like Bab ehd-Dhra [*sic* edh-Dhra], this exclusively Early Bronze III city [Numeira] was enclosed by a well-built defensive wall, averaging three meters in width. Also like Early Bronze III Bab edh-Dhra, its main gate was on the western side facing the open plain and the Dead Sea. Within the one-to-two-acre town were carefully planned areas consisting of many simple broadroom houses, often with attached storage rooms. A tower was built on the east during the last phase of the town's existence.[36]

For the terminal destruction of Numeira see Fact 39.

3. eṣ-Ṣafi

The EB I–III period site of eṣ-Ṣafi consists of "cist tombs built of cobble stones with a large flat stone over the top."[37] No architectural structures from this period have been discovered either at this site or nearby,

---

[28] Schaub, "Bab Edh-Dhra' (OEANE)," 249.

[29] Rast, "Bab Edh-Dhra' (ABD)," 1:560.

[30] Schaub and Rast, "Preliminary Report of the 1981 Expedition to the Dead Sea Plain, Jordan," 55–58.

[31] Rast, "Patterns of Settlement at Bab Edh-Dhra'," 33; Schaub, "Bab Edh-Dhra' (NEAEHL)," 1:135–36.

[32] Chesson, "Libraries of the Dead," 143 n.1; Schaub and Rast, "Preliminary Report of the 1981 Expedition to the Dead Sea Plain, Jordan," 36.

[33] Rast, "Settlement at Numeira," 36, 41–42.

[34] Coogan, "Numeira 1981," 75.

[35] Rast, "The Southeastern Dead Sea Valley Expedition, 1979," 60.

[36] Rast, "Bronze Age Cities along the Dead Sea," 47.

[37] MacDonald et al., "Southern Ghors and Northeast `Arabah Archaeological Survey 1986," 405; Rast and Schaub, "Survey of the Southeastern Plain of the Dead Sea, 1973," 15–16.

although Rast and Schaub speculate that: "From the sites of Bab edh-Dhra' and Feifeh it could be inferred that there should be a town site nearby to accompany this cemetery [at eṣ-Ṣafi]. The survey did not succeed in establishing a definite location."[38]

Rast and Schaub concluded that: "certainly the large number of tombs suggests that a sizeable population was supported in this area during Early Bronze."[39] They speculate that the settlement occupied the "area on the plateau"[40] although no architecture was discovered from this time period.

Meredith Chesson, Associate Professor at the University of Notre Dame, speculates that during the EB period:

> people traveled to the southeastern Dead Sea Plain to bury their dead in secondary ceremonies. . . . [such as] at Feifa, Safi/Naqa, and Bab edh-Dhra', where people traveled to these sites, set up temporary camp sites, and buried their dead as secondary burials in hundreds of rock-cut shaft (Bab edh-Dhra') or cobble–and slab–built cist tombs (Feifa and Safi/Naqa).[41]

The Ghor Safi archaeological project, under the direction of Konstantinos D. Politis, have located several sites since it began operating in 1997, including the early Byzantine-medieval Islamic urban centre of Khirbet Al Sheikh Isa, the industrial complex of Masna Al Sukkar (Byzantine sugar factory), and the Early Bronze Age and Byzantine cemeteries at Al Naqa, but no EB occupation at any of the sites.[42]

4. Feifa

Initially in 1973 Rast and Schaub speculated that the destruction at Feifa (or Fifa, Feifah) was dated to the end of the EB. They reported:

> A surface feature worthy of attention was the thick spongy charcoal across much of the site. Feifeh is much like Numeirah [sic Numeria] in this regard, the destruction dating probably to the end of the Early Bronze settlement.[43]

However, MacDonald et al. revised this hypothesis in their 1986 report.[44] Schaub summarized the finds in his 1991 report stating:

> Results from a sounding in the western walled town area of Feifa, supervised by Jack Lee, also confirmed that settlement first occurred in this area in the Iron Age, as had been proposed by MacDonald,[45] and not in the Bronze Age (an early hypothesis of the expedition). A substantial town wall from the eighth century B.C. [IA II] was built directly over Early Bronze Age cist tombs.[46]

In 1993 Nancy Lapp, from Pittsburgh Theological Seminary, reported the same thing:

> In the final season of the present series of excavations of the Expedition to the Dead Sea Plain (1990–1991), the walled site of Feifa was investigated and the EB cemetery that stretched to its east was excavated. The most recent surveys suggested that the visible structures of the walled site belonged to the Iron Age or Roman period.[47]

In summary, Feifa is not a MBA site but rather an EBI cemetery with no domestic occupation, except a small Iron Age II

---

[38] Rast and Schaub, "Survey of the Southeastern Plain of the Dead Sea, 1973," 10.

[39] Ibid., 11.

[40] Ibid., 15.

[41] Chesson, "Remembering and Forgetting in EBA Mortuary Practices," 113.

[42] Saeb Rawashdeh, "Ancient Ghor Safi Comes to Light with the Zoara Project," *Jordan Times*, July 3, 2017, http://www.jordantimes.com/news/local/ancient-ghor-safi-comes-light-zoara-project.

[43] Rast and Schaub, "Survey of the Southeastern Plain of the Dead Sea, 1973," 12.

[44] MacDonald et al., "Southern Ghors and Northeast `Arabah Archaeological Survey 1986," 408.

[45] MacDonald, "Southern Ghors and Northeast 'Arabah (OEANE)," 65.

[46] de Vries, "Archaeology in Jordan, 1991," 262; Schaub, "Southeast Dead Sea Plain," 63.

[47] Bert de Vries, "Archaeology in Jordan, 1993," ed. Pierre Bikai, *AJA* 97, no. 3 (1993): 482.

fortress built over the cemetery (see Map 12).⁴⁸

5. Khirbet al-Khanazir

In 1973 Rast and Schaub identified what they considered to be the walls of buildings. They reported:

> The promontory on which Khanazir is located is encompassed by a wall whose interior face was traced at several places. . . . On the southeast side a heap of stones provides a curious parallel to several of the other sites, and may again be the remains of a tower. The date of this heap is not certain. One or more sherds found near it were apparently Iron Age, but only excavation will tell the relation of the tower to the site as a whole.⁴⁹

Schaub summarized the excavation results in his 1991 report. He stated:

> this site [Khirbet Khanazir] was first discovered and dated to the Early Bronze Age IV period (2300–2000 B.C.) by MacDonald's survey team in 1986. The 88 well-preserved rectangular structures situated along the various terraces and hillsides of a 2 km² area appeared at first to be the components of an Early Bronze IV village settlement.
> Excavation of these structures, however, proved otherwise. Five buildings were cleared by MacDonald,⁵⁰ Nancy Lapp, and five volunteers. The structures yielded no occupational debris. Large slabs in the floor areas turned out to be ceiling stones of well-built stone-lined burial chambers.⁵¹

Chesson and Schaub described the sites this way:

> Unlike Bab adh-Dhra', ... Khirbet al-Khanazir is a one-period site with a cemetery from the EB IV. . . . There was no settlement associated with the al-Khanazir cemetery, and so the EB people came full-cycle in once again traveling to the cemetery to bury their dead in secondary ceremonies. Interestingly, they combined the more visible aspects of the EB II—III above-ground charnel houses with the earlier subterranean EB I shaft tombs.⁵²

The walls which Rast and Schaub identified in 1973 were in reality rectangular charnel burial houses marking EB IV shaft tombs.⁵³

FACT 44: THERE ARE FOUR MB SITES IN THE JORDAN VALLEY WITH EVIDENCE OF DESTRUCTION

The four sites which were occupied in the MB period are Tall el-Hammam, Tall Nimrin, Tall al-Kafrayn (see Fig. 38), and two sites which will be treated as one given their close proximity: Tall Bleibel and Tall el-Musṭāḥ.

1. Tall el-Ḥammâm (see Fig. 10, 12)

Khouri recounted that:

> Glueck, Mallon, de Contenson, and the 1975/76 Valley Survey team gathered much Iron Age I and II pottery from Tall el-Hammam, along with smaller quantities of pottery from the Early Bronze Age, the Middle Bronze Age and the Roman/Byzantine and Ayyubid/Mamluke periods.⁵⁴

The quantities of EB and MB pottery found were smaller than the quantities of IA pottery found because the IA settlement was exposed on the top of the upper level of the Tall which was surveyed.

Prag during her 1990 excavation of TeH reported that: "There is surface evidence for occupation in Phase 1 of the Intermediate EB–MB period on the west tell."⁵⁵ She also reported finding MB evidence in Areas H20–H50.

---

⁴⁸ http://followthepotsproject.org/?page_id=36.

⁴⁹ Rast and Schaub, "Survey of the Southeastern Plain of the Dead Sea, 1973," 13.

⁵⁰ "The structures excavated at Khirbet Khuneizir are EB IV tombs." MacDonald, "Southern Ghors and Northeast 'Arabah (OEANE)," 65.

⁵¹ de Vries, "Archaeology in Jordan, 1991," 262.

⁵² Chesson and Schaub, "Death and Dying on the Dead Sea Plain," 253, 258.

⁵³ de Vries, "Archaeology in Jordan, 1991," 262; Burton MacDonald, "EB IV Tombs at Khirbet Khanazir: Types, Construction, and Relation to Other EB IV Tombs in Syria-Palestine," *Studies in the History and Archaeology of Jordan* 5 (1995): 129–34; Schaub, "Southeast Dead Sea Plain," 62.

⁵⁴ Khouri, *Antiquities of the Jordan Rift Valley*, 76.

⁵⁵ Prag, "The Excavations at Tell Al-Hammam," 272.

36. The fenced site of Tall Nimrin overlooking the local school.

The presence of MB occupation has also been confirmed by Collins' nine seasons of excavation. Collins reported:

> Once again, surface sherding reveals that both MB1 and MB2 are well represented over most of the site. However, in excavated contexts, the MB1 assemblage seems to dominate on the lower tall, while the MB2 assemblage dominates on the upper tall. . . . .Presently, in the face of these observations, we theorize that virtually the entire fortified site footprint (30+ hectares) was occupied during both MB1 and MB2; however, the upper tall, surrounded by a massive earthen / mudbrick rampart (likely during MB2), became a true "acropolis" during MB2, the location of most of the city's monumental structures such as palaces, temples and administrative buildings.[56]

Of the 1,951 diagnostic pottery sherds read in the first 4 seasons, 38% were MB with the next highest number representing the IA2 at 32%.[57]

2. Tall Nimrin (see Fig. 36)

Flanagan, McCreery, and Yassine report that:

> The survey yielded some 41,000 sherds from the following periods: Early Bronze (EB) IV, Middle Bronze (MB), Late Bronze (LB)?, Iron I?, Iron II, Persian, Hellenistic, Roman, Byzantine, Umayyad, Abbasid, Ayyubid, Mamluk, Ottoman, and Moder [sic modern].[58]

They stated after the 1993 excavation that:

> The Middle Bronze occupation appears to have ended abruptly sometime in the 16th or early 15th century B.C., but up to this point, there is no clear evidence for a violent destruction of the Middle Bronze city. It may be that political and/or environmental factors led to the abandonment of the site.[59]

Then in their 1995 preliminary report they stated that: "there is abundant evidence of the latest phase of the MB II occupation immediately below the Iron IC remains."[60]

3. Tall al-Kafrayn (see Fig. 38)

In trench O14, Papadopoulos reported that: "the discovery of a few MBA and LBA sherds and many IA sherds indicated that this building was used over an extended period."[61]

Again, he confirmed the presence of MB in his statement that: "Pottery and other finds (Figs. 57, 58, 59, 60, 61 [in Papadopoulos' article]), suggest that tall Kafrayn was occupied from the EBA through to the Late IA."[62]

Collins confirmed the presence of MB pottery, comparing it with Tall al-Kafrayn. He

---

[56] Collins, Hamdan, and Byers, "Tall El-Hammam: Preliminary Report, Season Four, 2009," 407.

[57] Ibid., 406.

[58] James W. Flanagan, David W. McCreery, and Khair N. Yassine, "First Preliminary Report of the 1989 Tell Nimrin Project," *ADAJ* 34 (1990): 136.

[59] James W. Flanagan, David W. McCreery, and Khair N. Yassine, "Tell Nimrin: Preliminary Report on the 1993 Season," *ADAJ* 38 (1994): 219.

[60] James W. Flanagan, David W. McCreery, and Khair N. Yassine, "Tall Nimrin: Preliminary Report on the 1995 Excavation and Geological Survey," *ADAJ* 40 (1996): 283.

[61] Thanasis J. Papadopoulos and Litsa Kontorli-Papadopoulos, "Preliminary Report of the Seasons 2005-2008 of Excavations by the University of Ioannina at Tall Kafrayn in the Jordan Valley," *ADAJ* 54 (2010): 295.

[62] Ibid., 304.

stated: "There is a strong EBA and MBA presence, as at Tall Nimrin."⁶³

4. Tall Bleibel and Tall el-Musṭāḥ

While Glueck and the 1975/76 Valley Survey team did not identify any MB pottery, they "identified EB I, II and III pottery, as well as a few late Bronze Age and Byzantine sherds."⁶⁴ However, Collins reported:

> In fact, the three sites—Tall Nimrin, Tall Mustah, and Tall Bleibel—are so close together that Glueck thought they should, occupationally, be considered as one site. A cursory reading of the sherds at both sites confirmed what I already knew from previous sherding and survey activity. However, there was more surface pottery evidence of a Bronze Age presence at Tall Mustah and Tall Bleibel than pre-excavation analysis had revealed for Tall Nimrin, and Tall Nimrin turned out to contain the ruins of a major MB fortified city.⁶⁵

This has been confirmed by the author however until Tall Bleibel (see Fig. 37) and Tall el-Musṭāḥ are excavated there will be no official publication to verify the findings.

FACT 45: THERE IS NO LBA ARCHITECTURAL OCCUPATION IN THE JORDAN VALLEY

During the 1975–76 East Jordan Valley Survey, several sites are listed as LBA, identified on the basis of surface finds (see *Fact 14*) and some identified on the basis of their excavation reports, but none of the excavated sites in the *kikkār* have produced any LB evidence of occupation (except Jericho and a single building on the acropolis of TeH).⁶⁶ Yassine et al. reported at the end of

37. Tall Bleibel is the small hill in the foreground. It is an archaeological site that has been identified with Zeboiim north. It is located on the north side of the road that descends to the Jordan Valley. Tall Mustah (not shown), the southern of the two Zeboiim sites, is located on the south side of the road that descends from the highland plateau. Today an army post is located at the site of Tall Mustah.

their survey that "Many of the MB II sites . . . were not reoccupied in the Late Bronze period."⁶⁷ Yassine's survey reported that:

> The concentration of LB sites was restricted to the area between Wadi el-Yabis and the Zarqa River [*kikkār*]. . . . All of the sites found in the central Jordan Valley are associated with Tell Deir 'Allā; a religious center in the middle of these major sites. The excavations at Tell Deir 'Allā [See Map 4] have shown according to H. [Hendricus J.] Franken, a peaceful continuous development through the LB and Iron Ages.⁶⁸

In the 1996–2000 Survey in the Regions of 'Irāq Al-Amīr and Wādī Al-Kafrayn, only 5 sites (out of 216) indicated evidence of LB activity (2.31%), and in the 2000 survey only 2

---

⁶³ Collins et al., "Tall El-Hammam, Season Eight, 2013," 5 n.10.

⁶⁴ Khouri, *Antiquities of the Jordan Rift Valley*, 73.

⁶⁵ Collins, "Explorations," 22–23.

⁶⁶ Peter M. Fischer, "The Southern Levant (Transjordan) during the Late Bronze Age," in *The Oxford Handbook of the Archaeology of the Levant: C. 8000-332 BCE*, ed. Margreet L. Steiner and Ann E. Killebrew, Oxford Handbooks in Archaeology (Oxford, U.K.: Oxford University Press, 2013), 561–76.

⁶⁷ Khair Yassine, Moawiyah M. Ibrahim, and James A. Sauer, "The East Jordan Valley Survey 1975 (Part One)," in *The Archaeology of Jordan: Essays and Reports*, ed. Khair Yassine (Amman: Department of Archaeology, University of Jordan, 1988), 174.

⁶⁸ Yassine, Ibrahim, and Sauer, "The East Jordan Valley Survey 1975 (Part Two)," 197.

38. The site of Tall al-Kafrayn.

sites (out of 42) provided LB evidence (4.76%).[69]

James F. Strange, in his chapter on the LBA in Jordan, stated:

> It appears that the Jordan Valley south of Ayn Bassah (which is near Katarit ai-Samra) was *virtually uninhabited during the Late Bronze Age*. Only three sites, at Wadi Nimrin and Wadi Kufrayn, were found to be settled farther south. South of the Dead Sea, in the Southern Ghors and Northeast Arabah, *no Late Bronze Age sites are found*.[70]

While there is some LB pottery in the *kikkār* of the Jordan Valley, one must examine both the surface surveys and investigate the excavation reports to obtain a clearer picture (see *Fact 14*). Are there LB architectural remains? What follows are a few of the important sites on the *kikkār*:

---

[69] C. Ji Chang-Ho and Jong-Keun Lee, "The Survey in the Regions of 'Irāq Al-Amīr and Wādī Al-Kafrayn," *ADAJ* 49 (2002): 182.

[70] James F. Strange, "The Late Bronze Age," in *Jordan: An Archaeological Reader*, ed. Russell B. Adams (London, U.K.: Equinox, 2008), 288; Burton MacDonald, "Settlement Patterns Along the Southern Flank of Wadi Al-Hasa: Evidence from 'The Wadi Hasa Archaeological Survey,'" in *Studies in the History and Archaeology of Jordan*, ed. Muna Zaghloul et al., vol. 4, SHAJ (Amman, Jordan: Department of Antiquities, 1992), 71, 75.

Tall el-Ḥammâm

In Collins' report to the DOA he stated that: "Late Bronze Age pottery seems to be systematically absent, and consequently there is no discernable LBA architecture thus far."[71] After season eight, Collins reported: "Late Bronze Age sherds are extremely rare in the area, and there is no discernable LBA7 architecture thus far (the only LBA sherds from around the site were found in a tomb)."[72]

In 2017 a single LB structure was identified on the acropolis of tall that likely served as a watchtower given its prominent location overlooking the Jordan Valley.

Tall Nimrin

Flanagan, McCreery, and Yassine, reported in 1989 that:

> with the *possible exceptions of the Late Bronze and early Iron Ages*, the survey indicates that Tell Nimrin was occupied continuously from approximately 2,000 B.C. to the present. . . . .There is *no clear evidence of LB*

---

[71] Collins, Hamdan, and Byers, "Tall El-Hammam: Preliminary Report, Season Four, 2009," 388.

[72] Collins et al., "Tall El-Hammam, Season Eight, 2013," 4.

or Iron I occupation at this point [emphasis added]."[73]

In the 1993 Season, they acknowledged this mysterious phenomenon and call it "a *Late Bronze gap*."[74] They continue to speculate that: "The 500 year *gap* of occupation from *ca.* 1500 to 1000 B.C. [LB/IA] must be due to significant sociopolitical and/or environmental phenomena that remain to be explained."[75]

In Silvia's recent dissertation he points out that the absence could be explained by an air burst that he calls "the Civilization-Ending 3.7KYrBP Kikkar Event."[76]

Tall al-Kafrayn

In 2007 Papadopoulos reported on the 2000–2004 season, that: "Tall al-Kafrayn (see Fig. 38) has been inhabited since Early Bronze Age times with a floruit during the LBA/Early Iron Age."[77] Then in 2011, he adjusted his initial assumptions and reported:

> There is some evidence from pottery of a limited Late Bronze Age occupation, but *no architectural remains fill the gap* observed also at other sites of this area, such as Tall al-Hammam [see *Fact 45*], Tall Iktanu and Tall Nimrin" [emphasis added].[78]

Tall Iktanu

Glueck reported that:

> the sherds ranged from Middle Chalcolithic to Iron Age I–II, aside from a few Byzantine and mediaeval Arabic fragments. . . . There were some Chalcolithic sherds, most of which seemed to belong to Middle Chalcolithic, and in addition there were some EB IV–MB I and MB II sherds.[79]

While Glueck does not identify any LB pottery, Prag reported in the *American Journal of Archaeology* that the "surface survey suggests that the *north hill only was reoccupied in the Late Bronze Age* and Early Iron Age I, but *no remains* of this period have been *excavated* [emphasis added]."[80]

The presence of LB findings has yet to be identified below the surface of Tall Iktanu.[81]

Tell Al Sultan (Jericho)

In the *Anchor Bible Dictionary* article on Jericho, Holland stated:

> On the evidence of the Jericho pottery dated to the LB from the reused Tombs 4, 5, and 13,[82] it would appear that Jericho was reoccupied on a *small scale* in Area H on the E side of the tell during the second half of the 15th century BC. Bienkowski suggests for Tomb 5 a late LB I/first half of LB IIa date (*ca.* 1425–1350 BC or slightly later) and for Tombs 4 and 13 a mid-LB IIa/early LB IIb date, *ca.* 1350–1275 BC [emphasis added].[83]

In Negev's article on Jericho, he stated:

> There was *a little pottery* of the 14th century BC [LBA II]. It seems that the site was inhabited after the beginning of this century but deserted again by the second half. Nothing remained of the fortifications

---

[73] Flanagan, McCreery, and Yassine, "First Preliminary Report, 1989 Tell Nimrin," 136, 149.

[74] Flanagan, McCreery, and Yassine, "Tell Nimrin: Preliminary Report, 1993," 207.

[75] Ibid., 219; Flanagan, McCreery, and Yassine, "Tall Nimrin: Preliminary Report, 1995," 286.

[76] Silvia and Collins, "The Civilization-Ending 3.7KYrBP Kikkar Event: Archaeological Data, Sample Analyses, and Biblical Implications"; Silvia, *The Destruction of Sodom: What We Have Learned from Tall El-Hammam and Its Neighbors*.

[77] Thanasis J. Papadopoulos, "The Hellenic Archaeology Project of the University of Ioannina in Jordan: A Preliminary Synthesis of the Excavation Results at Ghawr as-Sāfī and Tall Al-Kafrayn (2000-2004)," in *Studies in the History and Archaeology of Jordan*, ed. Fawwaz al-Khraysheh, IX (Amman: Department of Antiquities, 2007), 189.

[78] Papadopoulos and Kontorli-Papadopoulos, "Preliminary Report of the Seasons 2005-2008: Tall Kafrayn," 308.

[79] Glueck, *Explorations in Eastern Palestine*, 394.

[80] de Vries, "Archaeology in Jordan," 515.

[81] Prag, "Iktanu, Tell," 143–44.

[82] Piotr Bienkowski, *Jericho in the Late Bronze Age*, Ancient Near East (Warminster, Wiltshire: Aris & Phillips, 1986), 32–102 and figs. 27–51.

[83] Thomas A. Holland, "Jericho (Place)," ed. David Noel Freedman et al., *ABD* (New York, N.Y.: Doubleday, 1996), 736.

of this period [emphasis added].⁸⁴

Jacobs' reports that:

> LB occupation appears to have been *restricted to a nonfortified village* in the 15–14th centuries. . . . From the end of the 15th to the 10th–9th centuries Tell es-Sulṭân *lay unoccupied*, at which time it was rebuilt [emphasis added].⁸⁵

Some LB structures have recently been identified at Jericho by the director Lorenzo Nigro.⁸⁶

Tall Bleibel (Tall Bulaybil)

In Glueck's 1951 report he stated: "we found *no Bronze Age sherds whatsoever* on this site" [emphasis added]⁸⁷ with only IA I–II sherds, along with Roman and Byzantine pottery. However, Khouri reports that: "the site has pottery sherds dating largely from the Iron Age, with only a few possible Early Bronze and some Roman/Byzantine sherds."⁸⁸ While there were a few EB sherds, along with MB, IA II, Persian, and Hellenistic sherds, no LB pottery was identified at the site in any of the surface surveys (see *Fact 14*).⁸⁹

Tall el-Musṭāḥ (Tall al-Musṭāḥ)

Glueck stated, based on his survey that Tall al-Musṭāḥ should be

> assigned exclusively to EB I. The modern road has cut a broad and revealing swath through the main part of this tell, showing house-foundations and burnings and large quantities of EB I pottery and some EB I flints.⁹⁰

Khouri stated that "the 1975/76 valley survey team identified EB I, II and III pottery, as well as *a few late Bronze Age* and Byzantine sherds."⁹¹ The Jordan Valley Team of Chang-Ho and Lee "found Early Bronze I–III and Byzantine sherds. According to our survey, at Tall el-Musṭāḥ, late Byzantine and early Islamic pottery dominates the ceramic assemblage."⁹² While a few LB surface sherds were reported by Khouri, Tall el-Musṭāḥ has not been excavated, therefore LB occupation and architecture has yet to be identified (see *Fact 14*).

The phenomenon of the lack of occupation during the LBA in the *kikkār* of the Jordan Valley, at sites such as Tall Iktanu, Tall al-Kafrayn and Tall Nimrin⁹³ is also repeated at TeH.⁹⁴ This "LBA gap" is a typical phenomenon in all Bronze Age sites in the *kikkār* of the Jordan Valley, with the possible exception of Jericho and the single structure at TeH.

Collins states:

> There is not a single Late Bronze Age sherd in the mix. Not one. Not at Tall el-Hammam. Not at Tall Nimrin. Not at Tall Iktanu. Not at Tall Kafrein. Not at talls Bleibel, Mustah, Barakat, Tahouneh,

---

⁸⁴ Avraham Negev, "Jericho," in *AEHL*, 3rd ed. (New York: Prentice Hall Press, 1996).

⁸⁵ Paul F. Jacobs, "Jericho," in *EDB*, ed. David Noel Freedman, Allen C. Myers, and Astrid B. Beck (Grand Rapids, Mich.: Eerdmans, 2000), 691.

⁸⁶ Lorenzo Nigro, "Tell Es-Sultan – A Pilot Project for Archaeology in Palestine," *The ASOR Blog* (blog), 2014, http://asorblog.org/tell-es-sultan-a-pilot-project-for-archaeology-in-palestine.

⁸⁷ Glueck, *Explorations in Eastern Palestine*, 371.

⁸⁸ Khouri, *Antiquities of the Jordan Rift Valley*, 73.

⁸⁹ Glueck, "Some Ancient Towns," 12; Yassine, Ibrahim, and Sauer, "The East Jordan Valley Survey 1975 (Part Two)," 197; Chang-Ho and Lee, "The Survey in the Regions of 'Irāq Al-Amīr and Wādī Al-Kafrayn," 187; Khouri, *Antiquities of the Jordan Rift Valley*, 73.

⁹⁰ Glueck, *Explorations in Eastern Palestine*, 370.

⁹¹ Khouri, *Antiquities of the Jordan Rift Valley*, 73; Yassine, Ibrahim, and Sauer, "The East Jordan Valley Survey 1975 (Part Two)," 176.

⁹² Chang-Ho and Lee, "The Survey in the Regions of 'Irāq Al-Amīr and Wādī Al-Kafrayn," 191–92.

⁹³ Rudolph H. Dornemann, "Preliminary Comments on the Pottery Traditions at Tell Nimrin, illustrated from the 1989 Season of Excavations," *ADAJ* 34 (1990): 153–81; Kay Prag, "The Intermediate Early Bronze-Middle Bronze Age: An Interpretation of the Evidence from Transjordan, Syria and Lebanon," *Levant* 6 (1974): 69–116; "Tell Iktanu and Tall El-Hammam 1990," 55–66; Strange, "The Late Bronze Age," 281–310.

⁹⁴ Collins et al., "Tall El-Hammam, Season Eight, 2013," 4, 14; Collins and Scott, *Discovering the City of Sodom*, 164.

Azeimah, Mwais, or Rama.⁹⁵

During the LBA the population settlement left the fertile Jordan Valley and moved up into the region above the *kikkār* to sites like Jerusalem, Tall Deir 'Allā (Succoth), Pella, Tell Abu Al-Kharaz and Amman (Rabbah-Ammon. See Map 4) and were under Egyptian control.⁹⁶ It is not significant that there are reports of a few pieces of LBA pottery found in the area, as pastoral nomads travelling through the region could have easily left them behind. What is significant and mysterious is that there are no LBA structures and settlements in the best agricultural land in the region.

Pollen studies (Palynology) have indicated that the entire eastern Mediterranean suffered from drought during the LBA and the Jordan Valley was likely not exempt from the affect of this collapse.⁹⁷ But TeH had ample water supplies, with numerous hot springs, and survived even when other sites, such as Tulaylat al-Ghassul, did not. It is well watered with springs, Wadi's and perennial rain from the mountains. So why did no one live in the best real estate in the region for about 500 years? Although archaeology has not definitively answered the why,⁹⁸ it does confirm the fact that no one had settled in the Jordan Valley during the LBA.

Fact 46: TeH is not MB Heshbon

One might ask: If TeH is not Sodom, then what other significant city is it, as it seems to have alluded being mentioned in the Bible. One would think that such a large city-state as TeH would have been mentioned in the biblical text somewhere. Clyde E. Billington, editor of *Artifax* magazine, argues that there were two Heshbons and TeH was the western Heshbon.⁹⁹ Billington proposed:

> I believe that the archaeological and biblical evidence strongly indicates that Tall el-Hammam is the ancient Bronze Age city of Heshbon, the capital city of the Amorite King Sihon who was defeated by none other than Moses himself. . . . Admittedly there is a problem in my identification of Tall el-Hammam with Heshbon. Almost any map of the Old Testament world places Heshbon at the site where the road eastward from Jericho connects with the King's Highway; about 12 miles directly to the east of Tall el-Hammam. For clarity's sake, I will refer to the Heshbon at the intersection with the King's Highway as "eastern Heshbon" and Tall el-Hammom [*sic* Hammam] in the Jordan Valley as "western Heshbon." I believe that there were two Heshbons.¹⁰⁰

Billington goes on to explain: "I believe that Tall el-Hammam—western Heshbon—was the original city of Heshbon that was captured by Moses, and that eastern Heshbon was built in the Iron Age and named after it."¹⁰¹

---

⁹⁵ Collins, "Tall El-Hammam Is Sodom," 6.

⁹⁶ Peter M. Fischer, ed., *Chronology of the Jordan Valley during the Middle and Late Bronze Ages: Pella, Tell Abu Al-Kharaz, and Tell Deir Alla*, Contributions to the Chronology of the Eastern Mediterranean 12 (Vienna: Österreichische Akademie der Wissenschaften, 2006); *Tell Abu Al-Kharaz in the Jordan Valley, Volume 2: The Middle and Late Bronze Ages*, Denkschriften Der Gesamtakademie, Band 39. Contributions to the Chronology of the Eastern Mediterranean 11 (Vienna: Österreichische Akademie der Wissenschaften, 2006); "The Southern Levant (Transjordan) during the Late Bronze Age," 561–62.

⁹⁷ William H. Stiebing, Jr., "When Civilization Collapsed: Death of the Bronze Age," *Archaeology Odyssey* 4, no. 5 (2001).

⁹⁸ Patrick E. McGovern, "Central Transjordan in the Late Bronze and Early Iron Ages: An Alternative Hypothesis of Socio-Economic Transformation and Collapse," in *Studies in the History and Archaeology of Jordan*, ed. Adnan Hadidi, vol. 4 (London, U.K.: Taylor & Francis, 1987), 267–73; Patrick E. McGovern and Robin Brown, *The Late Bronze and Early Iron Ages of Central Transjordan, the Baq'ah Valley Project, 1977-1981* (Pittsburgh, Penn: University of Pennsylvania, Museum of Archaeology, 1986), 2.

⁹⁹ Billington, "Tall El-Hammam Is Not Sodom," 2.
¹⁰⁰ Ibid.
¹⁰¹ Ibid., 3.

However, there is no evidence of any occupation at TeH in the LBA (the time of Moses), with only a single building on the acropolis during this time. There was no LBA occupation at sites in the southern Jordan Valley (see *Fact 45*). Heshbon is always associated with the cities Aroer, Dibon, Madaba, and Nebo, along the Kings highway (Judg 11:26; Num 21:30; 32:3; Josh 13:17) in the Transjordan Highlands, and never down in the Jordan Valley.

Also, if all scholars identifiy TeH as Abel-Shittim (see Fact 85), where Moses camped the Israelites prior to entering the promised land (Num 33:49; 22:1; 26:3; 31:12), how can it also be the Heshbon that Moses conquered (Num 21:26; 32:37)? There must be two separate sites.

Collins replied to Billington's suggestion with his own *Artifax* article (shorter version)[102] titled "Tall el-Hammam Is Sodom: Billington's Heshbon Identification Suffers from Numerous Fatal Flaws."[103] The archaeological research on Heshbon was carried out by the Madaba Plains Project and their published research is readily available.[104] There is no archaeological evidence to support Billington's claim.

FACT 47: THE PENTAPOLIS ARE NOT ALL MENTIONED TOGETHER IN THE EBLA TABLETS, AND MOST DOUBT THEY ARE LISTED AT ALL

With the discovery of the Ebla tablets at Tell Mardikh in 1974, many OT names, including many city names, were identified in the tablets. Wilson mentioned them as: "Salim, possibly the city of Melchizedec, Hazor, Lachish, Megiddo, Gaza, Dor, Sinai, Ashtaroth, Joppa and Damascus. Of special interest is Urusalima (Jerusalem), this being the earliest known reference to this city."[105]

As well, some scholars suggested that the five Cities of the Plain were listed in the tablets.[106] Freedman claimed that the same tablet listed the Pentapolis (five cities) in the precise order as Genesis 14,[107] and that his source (1976) was M. Dahood,[108] who was working with Giovanni Pettinato,[109] the original epigrapher of the excavation. Freedman's claim was picked up by others and confidently reported as fact.[110] But this claim was later denied by Pettinato. In a letter to Freedman from Dahood on October 8, 1978, Dahood states:

> Giovanni [Pettinato] tells me that he considers the reading of the first two names, Sodom and Gomorrah, quite certain, but that he is no longer ready to defend the next two city names because of his improvement in the reading of the signs, improvement that could only come with greater experience in reading the tablets. In any case, the cities 3 and 4 of the Genesis 14 list do not occur in the same tablet, so that the argument in favor of the antiquity of the Genesis list is weakened. I had not known that they were not in the same tablet. And as for tablet 1860, it deals with the alloys of metals, quite a long text but without these city names in

---

[102] A longer version was published in the BRB. http://www.tallelhammam.com/uploads/Collins_Answers_Billington.pdf.

[103] Collins, "Tall El-Hammam Is Sodom," 6–8.

[104] http://www.madabaplains.org/hisban/heshbon-expedition-publications.htm.

[105] Wilson, *Ebla Tablets*, 25.

[106] Wilson, "Ebla: Its Impact on Bible Records"; Mitchell J. Dahood, "Ebla, Ugarit E l'Antico Testamento," *La Civiltà Cattolica* 129, no. 2 (1978): 338; "Ebla, Ugarit and the Old Testament," 1978, 12; Freedman, "The Real Story of the Ebla Tablets," 149–150; Wilson, *Ebla Tablets*; Shea, "Two Palestinian Segments," 601, 604–605, 608–609.

[107] Freedman, "The Real Story of the Ebla Tablets," 149.

[108] Dahood, "Ebla, Ugarit E l'Antico Testamento," 338; "Ebla, Ugarit and the Old Testament," 1978, 99.

[109] Pettinato, "Gli archivi reali di Tell Mardikh-Ebla," 236.

[110] Freedman, "The Real Story of the Ebla Tablets," 143, 149; Shea, "Two Palestinian Segments," 605; René Labat, *Manuel D'épigraphie Akkadienne: Signes, Syllabaire, Idéogrammes*, 5th ed., Geuthner Manuels (Paris: Librairie orientaliste Paul Geuthner, 1976), 87, 231.

In an interview, on May 4, 1980, with Hershel Shanks, Pettinato stated: "Surely the five cities are not in the same tablet. I have never said that they were."[112] In the same interview with Shanks, Pettinato clarified his view on the presence of the Pentapolis in the Ebla tablets. Shanks asks:

> **BAR:** Do you think that these two cities [Sodom and Gomorrah] are the same cities that are mentioned in the Bible as the Cities of the Plain?
>
> **P:** We cannot say. For no city can we say that this is surely the same city as is mentioned in the Bible. We can say only that this is the name or that it is similar to the name. For example, when we find Mari, so frequently mentioned in the Ebla tablets, we cannot be sure that this is the famous city of Mari. Maybe it's only a name similar to that city. Maybe it's another city. We need much more analysis and discussion before we can prove that the identification of a city is really established. Now we can say only that the name reminds us of another city.
>
> **BAR:** It's been said that the Eblaite city resembling Sodom is in a list of deliveries of agricultural products and, therefore, it's probably a little city around Ebla rather than the city mentioned in the Bible.
>
> **P:** [That is what Mr. Archi says in reference to a city named] *Sa-du-ma* [in tablet TM.75.G.1992]. But I have never suggested a parallel between *Sa-du-ma* and Sodom of the Bible. I think *Si-da-mu* is the city mentioned in the Ebla tablets which recalls the Biblical city of Sodom. Mr. Archi thinks the only possible city is *Sa-du-ma* but there are many possibilities. I think that *Si-da-mu* is the city which reminds us of Sodom because in this period the long vowel *ou* is still written *au*.[113]

This clarification of Pettinato's views and his connection with the Bible has made some scholars question his research.[114]

Longman III pointed out that: "Some of the scholarly writings of G. Pettinato, Dahood, and D. H. Freedman[115] border on Pan-Eblaism, so it is not surprising that it has been developed to an extreme by less qualified writers".[116]

However, most scholars today even doubt the Sodom and Gomorrah readings,[117] claiming they are "exceptional and unsubstantiated claims"[118] and consider the Ebla tablets to have "no bearing on . . . . Sodom and Gomorrah,"[119] even though *si-da-mu*^{ki} does occur in a commercial text.[120]

Bimson perhaps best summarised the views of most today, when he stated: "Reservations have recently been expressed concerning the readings of the names espoused by Freedman, and it seems that the

---

[111] Freedman, "The Real Story of the Ebla Tablets," 143.

[112] Shanks, "BAR Interviews Giovanni Pettinato," 47.

[113] Ibid.

[114] Archi, "The Epigraphic Evidence from Ebla and the Old Testament"; "The Epigraphic Evidence from Ebla: A Summary," *BA* 43, no. 4 (1980): 200–203;

Archi, "Further Concerning Ebla and the Bible"; "Are 'The Cities of the Plain' Mentioned in the Ebla Tablets?"; Shanks, "BAR Interviews Giovanni Pettinato," 51.

[115] Pettinato, "Ebla and the Bible"; Dahood, "Appendix"; "Ebla, Ugarit and the Old Testament," 1979; "Ebla, Ugarit and the Old Testament," 1978; Freedman, "The Real Story of the Ebla Tablets."

[116] Tremper Longman III, *Fictional Akkadian Autobiography: A Generic and Comparative Study* (Winona Lake, Ind.: Eisenbrauns, 1991), 26.

[117] Freedman, "The Real Story of the Ebla Tablets"; Alfonso Archi, "Ebla Texts," in *OEANE*, ed. Eric M. Meyers, vol. 2, 5 vols. (Oxford, U.K.: Oxford University Press, 1997), 184–86; "The Epigraphic Evidence from Ebla and the Old Testament," 563 n. 21; Biggs, "The Ebla Tablets: An Interim Perspective," 82; Price, *The Stones Cry Out*, 85; Paolo Matthiae, "A Letter to the Editor," *Biblical Archaeologist* 43 (1980): 134; Mulder, "Sodom; Gomorrah," 156; Longman III, *Fictional Akkadian Autobiography*, 26; Hershel Shanks, "Ebla Evidence Evaporates," *BAR* 5, no. 6 (1979).

[118] Mark W. Chavalas and K. Lawson Younger, eds., *Mesopotamia and the Bible: Comparative Explorations* (Grand Rapids, Mich.: Baker Academic, 2002), 41.

[119] Ibid.

[120] Pettinato and Alberti, *Catalogo Dei Testi Cuneiformi Di Tell Mardikh-Ebla*, Tablet 6522; Pettinato, "Ebla and the Bible," 213; Archi, "The Epigraphic Evidence from Ebla: A Summary," 201.

The Location of Sodom

39. Early Bronze 3 bull's head motif with downturned horns on a storages jar with a rope decoration on the neck. The horn orientation is typically found in Minoean culture.

Photo courtesy of Michael Luddini

claim that the names of all five cities occur on one tablet was in any case erroneous."[121]

Sadly, Pettinato and Matthiae have taken opposite sides over this issue, ending their working relationship and resulting in a new epigrapher, Alfonso Archi, being assigned to the Ebla excavation.[122] But as Pettinato pointed out, A. Archi:

> is a teacher on annual contract of Hittitology at the University of Rome, hence a teacher of the culture and Indo-European (sic!) language of the Hittites. He is not an Assyriologist, nor a sumerologist, nor a Semitist, nor a Biblicist, nor a historian of religion, nor an economist, and yet he is the official epigraphist of Ebla![123]

However, the Ebla tablets do not provide anything useful to the argument concerning the location of the Pentapolis. As both Collins and Wood would agree, the Pentapolis existed during the EBA (Gen 10) at the time of the Ebla tablets. The question is: When were the Cities of the Plain destroyed (Gen 13)? But unfortunately, the Ebla tablets do not answer this question in spite of Shea's attempts to link some of the names with the southern region of the Dead Sea (See Chapter One under "Ancient Textual References").

Fact 48: There are reports of a Minoan connection at TeH

Several architectural features and ceramics at TeH have shown Minoan influence, a fact which has been documented at other Bronze Age sites in the region (i.e., Canaanite palace with Cretan-Theran Late Minoan IA frescos at Tel Kabri, Israel,[124] Alalakh, Turkey,[125] Tell el-Dab'a (Avaris), Egypt,[126] and Qatna, Syria[127]).

The pillared (hypostyle) building and gatehouse just inside the main gate at TeH

---

[121] Bimson, "Archaeological Data," 67.

[122] Shanks, "BAR Interviews Giovanni Pettinato," 46.

[123] Pettinato, "Ebla and the Bible," 203; Shanks, "BAR Interviews Giovanni Pettinato," 46.

---

[124] Eric H. Cline, Assaf Yasur-Landau, and N. Goshen, "New Fragments of Aegean-Style Painted Plaster from Tel Kabri, Israel," *AJA* 15, no. 2 (2011): 245–61; Eric H. Cline and Assaf Yasur-Landau, "Aegeans in Israel: Minoan Frescoes at Tel Kabri," *BAR* 39, no. 4 (2013): 37–44, 64, 66.

[125] Aharon Kempinski and Ronny Reich, *The Architecture of Ancient Israel: From the Prehistoric to the Persian Periods* (Jerusalem: Biblical Archaeology Society, 1992), 112–13.

[126] Manfred Bietak and N. Marinatos, "The Minoan Paintings of Avaris," *Ägypten Und Levante* 5 (1995): 49–62; Manfred Bietak, "The Setting of the Minoan Wall Paintings at Avaris," in *Aegean Wall Painting: A Tribute to Mark Cameron*, ed. Lyvia Morgan, British School at Athens Studies 13 (London, U.K.: British School at Athens, 2005), 83–90.

[127] Daniele Morandi Bonacossi, ed., *Urban and Natural Landscapes of an Ancient Syrian Capital: Settlement and Environment at Tell Mishrifeh/Qatna and in Central-Western Syria*, Proceedings of the International Conference held in Udine, 9-11 December 2004. collana Studi archeologici su Qatna (Udine: Forum Editrice, 2007); Ann Brysbaert, *The Power of Technology in the Bronze Age Eastern Mediterranean: The Case of the Painted Plaster*, Monographs in Mediterranean Archaeology 12 (London, U.K.: Equinox, 2008), 116, 129–39.

was unusual yet is mirrored in Minoan architecture (see Fig. 44).[128]

Collins asks:

> What was this seemingly-relentless cultural propensity that gave Tall el-Hammam a pillared building (EBA/IBA) and a pillared gatehouse (MBA)? Our initial research suggests that the influence was derived from Minoan Crete.[129]

Further, possible Minoan connections were suspected with the discovery of an EB III ceramic bull motif applique (see Fig. 39).[130]

While this does not help with the location of Sodom, Collins pointed out a possible literary link between Sodom, with their "sociological sexual practices"[131] and

> the attempted abduction of the angels by the "young and old" men of Sodom (Gen 19), suggest an affinity to the formal cultural institution of paiderastia found on Bronze Age Crete, including a unique feature: ritual kidnapping [See Strabo *Geogr.* 10.21.4].[132] Research in this vein is ongoing, but the results thus far support the idea that the link is more than coincidental.[133]

---

[128] Louise A. Hitchcock, "Minoan Crete: Understanding the Minoan Palaces," *Athena Review* 3, no. 3 (2003): 27–35; Louise A. Hitchcock, "Minoan Architecture," in *The Oxford Handbook of the Bronze Age Aegean*, ed. Eric H. Cline (Oxford, U.K.: Oxford University Press, 2012), 195; Jan Driessen, "The Proliferation of Minoan Palatial Architectural Style: (I) Crete," *Acta Archaeologica Louvanensia* 28–29 (1989 1990): 3–23, 14 n.85.

[129] Collins et al., "Tall El-Hammam, Season Eight, 2013," 8–9.

[130] Collins, Kobs, and Luddeni. *Introduction to Tall al-Hammam with Seven Seasons of Ceramics*, 73–75.

[131] Moore, "Dr. John Moore and Dr. Steven Collins Reflect on TeHEP's First Nine Years," 1.

[132] Strabo, *Geography: Books 10–12*, trans. Horace Leonard Jones, vol. 5, 8 vols., LCL 211 (Cambridge, Mass.: Harvard University Press, 1928).

[133] Collins et al., "Tall El-Hammam, Season Eight, 2013," 1 n.4; Robert B. Koehl, "The Chieftain Cup and a Minoan Rite of Passage," *JHS* 106 (1986): 99–110.

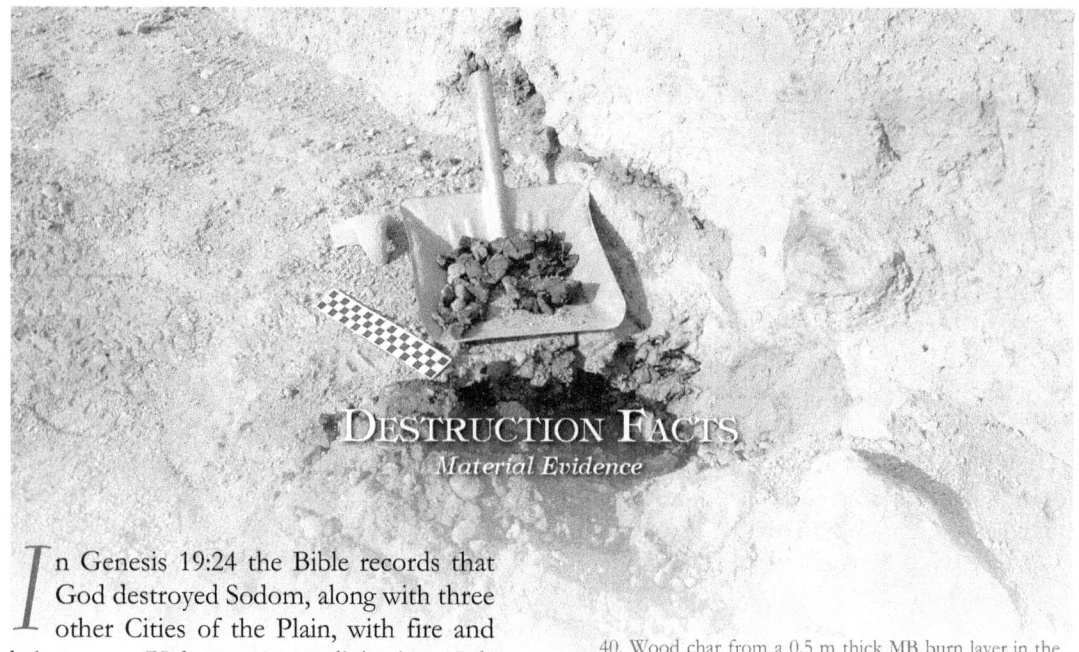

Destruction Facts
Material Evidence

In Genesis 19:24 the Bible records that God destroyed Sodom, along with three other Cities of the Plain, with fire and brimstone (Heb. *gopriyt* = lightning; Job 18:15; Ps 11:6; Isa 30:33; Ezek 38:22; cf. Gen 19:24) falling from the air.[1] The evidence of such a surgical destruction should still be visible, as only the city of Zoar escaped the catastrophe. This chapter will address the material evidence for any destruction in the two regions (N and S) that might match the account of the destruction found in the Bible.

FACT 49: BOTH SITES PROVIDE FIERY DESTRUCTION EVIDENCE

Some may argue that the destruction described in the biblical text should produce no physical remains and that the cities will never be found. This is an inaccurate assumption and based on the destruction of other cities in the past not reasonable. Even the destruction of Hiroshima and Nagasaki after the atomic

40. Wood char from a 0.5 m thick MB burn layer in the mud brick section of the city wall at Tall el-Ḥammâm, in season 1 (2006), dated by a MB handle (left of the dustpan) at the same location (see Fig. 17). The military cut a road through the wall and exposed this cross section, which was being clarified.

blast that ended the Second World War, left physical evidence that could be identified. There is no reason to believe that the site of Sodom and the other cities of the plain still had some visible remains following their destruction that can be excavated today.

Bâb edh-Dhrâʿ

Rast described the destruction at BeD this way:

> At approximately 2350 B.C., the EB III city suffered some sort of *trauma*, leaving it in ruins. In fields XIII and IV the upper part of the defensive wall made of brick fell onto the natural slopes of the site. The mudbrick superstructure of the sanctuary also *collapsed, apparently after burning*. . . . Although a natural disaster such as an earthquake may have been responsible for these events, an external attack against the city, as also at Numeira, cannot be ruled out [emphasis added].[2]

---

[1] Note that there is no mention of sulphur in the text and neither is there any association with the meaning of any of the terms used in the text. Further there is no evidence of any sulphurous burn layer at any of the sites in the southern region; although there is a sulphurous smell to the destruction layer in the MB II strata at TeH. Collins, "Tall El-Hammam Is Sodom," 5.

[2] Rast, "Bab Edh-Dhraʿ (ABD)," 1:560.

41. Wood char from a 0.5 m thick MB burn layer in the mud brick section of the city wall at Tall el-Ḥammâm, in season 1 (2006), dated by a MB handle (left of the dustpan) at the same location (see Figs. 17 and 40). The evidence of destruction is consistent through the tall in every square where there is an MB strata.

Rast continued to describe the destruction at BeD, comparing it with Numeira. He reported:

> At Numeira the evidence is *extensive that the town was burned* [3] during its last major phase, while the destruction of the EB III walled town at Bab edh-Dhra is attested by ruined and *abandoned structures* and by the demolished upper part of the town wall, the superstructure of which, made of mudbrick in some cases, had suffered *exposure to fire* [emphasis added].[4]

While Numeira suffered from extensive burning, Rast is cautious to contrast its destruction with the abandoned buildings at BeD which were ruined but only "suffered exposure to fire." In 1973 Rast and Schaub described the evidence of fire as "evidence of severe burning on many of the stones."[5] Schaub reports that it suffered "a major destruction near the end of EB III [2300 BC]" but was rebuilt in EB IV (2350–2100 BC).[6]

Tall el-Ḥammâm

In 2008, at the end of Season Four, Collins reported that:

> [In] LA.28 the EB3/IB1–2 domestic structures

---

[3] "The site [Numeira] as a whole is covered with ashy soil, suggesting that it was not utilized after the destruction which appears to be so evident on the surface. On the north side especially, the soil is spongy ash, and can be picked up in handfulls." Rast and Schaub, "Survey of the Southeastern Plain of the Dead Sea, 1973," 9.

[4] Rast, "Bab Edh-Dhraʽ and the Origin of the Sodom Saga," 194; Schaub and Rast, *The Southeastern Dead Sea Plain Expedition: 1977 Season*, 16–18.

[5] Rast and Schaub, "Survey of the Southeastern Plain of the Dead Sea, 1973," 8.

[6] Schaub, "Bab Edh-Dhraʽ (OEANE)," 249; Rast, "Bronze Age Cities along the Dead Sea," 48.

underwent *a major destruction with thick (30+ cm) layers of ash* over a *tumbled mudbrick and ash matrix*.[7]

.... In the "swale" of the upper tall we excavated part of a structure dating to MB1, containing two storage jars and a grey-burnished piriform juglet. One room contained a claylined silo or storage bin. All this was covered with approximately *1m of destruction matrix filled with dark ash*, broken mudbricks, pottery fragments and *severely burned* wattle-and-daub roofing material [emphasis added].[8]

Collins offers evidence of destruction in his 2013 *BAR* article where he reports that: "The latest Middle Bronze Age layer at Tall el-Ḥammâm consists of 1.5 to 3 ft. [.46 to .91 m] of heavy ash and destruction debris" (see Fig. 40 and 41)[9]

Collins described the destruction in greater detail in his response to Billington and stated:

The terminal ash layer at Tall el-Hammam runs from .5m to over a meter in depth across both the upper and lower talls. The stratum is dark-grey, heavy ash strewn with broken mudbricks, pottery, a vast array of artifacts, and even human bone scatter. The entire exterior MB2 gateway plaza surface is covered with a half-meter of dense, grey-black ash, and that is just what is left after thousands of years of erosion. It marks one of the most violent, enormous destruction events imaginable. We have pieces of pottery melted into glass, some bubbled like lava, found across the site. We have burned foundation stones, and bricks turned red or ceramic-like from extremely hot temperatures. Most of the MB2 mudbrick superstructures are seemingly blown off their foundations. It is a scene of utmost devastation and disintegration.[10]

In 2013 Collins reported in *BAR* that:

Across Tall el-Hammam, archaeologists found widespread evidence of an intense conflagration that left the Middle Bronze Age city in ruins. They found scorched foundations and floors buried under nearly 3 feet [.9 m] of dark grey ash, as well as dozens of pottery sherds covered with a frothy, "melted" surface; the glassy appearance indicates that they were briefly exposed to temperatures well in excess of 2,000 degrees Fahrenheit, the approximate heat of volcanic magma. Such evidence suggests the city and its environs were catastrophically destroyed in a sudden and extreme conflagration.[11]

In his 2013 book entitled *Discovering the City of Sodom*, Collins describes the evidence as:

The ash and destruction debris from Tall el-Hammam's terminal Middle Bronze 2 occupational level ranges from half a meter to two meters thick over both the upper and lower talls. Embedded in those layers are broken and tumbled muddricks, smashed and charred pottery vessels and other day to day objects, and human bones-all violently churned into a telltale, ashy matrix. Obviously, Tall el-Hammam suffered a violent end.[12]

Leen Ritmeyer added: "Nowhere else have I seen such a thick layer of destruction, with collapsed walls, burnt debris, and dramatic skeletal remains, all inside a meter-thick layer of ash."[13]

FACT 50: BOTH SITES HAVE A CITY GATE COMPLEX THAT WAS DESTROYED

Bâb edh-Dhrâʿ

Bâb edh-Dhrâʿ literally meaning "gate of the arm,"[14] also contained two gateways with towers. Rast described the construction of the defensive structures:

Encompassing more than 10 acres during this

---

[7] Collins confirms that the destruction "from the Chalcolithic through the Middle Bronze Age" is atypical of a military conflict and is more in line with an earthquake "followed immediately by rebuilding." Collins, "Tall El-Hammam Is Sodom," 4.

[8] Collins, Hamdan, and Byers, "Tall El-Hammam: Preliminary Report, Season Four, 2009," 402, 407.

[9] Collins, "Where Is Sodom?," 33.

[10] Collins, "Tall El-Hammam Is Sodom," 4.

[11] Collins, "Where Is Sodom?," 70–71.

[12] Collins and Scott, *Discovering the City of Sodom*, 156.

[13] Ibid., foreword.

[14] Rast, "Bab Edh-Dhraʿ (ABD)," 559.

42. Drawing of the 10 acre site of Bâb edh-Dhrâ' idenifying the gate, cemetery and terranced houses.

Illustration by E. Carlson. Lowest Point on Earth Museum, Jordan. Labels by David E. Graves

phase [EB III], a 7 m wide defensive wall girdled Bab edh-Dhra', and a gateway on the W provided access to the Mazra'a plain.[15]

Schaub pointed out that:

> The major gate on the west provided direct access to what appears to have been a plaza dominated by the higher sanctuary area to the south. Wooden beams along the southern face of the gate suggest that the gateway proper had a wooden door. In a later phase, during the Early Bronze Age III [100 years before its destruction][16], the gateway was blocked with a secondary wall made up of smaller stones, including discarded mortars.[17]

He also pointed out that the West Gate was small compared with other similar period gates.[18] He described the destruction of the gate at BeD and reported that: "The wall and *gate area* on the site's western edge underwent a *major destruction* near the end of EB III [2300 BC]."[19]

43. The city gate at Bab Edh-Dhra.

Rast and Schaub reported that the northeastern tower was built on "a layer of collapsed mudbricks and bricky debris (Locus 39) almost 1 m. deep."[20] This destruction debris was from an earlier destruction of the city and not a result of its final calamity.

Tall el-Ḥammâm

In January 2012 the monumental MBA II city gate complex was uncovered. In the season eight report, Collins stated:

---

[15] Rast and Schaub, *Bab Edh-Dhra': Excavations at the Town Site (1975-1981)*, 272.

[16] Schaub and Rast, "Preliminary Report of the 1981 Expedition to the Dead Sea Plain, Jordan," 46.

[17] Schaub, "Bab Edh-Dhra' (NEAEHL)," 1:134.

[18] Rast and Schaub, *Bab Edh-Dhra': Excavations at the Town Site (1975-1981)*, 279, 280.

[19] Schaub, "Bab Edh-Dhra' (OEANE)," 249.

[20] Rast et al., "Preliminary Report of the 1979 Expedition," 28.

44. Reconstruction of the TeH MB gate complex discovered in 2012 and drawn by L. Ritmeyer from the archaeological data provided by archaeologists. Note the inside pillared room of the gate chamber. This was distictive Minoan cultural influence.

© Ritmeyer Archaeological Design

The eastward expansion of this trench [LA] during Season Seven led to the discovery of a monumental MBA gateway system complete with both small and large defensive towers. Season Eight had as a goal the excavation and identification of the internal gatehouse accessed through the central axis of the main gate passage. . . . We soon determined that these penetrations represented not only the main entry to the city through a large gatehouse with towers, but also one of (likely) two flanking monumental towers creating a gateway system of significant proportion. During Season Eight we identified most of the structures associated with the city wall and external portions of the gateway system, and began excavating on the inside of the gate passage in order to determine the structure of the gatehouse. We were expecting to find a four-piered or six-piered gatehouse. What we unearthed was unexpected—and unprecedented. [see *Fact 48* and *55*][21]

Collins reported:

Several distinct features make this one of the most impressive gate systems ever unearthed in the southern Levant. First, the central gatehouse has two outside-corner towers with entrances into each through the city wall. . . . The width of the gatehouse is approximately seventy feet. . . . Second, we've unearthed the stone foundation and up to a dozen mudbrick courses of a large, external flanking tower measuring thirty-one by forty-six feet, not including the twelve-foot-thick section of Middle Bronze city wall to which it attaches.[22]

Collins stated in the 2013 *BAR* article that:

During the Middle Bronze Age, Tall el-Hammam was protected by an imposing rampart fortification system that greatly enhanced the already substantial defensive wall that surrounded the site during the Early Bronze Age. Excavations across the site and near the city's main gate revealed a sloped earthen rampart system constructed with millions of mudbricks. . . . built against the earlier stone city wall, producing fortifications that measured more than 100 feet thick. Positioned at regular intervals along the rampart were large square towers that likely stood to a height of 50 feet or more. Two of these towers flanked the multi-storied gatehouse of the city's main entrance, thereby creating a monumental gateway and spacious exterior plaza.[23]

At the end of the 2012 season, Collins reported in *Popular Archaeology* that: "thus far there are no evidences of conquest-destruction for the duration of the Bronze Age defenses."[24]

The MB city was destroyed by fire and while there was no evidence of the city gate being destroyed by a conquest, there was a lot of evidence of destruction commensurate with an earthquake or some

---

[21] Collins et al., "Tall El-Hammam, Season Eight, 2013," 6, 8.

[22] Collins and Scott, *Discovering the City of Sodom*, 168.

[23] Collins, "Where Is Sodom?," 38.

[24] "Archaeologists Excavate Massive Ancient Gateway in Jordan," *Popular Archaeology*, 1, accessed May 7, 2014, http://popular-archaeology.com/issue/september-2012/article/archaeologists-excavate-massive-ancient-gateway-in-jordan.

DESTRUCTION FACTS

other catastrophic event. All that remained were the foundations.

FACT 51: HUMAN REMAINS HAVE BEEN FOUND AT BOTH SITES

The fiery annihilation described in Genesis 13 suggests that there should be evidence of human remains in the destruction layer of Sodom, since the Cities of the Plain were destroyed and left unoccupied for a period of time afterward.

Bâb edh-Dhrâ'

While there have been human remains identified at Bâb edh-Dhrâ', they are confined to the cemetery (charnel house tombs) and are not found in the destruction layer of the city.[25] Some skeletons and bone fragments have been identified in Room V (NE 10/2 Locus 5) of Numeira but they were identified from an earlier destruction.[26]

Tall el-Ḥammâm

The discovery of human remains at TeH in the MB II destruction layer first happened in 2011, since up to that time much of the work was being done in the IA level above the MBA.[27]

Collins and Scott pointed out that:

> All the archaeologist on site agreed that the skeletal remains were intrinsic to the ash layer, which dates to the Middle Bronze 2 according to the ceramics. The material is within a half meter of the surface, at the level of the Middle Bronze 2 houses, streets, and alleyways. The human

45. Human remains in the Middle Bronze Age destruction layer at TeH.
Courtesy of TeHEP.

> remains are mixed in with fallen mudbricks, pottery, other artifacts, and lots of ash. . . . Some of their joints are hyperextended or twisted apart unnaturally, not in any normal or burial position. One is charred off at mid-femur. Their condition at death attests to "extreme trauma." This is terminology from our osteologists as they observed and documented the condition of the bones in situ.[28]

In an interview with Brian Nixon of ASSIST News Service, Collins reported that:

> Shortly after, we discovered a child body one meter north [from the previous skeleton]. The child's skeleton showed the same destruction, demonstrating traumatic demise." How so? I was quite curious. "The legs were flexed in the wrong way, the knee joints were ripped apart, one arm was broken with left palm up, and the other arm was smashed under the pelvis. In all, it showed the signs of a sudden, ghastly death." Any other skeletal remains? I prodded. "Yes. We're still investigating these. But, skeletal remains were found throughout the area, following the same patterns. One skeleton seems to be crouching, as if in fear, protecting itself from the destruction.[29]

In addition there is a large dolmen area known as the Al Rawda Field, next to TeH

---

[25] Donald J Ortner, "A Preliminary Report on the Human Remains from the Bab Edh-Dhra' Cemetery," in *The Southeastern Dead Sea Plain Expedition: An Interim Report of the 1977 Season*, ed. R. Thomas Schaub and Walter E. Rast, AASOR 46 (Boston, Mass.: American Schools of Oriental Research, 1979), 119–32.

[26] Coogan, "Numeira 1981," 79; Rast et al., "Preliminary Report of the 1979 Expedition," 44.

[27] Collins and Scott, *Discovering the City of Sodom*, 177.

[28] Ibid., 178–79.

[29] Brian Nixon, "Archaeological Evidence for Sodom: Recent Findings Shed Light on Discoveries of 'Biblical Proportions,'" *ASSIST News Service*, December 8, 2011, 3–4.

(see Fig. 34, 35 and Map 9).[30] Some human bone fragments were found in five of the twelve dolmens excavated in 2011, but dolmens appear to be used only for ceremonial purposes and not as burial tombs.[31]

FACT 52: THERE ARE VARIOUS THEORIES FOR THE DESTRUCTION OF THE PENTAPOLIS

Various scientists and scholars have sought to provide a natural explanation for the destruction of the Cities of the Plain. One or more of these means (secondary cause) may have been used by God (primary cause) to bring about their destruction; however most do not correspond to the biblical description of the final obliteration event.

Destroyed by a volcano

Nötling (1886) was a leading proponent of a volcanic eruption theory and proposed that the Cities of the Plain were located in the *Wady Zerka Ma'in*.[32] In 1931 Wyllie acknowledged the potential for a connection between volcanic activity and the destruction of the Pentapolis,[33] followed in 1975 by Block.[34] Recently, Trifonov, a Russian geologist, raised the idea once again, combining an earthquake with volcanic activity, which he claims, stimulated the biblical myth.[35]

However, in 1936 Frederick Clapp, a geologist, was skeptical, reporting that:

> after studying relationships of the western Transjordanian igneous and pyroclastic beds to existing and recent topography, [he] is not convinced that lava or ash eruptions have occurred in the locality as recently as 4000 years ago.[36]

Harland in 1943 agreed with Clapp and stated: "of course, in the case of Sodom and Gomorrah, there is no possibility of volcanic activity. Geologists have ruled that out."[37]

Destroyed by an earthquake

In the 1800's, Max Blanckenhorn was one of the earliest proponents of the tectonic earthquake theory[38] and placed the Cities of the Plain in the southern Dead Sea basin with the origin of the epic event occurring many thousands of years before Abraham.[39]

---

[30] Zeidan A. Kafafi and Hugo Gajus Scheltema, "Megalithic Structures in Jordan," *Mediterranean Archaeology and Archaeometry* 5, no. 2 (2005): 7.

[31] Schath, Collins, and Aljarrah, "Excavation of an Undisturbed Demi-Dolmen and Insights from the Al-Hammam Megalithic Field, 2011 Season," 341–42; Kafafi and Scheltema, "Megalithic Structures in Jordan," 13.

[32] Fritz Nötling, "Das Todte Meer Und Der Untergang von Sodom Und Gomorrha," in *Deutsches Montagsblatt* (Berlin: Rudolf Mosse, 1886), 27, 31, 33.

[33] B. K. N. Wyllie, "The Geology of Jebel Usdum, Dead Sea," *Geological Magazine* 68, no. 8 (1931): 360–72.

[34] J. W. Block, "Sodom and Gomorrah: A Volcanic Disaster," *Journal of Geological Education* 23 (1975): 74–77.

[35] Vladimir G. Trifonov, "The Bible and Geology: Destruction of Sodom and Gomorrah," in *Myth and Geology*, ed. L. Piccardi and W. Bruce Masse, Geological Society Special Publication 273 (London, U.K.: Geological Society, 2007), 133–42.

[36] Clapp, "The Site of Sodom and Gomorrah: A Diversity of Views," 339.

[37] Harland, "Sodom and Gomorrah Part II: Destruction," 43.

[38] Ewald, *History of Israel*, 1:313–14; Tristram, *The Land of Moab*, 348, 363; Robinson, "Jordan," 764; Power, "The Site of the Pentapolis: Part 1," 1:23; Neev and Emery, *The Destruction of Sodom, Gomorrah and Jericho*, 146; Wood, "Discovery of the Sin Cities," 75; Cocks, "The Discovery of Sodom, 1851," 1–27.

[39] Blanckenhorn, *Entstehung und Geschichte des Toten Meeres*, 51; *Noch eimal Sodom und Gomorrha*, Zeitschrift des deutschen Palästina-Vereins 21 (Leipzig: Baedeker, 1898), 79.

Clapp popularized the idea and proposed a natural explanation for the destruction. He explained:

> By contrast, exudations of bitumen, petroleum and probably natural gas (since the last-named is generally an accompaniment of these substances), emerging throughout historical time, may have been erratic and have taken place whenever disastrous earthquakes or controlling subterranean pressure impulses were manifested. The seepages, catching fire from lightning or human action, would adequately account for recorded phenomena without necessarily having recourse to super-natural or fanciful theories (except, perhaps, in the case of the obviously fictitious part of the story, where a human being was transformed into salt).[40]

Neev and Emery have suggested that the Jordan valley was destroyed by an earthquake in about 2350 BC which resulted in "light fractions of hydro-carbons escaping from underground reservoirs" raining "fire and brimstone" down upon the Cities of the Plain and Jericho.[41] However, Jericho's destruction occurred about 900 years later and thus their dating appears to be off.[42] But if an earthquake took out BeD, it could have also taken out TeH.

Destroyed by liquefaction

Harris and Beardow (1995), in their geotechnical analysis of the destruction of the Pentapolis, theorize that the cities were destroyed by an earthquake that toppled buildings and liquefied the rocks and soil underneath the cities. They proposed that this caused them to slide into "the southern extremity of the present-day North Basin of the Dead Sea" in the northeast corner of the Lisan Peninsula.[43]

Haigh and Madabhushi reported on testing this model and stated:

> It is thus shown that liquefaction-induced lateral spreading after an earthquake of these layered deposits is a plausible explanation for the disappearance of the cities of Sodom and Gomorrah, with displacements of hundreds of metres or even kilometres being possible even on fairly gentle slopes.
>
> It is not possible to state categorically whether this is what actually happened, as insufficient evidence is available at this time, approximately 4,000 years after the event is supposed to have taken place. In order to show this, archaeological evidence would need to be collected by searching for remains beneath the Dead Sea.[44]

However, with the Dead Sea at its lowest point in historical memory, there is no evidence at present of any ruins under the Dead Sea (see *Fact 56*).

Destruction by an air burst

Phillip J. Silvia in his dissertation has argued that the cities of the plain were destroyed by an air burst (3.7KYrBP Kikkar Event) and salt was scattered over the Jordan Valley preventing the vegetation from growing and explaining the 500-year hiatus during the LB period. He provides scientific evidence of soil samples from the MB period that indicates high levels of salt residue during this period preventing people from living in the Jordan valley during the IA period.[45] See also the 65-page Scientific Report that documents an air burst similar to Tunguska,

---

[40] Clapp, "The Site of Sodom and Gomorrah: A Diversity of Views," 340.

[41] Neev and Emery, *The Destruction of Sodom, Gomorrah and Jericho*, 139–41.

[42] David Hendel, "Review of D. Neev and K.O. Emery, Destruction of Sodom, Gomorrah and Jericho: Geological, Climatological and Archaeological Backgrounds," *BAR* 23, no. 1 (1997): 70.

[43] Harris and Beardow, "The Destruction of Sodom and Gomorrah: A Geotechnical Perspective," 349.

[44] Stuart K. Haigh and S. P. Gopal Madabhushi, "Dynamic Centrifuge Modelling of the Destruction of Sodom and Gomorrah," *Proceeding of the International Conference on Physical Modelling in Geotechnics*, 2002, 511.

[45] Silvia, MBA Civilization-Ending Destruction.

Russia in 1908 that destroyed the Jordan Valley at the end of the Middle Bronze period.[46]

Conclusion

All these theories, except the last, are merely based on speculation and because both BeD and TeH lie on the fault line of the Great Rift Valley (see *Fact 25*), this issue becomes redundant in determining which site is Sodom, as any seismic or tectonic activity would have affected both possible locations. Power points out that

> there is no suggestion of a volcanic eruption, or of a tectonic earthquake in an inflammable region. Such explanations of the destruction of the four cities, while not excluded by the scriptural narrative, must therefore be considered hypothetical conclusion when used to determine the site.[47]

A hypothetical geological description of the destruction of Sodom is no indication to its location.

However, the last theory, backed with scientific evidence, does hold a viable explanation for the location of Sodom north of the Dead Sea in the MB period, when following the destruction of the cities of the plain in the LB period, the soil showed high levels of salt.[48]

FACT 53: THE CEMETERY AT BeD WAS BURNED

Across the modern road (highway 50) from the occupational ruins of BeD lies a large cemetery at Khirbet Qazone (see Figs. 26, 46 and Map 10). Here there were different forms of burial, in different periods. In the EB III period the method used was rectangular mudbrick buildings called "charnel houses" or "body libraries." Chesson described their unique method of burial in this period and recounted:

> When the EBA people constructed their fortification walls with at least two gates at Bab adh-Dhra' around 2900 BCE (and built the walled settlement at an-Numayra slightly after that time), they abandoned the fully subterranean mortuary contexts for above-ground rectangular charnel houses in the cemetery at Bab adh-Dhra'.[49] While from a distance these buildings would have appeared to have been constructed on the ground surface, often they were technically semi-subterranean: built on a slope, with their back walls cut into the hillside and a short series of steps down into the building from the entrance at ground level. People stored the remains of the deceased with their grave goods in charnel houses, or body libraries, with pottery, beads, textiles, and stone and metal objects. In many ways, the rectangular charnel houses resembled the rectangular architecture in and surrounding the walled town, thus mirroring the houses inhabited by the living. . . . many of the structures had been severely burned in antiquity, thus destroying much evidence and rendering detailed interpretations and reconstructions of mortuary practices very difficult to make.[50]

Rast reported that "The tomb [at BeD] was also burned throughout."[51] Rast and Schaub provided more details:

> Bricks from the wall of this charnel house like

---

[46] Ted E. Bunch et al., "A Tunguska Sized Airburst Destroyed Tall El-Hammam a Middle Bronze Age City in the Jordan Valley near the Dead Sea," *Scientific Reports* 11, no. 1 (September 20, 2021): 18632.

[47] Power, "The Site of the Pentapolis: Part 1," 25.

[48] Silvia and Collins, "The Civilization-Ending 3.7KYrBP Kikkar Event: Archaeological Data, Sample Analyses, and Biblical Implications"; Silvia, *The Destruction of Sodom: What We Have Learned from Tall El-Hammam and Its Neighbors*; Graves, "Sodom And Salt in Their Ancient Near Eastern Cultural Context," 15–32.

---

[49] Rast and Schaub, *Bab Edh-Dhra': Excavations at the Town Site (1975-1981)*, 64–65; Rast and Schaub, *Bab Edh-Dhra': Excavations in the Cemetery*.

[50] Chesson and Schaub, "Death and Dying on the Dead Sea Plain," 256.

[51] Rast, "The Southeastern Dead Sea Valley Expedition, 1979," 60.

DESTRUCTION FACTS

46. A burial installation called a "charnel house" located in the cemetery at Bâb edh-Dhrâ' used during the urban occupation period (EB III). Dr. John Moore (foreground) and the author (background) are standing on the outside wall of the mudbrick house. It originally contained burned human remains and some 900 pottery vessels.

Photo Daniel Galissini

those in Fields XIII and IV were fired to a pink or orange hue by the burning that took place in this tomb. It was not clear whether the great amount of stone and mud-brick fall at the west end had occurred over time with successive erosion, or whether an intentional effort had been made during antiquity to topple parts of the wall at the time the burning took place. Such effacement apparently did occur in the case of Charnel House 22, where the walls gave evidence of having been pushed over intentionally when the charnel house was burned.[52]

Rast and Schaub suggested that the destruction of the city and the charnel houses are related. They stated: "The ashy debris in Area F 4 [of the BeD site] is paralleled in Area J 2 and Field XII, and the the [sic double the] burning of Charnel House G 1 may be related to the same event that produced it."[53]

Rast elaborated that:

At approximately 2350 B.C., the EB III city [BeD] suffered some sort of trauma, leaving it in ruins. . . . The charnel houses that were still in use *were burned*. Their brick walls *either fell in*, or as seems to be indicated by their position, were *pushed in*. Many of the *charnel house bricks were also burned in the conflagration*. Although a natural disaster such as an earthquake may have been responsible for these events, an external attack against the city, as also at Numeira, cannot be ruled out.[54]

The disarticulated bone piles, of the estimated 20,000 EB IA shaft tombs,[55] must be differentiated from: "the often jumbled human bone remains from the later EB II–III charnel houses. . . . which, it now seems evident, was caused by the successive displacement of originally primary burials."[56]

Chesson summarized that:

The 10 urban-phase charnel houses that have been published to date combine results from the excavations directed by Lapp from 1965 to 1967 (A8, A20, A21, A41, A42, A44, A51, C4), and those excavated in the following decade (A22,

---

[52] Rast and Schaub, *Bab Edh-Dhra': Excavations at the Town Site (1975-1981)*, 272.

[53] See also 62-65. Ibid., 103.

[54] Rast, "Bab Edh-Dhra' (ABD)," 1:560.

[55] The 20,000 shaft tombs were estimated to account for over half a million bodies. Lapp, "Bab Edh-Dhra' (RB 1966)"; "Bab Edh-Dhra' Tomb A 76"; "Bab Edh-Dhra' (RB 1968)."

[56] Rast, "Patterns of Settlement at Bab Edh-Dhra'," 9; Paul W. Lapp, "Palestine in the Early Bronze Age," in *Near Eastern Archaeology in the Twentieth Century: Essays in Honor of Nelson Glueck*, ed. James A. Sanders (Garden City, N.Y.: Doubleday, 1970), 107.

A55).⁵⁷ Analysis of the material culture demonstrates that these charnel houses are associated chronologically with the urban settlement of Bab edh-Dhraʿ. . . . The structure was constructed of mudbricks, with a stone-paved threshold. The builders cobbled the floor with wadi cobbles, and also built an entry way, slightly offcenter on the long wall. Charnel House A41 contained 231 vessels and a minimum number of 42 individuals. Also recorded was the areal extent of burned debris (wood, cloth, and ashy bone and brick), which can also be identified in the profile.⁵⁸

What is significant here is that the bodies in the charnel houses were dead before they were placed inside and burned from some kind of catastrophe which followed their internment. The cemetery may have been collateral damage from the destruction of the city either from divine or human means. However, to qualify as Sodom one should expect to find bodies among the ruins of the city and not only in the cemetery.

FACT 54: SHOOTING FLAMING ARROWS INTO THE AIR WAS COMMONLY USED BY ENEMIES IN THE ANE

Wood has suggested that because the evidence in Charnel house A22 in the cemetery at BeD "revealed that the fire started in the roof and spread to the interior when the roof collapsed" that "this provides powerful evidence that 'the Lord rained down burning sulphur on Sodom and Gomorrah—from the Lord out of the heavens'" (Gen 19:24).⁵⁹

However, in the ancient world it was common to destroy cities by means of shooting flaming arrows into the air, which would then land on the roofs of buildings and cause the wattle and daub (twigs and sticks) roof constructions to catch fire. This common practice is depicted on the Lachish reliefs in the British Museum, where fiery arrows are employed by the Babylonians in their siege of Lachish.⁶⁰

The roofs of buildings that have been set on fire are certainly not *proof* of divine destruction. Flaming arrows were used by ancient nations during military campaigns and charnel houses that appeared to be dwellings on the exterior would have certainly been attacked during war.

Prior to the destruction of Sodom and Gomorrah (Gen 18) we know that the region as far south as the Amorites who were dwelling in Ḥaṣaṣon-Tamar (=En-Gedi on the Israeli side of the Dead Sea, 2 Chron 20:2) had conflict with foreign nations (i.e., Shinar, Ellasar, Elam, Goiim; Gen 14:1–7).

As one of my students with a military background pointed out:

> From a military strategy perspective disrupting the enemy is a key tactic because it only takes a few weak links to break a defense—or one critical weak link. All of the people in this area have very specific burial practices for numerous deep-rooted reasons. Attacking the cemetery would be a direct mental and spiritual assault. The mental and spiritual well-being of any group is essential to its physical performance.⁶¹

There can be several explanations for why the roofs of the charnal houses burned.

---

⁵⁷ Rast and Schaub, *Bab Edh-Dhraʿ: Excavations in the Cemetery*.
⁵⁸ Chesson, "Libraries of the Dead," 150.
⁵⁹ Wood, "Have Sodom And Gomorrah Been Found?," 81.

⁶⁰ T. C. Mitchell, *Biblical Archaeology: Documents from the British Museum* (Cambridge, U.K.: Cambridge University Press, 1988).
⁶¹ Personal correspondence with Robert Hamilton, Jan 25, 2014.

Destruction Facts

Fact 55: Mysterious clinkers, identified as trinitite, were discovered at TeH

Thus far, the TeH excavation has uncovered a total of five pieces of superheated vitrified pottery (clinkers; see Fig. 47) from the MB destruction layer and desert glass at Tall Mwais, within five miles of TeH. Collins stated in *BAR* that:

> It marks one of the most violent, enormous destruction events imaginable. We have pieces of pottery melted into glass, some bubbled like lava, found across the site. . . . We have even documented pieces of desert glass (impact glass) strewn across the eastern Kikkar, created at temperatures exceeding 6,000 degrees Celsius.[62]

47. The 4.5-inch-long clinker of melted pottery (large piece to the left in the photo) that was discovered in the MB layer at TeH. To the right are two smaller pieces of trinitite from ground zero at Trinity New Mexico.

Photo by Michael C. Luddini. Courtesy of TeHEP

Something turned the pieces of pottery into glass, but only on one side. The material was blind tested at the U.S. Geological Survey Laboratory, on the campus of New Mexico Tech, and scientifically identified as "trinitite."[63] It derived its name from Trinity, New Mexico, where the first nuclear tests were conducted, the heat of which produced this same type of material.[64]

Dr. Dumbar, who tested the material at the laboratory, commented on the temperature necessary to create such a result. He reports:

> It would have to be at least two thousand degrees Fahrenheit at the zircon location. . . . Actually, the external air temperature would've had to be a lot higher than that, because ceramic material isn't a good conductor of heat, but it reached to the depth of the zircon to the tune of two thousand degrees. . . . An intensely burning room could only get to about sixteen hundred, maybe eighteen hundred degrees for a while, but not for long.[65]

Trinitite has unique characteristics different from obsidian (volcanic glass) and fulgurite (lightning glass), which scientists can easily identify. Given the unique characteristics of trinitite and according to Dr. Dumbar, this sample is "visually, materially and chemically"[66] the same as trinitite.

Collins reported in *BAR* that:

> Across Tall el-Ḥammâm, archaeologists found widespread evidence of an intense conflagration that left the Middle Bronze Age city in ruins. They found scorched foundations and floors buried under nearly 3 feet of dark grey ash, as well as dozens of pottery sherds covered with a frothy, "melted" surface; the glassy appearance indicates that they were briefly exposed to temperatures well in excess of 2,000 degrees Fahrenheit, the approximate heat of volcanic magma. Such evidence suggests the city and its environs were catastrophically destroyed in a sudden and extreme conflagration.[67]

The extreme heat required to melt pottery and produce trinitite indicates that there was an unusual phenomenon that took place at and around TeH.[68]

---

[62] Collins, "Tall El-Hammam Is Sodom," 4; Collins and Scott, *Discovering the City of Sodom*, 213.

[63] Collins and Scott, *Discovering the City of Sodom*, 207.

[64] Collins, "Where Is Sodom?, 71 n. 8, 9.

[65] Collins and Scott, *Discovering the City of Sodom*, 208–09.

[66] Ibid., 213.

[67] Collins, "Where Is Sodom?," 41.

[68] Bunch et al., "A Tunguska Sized Airburst Destroyed Tall El-Hammam".

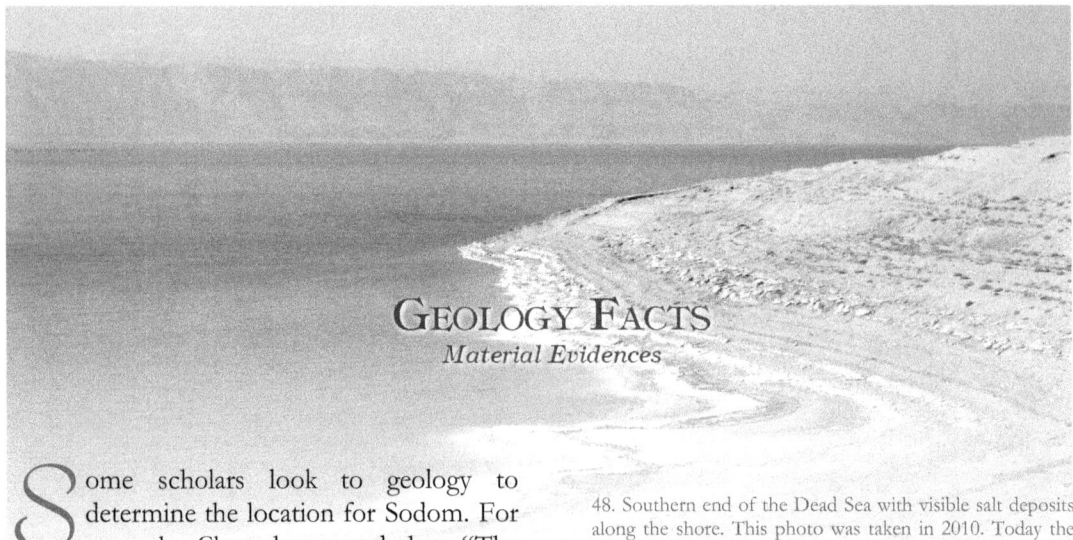

GEOLOGY FACTS
Material Evidences

Some scholars look to geology to determine the location for Sodom. For example, Clapp has stated that: "The strongest proof that Sodom and Gomorrah stood at the south end of the Dead Sea is offered by geology."[1]

There is a surprising amount of data that has been gathered on the Dead Sea region, largely produced by the petroleum and mining industries. This chapter will present the geological facts that are known based on much of this research.

FACT 56: THE DEAD SEA IS AT ITS LOWEST POINT IN HISTORY AND THERE ARE NO EXPOSED RUINS

The Dead Sea is one of the most interesting bodies of water in the world, particularly as it is the lowest point on earth along the Great Rift Valley in Jordan. Studies have shown that the Dead Sea levels have fluctuated over time. Bookman et al., describes the variations in the Dead Sea levels and states:

During historical periods,[2] the Dead Sea level

48. Southern end of the Dead Sea with visible salt deposits along the shore. This photo was taken in 2010. Today the Dead Sea is at its lowest point in history. There are no visible signs of EB or MB ruins comparable with Sodom along the shore. There Roman and Byzantine harbor ruins.

fluctuated around 400 below mean sea level (bmsl).[3] In the early 20th century the natural lake level reached a high-stand of ~390 m bmsl. However, since the 1930s, the construction of a dam at the Sea of Galilee outlet, and the increased diversion of the Jordan River water and industrial use of the Dead Sea brine, have initiated a continuous process of a drastic level drop, which has accelerated since the 1970s at a rate of >1 m/ year.[4]

---

[1] Clapp, "The Site of Sodom and Gomorrah: A Diversity of Views," 339.

[2] Based on radiocarbon dating, at 14,000 BC the level of the Dead Sea was -180 m bmsl. This however does not affect the argument being made here in the historical period. Revital Bookman et al., "Quaternary Lake Levels in the Dead Sea Basin: Two Centuries of Research," in *New Frontiers in Dead Sea Paleoenvironmental Research*, ed. Yehouda Enzel, Amotz Agnon, and Mordechai Stein, Special Papers: Geological Society of America 401 (Boulder, Colo.: Geological Society of America, 2006), 160.

[3] Revital Bookman (Ken-Tor) et al., "Late Holocene Lake Levels of the Dead Sea," *Geological Society of America Bulletin* 116, no. 5–6 (2004): 555–71; Bookman et al., "Quaternary Lake Levels in the Dead Sea Basin: Two Centuries of Research," 155–70; Mordechai Stein, "The Sedimentary and Geochemical Record of Neogene-Quaternary Water Bodies in the Dead Sea Basin - Inferences for the Regional Paleoclimatic History," *Journal of Paleolimnology* 26, no. 3 (2001): 271; Yuval Bartov et al., "Lake Levels and Sequence Stratigraphy of Lake Lisan, the Late Pleistocene Precursor of the Dead Sea," *Quaternary Research* 57 (2002): 9; Bookman (Ken-Tor) et al., "Late Holocene Lake Levels of the Dead Sea," 555–71; Adi Torfstein, Ittai Gavrieli, and Mordechai Stein, "The Sources and Evolution of Sulfur in the Hypersaline Lake Lisan (paleo-Dead Sea)," *Earth and Planetary Science Letters* 236 (2005): 63.

[4] Revital Bookman et al., "Possible Connection between Large Volcanic Eruptions and Level Rise Episodes in the Dead Sea Basin," *Quaternary Science*

49. The Dead Sea elevations over an 8-year period. See Fig. 48 for 2010 levels. Today the Dead Sea is at its lowest point in history due to modern irrigation and industrial plants along the southern end of the Dead Sea. There are no visible signs of EB or MB ruins comperable with Sodom along the shore.

Frumkin and Elitzur reported on the Dead Sea levels and stated that:

> Currently [2001] the lake is very low—around 1,350 ft. [-411 m[5]] below sea level; much of its southern basin, which in past low-water periods would have been exposed, now serves as a series of solar evaporation ponds for the extraction of minerals from water drawn from the northern basin. These ponds appear from space like cracked pieces of turquoise.[6]

According to the Israel Marine Data Center (ISRAMAR), which monitors the Dead Sea, "along with geological and archaeological evidence, today the Dead Sea is -423 meters (1,388 ft.) below sea level."[7]

Extensive geological and archaeological research, based on the ancient ruins along the Dead Sea shore, has been carried out by Frumkin and Elitzur to determine the ancient levels of the Dead Sea. They summarized their research and stated:

> There are three historically documented phases of the Dead Sea in the biblical record: low lake levels *ca.* 2000–1500 B.C.E. (before common era [MB]); high lake levels *ca.* 1500–1200 B.C.E. [LB]; and low lake levels between *ca.* 1000 and 700 B.C.E. [IA]. The biblical evidence indicates that during the dry periods the southern basin of the Dead Sea was completely dry, a fact that was not clear from the geological and archaeological data alone.[8]
>
> Whether Sodom and Gomorrah should be located on the southern shore of the Dead Sea or in the northern or central shore, . . . the implication of

---

Reviews 89 (2014): 123; N. G. Lensky et al., "Water, Salt, and Energy Balances of the Dead Sea," *Water Resources Research* 41, no. 12 (2005): 1–13.

[5] These are negative numbers because the Dead Sea is below sea level.

[6] Amos Frumkin and Yoel Elitzur, "The Rise and Fall of the Dead Sea," *BAR* 27, no. 6 (2001): 47.

[7] Isaac Gertman and A. Hecht, "The Dead Sea Hydrography from 1992 to 2000," *Journal of Marine Systems* 35 (2002): 169–81; Isaac Gertman, "Changes in the Surface Level of the Dead Sea and in the Total Stability of the Dead Sea Water Column.," *Israel Oceanographic & Limnological Research*, 2014,

http://isramar.ocean.org.il/isramar2009/DeadSea/LongTerm.aspx.

[8] Amos Frumkin and Yoel Elitzur, "Historic Dead Sea Level Fluctuations Calibrated with Geological and Archaeological Evidence," *Quaternary Research* 57 (2002): 334.

The Location of Sodom

Gen. 14 [time of the Patriarchs ca. 2100–1850 BC] is that in the time of the described war, the southern part of the lake was completely dry, so that the Dead Sea level must have been below −400 m amsl (1,300 ft.). On the other hand, when the chapter was written or edited, the plain was completely inundated.[9] The Dead Sea level would have been higher than −400 m amsl at that time.[10]

Frumkin reports that:

This suggests a maximum Dead Sea level below -351 m during the Early Bronze period…. [and] that the Dead Sea level was falling during Stage 4 [2,300–1,500 BC], and the south basin may have dried out [-380 m]."[11]

This would also indicate that during the period of the Patriarchs the level of the Dead Sea was higher than the present level (-423 m).[12] This agrees with Bookman et al. who stated: "The past drops in the lake never exceeded the modern artificial drop rates."[13] This indicates that if the Cities of the Plain were destroyed and slid into the Dead Sea, they should presently be visible along the shore (see *Fact 52*). However, the receding Dead Sea has not revealed any ruins that have been identified as Sodom. The Albrightan hypothesis, that the Cities of the Plain are submerged under the Dead Sea, is refuted by the geological evidence.

Both TeH and BeD are situated in the Great Rift Valley. BeD is positioned at an approximate elevation of -240 m. below sea level and TeH is -160 (lower tell) to -144 m (upper tell) below sea level. Both sites are well above the Dead Sea level in any period and neither could ever have been under the Dead Sea, as its lowest level in recorded history was -300 bmsl (3000 BC).

As Merrill puts it:

The destruction of these cities took place within historical times; but within historical times there has been no convulsion in that region, or change in the sea or land about it, to justify either of the opinions to which reference has been made.[14]

Josephus claims that Lake Asphaltites (the Dead Sea) was created overtop of the bitumen pits after the destruction of Sodom and Gomorrah (*Ant.* 1:9),[15] although geologists know from research that the Dead Sea existed long before that time (see Fact 61).[16]

Fact 57: Bitumen is Found All Around the Dead Sea

First, we must identify what is meant by *bitumen* (Gen 14:10; Heb. *ḥēmār*. See Chapter One: "Biblical References to Sodom: Genesis 14:1–12").[17] Nissenbaum and Goldberg defined it as ozocerite (Gr. *oze* stench + *kero* wax; an odorous paraffin earthwax) "a natural

---

[9] Frumkin and Elitzur, "The Rise and Fall of the Dead Sea," 48.

[10] Frumkin and Elitzur, "Historic Dead Sea Level Fluctuations Calibrated with Geological and Archaeological Evidence," 340.

[11] Amos Frumkin, "The Holocene History of Dead Sea Levels," in *The Dead Sea: The Lake and Its Setting*, ed. Tina M. Niemi, Zvi Ben-Avraham, and Joel R. Gat, Oxford Monographs on Geology and Geophysics 36 (New York, N.Y.: Oxford University Press, USA, 1997), 242–43.

[12] The only period of time when the Dead Sea was lower than today was during the Byzantine period (500 AD), when it was at about -440 m bmsl. This is evident from the Madaba map, where there is depicted only water evident in the northern basin and no evidence of the Lisan.

[13] Bookman (Ken-Tor) et al., "Late Holocene Lake Levels of the Dead Sea," 555.

[14] Merrill, *East of the Jordan*, 232–33.

[15] Montague held the idea that the Dead Sea did not exist prior to the destruction of Sodom and Gomorrah, but that the Jordan River continued to flow into the Gulf of Aquaba. Edward P. Montague, *Narrative of the Late Expedition to the Dead Sea* (Philadelphia, Pa.: Carey & Hart, 1849), 190.

[16] Gardosh et al., "Hydrocarbon Exploration in the Southern Dead Sea Area," 58.

[17] BDB states that bitumen was "used for cement in building Babel (Gen 11:3)"... and "used in coating Moses' 'ark' of bulrushes (Exod 2:3)." Briggs, Driver, and Brown, *A Hebrew and English Lexicon of the Old Testament with an Appendix Containing the Biblical Aramaic. Based on the Lexicon of William Gesenius as Translated by Edward Robinson*, 330.

50. Natural formed ashphalt called Bitumen collected along the shore of the Dead Sea.
Photo by Daniel Tzvi /Wikimedia Commons

mixture of predominantly high molecular weight paraffinic hydrocarbons."[18] However, it is often identified as asphalt, common in the Dead Sea. Josephus called it Lake Asphaltites (*Ant.* 1.9) and the Romans called it Asphalt Lake (Lat. *Palus Asphaltites;* see Fig. 50). Bitumen was also a major export from the Dead Sea region (Pliny the Elder *Nat. Hist.* 2.226; 5.72; 7.65; 28.80; 35.178).

Frumkin and Elitzur point out that:

> Although most ancient and modern versions and commentaries translate *h\emar* as bitumen or asphalt,[19] we believe, based on field evidence as well as etymological considerations, that the preferable translation might be "slime," which is more commonly found in the Dead Sea pits.[20]

The etymology of the term justifies using the term "slime pits," and is likely identified with the sink holes that form around the shores of the Dead Sea in dry periods (see Fig. 51). For this discussion, the term bitumen will be broadened to include all forms of petroleum products, including asphalt, oil, tar, and natural gas.[21]

There is no question that the Dead Sea is full of bitumen that floats to the surface (Josephus *J.W.* 4.479–80; Strabo *Geogr.* 16.2.42; Diodorus Siculus *Hist. Lib.* 19:98.84–88;[22] Tacitus *Hist.* 5.7),[23] being pushed up through the fault lines to the surface by earthquakes or movements of the plates.[24]

---

[18] Nissenbaum and Goldberg, "Asphalts, Heavy Oils, Ozocerite and Gases in the Dead Sea Basin," 172.

[19] In their research, Nissenbaum and Goldberg, decided that "The Dead Sea material has been so often referred to as asphalts, that for historial reasons it was decided to retain this term." Ibid., 167.

[20] Frumkin and Elitzur, "The Rise and Fall of the Dead Sea," 42 n.1.

[21] Gardosh et al., "Hydrocarbon Exploration in the Southern Dead Sea Area," 69; Nissenbaum and Goldberg, "Asphalts, Heavy Oils, Ozocerite and Gases in the Dead Sea Basin," 175.

[22] Diodorus Siculus, *Library of History: Books 19.66-20*, trans. Russel M. Geer, vol. 10, 12 vols., LCL 390 (Cambridge, Mass.: Harvard University Press, 1954).

[23] Arie Nissenbaum, "Dead Sea asphalts—Historical Aspects," *Bulletin of the Association of Petroleum Geologists* 62, no. 5 (1978): 840–45; Nissenbaum and Goldberg, "Asphalts, Heavy Oils, Ozocerite and Gases in the Dead Sea Basin," 167.

[24] Frederick G. Clapp, "Geology and Bitumens of the Dead Sea Area, Palestine and TransJordan," *Bulletin of the American Association of Petroleum Geologists* 20, no. 7 (1936): 901–903; Nissenbaum, "Dead Sea asphalts—Historical Aspects," 843.

Bitumen and asphalt are also found in the region around the Dead Sea.[25] Geikie testified that:

> the whole region is full of the materials for such a catastrophe as overtook them [Cities of the Plain]. Wells of liquid bitumen, or, as we may call it, petroleum, abounded in the neighbourhood, and vast quantities of it ooze through the chalky rocks, while the bottom of the lake is bedded with it, vast masses rising to the surface after any convulsion, as in the case of the great earthquake of 1837. Indeed, huge cakes float up, at times, even when there is no seismal disturbance, and are seized by the Bedouins, who carry what they can gather to Jerusalem for sale. Sulphur abounds, in layers and fragments, over the plains and along the shores of the lake.[26]

South

Udd, in her Ph.D. dissertation, made the erroneous statement that: "the geological features ascribed to the area surrounding the cities of the plain, such as bitumen and salt (Gen 14:10; 19:26), *are found only south of the Lisan* [emphasis added]."[27]

Students often repeat this error without checking the geological facts. Certainly there is bitumen in the southern end of the Dead Sea but it is also present in the regions to the east, west and north.[28] Today the area south of the Lisan Peninsula is occupied by shallow industrial salt evaporation ponds for extracting potash and other minerals.

North

Amit and Bein reported that in the north: "The only other asphalt occurrence in the Rift Valley is in the Hasbaya region in Lebanon, some 180 km north of the Dead Sea area."[29]

The reason it is so seldom associated with the northern end of the Dead Sea[30] is explained by Amit and Bein:

> To date, no exploration well has been drilled in the northern part of the Dead Sea north of the En Gedi-2 well. Most of this area is covered by the hypersaline, approximately 300-m-deep Dead Sea lake, and its hydrocarbon potential is poorly known.[31]

However, at TeH in the north, Collins reported that: "we have unearthed evidence of the bitumen-processing trade at Tall el-Hammam."[32]

East

Small seepages of asphalt have been reported on the southeastern side of the Jordan, south of the Wadi Mujib, and at BeD; but Clapp could not find anyone to verify these reports[33] and could not find evidence to justify calling them bitumen pits sufficient to trap an army. Nissenbaum and Goldberg reported that:

> the presence of ozocerite on the eastern shore of the lake has been known for a long time.[34] Picard (1933) described ozocerite veins from the area south of W.

---

[25] Nissenbaum, "Dead Sea asphalts—Historical Aspects," 837–44.

[26] Geikie, *Holy Land and the Bible*, 119; *Hours with the Bible or The Scriptures in the Light of Modern Discovery and Knowledge: From Creation to the Patriarchs with Illustrations*, vol. 1 (New York, N.Y.: Pott, 1882), 1:392.

[27] Udd, "Bab Edh-Dhra', Numeira, and the Biblical Patriarchs: A Chronological Study," 2.

[28] Wenham, *Genesis 1-15*, 1:309.

[29] Amit and Bein, "The Genesis of the Asphalt in the Dead Sea Area," 213.

[30] Nissenbaum and Goldberg, "Asphalts, Heavy Oils, Ozocerite and Gases in the Dead Sea Basin," 177.

[31] Gardosh et al., "Hydrocarbon Exploration in the Southern Dead Sea Area," 58; Ora Amit and Amos Bein, "The Evolution of the Dead Sea Floating Asphalt Blocks: Simulations by Pyrolisis," *Journal of Petroleum Geology* 2, no. 4 (1980): 429–47; Tina M. Niemi, Zvi Ben-Avraham, and Joel R. Gat, eds., *The Dead Sea: The Lake and Its Setting*, Oxford Monographs on Geology and Geophysics 36 (New York, N.Y.: Oxford University Press, USA, 1997).

[32] Collins, "The Geography of Sodom and Zoar," 5.

[33] Clapp, "Geology and Bitumens of the Dead Sea Area, Palestine and TransJordan," 901.

[34] Arie Nissenbaum and Z. Aizenshatat, "Geochemical Studies on Ozokerite From the Dead Sea Area," *Chemical Geology* 16 (1975): 121.

51. A sink hole on the eastern side of the Dead Sea during a visit in February 2014, although the majority of these are located on the western side.

Photo by Dan Galassini

Mujeib (River Arnon).³⁵ The largest occurrence is at Ein Humar (= 'Asphalt Spring' [See Map 7]), where the Nubian sandstone is characterized by fractures, 13 cm wide, that are filled with yellowish-gray, waxy ozocerite.³⁶

Bender reported that: "On the *eastern side of the graben, asphalt was recorded only in a fault breccia southeast of the Lisan Peninsula.*"³⁷

West

However, according to Amit and Bein, the main concentration of petroleum products is found on the western side of the Dead Sea graben³⁸ along what is called the "tar belt"³⁹ "from Hazeva in the south to Mezada in the north."⁴⁰ Nissenbaum and Goldberg reported that:

> Asphalts are found on both sides of the basin, although the quantities found in the western margins seem to be larger. . . . On the western margins of the Dead Sea Basin, asphalts are found mainly between Mt Sedom and Ein Gedi. Occasional reports of asphalts north of Ein Gedi have not as yet been verified.⁴¹

Oil seepage is concentrated around Wadi Mahawuat near Jebel Usdem and Wadi Sebbeh close to Masada (Strabo *Geogr.*

---

³⁵ See also Amit and Bein, "The Genesis of the Asphalt in the Dead Sea Area," 213.

³⁶ Nissenbaum and Goldberg, "Asphalts, Heavy Oils, Ozocerite and Gases in the Dead Sea Basin," 172.

³⁷ Friedrich Bender, *Geology of the Arabian Peninsula, Jordan*, U.S. Geological Survey Professional Paper 560 (Washington, D.C: United States Government Printing Office, 1975), 27.

³⁸ Gardosh et al., "Hydrocarbon Exploration in the Southern Dead Sea Area," 68.

³⁹ Ibid., 58.

⁴⁰ Amit and Bein, "The Genesis of the Asphalt in the Dead Sea Area," 213.

⁴¹ Nissenbaum and Goldberg, "Asphalts, Heavy Oils, Ozocerite and Gases in the Dead Sea Basin," 172.

16.2.44)[42] between Mount Sedom (Jebel Usdem) and En-Gedi,[43] as well as between En-Gedi and the end of the Jordan River at the northern tip of the Dead Sea (See Maps 4 and 7).[44]

Lynch described Wadi Zuweirah, at the north end of Jebel Usdum, as "a broad, flat, marshy delta, the soil coated with salt and bitumen, and yielding to the foot" (see *Fact 58*).[45]

Geikie described the presence of bitumen on the western sides and pointed out that:

> The chalk hills on the western side are marked by the presence of bitumen in them, both in a liquid and a solid form; in some places by layers of rocksalt. Between the mouth of the lake and Engedi, indeed, the marl is so strongly impregnated with bitumen at some points that it burns like our bituminous shale, and a strong odour of bitumen is given off by the hills.[46]

While the bitumen pits (Gen 14:10) are reported by many scholars[47] around the southern region of the Dead Sea (See Maps 4 and 7), geological research provides evidence for the concentration of asphalt (bitumen) seepage in the western side of the Dead Sea along the fault lines running north and south. While petroleum products are found along the southern regions of the Dead Sea, they are almost exclusively identified on the western side.

Location of bitumen pits

One of the difficulties in identifying the location of the bitumen pits (Gen 14:10) is that the formation of sink holes is triggered by "the declining level of the Dead Sea."[48] Since the level fluctuates, the exact location of sinkholes (bitumen pits) is unknown. If we use the present location of sinkholes as an example of where these were 3000 years ago, then they would have been concentrated on the western side of the Dead Sea, with a few possibly along the eastern shore. However, due to the variations in the levels of the Dead Sea, to determine the ancient location on the basis of modern research is mere speculation and not reliable. The fact that they are present in modern times does not necessarily mean they were in this exact location in ancient times. Certainly, this argument can be used for either the presence or the absence of bitumen pits in either location. All one can conclude is that the presence of sink holes alone does not determine the location of Sodom. Even if one could identify the location of ancient sink holes, this still does not determine the location of Sodom, since ancient people would not likely build their cities near these hazardous natural formations, nor go to battle close to where they lived (see *Fact 16*).

FACT 58: JEBEL USDUM IS NOT SODOM OR LOT'S WIFE

Some look to the southern end of the Dead Sea and see salt pillars around the salt formation of Jebel Usdum (Mount Sedom) that remind them of Lot's wife being turned into a pillar of salt (Gen 19:26), and conclude that Sodom must be close by. However, this is poor evidence since numerous pillars of salt

---

[42] Clapp, "Geology and Bitumens of the Dead Sea Area, Palestine and TransJordan," 901.

[43] Geikie, *Holy Land and the Bible*, 2:114–15.

[44] Blanckenhorn, *Noch eimal Sodom und Gomorrha*, 117; George Stanfield Blake, *The Mineral Resources of Palestine and Transjordan* (Jerusalem: Azriel, 1930), 13–25; Clapp, "Geology and Bitumens of the Dead Sea Area, Palestine and TransJordan," 900; Gardosh et al., "Hydrocarbon Exploration in the Southern Dead Sea Area," 58, 73.

[45] Lynch, *Narrative of the United States Expedition to the River Jordan and the Dead Sea*, 306.

[46] Geikie, *Holy Land and the Bible*, 2: 114–15.

[47] Wenham, *Genesis 1-15*, 1:310.

[48] Meir Abelson et al., "Evaluation of the Dead Sea Sinkholes," in *New Frontiers in Dead Sea Paleoenvironmental Research*, ed. Yehouda Enzel, Amotz Agnon, and Mordechai Stein, Special Papers: Geological Society of America 401 (Boulder, Colo.: Geological Society of America, 2006), 248.

can be found in the region and around the Dead Sea (see Fig. 19), each considered by successive generations to be Lot's wife. Clapp provided a survey of early explorers who witnessed the salt pillars around the region of Jebel Usdum.[49] As Taylor pointed out:

> Clearly, there was a pillar identified as Lot's wife situated conveniently close to the northern end of the Dead Sea, since in the account of Epiphanius the Monk (*Civ. Sana.* 32) it is 2 miles south of the cave of John the Baptist. By the 12th century (*Descriptio locorum* 26; Daniel the Abbot 56), however, the pillar is identified near Zoar.[50]

As Neev and Hall indicated: "Large salt diapirs (Mount Sedom; the Lisan Peninsula) are found along the coasts of the Dead Sea[51] as well as beneath it."[52]

However, no salt pillar around the Dead Sea has been archaeologically identified as Lot's wife and it may be impossible to positively identify any salt pillar as Lot's wife. On the role of salt in the biblical narrative see David E. Graves, "Sodom And Salt in Their Ancient Near Eastern Cultural Context," *NEASB* 61 (2016): 15–32.

Fact 59: TeH is well watered

While the water supply at some sites in the northern Jordan Valley, like as at Tulaylat al-Ghassul, may have dried up during the Early Bronze age, life at TeH continued uninterrupted. It was only when something happened in the LBA that life in the southern Jordan Valley was brought to a halt. The area around TeH is very well watered. As Graves and Stripling pointed out:

According to Prag, the name Tall el-Ḥammâm translates as "Hill of the Hot Baths."[53] The word Ḥammâm in Arabic means "hot spring/well"[54] and most commonly refers to "hot baths" similar to the Hebrew *ḥamat* which means "hot springs." It is the only site in the region with a name associated with thermal springs.[55]

As Collins described:

> The Kikkar of the Jordan was watered [in ancient times] by the flooding of the Jordan River, by the runoff from major wadis that brought water from both the Cisjordan and Transjordan highlands, and by numerous perennial springs.[56]

Indeed, numerous hot springs exist in and around TeH, testified by William Thomson[57] in the 1880's and the author. Today three of the springs are capped and used for agricultural irrigation. These waters would have provided a lush environment for a variety of crops (see *Fact 62*).

While most sites in the region that relied on water from wadis during the winter months would have to go without, Tall el-Ḥammâm would have water year-round, one of the main reasons they survived for so many centuries.

Fact 60: The southern Jordan Valley was well-watered in ancient times

Today, the southern Jordan Valley is well-watered and full of agriculture, and it was the same in ancient times. As Neev and Emery point out:

> During the Early Bronze ages overall the climatic conditions in the Dead Sea region were not appreciably different from those at present, as

---

[49] Clapp, "The Site of Sodom and Gomorrah: A Diversity of Views," 327–32.

[50] Taylor, "The Dead Sea in Western Travellers' Accounts," 11.

[51] I. Zak, "The Geology of Mt. Sedom" (Ph.D. diss., Hebrew University of Jerusalem, 1967), 209.

[52] David Neev and John K. Hall, *The Dead Sea Geophysical Survey 19 July-1 August 1974: Final Report No. 2*, vol. 76, Geological Survey of Israel 6 (Jerusalem: Marine Geology Division, 1976).

[53] Prag, "Tell Iktanu and Tall El-Hammam 1990," 57.

[54] The word *Hammam* can also mean "pigeon" depending on how it is pronounced.

[55] Graves and Stripling, "Re-Examination of the Location for the Ancient City of Livias," 189.

[56] Collins and Scott, *Discovering the City of Sodom*, 116; Collins, "Where Is Sodom?," 5.

[57] Thomson, *Land and the Book: Lebanon, Damascus, and Beyond Jordan*, 3:670.

attested by fossil flora found in excavations at Bab edh-Dhr'a and Numeira [see *Fact 62*].[58]

As T. E. Lawrence (of Arabia) observed in the early 1900's: "Abdulla. . . . was camped beneath us in the paradise of the Dead Sea's southern shore, a plain gushing with brooks of sweet water, and rich in vegetation."[59]

In the space of just one hundred years, it is clear to see that a lush region has turned into a desert. What looks like a cursed region to our eyes may have once been an oasis.

FACT 61: THE DEAD SEA EXISTED PRIOR TO GENESIS 19

Some maintain, based on Josephus (*Ant.* 1:9), that the Dead Sea was created from the destruction of the Cities of the Plain and did not exist until Gen 19.

However, as early as 1896, Blanckenhorn described the events and upheaval, which in his estimation, created the Dead Sea graben: "With the end of the Tertiary period,[60] in an event of extreme violence . . . the entire Syrian land, from its south end to its north end, was torn apart and the ground in between sank into the depths."[61]

In 1977 Garfunkel described it this way: "The basin is a young intracontinental plate boundary formed as a result of the late-Cenozoic [15–20 million years] breakup of the once continuous Arabo-African continent."[62]

Lyakhovsky, Ben-Avraham, and Achmon in 1985 described its creation from two processes and stated that:

> Geological and geophysical evidence from the Gulf of Elat, at the southern part of the Dead Sea rift, and other parts of the rift indicate that two kinds of geodynamical processes occur here simultaneously.[63] The first is a transform motion which has led to a total displacement of 105 km on the faults along the Dead Sea rift since the time of its formation less than 20 Ma [mega-annum; million years][64] and to the formation of a series of pull-apart basins along the entire length of the rift zone. The other process is a propagation of actual crustal spreading activity from the Red Sea northward into the Gulf of Elat.[65]

Regardless of whether one agrees with the early age of millions of years, Power provides a suitable conclusion and stated that: "From the geological exploration of the great Syro-Palestinian depression we now know that the Dead Sea existed long before the destruction of the four cities."[66]

FACT 62: THERE IS PALEO-BOTANICAL EVIDENCE AT BOTH SITES

All cities in the Jordan Valley require water to survive and it is no surprise to find that both the northern and southern sites were strategically located near flowing springs.

---

[58] Neev and Emery, *The Destruction of Sodom, Gomorrah and Jericho*, 139.

[59] I am indebted to Glen Ruffle for bringing this to my attention. T. E. Lawrence, *Seven Pillars of Wisdom*, Wordsworth Classics of World Literature (Ware, Hertfordshire: Wordsworth, 1997), 474.

[60] Then in 1908 Blanckenhorn proposed the Jordan Valley was created in the pluvial, or the start of the first glacial age. Max Blanckenhorn, *Naturwissenschaftliche Studien Am Toten Meer Und Im Jordental* (Berlin: Friedländer & Sohn, 1912).

[61] Blanckenhorn, *Entstehung und Geschichte des Toten Meeres*, 16.

[62] Zvi Garfunkel, "The History and Formation of the Dead Sea Basin," in *The Dead Sea: The Lake and Its Setting*, ed. Tina M. Niemi, Zvi Ben-Avraham, and Joel R. Gat, Oxford Monographs on Geology and Geophysics 36 (New York, N.Y.: Oxford University Press, USA, 1997), 36.

[63] Zvi Ben-Avraham, "Rift Propagation along the Southern Dead Sea Rift (Gulf of Elat)," *Tectonophysics* 133 (1987): 193–200.

[64] R. Freund et al., "The Shear along the Dead Sea Rift," *Philosophical Transactions of the Royal Society of London: Series A, Mathematical and Physical Sciences* 267 (1970): 107–130; Garfunkel, "Internal Structure of the Dead Sea Leaky Transform (Rift) in Relation to Plate Kinematics," 81–108.

[65] Lyakhovsky, Ben-Avraham, and Achmon, "The Origin of the Dead Sea Rift," 29; Zvi Ben-Avraham, "Structural Framework of the Gulf of Elat (Aqaba), Northern Red Sea," *Journal of Geophysical Research* 90 (1985): 703–26.

[66] Power, "The Site of the Pentapolis: Part 1," 26.

These springs would have provided the lush landscape and crops to sustain life.

McCreery reported on the paleo-botanical studies from BeD. He documented that" "A total of 13 different cultigens [crops] have been identified from the 61 samples coming from primary loci."[67]

The species included barley, wheat, flax, lentil, pea, bean, chickpea, olives, grapes, figs, dates, almonds, wild plums, coriander, peaches and a variety of wild edible plants.[68]

Curtis Smith, the TeH paleo-botanist, reported that, based on what was found in the floatation samples:

> I found at Tall el Hammam this season (2014): grain seeds – barley or wheat, grass-type seed, . . . lentil seed (one), grape seeds and fragments (fairly numerous), perhaps a coriander (cilantro) seed – would have been for seasoning/spice, . . . perhaps flax seeds. All of these seeds were carbonized, but retained the form of the original. . . . The most productive site for finding the seeds was the area at first called "tabun/taboon", but lacking the clay structure, so perhaps an open-fire cooking site.[69]

Both sites reveal the presence of ample food and water to sustain a large population with a suitable diet via the presence of a variety of edible plants.

But does this help in the identification of either site as Sodom? What site would not have this kind of evidence to survive as a city in such a harsh climate?

Conclusion

Collins provided a word of caution here: "people who look only at geological features to ascertain the location of a site for an event and ignore the geographical details in the only ancient document that describes the event, become etiological legend-spinners themselves."[70]

---

[67] David W. McCreery, "The Paleoethnobotany of Bab Edh-Dhraʿ," in *Bab Edh-Dhraʿ: Excavations at the Town Site (1975-1981): Part 1: Text*, ed. Walter E. Rast and R. Thomas Schaub, vol. 2, Reports of the Expedition to the Dead Sea Plain, Jordan (Winona Lake, Ind.: Eisenbrauns, 2003), 451.

[68] Ibid., 449–61.

[69] Curtis Smith, "Paleo-Botanical Report for Tall El-Hammam, 2014," May 22, 2014, 1.

[70] Collins and Scott, *Discovering the City of Sodom*, 102.

Testimony Facts

Apart from the testimonial facts presented by early explorers for the NST and the traditional views of Josephus and Jerome for the SST it is good to hear from contemporary scholars. Certainly, the debate will not be settled by counting scholars and this chapter is not meant to be a contest of credentials, but it is always good to hear what others have to say.

Some of the supporters of Bâb edh-Dhrâ' wrote prior to the excavation of Tall el-Ḥammâm and will not be considered here as they had not entered into the debate of the two candidates for Sodom examined in this treatment.

Testimonies supporting Bâb edh-Dhrâ'

Todd Bolen

Todd Bolen is a biblical studies faculty member with The Master's College and a photographer who has a collection of photographs in 18 vols. of the Holy Land called *The Pictorial Library of Bible Lands*. He has written extensively, on his blog, against the research that Collins has been doing at TeH,[1] but has also been critical of BeD. On

52. Southern end of the Dead Sea seen from Numeira with white salt deposits visible along the shore. The Arab Potash Company (APC) is visible to the right and is primarily involved in harvesting minerals from the Dead Sea. It is the eighth largest potash producer worldwide by volume of production and the sole Arab producer of potash. The company also produces magnesium chloride, industrial salts, de-icers, bath salts, table salt, and raw materials for the cosmetic industry. Visible in the distance are the solar ponds where the water is evaporated to leave behind the raw materials. There are no visible signs of EB or MB ruins comperable with Sodom along the shore.

his *BiblePlaces* website he stated:

> Bab edh-Dhra ("Gate of the Arm") is on the southeastern corner of the Dead Sea, on the south bank of Wadi Kerak. It has been suggested as one of the five "cities of the plain" in Genesis 13 and 19, and has been proposed by some to be the city of Sodom. One difficulty with this identification is that the destruction of the Bab edh-Dhra is typically dated to c. 2300 BC, about 200 years earlier than the biblical date for the destruction of Sodom and Gomorrah.[2]

In one of his replies to Collins he states:

> For the record, *Bab edh-Dhra is not "my site."* I am open to the possibility, but it too must meet the historical, geographical, and archaeological criteria. You are right to note that its destruction appears to be too early for Abraham's time [emphasis added].[3]

---

[1] Todd Bolen, "Sodom Identified?," *BiblePlaces*, May 13, 2006, http://blog.bibleplaces.com/2006_05_01_archive.html; "Arguments Against Locating Sodom at Tall El-Hammam"; Todd Bolen, "Video: Search for Sodom and Gomorrah," *BiblePlaces*, August 10, 2009, http://blog.bibleplaces.com/2009/08/video-search-for-sodom-and-gomorrah.html; Todd Bolen, "Excavator Finds Evidence of Destruction at 'Sodom,'" *BiblePlaces*, December 19, 2011, http://blog.bibleplaces.com/2011/12/excavator-finds-evidence-of-destruction.html.

[2] Todd Bolen, "Bab Edh-Dhra," *Pictorial Library of Bible Lands*, 2014, http://www.bibleplaces.com/babedhdhra.htm.

[3] Bolen, "Video: Search for Sodom and Gomorrah."

Clyde Billington

Clyde Billington is Professor of History at University of Northwestern St. Paul, Executive Director of the Institute for Biblical Archaeology, and the Secretary of the Near East Archaeological Society.[4] He is also the editor of *Artifax* magazine in which he wrote an article and argued that Tall el-Ḥammâm is Heshbon.

> The largest of these villages was Bab edh Dhra, which was only about 10 acres. *I do not believe that any of these villages were Sodom or Gomorrah, but they were almost certainly ancillary villages that belonged to Sodom, Gomorrah,* and also to the other three cities mentioned in the Genesis account. It is true that Rast and Schaub dated these villages to ca. 2350–2300 BC, and it is also true that Abraham and Lot date closer to ca. 2100 BC, but this dating discrepancy can be easily explained, i.e. not all Early Bronze Age cities fell at the same time in Canaan as is generally assumed [emphasis added].[5]

Eugene H. Merrill

Eugene Merrill is the retired distinguished professor of Old Testament studies at Dallas Theological Seminary and 2010 president of the Evangelical Theological Society. Merrill who has been critical of the chronology of TeH earlier stated:

> Excavations at Bab edh-Dhra' and other sites on and near the el-Lisan Peninsula at the southeast end of the Dead Sea have revealed the remains of at least five ancient urban complexes, the latest of which is apparently earlier than 2000 BC. One is tempted to suppose that some or all of these are the biblical cities of the plain, since both their locations and dates are compatible with the witness of the Old Testament. It is impossible to be dogmatic on this point in light of the absence of extrabiblical literary attestation from these sites, but clearly the patriarchal history does seem to have more corroboration on this point than ever before.[6]

J. Randall Price

J. Randall Price is Distinguished Research Professor and Executive Director of the Center for Judaic Studies at Liberty University in Lynchburg, Virginia and founder and President of World of the Bible Ministries. Randall is also a visiting professor of Archaeology at Trinity Southwest University. In 1997 Price argued for the SST in his book *The Stones Cry Out* presenting the research done by Wood.[7] However, when Price wrote *The Stones Cry Out* in 1997 Tall el-Ḥammâm was still unexcavated.[8] Also, in personal conversations with Price, he has continued to support his earlier view of the location of BeD for Sodom. In his new book *Zondervan Handbook to Biblical Archaeology,* Price does not address Sodom or consider either Bâb edh-Dhrâ' or Tall el-Ḥammâm, but does place the destruction of Sodom and Gomorrah in 2067 BC at the end of the EB III period (although he lists this date in the EB IV ca. 2176–1973 BC).[9] He also mentions that the MB I–III dates (2000–1700 BC) are held by some scholars for the Patriarchs.

TESTIMONIES NOT SUPPORTIVE OF BED

Eric Cline

Eric Cline is currently Chair of the Department of Classical and Near Eastern Languages and Civilizations and Director of the Capitol Archaeological Institute at The George Washington University. As Eric Cline recently admitted in his chapter on "Sodom and Gomorrah", after assessing the current state of the "southern" evidence:

> [There] is no longer any particular reason to insist

---

[4] https://www.unwsp.edu/web/history-dept/clyde-billington.
[5] Billington, "Tall El-Hammam Is Not Sodom," 1.
[6] Merrill, *Kingdom of Priests,* 57.

[7] Price, *The Stones Cry Out,* 109–124.
[8] Collins and Scott, *Discovering the City of Sodom,* 35.
[9] J. Randall Price and H. Wayne House, *Zondervan Handbook of Biblical Archaeology: A Book by Book Guide to Archaeological Discoveries Related to the Bible* (Grand Rapids: Zondervan, 2018), 41.

that Bâb edh-Dhrâ' and Numeira are definitely Sodom and Gomorrah, especially if we wish to have Abraham both as an eyewitness and living in the Middle Bronze Age.. . . . Perhaps it would be wise to untether Sodom and Gomorrah from Bâb edh-Dhrâ' and Numeira and search elsewhere for them. But where?[10]

As an alternative Cline, told *Christianity Today* in 2008, that Collins:

> might be on to something but that he "has not yet produced any compelling archaeological evidence." Furthermore, Cline said, Collins's research was "putting the proverbial cart before the horse and excavating with an *a priori* bias." Cline said all Collins had so far was a hypothesis.[11]

More archaeological evidence has certainly been uncovered since 2008.

TESTIMONIES SUPPORTING TALL EL-ḤAMMÂM

Norman L. Geisler and Joseph M. Holden (2013)

Norman L. Geisler, is co-founded and chancellor of Veritas Evangelical Seminary in Murrieta, California, and Joseph M. Holden, President of Veritas Evangelical Seminary have argued for Tall el-Ḥammâm for the location of Sodom based on the strong evidence. Holden spent a season excavating at TeH and can speak firsthand of the evidence. In their new book they stated:

> More recent ongoing research conducted by Dr. Steven Collins at the northeastern end of the Dead Sea region (in Jordan) has offered promising evidence supporting the northern location of Tall el-Hammam as the city of Sodom.[12]
>
> In the case of Tall el-Hammam, the geographical information appears to have exceeded the customary criteria needed to typically consider an ancient ruin a confirmed biblical city. Many existing biblical sites have been confirmed based on much less geographical evidence than that offered by Tall el-Hammam. Indeed, after reviewing the still-increasing amount of archaeological, biblical, and geographical evidence, if one denies that Tall el-Hammam is the biblical city of Sodom, every biblical city that has been confirmed on less than epigraphical evidence must be called in question.[13]

Holden in describing Collins book states: "I don't know of a more convincing case for Sodom's long-awaited identification."[14]

Robert A. Mullins

Robert A. Mullins is the Professor of archaeology and Old Testament at Azusa Pacific University and stated:

> In this book [Collins and Scott, *Discovering the City of Sodom*], Collins provides the most complete discussion to date of all of the relevant biblical texts. The most compelling part of the book is Dr. Collin's argument for locating Sodom northeast of the Dead Sea, rather than farther to the south as many have assumed. Much of the skepticism about the historicity of Sodom over the years has been conducted in an archaeological vacuum. Now, with the excavations of Tell el-Hammâm and Collin's extensive presentation of the historical, geographical, and archaeological data, we now have a better material basis, for further discussion.[15]

James D. Tabor

James D. Tabor is the Chair of the Department of Religious Studies at the University of North Carolina at Charlotte. In personal correspondence with Collins in the summer of 2005, Tabor states:

> I have favored the "northern Sodom" theory for years now, not because of any archaeological evidence of which I am aware, but mostly just based on my reading of Genesis and the translation work I have done. In the Transparent English Version, of which I am the editor, we translated Genesis 13:10-11 (with the note): "And Lot lifted his eyes and saw all the circuit of the Jordan, that it was completely

---

[10] Eric H. Cline, *From Eden to Exile: Unraveling Mysteries of the Bible* (Tampa, Fla.: National Geographic, 2007), 59–60.

[11] Govier, "Looking Back: Claims to New Sodom Location Are Salted with Controversy," 15–16.

[12] Ibid., 215.

[13] Ibid., 219.

[14] Collins and Scott, *Discovering the City of Sodom*, back cover.

[15] Ibid., Preface.

watered—before YHVH ruined Sodom and Gomorrah—as the garden of YHVH, as the land of Egypt in your coming toward Zoar. And Lot chose for himself all the circuit* of the Jordan, and Lot pulled up stakes from the east, and they were separated, a man from upon his brother. . . . [Note:] *Heb *kikkār*, something round, a coin, a loaf of bread, or here, an area." Also, my reading of Josephus supports the same conclusion. Even though he is a very late witness, he seems to reflect/preserve older traditions. . . . I am very excited and encouraged by your work.[16]

Anson F. Rainey

Anson F. Rainey was the late (2011) Professor Emeritus of Ancient Near Eastern Cultures and Semitic Linguistics at Tel Aviv University. While Rainey did not believe in the historicity of the cities of the Plain, Collins quotes correspondence from Rainey about the location of the *kikkār* and stated:

> In recent conversations with A. Rainey regarding the location of the "plain (*kikkār*) of the Jordan" on which the Cities of the Plain, including Sodom and Gomorrah, were located, he stated that "Your arguments about the *Kikkar* are the most cogent…The map in the Atlas [*The Sacred Bridge: Carta's Atlas of the Biblical World*.] does need revision. I should have tagged it like the Shishak map, "highly conjectural." Gen 13 has to do with the high ground east of Bethel. As I said earlier, the references to the *kikkar* fit better with the area N. of the Dead Sea…As a sideline, it is usually ignored that the term "arabah" applies to the Jordan Valley north of the Dead Sea (2 Sam 4, about the assassins of Ish-baal). Too bad the author there did not use the term *kikkar*."[17]

Hershel Shanks

Hershel Shanks is the owner/editor of *Biblical Archaeology Review* and in correspondence with Collins over the publication of an article for the magazine Shanks stated:

> The tack I would like to take [for your BAR article] is whether the destruction of Sodom is a historical event or a matter of faith. But in any event, it is likely that it was this site [Tall el-Hammam] that inspired the Biblical description.[18]

Shanks visited Tall el-Ḥammâm on January 16, 2012.

Amahai Mazar

Amahai Mazar is the Professor at the Institute of Archaeology of the Hebrew University of Jerusalem. In 1992, with only the excavation of the sites in the southern end of the Dead Sea available for study, Mazar stated:

> The attempts to relate Genesis narratives to Early Bronze Age features cannot be completely excluded. The most tempting supposition is to relate the narrative in Genesis 14 about the five "cities of the plain" (Sodom, Gomorrah, Admah, Zeboiim, Zoar) to the discovery of five Early Bronze Age sites close to the eastern shores of the Dead Sea. At least two of these sites were fortified (Bab edh-Dhra and Numeira).[19]

Later in 2005 with regards to Collins' view of the *Kikkār* Mazar replied in personal correspondence that:

> I agree with you that real geographical background can be found in many biblical stories… such as the patriarchal stories…. I also agree with you that a straightforward reading of Gen 13:1-12 would call for the conclusion that when the author wrote *Kikkar Hayarden* he meant the southern Jordan Valley north of the Dead Sea…its supposed location in the mind of the biblical author.[20]

Mazar visited TeH February 2014 and was impressed with the size and prominence of the remains.

Leen Ritmeyer

Leen Ritmeyer is a free lance archaeological architect who works with the Tall el-Ḥammâm excavation on contract to draw the remains. In the forward to Collins's book

---

[16] Collins, "A Response to Bryant G. Wood," 17.
[17] Ibid., 4–5 n.13.
[18] Steven Collins, "Trowling Down: Tall El-Hammam News Letter," December 31, 2011, 1.
[19] Amihai Mazar, *Archaeology of the Land of the Bible: 10,000-586 B.C.E.*, vol. 1, The Anchor Yale Bible Reference Library (New Haven, Conn.: Yale University Press, 1992), 143.
[20] Collins, "A Response to Bryant G. Wood," 17.

Ritmeyer writes:

> As I see it, the location of Tall el-Hammam corresponds indeed to the biblical location of Sodom. For me, the identification of Tall el-Hammam with Sodom ticks all the required boxes but one—the time of its destruction. Instead of rejecting the identification of this singular site with Sodom on this point only, I suggest that this unticked box of the accepted chronology needs closer examination.[21]

Leen has also promoted Tall el-Hammam as Sodom on his website.[22]

William J. Fulco

As Dr. William J. Fulco, the National Endowment of the Humanities Professor of Ancient Mediterranean Studies, Loyola Marymount University, states:

> Among the several sites or collection of sites that have been proposed for the notorious Cities of the Plain, which includes Sodom as its nucleus, Collins' proposal of Tall el-Ḥammâm as this very place is convincing indeed. The evidence that the Tall al-Hammâm Excavation Project (TeHEP) has brought to light and which Prof. Collins marshals to demonstrate the correlation between Tall Hammâm and the biblical narrative must now enter the discussion as by far the strongest candidate for the site of Sodom.[23]

---

[21] Collins and Scott, *Discovering the City of Sodom*, forward xi.

[22] www.ritmeyer.com/2015/05/12/sodom-and-gomorrah; www.ritmeyer.com/2015/05/04/the-search-for-sodom.

[23] Ibid., Preface.

Summary

I have always been a northern resident, growing up in Canada, although I visited the southern United States numerous times.[1] I'm definitely not a "southern boy", but this was not always the case when it came to the identification of a suitable candidate for the destroyed city of Sodom. In this regard you might say I'm a "southern boy" turned "northern renegade"!

Background

In 1979 following research for an undergraduate paper in archaeology on the location of Sodom, I concluded that the best candidate for Sodom at that time was Bâb edh-Dhrâʿ (BeD) at the southern end of the Dead Sea (Southern Sodom Theory SST). The argument seemed compelling and since I did not doubt Sodom's historicity it was the best candidate at that time. In 1979 I had not given the date of destruction a lot of thought or consideration.

In 2006 I had plans to join the excavation at Khirbet el-Maqatir (Ai?) with Dr. Bryant Wood but it was cancelled due to security reasons, so instead I joined the Tall el-Ḥammâm (TeH) excavation during the first season. I had no idea at the time that Dr. Steven Collins believed this site to be Sodom (Northern Sodom Theory NST), but soon came to hear him explain and appreciate his reasons for his hypothesis. It was during those

53. Tall el-Ḥammâm, Jordan, which is the likely location for Sodom (MBA). Later in the Late Bronze age it became Abel-shittim (the meadow of the acacias), a Solomonic administrative site in the Iron Age and in the Roman Period was part of the city of Livias. An important biblical site throughout history and one of the largest strategic sites in the Levant.

nine seasons that Scott Stripling and I also identified the Roman/Byzantine remains at Tall el-Ḥammâm as part of Livias (see *Fact 28)*[2] and located TeH on the Madaba Map (see *Primary Sources: Madaba Map*).[3]

Not a Debate Over Minimalism

First, this is not a debate by a maximalist vs minimalist, as both Dr. Wood and Dr. Collins are maximalists and agree that the story of Sodom, as presented in the biblical text, is both historical and reliable. Also, the southern/northern debate is not new, although the sites of Bâb edh-Dhrâʿ and Tall el-Ḥammâm were not known to the following early writers. The southern location was argued by the likes of Thomas Fuller (1650), Peter Graham (1836), William F. Lynch (1849), Louis Félix de Saulcy (1851), Samuel Wolcott (1868), Georg H. Ewald (1869), Charles Clermont-Ganneau (1846–1923), Sir Charles Warren (1899), William F. Albright (1891–1971), and James Penrose Harland (1943). The northern location has been argued by the likes of Charles W. Wilson (1869),

---

[1] This chapter will be published as David E. Graves, "My Journey to Locate the Genesis Pentapolis North of the Dead Sea," in *Kikkar Dialogues*, ed. Steven Collins, 2nd ed., Research & Discovery Series 1 (Albuquerque, N.M.: Trinity Southwest University Press, Forthcoming), 100–128.

[2] Graves and Stripling, "Re-Examination of the Location for the Ancient City of Livias."

[3] Graves and Stripling, "Identification of Tall El-Hammam"; "Is Tall El-Hammam on the Madaba Map?," in *Near East Archaeological Society* (Near East Archaeological Society, San Diego: Near East Archaeological Society, 2007), 1–20; "Locating Tall El-Hammam."

Edward H. Palmer (1871), Henry Baker Tristram (1873), Selah Merrill (1876, 1881), William F. Birch (1879), Claude Reignier Conder (1879–1883), William M. Thomson (1882–85), George Grove (1884), John Cunningham Geikie (1887), E. Power (1930), and Père Alexis Mallon (1929–1934).[4] However, Wood and Collins draw from many of the same arguments advanced by these early pioneers to support their research. Most, if not all, of the following arguments are not new and have been argued by many before me but will summarize some of them here.

Moot arguments

Second, many of the arguments for the location of Sodom are moot issues that do not make a significant difference toward locating the site north or south of the Dead Sea. Many of the arguments used to support Bâb edh-Dhrâ' as Sodom in the south are equally true of Tall el-Ḥammâm in the north. These are considered moot arguments, although some may be stronger in supporting the NST.

Both were large cities

Both were large cities in their region and in their own time. Sometimes the claim is made that "Bab edh-Dhra is the largest site from the pre-Hellenistic period in the area,"[5] as it covers 10 acres. Certainly, this is true if one is only talking about the southern end of the Dead Sea. However, after many seasons of excavations at TeH, it is known that TeH has "over 100 acres of Bronze Age occupational footprint and over 60 acres of that situated behind an enormous defensive system, Tall el-Hammam was—on average over its 3,000–year history prior to its destruction toward the end of the Middle Bronze Age—the largest continuously-occupied city in the southern Levant."[6] TeH was certainly a large city-state controlling the southern Jordan Valley in the EB and MB periods. It would be reasonable that one of the largest cities in the Levant would be mentioned in the Bible (i.e., Sodom and the Cities of the Plain).

Both have a large cemetery

Bâb edh-Dhrâ has a large cemetery (Khirbet Qazone), with possibly half a million-people buried there from various periods. However the EB IA, B shaft tombs, which make up the bulk of the graves,[7] predate the EB II and III occupation of the city of BeD and its destruction.[8] The EB cemetery is much smaller.

Next to TeH there is a large dolmen area known as the Al Rawda Field (see Fig. 34, 35 and Map 9).[9] Some human bone fragments were found in five of the twelve dolmens excavated in 2011, but dolmens appear to be used only for ceremonial purposes and not as burial tombs.[10] The dead were buried in surrounding caves. However, the evidence for Sodom's cataclysm should reveal human remains in the destruction layer; not neatly buried in cemeteries.

Both have evidence of a fiery destruction

Both have evidence of a fiery destruction to

---

[4] For a list of their sources see Fact 2 and 3.
[5] Wood, "Discovery of the Sin Cities," 68.
[6] Collins, "Tall El-Hammam Is Still Sodom," 6; Collins, Hamdan, and Byers, "Tall El-Hammam: Preliminary Report, Season Four, 2009," 386; Collins et al., "Tall El-Hammam, Season Eight, 2013," 4.
[7] Schaub, "Bab Edh-Dhra' (NEAEHL)," 1:131.
[8] Lapp, "The Cemetery at Bab Edh-Dhra', Jordan," 111.
[9] Kafafi and Scheltema, "Megalithic Structures in Jordan," 7.
[10] Schath, Collins, and Aljarrah, "Excavation of an Undisturbed Demi-Dolmen and Insights from the Al-Hammam Megalithic Field, 2011 Season," 341–42; Kafafi and Scheltema, "Megalithic Structures in Jordan," 13.

their city gate[11] and human remains in the destruction layers,[12] although at BeD charred human remains were only found in the cemetery.[13]

Wood has suggested that because the evidence in Charnel house A22 in the cemetery at BeD "revealed that the fire started in the roof and spread to the interior when the roof collapsed" that "this provides powerful evidence that 'the Lord rained down burning sulphur on Sodom and Gomorrah—from the Lord out of the heavens' " (Gen 19:24).[14] However, in the ancient world it was common to destroy cities by means of shooting flaming arrows into the air (i.e., the Lachish reliefs in the British Museum),[15] which would then land on the roofs of buildings and cause the wattle and daub (twigs and sticks) roof constructions to catch fire. The roofs of buildings that have been set on fire are certainly not *proof* of divine destruction. Charnel houses that appeared to be dwellings on the exterior would have certainly been attacked during war. There can be several explanations for why the roofs of the charnel houses burned.

The destruction at Tall el-Hammam is also unusual. Thus far, the TeH excavation has uncovered a total of five pieces of super-heated vitrified pottery (clinkers) from the MB destruction layer that have been identified as "trinitite"[16] and desert glass (impact glass) at Tall Mwais, near TeH.[17] Trinitite has unique characteristics different from obsidian (volcanic glass) and fulgurite (lightning glass), which scientists can easily identify. The extreme heat required to melt pottery and produce trinitite indicates that there was an unusual phenomenon that took place at and around TeH.

Both were well-watered

Both locations were well-watered in ancient times,[18] Although TeH was supplied with perennial water from several hot springs and BeD relied on seasonal water supplied from the Wadi al-Karak. Paleo-botanical evidence collected from both BeD[19] and TeH[20] indicate that the residents ate a variety of foods but does not indicate where these were grown and may have been imported. All cities in the Jordan Valley require water to survive in such a harsh climate and it is no surprise to find that both the northern and southern sites were strategically located near a water source. Both sites reveal the presence of ample food and water to sustain a large population with a suitable diet via the presence of a variety of edible plants. When the water dried up, the

---

[11] Schaub, "Bab Edh-Dhraʿ (OEANE)," 249; Collins et al., "Tall El-Hammam, Season Eight, 2013," 6, 8; "Where Is Sodom?," 38; Collins and Scott, *Discovering the City of Sodom*, 168.

[12] Collins and Scott, *Discovering the City of Sodom*, 177–79; Nixon, "Archaeological Evidence for Sodom," 3–4.

[13] Ortner, "A Preliminary Report on the Human Remains from the Bab Edh-Dhraʾ Cemetery," 119–32; Rast, "The Southeastern Dead Sea Valley Expedition, 1979," 60.

[14] Wood, "Have Sodom And Gomorrah Been Found?," 81.

[15] Mitchell, *Biblical Archaeology*.

[16] It derived its name from Trinity, New Mexico, where the first nuclear tests were conducted, which produced this same type of material. Collins, "Where Is Sodom?," 41; Collins and Scott, *Discovering the City of Sodom*, 207.

[17] Collins, "Tall El-Hammam Is Sodom," 4; Collins and Scott, *Discovering the City of Sodom*, 213.

[18] See *Facts 59* and *60*. David E. Graves, *Key Facts for the Location of Sodom Student Edition: Navigating the Maze of Arguments* (Moncton, N.B.: Graves, 2014), 139–40; Graves and Stripling, "Re-Examination of the Location for the Ancient City of Livias," 189; Thomson, *Land and the Book: Lebanon, Damascus, and Beyond Jordan*, 3:3:670; Neev and Emery, *The Destruction of Sodom, Gomorrah and Jericho*, 139.

[19] McCreery, "The Paleoethnobotany of Bab Edh-Dhraʿ," 451.

[20] Smith, "Paleo-Botanical Report for Tall El-Hammam, 2014," 1.

people moved to another location.

Both are in the Great Rift Jordan Valley

Both are located in the Great Rift Jordan Valley along the same geological fault lines which are known to have bitumen[21] (i.e. "slime pits")[22]/asphalt pits,[23] sulphur, tar, and natural gas[24] in this region and be susceptible to seismic activity.[25] And the hypothetical geological description of the destruction of Sodom by volcano,[26] earthquake[27] or liquefaction[28] is no indication to its location,[29] because if tectonic or seismic activity took out BeD, it could have also taken out TeH.

Wood suggests that the mention of bitumen pits in Genesis 14:10 "tips the scales in favour of a southern location"[30] for the Cities of the Plain.[31] There is no question that the Dead Sea is full of bitumen that floats to the surface (Josephus *J.W.* 4.479–80; Strabo *Geogr.* 16.2.42; Diodorus Siculus *Hist. Lib.* 19:98.84–88;[32] Tacitus *Hist.* 5.7),[33] being pushed up through the fault lines to the surface by earthquakes or movements of the plates.[34] However, one of the difficulties in identifying the location of the bitumen pits is that the formation of sink holes is triggered by

---

[21] Bitumen was also a major export from the Dead Sea region (Pliny the Elder *Nat. Hist.* 2.226; 5.72; 7.65; 28.80; 35.178). Nissenbaum and Goldberg defined *bitumen (Heb. ḥēmār; Gen 14:10)* as ozocerite (Gr. *oze* stench + *kero* wax; an odorous paraffin earthwax) "a natural mixture of predominantly high molecular weight paraffinic hydrocarbons." Nissenbaum and Goldberg, "Asphalts, Heavy Oils, Ozocerite and Gases in the Dead Sea Basin," 172.

[22] Frumkin and Elitzur, "The Rise and Fall of the Dead Sea," 42 n.1.

[23] It is often identified as asphalt, common in the Dead Sea. Josephus called it Lake Asphaltites (*Ant.* 1.9) and the Romans called it Asphalt Lake (Lat. *Palus Asphaltites*). In their research, Nissenbaum and Goldberg, decided that "The Dead Sea material has been so often referred to as asphalts, that for historical reasons it was decided to retain this term." Nissenbaum and Goldberg, "Asphalts, Heavy Oils, Ozocerite and Gases in the Dead Sea Basin," 167.

[24] Gardosh et al., "Hydrocarbon Exploration in the Southern Dead Sea Area," 69; Nissenbaum and Goldberg, "Asphalts, Heavy Oils, Ozocerite and Gases in the Dead Sea Basin," 175.

[25] Niemi and Ben-Avraham, "Active Tectonics in the Dead Sea Basin," 73–81; Amit and Bein, "The Genesis of the Asphalt in the Dead Sea Area," 211–25; Gardosh et al., "Hydrocarbon Exploration in the Southern Dead Sea Area," 58; Garfunkel, "Internal Structure of the Dead Sea Leaky Transform (Rift) in Relation to Plate Kinematics," 81–108; Neev and Emery, *The Destruction of Sodom, Gomorrah and Jericho*, 167–77.

[26] Nötling, "Das Todte Meer Und Der Untergang von Sodom Und Gomorrha"; Wyllie, "The Geology of Jebel Usdum, Dead Sea," 360–72; Block, "Sodom and Gomorrah: A Volcanic Disaster," 74–77; Trifonov, "Bible and Geology," 133–42.

[27] Blanckenhorn, *Entstehung und Geschichte des Toten Meeres*, 51; *Noch eimal Sodom und Gomorrha*, 79; Ewald, *History of Israel*, 1:313–14; Tristram, *The Land of Moab*, 348, 363; Robinson, "Jordan," 764; Power, "The Site of the Pentapolis: Part 1," 1:23; Neev and Emery, *The Destruction of Sodom, Gomorrah and Jericho*, 139–141, 146; Wood, "Discovery of the Sin Cities," 75; Cocks, "The Discovery of Sodom, 1851," 1–27; Clapp, "The Site of Sodom and Gomorrah: A Diversity of Views," 340.

[28] Harris and Beardow, "The Destruction of Sodom and Gomorrah: A Geotechnical Perspective," 349; Haigh and Madabhushi, "Dynamic Centrifuge Modelling of the Destruction of Sodom and Gomorrah," 511.

[29] Clapp, "The Site of Sodom and Gomorrah: A Diversity of Views," 339; Harland, "Sodom and Gomorrah Part II: Destruction," 43; Hendel, "Review of D. Neev and K.O. Emery, Destruction of Sodom, Gomorrah and Jericho: Geological, Climatological and Archaeological Backgrounds," 70.

[30] Wood, "Discovery of the Sin Cities," 67; Howard, Jr., "Sodom and Gomorrah Revisited," 390.

[31] See also Wade, "Jordan," 853; Driver, "Jordan," 4:512; Astour, "Siddim," 6:15–16.

[32] Siculus, *Library of History: Books 19.66-20*.

[33] Nissenbaum, "Dead Sea asphalts—Historical Aspects," 840–45; Nissenbaum and Goldberg, "Asphalts, Heavy Oils, Ozocerite and Gases in the Dead Sea Basin," 167.

[34] Clapp, "Geology and Bitumens of the Dead Sea Area, Palestine and TransJordan," 901–903; Nissenbaum, "Dead Sea asphalts—Historical Aspects," 843.

"the declining level of the Dead Sea."³⁵ Since the level fluctuates, the exact location of sinkholes (bitumen pits) in antiquity is unknown along with the Valley of Siddim (Genesis 14:3, 8, 10).³⁶

If we use the present location of sinkholes as an example of where these were 3000 years ago, then they would have been concentrated on the western side of the Dead Sea graben³⁷ along what is called the "tar belt"³⁸ "between Mt Sedom and Ein Gedi"³⁹ with a few possibly along the eastern shore.⁴⁰ However, due to the variations in the levels of the Dead Sea, to determine the ancient location on the basis of modern research is mere speculation and not reliable. The fact that they are present in modern times does not necessarily mean they were in this exact location in ancient times. Certainly, this argument can be used for either the presence or the absence of bitumen pits in either location. All one can conclude is that the presence of sink holes alone does not determine the location of Sodom.

But even if one could identify the location of ancient sink holes, this still does not determine the location of Sodom, since ancient people would not likely build their cities near these hazardous natural formations, nor go to battle in location close to where the peoples lived. In addition, as Howard points out: "the implication in v 3 (and also in v 8 [of Gen 14]) is that the kings (or at least some of them) did not live in the place where they joined forces and prepared for war but rather that this was a rendezvous point and that they lived nearby."⁴¹

Both are visible from the Hebron plateau

Thick smoke rising from either the northern Jordan Valley or southern Ghor would be visible from the Hebron plateau (Genesis 19:28). While there are reports from both the NST⁴² and the SST⁴³ proponents, claiming that only smoke from their site could be visible from Hebron, the fact is that thick smoke rising from either the northern Jordan Valley or south Ghor would be visible from the Hebron plateau, which rises 3,094 ft. (943 m) above sea level and is about halfway between BeD and TeH, a fact that can be verified by looking at any good Bible map.

There are not two destructions of Sodom mentioned in the Bible.

Wood has made a lot of the fact that Bâb edh-Dhrâʿ has evidence of two destructions and connects this with the events of Genesis 14. Under his heading "Two Destructions" he states: "the Bible tells of not one, but two, traumatic events that occurred in the final days of Sodom and Gomorrah. Genesis 14 describes an attack against the Cities of the Plain by a coalition of four Mesopotamian

---

³⁵ Lynch, *Narrative of the United States Expedition to the River Jordan and the Dead Sea*, 306; Geikie, *Holy Land and the Bible*, 2: 114–15; Abelson et al., "Evaluation of the Dead Sea Sinkholes," 248.

³⁶ Albright places it on the "southwestern part of the Dead Sea." Albright, "The Archaeological Results of an Expedition to Moab and the Dead Sea," 9.

³⁷ Gardosh et al., "Hydrocarbon Exploration in the Southern Dead Sea Area," 68.

³⁸ Ibid., 58.

³⁹ Nissenbaum and Goldberg, "Asphalts, Heavy Oils, Ozocerite and Gases in the Dead Sea Basin," 172; Amit and Bein, "The Genesis of the Asphalt in the Dead Sea Area," 213.

⁴⁰ Nissenbaum and Aizenshatat, "Geochemical Studies on Ozokerite From the Dead Sea Area," 121; Amit and Bein, "The Genesis of the Asphalt in the Dead Sea Area," 213; Nissenbaum and Goldberg, "Asphalts, Heavy Oils, Ozocerite and Gases in the Dead Sea Basin," 172; Bender, *Geology of the Arabian Peninsula, Jordan*, 27.

---

⁴¹ Howard, Jr., "Sodom and Gomorrah Revisited," 389.

⁴² Geikie, *Holy Land and the Bible*, 118–119.

⁴³ Harland, "Sodom and Gomorrah Part I: Location," 22; Simons, *The Geographical and Topographical Texts of the Old Testament*, 409; Howard, Jr., "Sodom and Gomorrah Revisited," 390; Wood, "Discovery of the Sin Cities," 67.

kings."[44]

However, the events as described in Genesis, can be classified as traumatic but can hardly be described as a destruction. The text states that, after doing battle in the Valley of Siddim, that Chedorlaomer king of Elam "took all the possessions of Sodom and Gomorrah, and all their provisions, and went their way. They also took Lot, the son of Abram's brother, who was dwelling in Sodom, and his possessions, and went their way" (Gen 14:11–12). One may assume that Chedorlaomer destroyed the cities of Sodom and Gomorrah but the text only states that he took their possessions after doing battle out in the Valley of Siddim. The text makes it clear that all the kings armies *"joined forces* in the Valley of Siddim," (emphasis added; Gen 14:3) and "then the king of Sodom, the king of Gomorrah, the king of Admah, the king of Zeboiim, and the king of Bela (that is, Zoar) *went out*, and they joined battle in the Valley of Siddim with Chedorlaomer king of Elam (emphasis added; Gen 14:8–9). After the victory out on the battlefield in the Valley of Siddim, Chedorlaomer marched in and took the possessions that were his by virtue of his victory. Hardly a destruction, and thus a moot argument.

Both were resettled

Some people have argued that Jeremiah 50:39–40, which compares the curse on Babylon, "As when God overthrew Sodom and Gomorrah and their neighboring cities, declares the LORD, so no man shall dwell there, and no son of man shall sojourn in her" (Jeremiah 50:40) indicates that Sodom will be abandoned forever. Therefore, the archaeological site, identified as the location of Sodom, must be a site with signs of destruction and with no signs of later resettlement.

According to this interpretation of Jeremiah, TeH is ruled out as a candidate for Sodom because it was resettled in the Iron Age and Roman, Byzantine and Umayyad periods.[45] However, if this is the criteria, then BeD must also be ruled out, as it was also reoccupied in the EBIV period after the major destruction of 2350 BC, which some claim was the Sodom destruction.[46]

But Ezekiel also promises that "Sodom and her daughters shall return to their former state" (Ezekiel 16:53–55). So, if these prophetic passages are treated literally, then both TeH and BeD were resettled to some extent and this argument becomes moot.

Both have possible locations for Zoar

Both sites have possible locations for Zoar, but no one really knows for sure where Zoar is located, and over the years scholars have proposed several locations, though no clear archaeological evidence has ever emerged to positively identify it.[47]

The site of *Ghor eṣ-Ṣafi*,[48] at the southern end of the Dead Sea is a popular location for Zoar for SST proponents because it has traditionally retained the name of Zoar (then Zoora; see Fig. 8) since Roman and Byzantine times.[49] This is the location preserved in Greek on the 6th cent. AD Madaba Map, in the Greek Orthodox Parish Church of St. George, in Madaba, Jordan. It reads: "Balak,

---

[44] Wood, "Discovery of the Sin Cities," 70–71.

[45] Graves and Stripling, "Re-Examination of the Location for the Ancient City of Livias," 178–200.
[46] For further discussion see *Fact 20*. Graves, *Key Facts for the Location of Sodom*, 75–76.
[47] Albright believed that Zoar was buried under the Dead Sea with the rest of the Cities of the Plain. Albright, "The Archaeological Results of an Expedition to Moab and the Dead Sea," 8.
[48] Astour, "Zoar (Place)," 6:1107.
[49] Politis, "Death at the Dead Sea," 45; Saldarini, "Babatha's Story," 29; Lewis, Greenfield, and Yadin, *Documents from the Bar Kokhba*; Yardeni et al., *Documents from the Bar Kokhba: Hebrew*, 1–4, 6–10; Negev, "Zoar," op. cit.

also Segor [Rom. Seghor], now Zoora [Byz. Zoara]".[50] However, early surveys of the area reported no archaeological evidence uncovered at this site earlier than the Hellenistic Period[51] and Schuab, who excavated BeD, states that the 6th cent. Zoar on the Madaba map is not the same as the Middle Bronze age Zoar as listed in Genesis.[52]

In the *northern Jordan Valley*, Selah Merrill has identified *Tall Iktanu (also Ektanu) for the location of Zoar*.[53] It was excavated between 1987 and 1990 by Kay Prag, identifying Early Bronze I and II (ca. 3200–2800 BC) and Intermediate EB–MB (= EB IV) occupations.[54] Also north of the Dead Sea, William Birch was the first to identify *Tell eš-Šāġūr (Hill of Zoar;* Tell esh Shaghur; Um Sheggar; or M'Shuggar*)* with Zoar (Σηγώρ Gr. Segor or *Ṣo'ar*)[55] which Taylor identified with the modern village of el-Makhayyat (or *Serâbît el-Mushaqqar*).[56] There is only early IA pottery at the site, [57] but a significant MB site at Khirbet Qarn al Qubish (Kh. Qurn el-Kibsh) is only 3 km east of *Serâbît el-Mushaqqar and 1 km south of the modern village of el-Mushaqqar*.[58]

And finally, Collins proposed that Zoar was a "tent city"[59] and a "port" on the Arnon River, since it was the southern border for the land of Israel promised to Moses (Deut 2:4–5, 9; 34:1–4; Josh 13:9–10).[60] Also, eṣ-Ṣafi is located well inside the territories of Moab and Edom which "were off-limits to the Israelites" (Deut 2:4–5, 9).[61]

With four, possibly more, locations for Zoar in the northern and southern regions, but with none positively identified, the question whether Zoar can help in the location of Sodom is still open. But even if Zoar were located, this still does not help in locating the city of Sodom, as the narrative indicates that it was situated at a distance from the destruction that covered most of the Cities of the Plain. If Zoar was found, we would know where the destroyed Cities of the Plain were NOT located. Thus, the location of Zoar is a moot argument.

The Ebla Tablets do not help

The proposed identification of Sodom on the

---

[50] Donner, *Mosaic Map of Madaba*, op. cit.; Avi-Yonah, *Madaba Mosaic Map*, 42–43 pl. 4.

[51] Palmer, *The Desert of the Exodus*, 1:1:29; Mallon, "Biblica," 438; Albright, "The Jordan Valley in the Bronze Age," 57; Rollin and Streetly, *Jordan*, 164–65; Politis et al., "Survey and Excavations in the Ghawr as-Safi 2004," 314–18; Graf, "Zoora Rises from the Grave: New Funerary Stelae from Palaestina Tertia," 752–58; Politis et al., "Survey and Excavations in the Ghawr as-Safi 2006–07," 199–210; Politis, Sampson, and O'Hea, "Ghawr As-Safi Survey and Excavations 2008-2009," 303–304.

[52] Schaub, "Southeast Dead Sea Plain," 5:64; Sarna, *Genesis*, 388–89.

[53] Merrill, "Modern Researches in Palestine, PEFSt.," 149.

[54] Prag, "Excavations at Tell Iktanu, 1987," 33–45; "Excavations at Tell Iktanu, 1989," 119–30; "Tell Iktanu and Tall El-Hammam 1990," 55–57; "Tell Iktanu and Tell Al-Hammam. Excavations in Jordan," 15–19; "The Excavations at Tell Iktanu 1989 and 1990," 269–73; de Vries, "Archaeology in Jordan," 515.

[55] Birch, "Zoar," 17; Culver, "Zoar," 5:1240.

[56] Joan E. Taylor, "The Dead Sea in Western Travellers' Accounts from the Byzantine to the Modern Period," *Bulletin of the Anglo-Israel Archaeological Society* 27 (2009): 11–12; Sylvester J. Saller, *The Memorial of Moses on Mount Nebo I: The Text; II: The Plates*, Studium Biblicum Franciscanum Collection 1 (Jerusalem: Studium Biblicum Franciscanum, 1941), 1:6–7, 2:Plate 6, 1; Sylvester J. Saller and Bellarmino Bagatti, *The Town of Nebo (Khirbet El-Mekhayyat): With a Brief Survey of Other Ancient Christian Monuments in Transjordan*, Publications of the Studium Biblicum Franciscanum 7 (Jerusalem: Franciscan, 1949). Contra Gottlieb Schumacher, *Across the Jordan: Being an Exploration and Survey of Part of Hauran and Jaulan* (London, U.K.: Watt, 1889), 317–21.

[57] Schumacher, *Across the Jordan*, 317–21.

[58] Glueck, *Explorations in Eastern Palestine II*, 111.

[59] Collins, "Rethinking the Location of Zoar," 3; Collins, *The Search for Sodom and Gomorrah*, 15.

[60] Collins, "Rethinking the Location of Zoar," 1–5; "The Geography of Sodom and Zoar," 1–14.

[61] Collins, "Rethinking the Location of Zoar," 2; Neev and Emery, *The Destruction of Sodom, Gomorrah and Jericho*, 131–38.

The Location of Sodom

Ebla tablets from Tell Mardikh[62] is used by Shea, Freedman[63] and others[64] to support the SST. The Pentapolis are purported to be places visited by merchants from Ebla and "listed in geographical order,"[65] placing them in the southern end of the Dead Sea. This argument proposed by Shea and Freedman, is picked up by Wood to argue for the SST,[66] but their arguments are very subjective and arbitrary.[67]

The only two sites that are even remotely recognizable in the Ebla tablets are Admah (*ad-mu-ut*^{ki}) and Sodom[68] (*si-da-mu*^{ki}),[69] which could easily be in the northern region of the Jordan Valley since the other sites are impossible to identify with any degree of certainty. All the other place names could be located anywhere in the region. Matthiae dates the Ebla tablets to the EB III period (2400 and 2250 BC),[70] which would be the earliest mention of the Pentapolis outside the biblical text (Gen 10) and the time period would indicate that merchants from Ebla were trading with these cities prior to their destruction.

However, even if Sodom was named in the Ebla tablets (and that is debated)[71] it does not indicate if Sodom was north or south of the Dead Sea. As all would agree, the Pentapolis existed during the Early Bronze Age (Gen 10) at the time of the Ebla tablets and both sites (BeD and TeH) were occupied in the EB age. The important questions concerning the location and destruction of the Pentapolis are not answered by the Ebla tablets. The use of the Ebla tablets is a moot argument.

Compelling Arguments

Given these moot arguments, what was it that finally swayed me from the southern to a northern location for the Pentapolis? The two main arguments are geography and chronology, with some supportive evidence from the ancillary elements of the moot arguments.

Serial Geography is Central in Determining the Location of the Pentapolis

Usually scholars use geographic indicators, as opposed to inscriptions,[72] to identify a cities location (i.e., by the Jordan River, below Mt.

---

[62] Archi, "The Epigraphic Evidence from Ebla and the Old Testament"; "The Archives of Ebla," 78; Pettinato, "Report on Ebla"; "Gli archivi reali di Tell Mardikh-Ebla"; "Ebla and the Bible," 203–16.

[63] Freedman, "The Real Story of the Ebla Tablets"; Shea, "Two Palestinian Segments"; Wilson, *Ebla Tablets*; "Ebla: Its Impact on Bible Records"; *Ebla Tablets*, 12; Dahood, "Ebla, Ugarit E l'Antico Testamento," 129, no. 2.

[64] Pettinato, "Ebla and the Bible"; Dahood, "Appendix"; "Ebla, Ugarit and the Old Testament," 1979; "Ebla, Ugarit and the Old Testament," 1978; Freedman, "The Real Story of the Ebla Tablets"; Wilson, *Ebla Tablets*; *The Impact of Ebla on Bible Records*.

[65] Shea, "Two Palestinian Segments," 591.

[66] Wood, "Discovery of the Sin Cities," 13.

[67] Archi, "Ebla Texts"; "The Epigraphic Evidence from Ebla and the Old Testament," 563 n. 21; Biggs, "The Ebla Tablets: An Interim Perspective," 82; Price, *The Stones Cry Out*, 85; Matthiae, "A Letter to the Editor," 134; Mulder, "Sodom; Gomorrah," 156; Longman III, *Fictional Akkadian Autobiography*, 26; Shanks, "Ebla Evidence Evaporates."

[68] Shea, "Two Palestinian Segments," 601.

[69] Pettinato and Alberti, *Catalogo Dei Testi Cuneiformi Di Tell Mardikh-Ebla*, Tablet 6522; Pettinato, "Ebla and the Bible," 213; Archi, "The Epigraphic Evidence from Ebla: A Summary," 201.

[70] Matthiae, "Ebla Recovered," 134–137.

[71] Archi, "The Epigraphic Evidence from Ebla and the Old Testament," 563; Biggs, "The Ebla Tablets: An Interim Perspective," 76–86; Archi, "Further Concerning Ebla and the Bible"; "Are 'The Cities of the Plain' Mentioned in the Ebla Tablets?," 54–55; Mark W. Chavalas and K. Lawson Younger, eds., *Mesopotamia and the Bible: Comparative Explorations* (Grand Rapids, Mich.: Baker Academic, 2002), 41.

[72] See Appendix C, "How are Biblical Cities and Towns Identified and Placed on Bible Maps?" in Collins and Scott, *Discovering the City of Sodom*, 277.

Nebo, near Jerusalem, etc.).[73] Collins is quoted stating that: "the Tall el-Hammam site has 25 geographical indicators that align it with the description in Genesis. Compare this with something well known—like Jerusalem—that has only 16. Other sites have only 5 or 6. So, this site has many times more indicators than any other Old Testament site."[74]

While several passages in the Bible mention geographic indicators for the location of Sodom (Gen 13:10; 14:3; 19:28), there is debate as to which is more helpful. Wood claims that "the reference to 'bitumen pits' [see *Fact 57*] in Genesis 14:10, however, tips the scale in favor of a southern location."[75] However, the bitumen pits (Gen 14:10) are referring to the battle of the Mesopotamian kings and not the location of the Pentapolis.[76] Context is vital. Poetic and prophetic passages (i.e., Jer 50:35–46; Ezek 16:46; Is 15:4–7) are also often referenced for Sodom's location, but these must not be treated as narrative texts.[77] Thus, Collins asserts, on good grounds, in his reply to Wood's criticism,[78] that: "the only *definitive* biblical text on the geography of the Cities of the Plain: [is] Genesis 13:1–12.[79]"[80]

The destroyed cities of the Pentapolis are repeatedly mentioned located in "the plain" or "valley" (Gen 13:12; Heb. *kikkār*), also called "the land of the valley" (Gen 19:28) and "Jordan Valley" (Gen 13:10f). This distinctive Hebrew term (*kikkār*) is central in identifying the location of the city of Sodom. The etymology of the root word indicates that *kikkār* refers to something round, as in a "round loaf of bread" (1 Sam 2:36; Prov 6:26; Exod 29:23; Jer 37:21; 1 Chr 16:3; 1 Sam 10:3, Jud 8:5) or a "circular disk for payment" (2 Sam 12:30, 1 Kgs 20:39, 2 Kgs 5:5; 1 Chr 29:7; 2 Kgs 9:14).[81] Other references to the *kikkār* place it between Zarethan (*Tell es-Saidiyeh*,[82] Josh 3:16; 1 Kgs 7:46; 2 Chron 4:17) and Succoth (*Tall Deir 'Allā* ;[83] Josh 13:27) in the Jordan Valley near the Jabbok River, east of the Jordan River (1 Kgs 7:46; 2 Chron 4:17; 2 Sam 18:23). This would place the *kikkār* in the northern region between the Sea of Galilee and the Dead Sea. Later, during Nehemiah's time, the term *kikkār* was used to refer to an area surrounding (Heb. *sbybwt*) Jerusalem (Heb. *hakkikkār*; Neh 3:22; 12:28).[84] It would appear that *kikkār was adopted as a technical geographical term due to the round appearance of the Jordan Valley when viewed from the surrounding hills*. The term *kikkār* is still used in Israel for a traffic circle or a roundabout.

However, some arguing for the SST, have suggested that the roundness of the term *kikkār* must not be pressed too hard, as the Jordan Valley has an oval or rectangular shape, since it extends to Zarethan and

---

[73] Rainey, "Historical Geography," 353–68.

[74] Nixon, "Sodom Found? The Quest For The Lost City Of Destruction -- Part 3"; Collins and Scott, *Discovering the City of Sodom*, 278–96.

[75] Wood, "Discovery of the Sin Cities," 67; Wood, "Locating Sodom: A Critique of the Northern Proposal," 78–79.

[76] See the section "Both are located in the Great Rift Jordan Valley" above.

[77] See *Fact 17: Jeremiah 50:35-46 is prophetic literature*; *Fact 18: Ezekiel is poetry and not narrative*. Graves, *Key Facts for the Location of Sodom*, 72–74.

[78] Wood, "Locating Sodom: A Critique of the Northern Proposal," 81–82; Rast, "Sodom and Its Environs: Can Recent Archaeology Offer a Perspective?," 21; Collins, "A Response to Bryant G. Wood," 5–6.

[79] For Collins' exegesis of Genesis 13:1-12 and other passages, see his article on the "Geography of the Cities of the Plain." Collins, "Geography of the Cities of the Plain," 1–17.

[80] Collins, "A Response to Bryant G. Wood," 5.

[81] Robinson, "Jordan," 761; Harris, Archer, Jr., and Waltke, "503 כָּפַר," no. 4673; Briggs, Driver, and Brown, "כָּפַר," no. 1046c.

[82] Tubb, "Sa'idryeh. Tell Es-," 452.

[83] Franken, "Deir 'Alla, Tell," 138.

[84] Collins, "Reassessing the Term Hakikkar in Nehemiah," 1–4.

Succoth,⁸⁵ and they include the entire southern "region"⁸⁶ of the Dead Sea into the *kikkār*.⁸⁷ Also, the idea that Lot saw "all" the Plain from between Bethel and Ai must be figurative, since as Driver points out, "not even the entire valley north of the Dead Sea is visible from near Bethel."⁸⁸ But this was challenged in the 1800's by Merrill, who protested the extension of the meaning of the word *kikkār* to include the entire Dead Sea valley. He stated:

> But I think it is to do violence to the language and to the facts of the case to attempt to make the phrase "all the plain of the Jordan" include the salt marsh at the southern end of the Dead Sea, which is fifty miles from that river, and has nothing to do with it. Indeed, the region there belongs to another water-system altogether-entirely distinct from that at the northern end of the Dead Sea, with which the Jordan is connected.⁸⁹

And today Sarna agrees, stating several arguments in support of the northern location for the *kikkār*:

> The statement that King Solomon cast the bronze vessels for the Temple "in the plain of the Jordan [*kikkār*] between Succoth and Zerethan" (2 Chron 4:17), referring to the middle section of the Jordan Valley, between the Sea of Galilee and the Dead Sea, seems to imply that the northern shore of the Dead Sea is the southern extremity of the *Kikkār*. This conclusion is supported by the report that from the summit of Mount Nebo in Transjordan "facing Jericho" (Deut 32:49), Moses was able to see . . . "the Negeb, and the Plain, that is, the Valley of Jericho the city of palm trees, as far as Zoar" (Deut 34:3). Finally, as we noted above, Lot is said to have been able to view the entire Jordan Plain from a location between Bethel and Ai (Gen 13:3, 10), which would have been impossible if the cities were south of the Dead Sea.⁹⁰

Even the strong SST advocate Samuel R. Driver admits that Genesis 13 suggests a northern site.⁹¹ Regardless of the exact geometrical shape of the Jordan Valley, the *kikkār* is described as the "*kikkār* of the Jordan" (Gen 13:10) and "*kikkār* of Jericho" (Deut 34:3) indicating that it is in the northern region of the Dead Sea, where the Jordan River and Jericho are located. The biblical text provides a clear geographic indicator for the location of the Pentapolis. The large site of Tall el-Ḥammâm is situated up against the eastern side of the Jordan Valley (*kikkār*), enabling it to exercise control over much of the Jordan Valley.

The Chronology fits with the Date of the Patriarchs

Destruction of TeH.

Preliminary reports, even as late as 2013, identified the terminal destruction of TeH in the MBA at ca. 1600 BC.⁹² However, later in 2013, following eight seasons of excavations and reading over 40,000 separate vessels,⁹³ Collins published that "our refined date-range for Tall el-Ḥammâm's destruction is 1750–1650 BCE, [MB IIB] not 1600."⁹⁴

Collins also reports that "virtually no Late Bronze Age pottery has been found at

---

⁸⁵ Simons, *The Geographical and Topographical Texts of the Old Testament*, 407; Wood, "Locating Sodom: A Critique of the Northern Proposal," 81.

⁸⁶ Howard, Jr., "Sodom and Gomorrah Revisited," 388.

⁸⁷ Harland, "Sodom and Gomorrah Part I: Location," 20; Craigie, *The Book of Deuteronomy*, 405; Har-El, "The Pride of the Jordan–The Jungle of the Jordan," 66–67.

⁸⁸ Howard, Jr., "Sodom and Gomorrah Revisited," 388; Driver, "Zoar," 4:986.

⁸⁹ Merrill, "Modern Researches in Palestine, 1877," 117; Merrill, "Modern Researches in Palestine, PEFSt.," 145; Collins, "Forty Salient Points," 3.

⁹⁰ Sarna, *Genesis*, 387; Fields, *Sodom and Gomorrah*, 36 n. 28.

⁹¹ Driver, "Zoar."

⁹² Collins, "Where Is Sodom?," 70; Merrill, "Texts, Talls, and Old Testament Chronology," 1.

⁹³ Collins and Scott, *Discovering the City of Sodom*, 33.

⁹⁴ Collins, "Tall El-Hammam Is Still Sodom," 9; "Tall El-Hammam Is Sodom," 8; Moore, "Dr. John Moore and Dr. Steven Collins Reflect on TeHEP's First Nine Years," 1; Collins and Scott, *Discovering the City of Sodom*, 226.

Tall el-Ḥammâm."[95] In the 2013 report, after eight seasons, Collins reports:

> Late Bronze Age [1550–1200 BC] sherds are extremely rare in the area, and there is no discernable LBA architecture thus far (the only LBA sherds from around the site were found in a tomb)... Material from the Late Bronze Age are systematically absent from the tall proper. However, LB2 pottery vessels were found in a nearby tomb containing vessels dating from the Chalcolithic Period through the Iron Age. Thus, some kind of LB2 presence in the area can be surmised; however, no architecture from that period is known in this vicinity of the valley E of the Jordan River.[96]

Since TeH is considered Abel-Shittim,[97] and Moses camped here with the Israelites for a few years, it is not surprising to find some LB pottery lying around, with only a small structure (watchtower?) on the acropolis dating to the LB period. Following the destruction of TeH in the MBA, it lay unoccupied for over 500 years only to be resettled in the IAII,[98] about five centuries later. What is also compelling is that there are at least four other sites in the Jordan Valley with the same archaeological footprint (MB destruction with no LBA occupation)[99] to easily fulfill the requirements for the Pentapolis.

Destruction of BeD

According to Paul Lapp, Walter E. Rast and R. Thomas Schaub, who excavated Bâb edh-Dhrâ' between 1975 and 1981[100] the material finds indicate at least five periods of occupation between ca. 3150 and 2200 BC.[101] The permanent occupation dates to the EB IB (3150–3000 BC), EB II and III (3000–2300 BC).[102] A massive EB III destruction took place around 2350 BC[103] or 2300 BC.[104] This is the destruction that Wood and others have connected with the destruction of Sodom.[105] Additionally, in this period the ancient Near East (ANE) suffered an unidentified regional catastrophe which affected life in Egypt and Mesopotamia.[106] It is speculative whether the two catastrophes of BeD and the rest of the ANE are connected.

However, BeD was not permanently abandoned but resettled for about 100 years in EB IV [2350–2100 BC] until the water dried up.[107] Wood has tried to nullify the EB IV occupation by highlighting in the 1981 report that "the EB IV peoples chose areas

---

[95] Collins, "Where Is Sodom?," 70–71 n.6; Collins and Scott, *Discovering the City of Sodom*, 164; Collins, Hamdan, and Byers, "Tall El-Hammam Activity Report Season Four, 2009," 406, 408.

[96] Collins et al., "Tall El-Hammam, Season Eight, 2013," 4, 13.

[97] Thomson, *Land and the Book: Lebanon, Damascus, and Beyond Jordan*, 3:3:669; Glueck, *Explorations in Eastern Palestine*, 378; Merrill, "Modern Researches in Palestine, 1877," 117; "Modern Researches in Palestine, PEFSt.," 144; "Some Ancient Towns," 15; Miller and Tucker, *The Book of Joshua*, 199; Harrison, "Shittim," 413; Khouri, *Antiquities of the Jordan Rift Valley*, 76; MacDonald, *East of the Jordan*, 90; Kaiser, Jr. and Garrett, *NIV Archaeological Study Bible*, 233.

[98] Collins et al., "Tall El-Hammam, Season Eight, 2013," 13.

[99] See *Fact 44* and *45*.

[100] Rast and Schaub, *Bab Edh-Dhra': Excavations at the Town Site (1975-1981)*; Schaub, "Bab Edh-Dhra' (OEANE)," 1: 249.

[101] Rast and Schaub, *Bab Edh-Dhra': Excavations in the Cemetery*; Lapp, "Bab Edh-Dhra' (RB 1966)"; "Bab Edh-Dhra' Tomb A 76"; "Bab Edh-Dhra' (RB 1968)"; Schaub, "Bab Edh-Dhra' (OEANE)," 249.

[102] Rast, "Patterns of Settlement at Bab Edh-Dhra'," 9–31; Rast, "Bronze Age Cities along the Dead Sea," 46–47; Schaub, "Bab Edh-Dhra' (NEAEHL)," 1: 132–35.

[103] Rast, "Bronze Age Cities along the Dead Sea," 47; "Bab Edh-Dhra' (ABD)," 1:560; "Bab Edh-Dhra' and the Origin of the Sodom Saga," 194.

[104] Schaub, "Bab Edh-Dhra' (OEANE)," 1:249.

[105] Collins and Scott, *Discovering the City of Sodom*, 78.

[106] Grimal, *A History of Ancient Egypt*, 137ff; Redford, *Egypt, Canaan, and Israel in Ancient Times*, 63–64; Pollock, *Ancient Mesopotamia: The Eden That Never Was*, 117–48.

[107] Rast and Schaub, *Bab Edh-Dhra': Excavations at the Town Site (1975-1981)*, 7–8.

away from the town for settlement."[108] But new evidence, reported in their 1981 excavation reports, indicated that there was EB IV settlement inside the city.[109] The site was finally destroyed and abandoned after 2200[110]–2250 BC (EB IV).[111] Although Rast and Schaub question the reliability of some of their C-14 dates,[112] the evidence is clear that there was a reoccupation at BeD following the EB III destruction and hiatus with structural resettlement in the EB IV period.

BeD and Numeira were destroyed at different times.

In 1977 Rast and Schaub reported on the destruction at Numeira, which is well documented.[113] The question is: Were BeD and Numeira destroyed at the same time? The evidence at first (1977–1980) suggested that the destruction occurred simultaneously.[114] However, there was initial difficulty with the C-14 samples and the calibrated dates, but they continued to re-examine the evidence[115] and stated that "The possibility that Numeira lasted somewhat longer than the EB III city at Bâb edh-Dhrâʿ also cannot be ruled out."[116]

While in 1987 Rast reported that BeD and Numeira "were terminated at *approximately the same time* toward the end of EB III.[117] [emphasis added],[118] in 2007, Schaub and Chesson reported that it was an earthquake[119] that brought the final destruction[120] in 2600 BC,[121] 250 years before the destruction of BeD in 2350 BC.

The early conclusions of Rast and Schaub that BeD and Numeira were both destroyed at approximately the same time (i.e., 2350–2067 BC), are often recounted. However, it is now known that their individual destructions were separated by approximately two and a half centuries, with the destruction of BeD identified at ca. 2350 BC and Numeira at ca. 2600 BC. If BeD is Sodom, then Numeira cannot possibly be one of the cities of the Pentapolis and vice versa.

In addition, the southern EB I–III period sites of eṣ-Ṣafi,[122] Feifa,[123] and Khirbet al-Khanazir,[124] which have been identified as

---

[108] Rast and Schaub, "A Preliminary Report of Excavations at Bab Edh-Dhraʿ, 1975," 14.

[109] Chesson and Schaub, "Life in the Earliest Walled Towns," 247; Schaub, "Bab Edh-Dhraʿ (OEANE)," 1:249; Rast, "Bronze Age Cities along the Dead Sea," 48; "Patterns of Settlement at Bab Edh-Dhraʿ," 17, 31–34.

[110] 2200 may be too early for the EBIV period based on suspicious C-14 dating. Schaub, "Bab Edh-Dhraʿ (NEAEHL)," 136.

[111] Rast and Schaub, *Bab Edh-Dhraʿ: Excavations in the Cemetery.*

[112] Rast et al., "Preliminary Report of the 1979 Expedition," 46–47.

[113] Rast, "Settlement at Numeira," 36.

[114] Harlan, "Natural Resources of the Southern Ghor," 160; Rast et al., "Preliminary Report of the 1979 Expedition," 47.

[115] Rast, "Settlement at Numeira," 41.

[116] Rast et al., "Preliminary Report of the 1979 Expedition," 46.

[117] Ibid., 46–47.

[118] Rast, "Bab Edh-Dhraʿ and the Origin of the Sodom Saga," 194; Schaub and Rast, *The Southeastern Dead Sea Plain Expedition: 1977 Season*, 16–18.

[119] See also Donahue, "Geologic Reconstruction of Numeira," 87; Coogan, "Numeira 1981," 81.

[120] Wenham suggests that the destruction was not natural or supernatural but brought about through military means Wenham, *Genesis 1-15*, 1:309.

[121] Chesson and Schaub, "Life in the Earliest Walled Towns," 247.

[122] Rast and Schaub, "Survey of the Southeastern Plain of the Dead Sea, 1973," 10; Chesson, "Remembering and Forgetting in EBA Mortuary Practices," 113.

[123] de Vries, "Archaeology in Jordan, 1991," 262; Schaub, "Southeast Dead Sea Plain," 63; MacDonald, "Southern Ghors and Northeast ʾArabah (OEANE)," 65; de Vries, "Archaeology in Jordan, 1993," 482.

[124] "The structures excavated at Khirbet Khuneizir are EB IV tombs." MacDonald, "Southern Ghors and Northeast ʾArabah (OEANE)," 65; Rast and Schaub, "Survey of the Southeastern Plain of the Dead Sea, 1973," 13; de Vries, "Archaeology in Jordan, 1991," 262; Chesson and Schaub, "Death and Dying on the Dead Sea Plain," 253, 258; MacDonald, "EB IV Tombs at

the remaining cities of the Pentapolis,[125] are nothing more than cemeteries, with no architectural structures or domestic settlement. If BeD is Sodom, then there are no other candidates for the cities of the Pentapolis. In the EBA the southern region was one large burial site, perhaps managed by Bâb edh-Dhrâʿ and Numeira.

Most maximalists believe that the Patriarchs lived in the Middle Bronze Age.

Most conservative evangelical scholars and maximalists would place the period of the Patriarchs (including Abraham and Lot) in the Middle Bronze Age.[126] This is based not so much on archaeological finds as on correlating characteristics in the biblical text with the cultural markers of the MB periods. Scholars who hold to a MB I period for the Patriarchs[127] base their position on the literal biblical chronology based on a mid-15th cent. BC date for the Exodus, the antiquity of the biblical accounts (Gen 14), the geopolitical conditions and climate of the regions in the MB I period, nomadism and migration exemplified in the domestication of camels, and personal names and places identified in MB texts from Egypt, Ur, Mari, Ebla, Nuzi and Anatolia (20th–18th cent. BC).[128] Those who support a MB IIA/B date for the Patriarchs[129] rely on the 13th cent. BC date for the Exodus, the presence of the Hyksos in Egypt, pottery in Negev, the Beni-Hasan mural (1890 BC), Middle kingdom Egyptian chronology, the geopolitical conditions (Gen 14), parallels with the MB culture and the price of slaves, and the structure of covenants. Collins explains some of the issues surrounding the question of chronology when he states:

Khirbet Khanazir," 129–34; Schaub, "Southeast Dead Sea Plain," 62.

[125] Wood, "Have Sodom And Gomorrah Been Found?," 67; Wood, "Discovery of the Sin Cities," 67–80.

[126] See the chart in Price, *The Stones Cry Out*, 106.

[127] Kenyon identifies the patriarchs with a Canaanite migration and "invasion of Palestine by nomad tribes of Amorites." Kathleen M. Kenyon, "Excavations in Jerusalem, 1965," *PEQ* 98, no. 1 (1966): 75; *Amorites and Canaanites*, Schweich Lectures on Biblical Archaeology (Oxford, U.K.: Oxford University Press, 1967), 76; Paul W. Lapp, *The Dhahr Mirzbaneh Tombs: Three Intermediate Bronze Age Cemeteries in Jordan* (Philadelphia, Pa.: American Schools of Oriental Research, 1966), 114; John H. Walton, *Chronological and Background Charts of the Old Testament* (Grand Rapids, Mich.: Zondervan, 1994), 15; Price, *The Stones Cry Out*, 92, 350; Ed Hindson and Elmer L. Towns, *Illustrated Bible Survey: An Introduction* (Nashville, Tenn.: B&H, 2013), 36; Bimson, "Archaeological Data," 84–85; Nelson Glueck, *Rivers in the Desert: A History of the Negev* (New York, N.Y.: Farrar, Straus and Cudahy, 1959), 61–84; *The Other Side of the Jordan* (New Haven, Conn.: ASOR, 1970), 15–16; Merrill, *Kingdom of Priests*, 47–48, 83–96; "Texts, Talls, and Old Testament Chronology," 20–21.

[128] Bimson, "Archaeological Data," 59–92; Merrill, *Kingdom of Priests*, 47–48; "Texts, Talls, and Old Testament Chronology," 20–21.

[129] Albright, *The Archaeology of Palestine and the Bible*, 10; "A Revision of Early Hebrew Chronology," 68, 79; Glueck, *Rivers in the Desert*, 61–84; *The Other Side of the Jordan*, 15–16; Samuel J. Schultz and Gary V. Smith, *Exploring the Old Testament* (Wheaton, Ill.: Crossway, 2001), 209; Wright, *Biblical Archaeology*, 50; Hoffmeier, *The Archaeology of the Bible: Reassessing Methodologies and Assumptions*, 68; Kitchen and Mitchell, "Chronology of the Old Testament," 190; Millard, "Methods of Studying the Patriarchal Narratives as Ancient Texts," 43–58; Free and Vos, *Archaeology and Bible History*, 101; Gleason L. Archer, *A Survey of Old Testament Introduction*, Rev Upd (Chicago, Ill.: Moody, 1996), 184; Bruce K. Waltke and Cathi J. Fredricks, *Genesis: A Commentary* (Grand Rapids, Mich.: Zondervan, 2001), 30; John E. Goldingay, "The 'Salvation History' Perspective and the 'Wisdom' Perspective within the Context of Biblical Theology," *The Evangelical Quarterly* 51, no. 4 (1979): 11; William Sanford La Sor et al., *Old Testament Survey: The Message, Form, and Background of the Old Testament*, 2nd ed. (Grand Rapids, Mich.: Eerdmans, 1996), 38–43; Bill T. Arnold, *Encountering the Book of Genesis* (Grand Rapids, Mich.: Baker, 2003), 86; Geisler and Holden, *Popular Handbook of Archaeology and the Bible*, 191; Sarna, "The Patriarchs Genesis 12-36," 118.

While high, middle, and low ANE chronologies exist—tied principally to the chronology(ies) of Egypt—the differences between them consist of one or two decades, not centuries. (I am talking about the well-worked-out chronologies of mainline scholars like W. F. Albright, K. Kenyon, A. Ben-Tor, B. Mazar, A. Mazar,[130] K. A. Kitchen, D. Redford, Wente and Van Siclen, J. Hoffmeier, J. Currid, and W. Dever; not the fringe, radical revisions of ANE chronology suggested by D. Rohl, G. Aardsma, and a few others.).[131]

Almost all scholars place the Patriarchs in the Middle Bronze Age, including Wood (2166–1991 BC MB I)[132] and Collins (2000–1600 MB IIA/B).[133] Freedman and van Hattem place the Patriarchs in the EB age,[134] to support a SST.[135] The proponents who place them in the LB,[136] Iron IA,[137] and Persian/Greek[138] periods are in the minority. Even Wood, who supports the idea of the EB destruction of BeD as supporting his claim on being Sodom, places the Patriarchs in the Middle Bronze I (2166–1991 BC) along with other scholars.[139] Wood acknowledges the discrepancy and explains:

> If we assume a mid-15th century BC date for the Exodus, the date for the destruction [of Sodom] would then be ca. 2070 BC. The archeological date for the destruction of Bab eh-Dhra and Numeira, however, is considerably earlier than this. . . . This leaves a discrepancy between the Biblical date and the archaeological date of 230–280 years.[140]

The fact remains that most scholars believe that the Patriarchs lived in the Middle Bronze age (2nd millennium BC).

Logical Conclusion

If Bâb edh-Dhrâʿ was destroyed in the EBA (2350 BC), and yet all conservative

---

[130] Mazar, *Archaeology of the Land of the Bible*, 1:225–226; Amihai Mazar, "The Patriarchs, Exodus and Conquest Narratives in Light of Archaeology," in *The Quest for the Historical Israel*, ed. Israel Finkelstein and Brian B. Schmidt, Archaeology and Biblical Studies 17 (Atlanta, Ga.: SBL, 2007), 59.

[131] Collins, "Tall El-Hammam Is Still Sodom," 10.

[132] Wood claims that the date for the destruction of Sodom is ca. 2070 BC based on a 1446 BC date for the Exodus. The date of the destruction of Bab edh-Dhra according to Rast and Schaub is 2350 BC. Wood, "Discovery of the Sin Cities," 78; "Locating Sodom: A Critique of the Northern Proposal," 81.

[133] Collins has a slightly narrower date of 1950–1550 in his response to Bryant Wood. Collins, "A Response to Bryant G. Wood," 27; "Sodom: The Discovery of a Lost City," 72.

[134] Freedman states, "If Abraham and Lot had anything to do with the Cities of the Plain, then that link could only have existed in the Early Bronze Age, certainly not in the Middle Bronze Age." Freedman, "The Real Story of the Ebla Tablets," 157; Albright, "The Jordan Valley in the Bronze Age," 58–61; Willem C. van Hattem, "Once Again: Sodom and Gomorrah," *BA* 44, no. 2 (Spring 1981): 90; Shanks, "BAR Interviews Giovanni Pettinato," 47. Pettinato replied to Freedman's dating the Patriarchal Age to the third millennium as "impossible."

[135] Recently Kris Udd wrote his dissertation on the subject and states in his abstract "Combining the new lower archaeological chronologies and the higher dates for the patriarchs indicates the possibility that Bâb edh-Dhrâʿ and Numeira could be two of the biblical cities of the plain." Udd applies two extreme views to propose this speculative hypothesis. Udd, "Bab Edh-Dhraʿ, Numeira, and the Biblical Patriarchs: A Chronological Study."

[136] Cyrus H. Gordon, "The Patriarchal Narratives," *JNES* 13 (1954): 56–59; *Introduction to Old Testament Times* (Ventnor, N.J.: Ventnor, 1953), chapter 8; "Biblical Customs and the Nuzu Tablets," *BAR* 2 (1964): 1–12; "The New Amarna Tablets," *Orientalia* 16 (1947): 1–21; "Hebrew Origins in the Light of Recent Discovery," in *Biblical and Other Studies*, ed. Alexander Altmann (Cambridge, Mass.: Harvard University Press, 1963), 5–6.

[137] Benjamin Mazar, *The World History of the Jewish People: Ancient Times: Patriarchs*, vol. 2 (London, U.K.: Rutger's University Press, 1970), 169–87, 276–78; Aharoni, *The Land of the Bible*, 133–90; Ze 'ev Herzog, "Deconstructing the Walls of Jericho," *Ha'aretz Magazine*, 1999, 4–5.

[138] Thompson, *Historicity of the Patriarchal Narratives*, 89; John Van Seters, *Abraham in History and Tradition* (New Haven, Conn.: Yale University Press, 1975); S. M. Warner, "The Patriarchs and Extra-Biblical Sources," *JSOT* 2 (1977): 50–61.

[139] Wood, "Discovery of the Sin Cities," 78.

[140] Ibid.

maximalists would place Abraham in the MBA (2100–1600 BC), then BeD cannot be Sodom, as it no longer existed. However, TeH was still a thriving city state until it was destroyed in 1750–1650 BC (MB II) at the time of the Patriarchs and lay dormant for some 500 years until the Iron Age.

Criteria for the Identification of Sodom for the SST and NST			
Criteria	Scripture	BeD	TeH
East of Canaan boundary	Gen 12:4–5	Yes	Yes
Large city listed first in pentapolis	Gen 14:2	10 acres	62 acres
Time of the patriarchs (MBA)	Gen 13	No EB3	Yes MB2
Well watered	Gen 13:10	No[1]	Yes[2]
Located on the *kikkār* (Jordan Valley)	Gen 13:11	No	Yes
Visible from Bethel and Ai	Gen 13:3–12	No	Yes
Distinct from the battlefield (Kedorlaomer)	Gen 14:1–8	No	Yes
Fortified city	Gen 19:1	Yes	Yes
Near Zoar[3]	Gen 19:23	Yes	Yes
Fiery destruction	Gen 19:24	Yes EB3	Yes MB2
Human remains in the destruction	Gen 19:25	No[4]	Yes
Large cemetery	Gen 19:25	Yes	Yes[5]
On a geological fault line[6]	Gen 19:25	Yes	Yes
Evidence of four destroyed Cities of the Plain	Gen 19:25	No[7]	Yes
Visible from Hebron	Gen 19:28; 13:18	No	Yes
A wasteland in Late Bronze age	Num 21:20; 22:1	Yes	Yes
Visible from Mount Nebo	Deut 34:3	No	Yes
Abandoned forever	Jer 50:39–40	No EB4	No IA2

[1] Water supplied by wadi's that only flow during the rainy season and dry the rest of the year.

[2] Water supplied by several hot springs on the site providing water year-round.

[3] Both BeD and TeH have possible locations for Zoar, but no one really knows for sure where Zoar is located, and over the years scholars have proposed several locations, though no clear archaeological evidence has ever emerged to positively identify it.

[4] Bodies were only identified in the cemetery.

[5] Large dolmen fields (Al Rawda Field) next to TeH that served as family memorials for the deceased.

[6] Some have suggested that Sodom was destroyed by an earthquake since it was located on a fault line. However, this is a moot criterion as both sites are located on the same fault line.

[7] Numeira and Bâb edh-Dhrâ' were destroyed at different times, about 250 years apart. Feifa and Khirbet Khanazir, proposed for the other Cities of the Plain, do not have Early Bronze 3 domestic occupation, as they were both only cemeteries during this period.

The Location of Sodom

| Returned to former state | Ezek 16:53–55 | No only small EB4 | Yes IA2 |
| Three other sites from the same period | Gen 14:2 | No | Yes |

Conclusion

The research into the location of Sodom is certainly not finished and proves to be an ongoing project. Perhaps with the passage of time more evidence will come to light at both TeH and BeD. For example, the excavation reports from BeD are due to be published soon, making available facts as yet unknown. Excavations at TeH are also scheduled to continue for at least another few years and there is no telling what might be discovered in that time.

Certainly, the facts that have been presented here, in the areas of methodology, hermeneutics, geography, chronology, archaeology, destruction, and geology, will guide the reader to a better understanding of the debate over Sodom's location. What is evident from most of the facts presented is that few of them have any real bearing on the location of the ancient city of Sodom.

The biblical text indicates that Sodom is the only major Bronze Age city mentioned on the eastern Jordan Valley. In fact, for Sodom to be mentioned first in the list of the Cities of the Plain seems to indicate that it was a large city-state. While there are many smaller sites in the area, one should be looking for a large, prominent ruin on the eastern side of the Jordan. TeH (62 acres) and BeD (10 acres) are really the only two options to be considered in this category and TeH is much larger than BeD (see Figs. 32, 33).

However, the geography of the biblical text (Gen 13) places the Pentapolis on the

54. The balk of a room in the monumental palace in the Upper Area of Tall el-Ḥammâm 2015 (season 10) with the stratigraphy marked for the various loci. The destruction layer (black line Locus 27) of the Middle Bronze age period is clearly visible in the middle of the balk with the Late Bronze occupation sitting above the Middle Bronze age walls. A distinctive palace ware type pottery was recovered from these rooms in subsequent seasons. If this is Sodom, this would be part of King Bara's palace (Gen 14:2).

kikkār in the Jordan Valley north of the Dead Sea. This is precisely where Tall el-Ḥammâm is situated on the eastern edge of the *kikkār*. With a size of 62 acres, it would have been clearly visible from between Bethel and Ai, where the text states Abraham and Lot were standing looking east (Gen 13:3 and 12:8). If this was the only argument for the location of the Pentapolis, it would be sufficient; but there is more.

A significant unusual destruction took place at Tall el-Ḥammâm in the Middle Bronze II period, the time of the Patriarchs (see Fig. 54). Human remains were found contorted in the ash layer of the MB II ruins obviously not buried following their natural deaths but smothered in the destruction (see Fig. 45). A catastrophic event took place here with such high temperatures, it turned pottery into glass (see Fig. 47).

The proverbial icing on the cake has been the recent identification of several architectural features and ceramics at Tall el-Ḥammâm that have shown Minoan influence (see Fig. 39).¹ While this, in itself is not unique,² and does not help with the location of Sodom, Collins pointed out a possible literary link between Sodom, with their "sociological sexual practices"³ and

> the attempted abduction of the angels by the "young and old" men of Sodom (Gen 19), suggest an affinity to the formal cultural institution of paiderastia found on Bronze Age Crete, including a unique feature: ritual kidnapping [See Strabo *Geogr.* 10.21.4]. Research in this vein is ongoing, but the results thus far support the idea that the link is more than coincidental.⁴

Thus, Tall el-Ḥammâm is in the right location on the *kikkār*, at the appropriate MB period for the Patriarchs, and contains the suitable material remains and destruction to be Sodom. To date Tall el-Ḥammâm is the best candidate for the lost city of Sodom and no longer is there any reason to look south of the Dead Sea for its location. Based on the most up-to-date archaeological evidence, while once a southern supporter, I am now a persuaded northern defector!!

---

¹ Collins et al., "Tall El-Hammam, Season Eight, 2013," 8–10.

² Minoan influence has also been identified at Tel Kabri, Israel, Alalakh, Turkey, Tell el-Dab'a (Avaris), Egypt, and Qatna, Syria.

³ Moore, "Dr. John Moore and Dr. Steven Collins Reflect on TeHEP's First Nine Years," 1.

⁴ Collins et al., "Tall El-Hammam, Season Eight, 2013," 1 n.4; Koehl, "The Chieftain Cup and a Minoan Rite of Passage," 99–110.

Maps and Charts

MAP 1: Proposed Sites for the Cities of the Plain

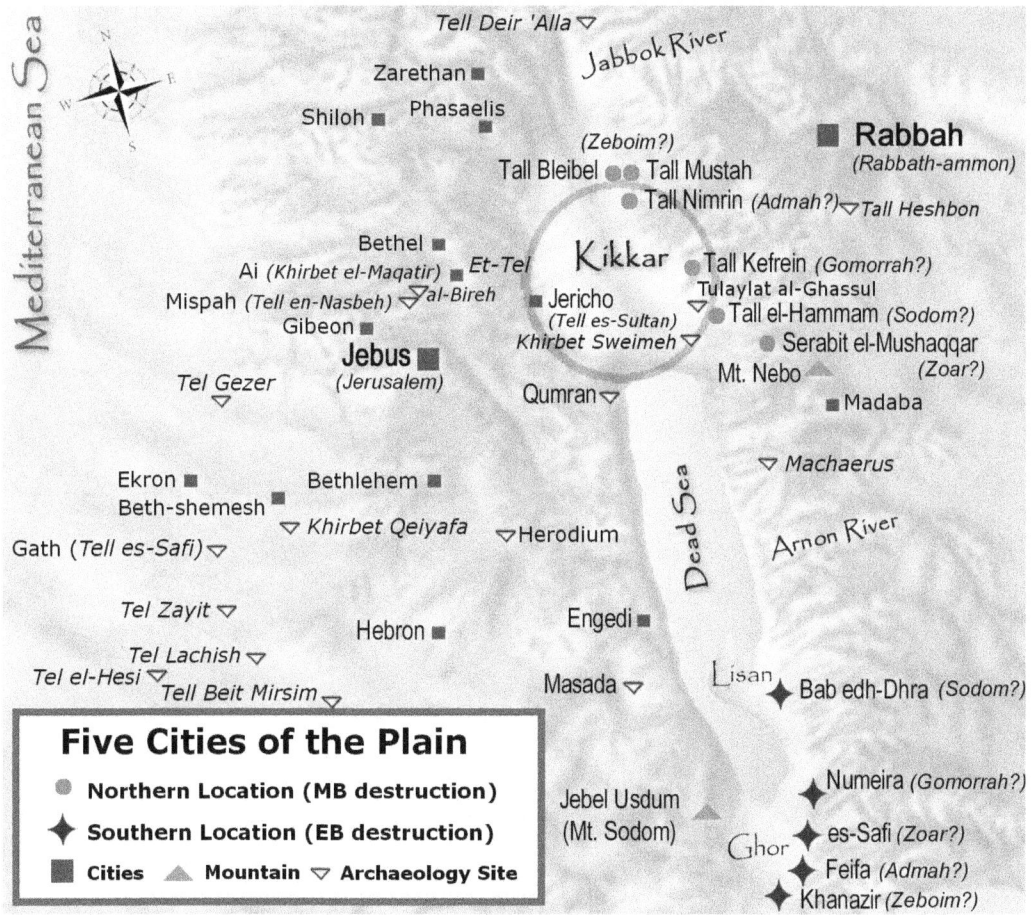

55. **MAP 1:** Proposed sites for the northern and southern location of the Cities of the Plain.

The Location of Sodom

Map 2: Proposed Northern Sites for the the Cities of the Plain

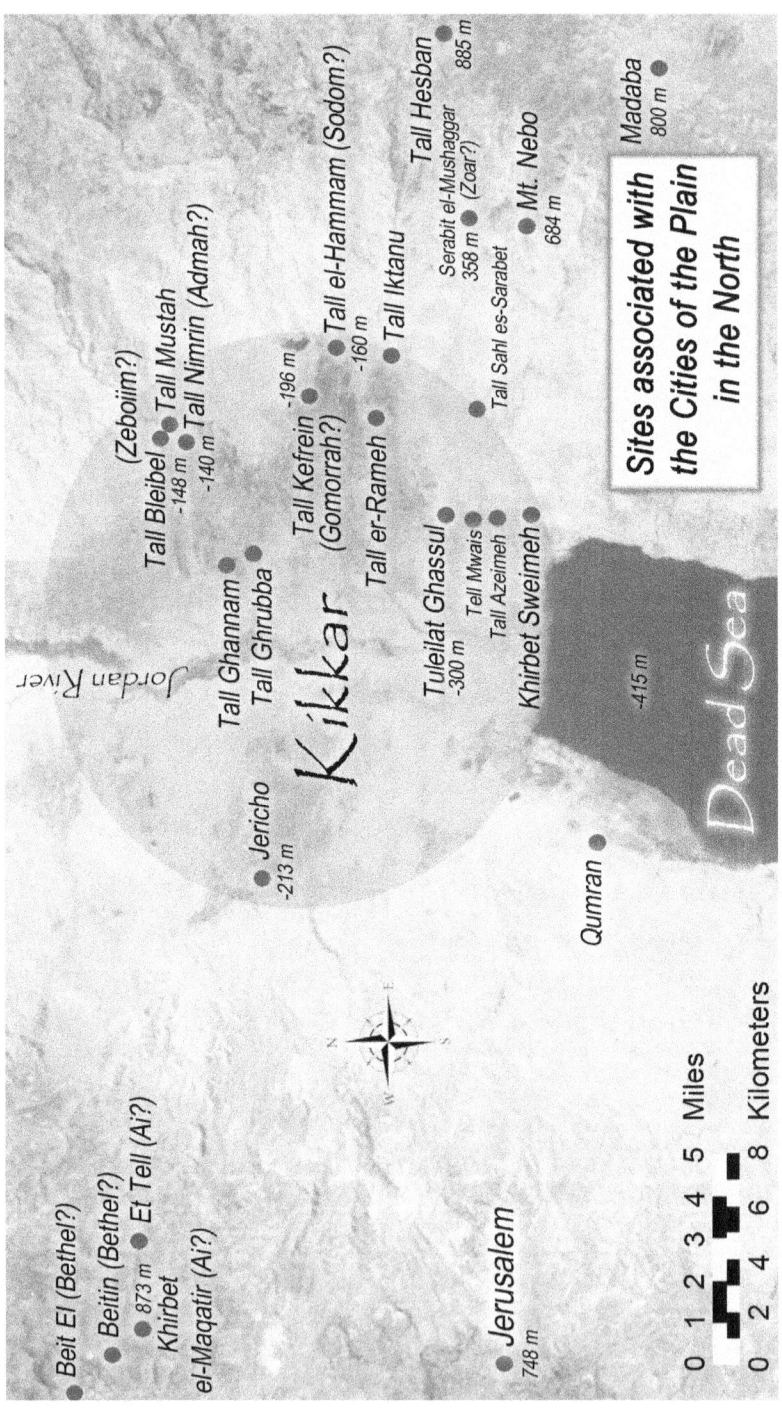

56. **MAP 2:** The proposed northern locations for the Cities of the Plain. The *kikkār* is indicated by the circle in the centre. The altitude in the Jordan Valley is given in negative numbers. In the upper left hand corner, the several options for Bethel and Ai are indicated; though these do not affect the general location from where Lot looked East across the *kikkār* to see the city of Sodom.

MAP 3: PROPOSED SOUTHERN SITES FOR THE CITIES OF THE PLAIN

57. **MAP 3:** Proposed southern locations for the Cities of the Plain. The southern basin of the Dead Sea was once covered by water but is now an artificial industrial pond filled with water from the northern basin and used to extract salts and minerals.

The Location of Sodom

Map 4: Dead Sea Fault Lines and Chedorlaomer's Campaign of the Region

58. **MAP 4:** representing the fault lines and the level of the Dead Sea in the Middle Bronze Age (about 2000 BC; A. D. Riddle, and David Parker, "Interactive Dead Sea Map," The Dead Sea: A History of Change, December 2013. http://www.riddlemaps.com/deadSea/map.swf). This map also depicts the southern campaign (① – ⑧) of Chedorlaomer, the king of Elam described in Genesis 14:1–12. Following his attack on Ḥaṣaṣon-Tamar (En-Gedi) ⑥ he encountered the confederation of the kings of the Cities of the Plain. Unfortunately the location of the Valley of Siddim is uncertain and bitumen deposits can be found in several locations around the Dead Sea (See Map 7 for the location of Sink holes). Chedorlaomer would have needed to have backtracked to encounter the Cities of the Plain in the south ⑦. Whereas traveling north ⑦ he would be traveling in the direction of Dan ⑧ where he was pursued by Abraham.

Glossary

Map 5: Borders of the Promised Land

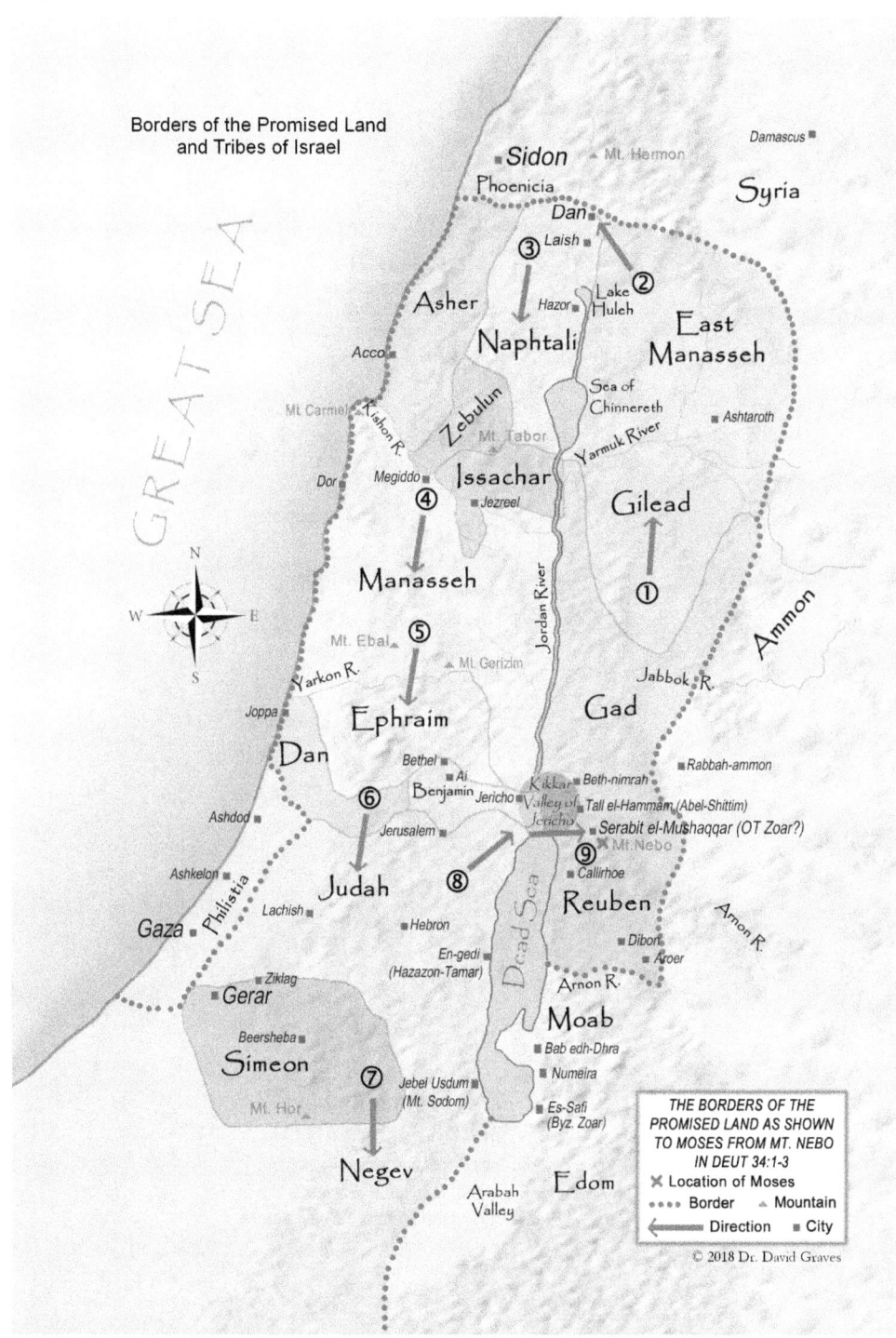

59. **MAP 5:** representing the outside borders of the Promised Land that God showed to Moses on Mount Nebo, described in Deuteronomy 34:1-3. It is unlikely that es-Safi (Byzantine Zoar) is the location of the eastern boundary of the Promised Land, as it would lay in Moabite territory, south of the Arnon River. It is more likely that Serâbît el-Mushaqqar, located on the ascent to Mount Nebo, or another site nearby, was the OT Zoar ⑨ and represents the eastern boundary of the Promised Land.

The Location of Sodom

Map 6: Boundaries of Palestinae

60. **MAP 6:** Historical boundaries of Roman / Byzantine / Islamic Palestine (sourced from Irfan Shahid, Byzantium and the Arabs in the Sixth Century, 683, Bernard Lewis, Islam in History: Ideas, People, and Events in the Middle East, 155 and the borders of Mandate Palestine from multiple sources). CM 01

MAP 7: LOCATION OF THE TARPITS AROUND THE DEAD SEA

61. **MAP 7:** The location of sinkholes from recent surveys overlayed on the map of the Dead Sea as it would have appeared during the time of Chedorlaomer, in the Middle Bronze Age (2000-1550 BC). The slime pits or bitumen pits were probably these sinkholes.

The Location of Sodom

Map 8: *Kikkār* Region North of the Dead Sea

62. **MAP 8:** The region of the *Kikkār* indicating the Roman road from Esbus to Livias and sites mentioned in this book.

MAP 9: AREA AROUND TALL EL-ḤAMMÂM

63. **MAP 9:** Map close-up of the area around Tall el-Ḥammâm. Multi-period site plan showing the excavation fields of the upper and lower tall. The survey plot of Tall el-Ḥammâm was used with permission from Leen Ritmeyer, architect and Qutaiba Dasouqi, Surveyor.

© Map drawn by David E. Graves

The Location of Sodom

Map 10: Area Around Bâb Edh-Dhrâ'

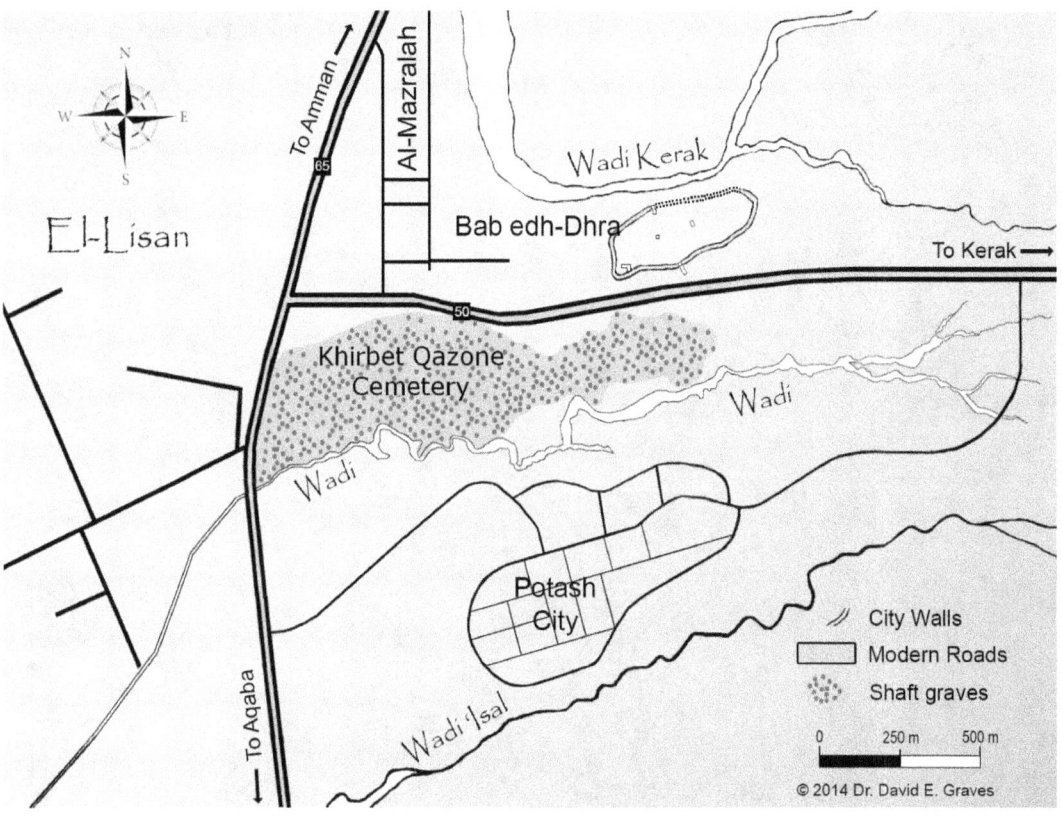

64. **MAP 10:** Map close-up of the area around Bâb Edh-Dhrâ' and Khirbet Qazone cemetery.
© Map drawn by David E. Graves

MAPS

MAP 11: SITE PLAN OF TALL EL-ḤAMMÂM

65. **MAP 11**. Multi-period site plan of Tall el-Ḥammâm showing excavation Fields.
Courtesy of Leen Ritmeyer. Used with permission

The Location of Sodom

Map 12: Site Plan of Feifa

66. **MAP 12**. Site plan for the EB and IAII remains at Feifa (or Fifa).
Used with permission of Hugh Barnes, The Follow the Pots Project.

CHART 1: ARCHAEOLOGICAL PERIODS

Period	Abbreviation	Historical Period	Dates
PREHISTORIC PERIOD			
Pre-Pottery Neolithic A, B	PPNA, PPNB	Post Creation	8500–6000 BC
Pottery Neolithic A, B	PNA, PNB	Ubaid Period (Sumer)	6000–4300 BC
Chalcolithic Period	Cal.	Ubaid Uruk Period	4300–3600 BC
BIBLICAL PERIOD			
Early Bronze Age I	EB I EB IA to EB IB*B IB to EB II*	Uruk Period (Sumer) Writing	3600–3000 BC[1] 3450–3100 BC*[2] 3200–2900 BC*
Early Bronze Age II–III	EB II–III EB II to EB III* EB IV*	Dynastic Period (flood?)	3000–2350 BC 2900–2450 BC*[3] 2500 BC*
Intermediate Bronze Age	IB (formerly EB IV–MB I)	Third Dynasty of Ur	2350–2000 BC
Middle Bronze Age IIA	MB IIA	Israel's Patriarchs	2000–1750 BC
Middle Bronze Age IIB	MB IIB	Middle Kingdom Egypt	1750–1650 BC
Middle Bronze Age IIC	MB IIC	New Kingdom Egypt	1650–1550 BC
Late Bronze Age I	LB I	Mosaic Period	1550–1400 BC
Late Bronze Age IIA	LB IIA	Early Exodus & Conquest	1400–1300 BC
Late Bronze Age IIB	LB IIB	Late Exodus & Conquest	1300–1200 BC
Iron Age I A, B	IA IA, IA IB	Judges	1200–1000 BC
Iron IIA	IA IIA	United Monarchy	1000–900 BC
Iron Age IIB–C	IA IIB–C	Divided Monarchy and Babylonian Conquest	900–586 BC
Iron Age III	IA III	Neo-Babylonian Period	586–539 BC
Persian Period	Pers.	Exile	539–332 BC

---

[1] Graham Philip, "The Early Bronze Age I–III," in *Jordan: An Archaeological Reader*, ed. Russell B. Adams (London, U.K.: Equinox, 2008), 167.

[2] * New High Chronology dates based on 313 C-14 date from 41 sites. Johanna Regev et al., "Chronology of the Early Bronze Age in the Southern Levant: New Analysis for a High Chronology," *Radiocarbon* 3–4 (2012): 561.

[3] Regev state that this "is at least 200 yr earlier than the traditionally accepted dates." Regev "Chronology," 561

THE LOCATION OF SODOM

Period	Abbreviation	Historical Period	Dates

CLASSICAL PERIOD

Hellenistic Period	Hell.	Alexander the Great	332–63 BC
Maccabean / Hasmonean Period	Macc.	Maccabean Revolt	165–63 BC
Early Roman Period	ER or E. Rom.	Herodian/ NT Period	63 BC–70 AD
Middle Roman Period	MR or M. Rom.	Yavne Period	70–135 AD
Late Roman Period	LR or L. Rom.	Mishnaic Period	135–200 AD
Late Roman Period	LR or L. Rom.	Talmudic Period	200–330 AD
Byzantine Period	Byz.	Eastern Roman Empire	330–638 AD

ISLAMIC PERIOD

Umayyad Period	Umay.	Arab Caliphate Period	638–750 AD
Abbasid Period	Abb.	Arab Caliphate Period	750–969 AD
Fatimid Period	Fat.	Caliphate Egyptians	969–1171 AD
Kingdom of Jerusalem Period	Crus.	Crusader Period	1099–1187 AD
Ayyubid Period	Ayy.	Crusader Period	1187–1244 AD
Mamluk Period	Mam.	Crusader Period	1244–1517 AD
Ottoman Period	Ott.	Ottoman Empire	1517–1917 AD

MODERN PERIOD

British Mandate Period	Brit. Man.	British Occupation and Arab States	1917–1948 AD
Israeli Period	Isr.	Modern Israel	1948–Present

CHART 2: COMPARATIVE ARCHAEOLOGICAL DATING

Period	Geisler[4]	ABD[5]	Collins[6]	Price[7]
Neolithic Age	8500–4600	8300–5000	6600–4500	8000–4300
Chalcolithic Period	4600–3600	5000–3500	4500–3600	4300–3300
Early Bronze I	3600–2900	3500–3100	3600–3100	3300–2900
Early Bronze II[8]	2900–2700	3100–2650	3100–2800	2900–2600
Early Bronze III[9]	2700–2500	2650–2350[10]	2800–2350	2600–2300
Early Bronze IV	2500–2350	2400–2000[11]		2300–2100
Intermediate Bronze	2350–2000		2350–1950[12]	
Middle Bronze I	2000–1800	2000–1800	1950–1800	2100–1900
Middle Bronze II	1800–1550	1800–1650	1800–1550	
Middle Bronze IIA				1900–1700
Middle Bronze IIB				1700–1600
Middle Bronze IIC				1600–1550
Middle Bronze III		1650–1500		
Late Bronze I	1550–1400	1500–1400	1550–1400	1550–1400
Late Bronze II	1400–1200	1400–1200	1400–1200	1400–1200

---

[4] Geisler and Holden, *Popular Handbook of Archaeology and the Bible*, 191–92.

[5] William G. Dever et al., "Palestine, Archaeology of," ed. David Noel Freedman et al., *ABD* (New York, N.Y.: Doubleday, 1996), 5:99–119.

[6] Collins et al., "Tall El-Hammam, Season Eight, 2013," 12–13.

[7] Price, *The Stones Cry Out*, 350–51.

[8] "The transition between EB II and EB III is not as clearly connected to Egyptian chronology due to the cessation of trade connections between the regions from the 2nd Dynasty onwards. Thus, the traditional correlation of later EB II with the 2nd Dynasty, or even the 3rd Dynasty, is based on virtually no material evidence." Regev et al., "Chronology of the Early Bronze Age in the Southern Levant: New Analysis for a High Chronology," 526.

[9] "EB III is traditionally defined as coinciding with [Egyptian] dynasties 3–6. These correlations, however, have no secure material basis. The end of the period is conventionally placed around 2300 BC, during the reign of Pharaoh Pepi I, when there is evidence of Egyptian military intervention along the southern Coastal Plain of Israel. The date of Pepi's reign, however, is disputed and could be somewhat earlier." Ibid., 527.

[10] The end of EB III is given as 2350 BC in the *ABD* (William G. Dever et al., "Palestine, Archaeology of," ed. David Noel Freedman et al., *ABD* (New York, N.Y.: Doubleday, 1996), 5:110), 2200 BC in the *New Encyclopedia of Archaeological Excavations in the Holy Land* (Edited by Ephraim Stern, Ayelet Levinson-Gilboa, and Joseph Aviram, 4 vols. (New York, N.Y.: MacMillan, 1993), 4:1529), and 2300 BC in *The Oxford Encyclopedia of Archaeology in the Near East*" (Edited by Eric M. Meyers, 5 vols. (Oxford, U.K.: Oxford University Press, 1997), 413).

[11] According to Dever this was "Albright's 'Middle Bronze I,' Kenyon's 'Intermediate EB–MB'" William G. Dever et al., "Palestine, Archaeology of," ed. David Noel Freedman et al., *ABD* (New York, N.Y.: Doubleday, 1996), 5:111.

[12] 2350-2200 BC IB1, formerly EB IV. 2200-1950 IB2, formerly MB I.

The Location of Sodom

COMPARATIVE ARCHAEOLOGICAL DATING (*cont.*)				
Period	Geisler	ABD	Collins	Price
Iron I	1200–1000	1200–900	1200–1000	1200–918
Iron II	1000–586	900–600	1000–539	918–586
Iron III/Persian	586–332	586–332	539–332	586–332
Hellenistic	332–63	332–50	332–63	
NT Period		50 BC–AD 150		
Roman Period	63 BC–AD 324			
Early Roman			63 BC–AD 135	

CHART 3: THE REGIONS FOR THE CHURCH COUNCIL REPRESENTATIVES

Year	Event	Representative	Eccles. Region	Eccles. Province
AD 325	Council of Nicaea I	Severus	Bishop of Sodom	Arabia[1]
AD 325	Council of Nicaea I	Cyprion	Bishop of Philadelphia	Arabia[2]
AD 325	Council of Nicaea I	Asterius Germanus	Bishop of Petra	Palæstina
AD 325	Council of Nicaea I	Petrus	Bishop of Abila	Palæstina [3]
AD 325	Council of Nicaea I	Januarius	Bishop of Jericho	Palæstina [4]
AD 325	Council of Nicaea I	Eusebius	Bishop of Caesarea	Palæstina [5]
AD 357	Split of Palaestina into Palaestina Prima I, Palaestina Secundae II and Palaestina Salutaris (later Terti) III[6]			Palæstina I, II & III
AD 381–84	Egeria's visit	?	Priest of Livias[7]	Palæstina I?
AD 381–84	Egeria's visit	Musonius?	Bishop of Zoar (Segor)[8]	Arabia?[9]
AD 409	Creation of Palaestina[10]			Palæstina I, II & III
AD 431	Council of Ephesus I	Letoius	Bishop of Livias	Palæstina I[11]
AD 449	Council of Ephesus II	Musonius	Bishop of Zoar (Segor)	Palæstina III[12]
AD 449	Council of Ephesus II	Anastasius	Bishop of Areopolis	Palæstina III[13]
AD 449	Council of Ephesus II	Pancratius	Biship of Livias	Palæstina I[14]

---

[1] Mouchy, *Christianae religionis institutionisque*, 85 no. 78; Le Quien, *Oriens christianus*, 3:743.

[2] Mouchy, *Christianae religionis institutionisque*, 85 no. 76.

[3] Ibid., 85 no. 40.

[4] Ibid., 85 no. 34.

[5] Le Quien, *Oriens christianus*, 3:551; Power, "The Site of the Pentapolis: Part 1," 1:51–52.

[6] Dan, "Palaestina Salutaris (Tertia) and Its Capital," 134–35; Lionel Casson, "The Administration of Byzantine and Early Arab Palestine," *Aegyptus* 32, no. 1 (1952): 54.

[7] Egeria, *The Pilgrimage of Etheria*, 21.

[8] Ibid., 24.

[9] Dan, "Palaestina Salutaris (Tertia) and Its Capital," 136 n. 20.

[10] Kazhdan, "Arabia, Province of," 147.

[11] "A titular see in Palestina Prima, suffragan of Cæsarea" which would be the capital of Palaestina. Vailhé, Siméon. "Livias." Translated by Mario Anello. *CE*. New York, N.Y.: Appleton Company, 1913; Le Quien, *Oriens christianus*, 3:655.

[12] Ibid., 3:743.

[13] Ibid., 3:733–35.

[14] Ibid., 3:655.

| AD 451 | Council of Chalcedon | Musonius | Bishop of Zoar (Segor) | Palæstina III[15] |
| AD 451 | Council of Chalcedon | Pancratius | Bishop of Livias | Palæstina I[16] |

---

[15] Ibid., 3:743.
[16] Ibid., 3:655.

CHART 4: PROPOSED DATING FOR THE PATRIARCHS[1]

Period	Proponents	Dates BC	Evidence
Early Bronze III 2750–2350 BC	D. N. Freedman	2650–2350[2]	Support the SST
	W. van Hattem	2400–2300[3]	Ebla tablets
			Destruction of Bâb edh-Dhrâ' in 2350 BC
Middle Bronze I or Intermediate Bronze (formerly under the early chronology EBIV) 2350–1950 BC	K. Kenyon	2300–1900[4]	Literal biblical chronology based on a mid–15th cent. BC date for the Exodus
	B. Wood	2166–1991 (Abraham)[5]	
	J. Walton	2166–1805[6]	
	E. Hindson & E. Towns	2166–1806[7]	Antiquity of Accounts (Gen 14).
	J. Bimson	2150–1992[8]	Geopolitical conditions and climate of region in MB I.
	R. Price	2150–1850[9]	
	N. Glueck	2100–1900[10]	
	E. Merrill	2100–1700[11]	Nomadism-migration
			Personal names & places
			Texts from Egypt, Ur, Mari, Ebla, Nuzi and Hittites (20th–18th cent. BC)
Middle Bronze IIA/B	K. Kitchen, A. Millard	1991–1825[12]	13th cent. BC date for the Exodus. Hyksos in

---

[1] Adapted from J. Randall Price, *The Stones Cry Out: What Archaeology Reveals About the Truth of the Bible* (Eugene, Oreg.: Harvest House, 1997), 106. Also, see Chart 2 for different dates for the archaeological periods used by various scholars.

[2] Freedman states, "If Abraham and Lot had anything to do with the Cities of the Plain, then that link could only have existed in the Early Bronze Age, certainly not in the Middle Bronze Age." Freedman, "The Real Story of the Ebla Tablets," 157; Shanks, "BAR Interviews Giovanni Pettinato," 47; Albright, "The Jordan Valley in the Bronze Age," 58–61. Pettinato replied to Freedman's dating the Patriarchal Age to the third millennium as "impossible."

[3] Hattem, "Once Again," 90.

[4] Kenyon identifies the patriarchs with a Canaanite migration and "invasion of Palestine by nomad tribes of Amorites." Kenyon, "Excavations in Jerusalem, 1965," 75; *Amorites and Canaanites*, 76; Lapp, *Dhahr Mirzbaneh Tombs*, 114.

[5] Wood claims that the date for the destruction of Sodom is *ca.* 2070 BC based on a 1446 BC date for the Exodus. The date of the destruction of Bab edh-Dhra according to Rast and Schaub is 2350 BC. Wood, "Discovery of the Sin Cities," 78; "Locating Sodom: A Critique of the Northern Proposal," 81.

[6] Walton, *Chronological and Background Charts of the Old Testament*, 15; Price, *The Stones Cry Out*, 92.

[7] Hindson and Towns, *Illustrated Bible Survey*, 36.

[8] Bimson, "Archaeological Data," 84–85.

[9] Price identifies MBI from 2100-1900 BC and MB IIA from 1900-1700 BC. Price, *The Stones Cry Out*, 350.

[10] Glueck, *Rivers in the Desert*, 61–84; *The Other Side of the Jordan*, 15–16.

[11] Merrill, *Kingdom of Priests*, 47–48, 83–96; "Texts, Talls, and Old Testament Chronology," 20–21.

[12] Kitchen and Mitchell, "Chronology of the Old Testament," 190; Millard, "Methods of Studying the Patriarchal Narratives as Ancient Texts," 43–58.

The Location of Sodom

Period	Scholars	Dates	Evidence
1950–1650 BC	W. Albright, N. Glueck, S. Schultz, G. Wright, J. Hoffmeier	2000–1700[13]	Egypt
			Pottery in Negev
	S. Collins	2000–1600[14]	Beni-Hasan mural (1890 BC)
	J. P. Free, A. Horeth & J. McRay	2000–1500[15]	Egyptian chronology (middle kingdom)
	G. Archer	2100–1500[16]	Geopolitical conditions (Genesis 14)[20]
	B. Walke, J. Goldingay, W. La Sor	1950–1550[17]	Price of slaves and covenant structure
	B. Arnold	1800–1650[18]	Amorite Hypothesis
	J. Holden & N. Geisler	1800–1550[19]	
Middle Bronze IIB/C 1750–1550 BC	A. Mazar	1750–1550[21]	Remembered traditions.
			Mari/Nuzi archives
			Prosperous urban culture
			Hyksos Dynasty
Late Bronze 1550-1200 BC	C. Gordon	1550-1200[22]	Cuneiform and Egyptian parallels
			Amarna and Nuzi Tablets
Iron IA	B. Mazar	1250–1150[23]	Remembered in

---

[13] Albright states on the basis of the evidence at Bab edh-Dhra that "it does suggest very strongly that the date of Abraham cannot be placed earlier than the nineteenth century BC" (1900 to 1801 BC). Albright, *The Archaeology of Palestine and the Bible*, 10; "A Revision of Early Hebrew Chronology," 68, 79; Glueck, *Rivers in the Desert*, 61–84; *The Other Side of the Jordan*, 15–16; Schultz and Smith, *Exploring the Old Testament*, 209; Wright, *Biblical Archaeology*, 50; Hoffmeier, *The Archaeology of the Bible: Reassessing Methodologies and Assumptions*, 68. Hoffmeier narrows the date to 1800-1540 in his *Israel in Egypt* book.

[14] Collins has a slightly narrower date of 1950–1550 in his response to Bryant Wood. Collins, "A Response to Bryant G. Wood," 27; "Sodom: The Discovery of a Lost City," 72.

[15] Free and Vos, *Archaeology and Bible History*, 64; Hoerth and McRay, *Bible Archaeology*, 101.

[16] Archer identifies these dates as the Middle Bronze Age. Archer, *A Survey of Old Testament Introduction*, 184.

[17] Waltke and Fredricks, *Genesis*, 30; Goldingay, "The Patriarchs in Scripture and History," 11; La Sor et al., *OT Survey*, 38–43.

[18] Arnold, *Encountering the Book of Genesis*, 86.

[19] Geisler and Holden base part of their arguments on the Excavations at Tall el-Hammam. Geisler and Holden, *Popular Handbook of Archaeology and the Bible*, 191.

[20] Sarna, "The Patriarchs Genesis 12-36," 118.

[21] Mazar, *Archaeology of the Land of the Bible*, 1:225–226; Mazar, "The Patriarchs, Exodus and Conquest Narratives in Light of Archaeology," 59.

[22] Gordon, "The Patriarchal Narratives," 56–59; *Introduction to Old Testament Times*, chapter 8; "Biblical Customs and the Nuzu Tablets," 1–12; "The New Amarna Tablets," 1–21; "Hebrew Origins in the Light of Recent Discovery," 5–6.

[23] Mazar, *Patriarchs*, 2:169–87, 276–78; Aharoni, *The Land of the Bible*, 133–90; Herzog, "Deconstructing the Walls of Jericho," 4–5.

1200-1000 BC	Y. Aharoni		monarchy.
	Z. Herzog		Excavations at Beersheba (no MB)
			Anarchronisms in Gen Account
			Mention of Philistines and Arameans
Persian/Greek tradition 400-165 BC	T. L. Thompson	400–165[24]	Literary and oral tradition
	J. Van Seeters		
	S. M. Warner		Use of folklore

---

[24] Thompson, *Historicity of the Patriarchal Narratives*, 89; Seters, *Abraham in History and Tradition*; Warner, "The Patriarchs and Extra-Biblical Sources," 50–61.

CHART 5: NORTHERN LOCATION SITES

Site[1]	Identification	Directors	Excavation Date	Occupation Periods	Date of Destruction
Tall el-Ḥammâm[2]	Sodom	Kay Prag Steven Collins	1990[3] 2009-2014[4]	Neol.ithic, Chal. (4600-3600 BC), EB-IB (ca. 3000–2350 BC), MB[5] (ca. 2000–1600 BC),[6] no LB except in a tomb, few IA I sherds, IA II, Rom., Byz., & Umay.[7]	1750–1650 BC[8]
Tall al-Kafrayn[9] (or Kefrein) Not to be confused with	Gomorrah[10]	Thanasis J. Papadopoulos[11]	2000-2009 Papadopoulos, Thanasis J. "Tall Al-Kafrayn: The	EB I-III cemetery LB pottery but no LB or IA	"Destruction of the settlement by fire

---

[1] S. Merrill identified Tell er-Rameh or Beth Haram, and Suweimeh or Beth Jeshimoth, as two of the Cities of the Plain, but does not indicate which cities. Merrill, "Modern Researches in Palestine, 1877," 119; "Modern Researches in Palestine, PEFSt.," 144.

[2] Merrill identifies Tall el-Hammam as one of the Cities of the Plain but does not indicate which city. Merrill, "Modern Researches in Palestine, 1877," 119; "Modern Researches in Palestine, PEFSt.," 144.

[3] University of Durham, UK. Prag, "Tell Iktanu and Tall El-Hammam 1990"; "Tell Iktanu and Tell Al-Hammam. Excavations in Jordan"; "The Excavations at Tell Al-Hammam."

[4] Trinity Southwest University, Albuquerque, N. M. Collins et al., "Tall El-Hammam, Season Eight, 2013," 1–20; Collins, Hamdan, and Byers, "Tall El-Hammam: Preliminary Report, Season Four, 2009," 385–414.

[5] In 1988 Yassine stated that few EB-MB were identified at TeH. Subsequent excavations have shown that surface surveys do not indicate the true occupational history. Yassine, Ibrahim, and Sauer, "The East Jordan Valley Survey 1975 (Part Two)," 192.

[6] Collins, "Where Is Sodom?," 40.

[7] Based on over *ca.* 2,000 pottery sherds read in the first four seasons and 40,000 separate vessels by Season eight. Collins, Kobs, and Luddeni, *Introduction to Tall Al-Hammam with Seven Seasons of Ceramics*; 4, 12–14; Collins, Hamdan, and Byers, "Tall El-Hammam Activity Report Season Four, 2009," 408; Collins and Scott, *Discovering the City of Sodom*, 33.

[8] Collins, "Tall El-Hammam Is Still Sodom," 9; Moore, "Dr. John Moore and Dr. Steven Collins Reflect on TeHEP's First Nine Years," 1.

[9] S. Merrill identified Tall Kefrein (or Abel-Shittim) as one of the Cities of the Plain, but does not indicate which city. Merrill, "Modern Researches in Palestine, 1877," 119; "Modern Researches in Palestine, PEFSt.," 144.

[10] Steven Collins, "Sodom and the Cities of the Plain," *Bible Dictionary* (Albuquerque, N.M.: TSU Press, 2013), 2.

[11] University of Ioannina, Greece. Papadopoulos and Kontorli-Papadopoulos, "Preliminary Report of the Seasons 2005-2008: Tall Kafrayn," 283–310.

Khirbet Kefrein 1 km SW			University of Ioannina Hellenistic-Jordan Expedition, Preliminary Report on the Ninth Excavation Season (2009)." ADAJ 55 (2011): 131–46.	I structures,[12] IA I-III.[13] "EBA through to the Late IA" which includes MB.[14] Chal., IA, Rom., Byz., Umay., & Hell.[15]	during the transitional period LBA/Early Iron Age."[16]
Tall Nimrin	Admah[17]	James W. Flanagan,[18] David W. McCreery,[19] and, Khair N. Yassine[20]	1989, 1990, 1993, 1995	Glueck[21] reports EBI, (no LB) IAI, IA II, Rom.-Umay.[22] Following excavations: EB IV, MB IIC, IA II, Pers., Hell., Rom., Byz., Umay., Mam., Ayy.[23] EB IV, IB, MB I & II	

---

[12] "On the basis of the evidence available from the tall and the adjacent EBA cemetery, one might provisionally suggest that the site of Tall al-Kafrayn was inhabited from Early Bronze Age times with the floruit during the Iron Age. There is some evidence from pottery of a limited Late Bronze Age occupation, but no architectural remains fill the gap observed also at other sites of this area, such as Tall al-Hammam, Tall Iktanu and Tall Nimrin." Ibid., 308.

[13] Papadopoulos, "Hellenic Archaeology Project: Ghawr as-Sāfī and Tall Al-Kafrayn (2000-2004)," 180, 189; Khouri, *Antiquities of the Jordan Rift Valley*, 75.

[14] Collins reports "Although not much has been published on the ongoing excavation at Tall Kufrayn, our personal contact with the director of the excavation [Papadopoulos] confirms that there is not an LBA architectural presence at the site. There is a strong EBA and MBA presence, as at Tall Nimrin." Collins, "Tall El-Hammam, Season Eight, 2013", 5 n.10. Papadopoulos and Kontorli-Papadopoulos, "Preliminary Report of the Seasons 2005-2008: Tall Kafrayn," 304.

[15] Khouri, *Antiquities of the Jordan Rift Valley*, 75.

[16] Papadopoulos, "Hellenic Archaeology Project: Ghawr as-Sāfī and Tall Al-Kafrayn (2000-2004)," 189.

[17] Collins, "Sodom and the Cities of the Plain," 2.

[18] 1978-2007, Case Western Reserve University, Cleveland, Ohio

[19] Willamette University, Salem, Oregon

[20] Khair N. Yassine, University of Jordan

[21] Previously Glueck reported "not a single one [sherd] from any pre-Roman period." Glueck, *Explorations in Eastern Palestine*, 368.

[22] Glueck, "Some Ancient Towns," 12.

[23] Dornemann, "Preliminary Comments on the Pottery Traditions at Tell Nimrin, 1989," 153–81; Khouri, *Antiquities of the Jordan Rift Valley*, 70–72.

				(Stratum I),[24] IA II, Pers., Byz.,[25] Umay., & Mam.[26] (no LB or IA I)[27]	
Tall Bleibel (Bulaybil) & Tall el-Musṭāḥ[28]	Zeboiim	N/A	Never excavated only surface surveys such as Glueck (1951), Ibrahim, Yassine, and Sauer (1975-76)[29] and Chang-Ho and Lee (2000).[30]	Surface survey: Tall Bleibel: Few EB, IA II, Per., Hell., Flints Tall el-Musṭāḥ EB I, II, III, Few LB, Few Byz, Umay, Flints[31] EB, IB, MB, (no LB or IA I), IA II,[32] Rom.[33] EBI, (no LB) IA I–II, Rom.–Umay.[34]	Khouri reports "When the modern road cut through a portion of the tell [Tall el-Musṭāḥ], it revealed the remains of ancient walls and house foundations, burning, and much pottery."[37]

---

[24] Flanagan, McCreery, and Yassine, "Tell Nimrin: Preliminary Report, 1993," 217–18; Steven Falconer, "The Middle Bronze Age," in *Jordan: An Archaeological Reader*, ed. Russell B. Adams (London, U.K.: Equinox, 2008), 268.

[25] James W. Flanagan, David W. McCreery, and Khair N. Yassine, "Tall Nimrin: The Byzantine Gold Hoard from the 1993 Season," *ADAJ* 38 (1994): 245–65.

[26] Patrick E. McGovern, "A Neutron Activation Analysis Study of Bronze Age-Mamluk Period Pottery From Tell Nimrin, Jordan," *Virtual Nimrin*, 1998, 1, http://www.cwru.edu/affil/nimrin/data/geol/gpm_0001.pdf; Flanagan, McCreery, and Yassine, "First Preliminary Report, 1989 Tell Nimrin," 131–52; "Preliminary Report of the 1990 Excavation at Tell Nimrin," *ADAJ* 36 (1992): 89–111; "Tell Nimrin: Preliminary Report, 1993," 205–44; "Tall Nimrin: Preliminary Report, 1995," 271–92.

[27] "As in past seasons, all periods from EBIV/MBI through the modern era were represented in the ceramics assemblage with the exception of LB and early Iron I." Flanagan, McCreery, and Yassine, "Tall Nimrin: Preliminary Report, 1995," 287.

[28] Collins points out "Tall Bleibel and Tall Mustah, separated only by the wadi (stream) running between them [200 m]. They are so close together that not a few scholars have thought they should be considered one site." Collins, "Sodom and the Cities of the Plain," 3; Khouri, *Antiquities of the Jordan Rift Valley*, 70–86.

[29] Yassine, Ibrahim, and Sauer, "The East Jordan Valley Survey 1975 (Part One)," 159–89; "The East Jordan Valley Survey 1975 (Part Two)," 189–207.

[30] Chang-Ho and Lee, "The Survey in the Regions of 'Irāq Al-Amīr and Wādī Al-Kafrayn," 187–92.

[31] Yassine, Ibrahim, and Sauer, "The East Jordan Valley Survey 1975 (Part Two)," 192.

[32] Collins reports that "Bleibel and Mustah sherd identically to Hammam EB, IB, MB, IA2, but no LB." Correspondence with Steven Collens March 29, 2014.

[33] Identified from surface finds and an aqueduct by the author in 2010.

[34] Glueck, "Some Ancient Towns," 12.

CHARTS

				EB I–III, LB,[35] IA I & II, Rom, Byz. & Islamic.[36]	
Seaport on the Arnon River	Zoar		?	Rom.[38]	N/A
Serâbît el-Mushaqqar (also Tell esh Shaghur; Um Sheggar; or M'Shuggar)	Zoar	Sylvester J. Saller,[39] and Bellarmino Bagatti[40]		EB,[41] Moabite Early IA I–II,[42] IA,[43] Rom., & Byz.[44]	
Tall Iktanu	Zoar[45] Gomorrah[46]	Kay Prag	1966, 1987–1990	Cal., EB, IB,[47] MB I[48], & IA[49]	N/A

---

[37] Ibid.

[35] Yassine, Ibrahim, and Sauer, "The East Jordan Valley Survey 1975 (Part Two)," 197.

[36] Khouri, *Antiquities of the Jordan Rift Valley*, 73.

[38] See *Fact 33*.

[39] Franciscan priest and archaeologist.

[40] 1905-1990, Italian Franciscan priest and archaeologist.

[41] Taylor, "The Dead Sea in Western Travellers' Accounts," 11–12.

[42] There is a significant MB site at Khirbet Qarn al Qubish (Kh. Qurn el-Kibsh), only 3 km east of Serâbît el-Mushaqqar and 1 km south of el-Mushaqqar. Glueck, *Explorations in Eastern Palestine II*, 111.

[43] Saller and Bagatti, *Town of Nebo (Khirbet El-Mekhayyat)*; Saller, "Iron Age Tombs at Nebo," 165–298.

[44] Waterhouse and Ibach, "Heshbon 1973: The Topographical Survey," 221, 226.

[45] Merrill, *East of the Jordan*, 236–39; "Modern Researches in Palestine, 1877," 117–21; "Modern Researches in Palestine, PEFSt.," 144.

[46] Collins, "Sodom and the Cities of the Plain," 2.

[47] Prag, "Excavations at Tell Iktanu, 1987"; "Excavations at Tell Iktanu, 1989"; "The Excavations at Tell Iktanu 1989 and 1990"; "Tell Iktanu and Tall El-Hammam 1990"; "Tell Iktanu and Tell Al-Hammam. Excavations in Jordan"; de Vries, "Archaeology in Jordan."

[48] "Iktanu is claimed to be only EB, IB by Prag, but we've sherded the upper tall there and have had many, many MB reads from there." Personal correspondence with Steven Collins, March 29, 2014. The author can also verify the identification of MB sherds at Iktanu.

[49] Khouri, *Antiquities of the Jordan Rift Valley*, 76–79.

CHART 6: SOUTHERN LOCATION SITES

Site	Identification[50]	Directors	Excavation Date	Occupation Periods	Date of Destruction
Bâb edh-Dhrâ'	1. Zeboiim 2. Sodom	Paul Lapp Walter E. Rast and R. Thomas Schaub[51]	1965–1967[52] 1975, 1977, 1979, and 1981[53]	ca. 3300–2100 BC[54] Five periods of EB occupation in EB IA, EB IB, EB II, EB III, and EB IV[55] Pastoral nomads-PPNA, Chal., EB I, EB IA (ca. 3150–3050 BC)[56] Domestic occupation – EB IB (3050–2950), EB II (2950–2800), III (2800–2300)[57] Sedentary, non-urban occupation in EB IVA (2300–2150) after hiatus at the end of EB III destruction.[58]	EBIII destruction between 2350[59] and 2300 BC[60] The site is unoccupied after 2200–2150 BC[61]

---

[50] The first identification was proposed by Wood in his 1974 article "Have Sodom And Gomorrah Been Found?" *Bible and Spade* 3, no. 3 (1974): 67. The second identification was changed in Wood's later work "The Discovery of the Sin Cities of Sodom and Gomorrah." *Bible and Spade* 12, no. 3 (1999): 70.

[51] Rast (1930-2003), University of Chicago. Schaub, Indiana University of Pennsylvania.

[52] Rast and Schaub, *Bab Edh-Dhra': Excavations in the Cemetery*, 36; Lapp, "Bab Edh-Dhra' (RB 1966)," 556–61; "Bab Edh-Dhra' Tomb A 76," 12–41; "Bab Edh-Dhra' (RB 1968)," 86–93; Schaub, "Bab Edh-Dhra' (OEANE)," 249.

[53] http://expeditiondeadseaplain.org. Rast and Schaub, *Bab Edh-Dhra': Excavations at the Town Site (1975-1981)*; Schaub, "Bab Edh-Dhra' (OEANE)," 1: 249.

[54] In this section the dates and periods are according to Rast and Schaub. Schaub and Rast, "Preliminary Report of the 1981 Expedition to the Dead Sea Plain, Jordan," 36; Rast, "Bab Edh-Dhra' (ABD)," 1: 559; Schaub, "Bab Edh-Dhra' (NEAEHL)," 1:131–36; Chesson, "Libraries of the Dead," 143 n.1.

[55] Based on the C-14 dates the Regev study suggested that: "the transition from EB IB to EB II occurred sometime between 3080–2610 BC." Regev et al., "Chronology of the Early Bronze Age in the Southern Levant: New Analysis for a High Chronology," 552.

[56] Rast, "Bronze Age Cities along the Dead Sea," 44; "Patterns of Settlement at Bab Edh-Dhra'," 7–9.

[57] Rast, "Bronze Age Cities along the Dead Sea," 46–47; Rast, "Patterns of Settlement at Bab Edh-Dhra'," 9–31; Chesson and Schaub, "Life in the Earliest Walled Towns," 247; Chesson, "Remembering and Forgetting in EBA Mortuary Practices," 111–12.

[58] Schaub, "Bab Edh-Dhra' (OEANE)," 1: 249; "Bab Edh-Dhra' (NEAEHL)," 1:135–36; Rast, "Bronze Age Cities along the Dead Sea," 48; "Patterns of Settlement at Bab Edh-Dhra'," 17, 31–34; Chesson, "Libraries of the Dead," 143 n.1.

Charts

Site	Identification[25]	Directors	Excavation Date	Occupation Periods	Date of Destruction
Numeira (also an-Numayra, Numeirah, or Numeireh)	1. Admah 2. Gomorrah	Walter E. Rast and R. Thomas Schaub Meredith S. Chesson	1977, 1979, 1981, and 1983[62] 2004[63]	Ras an-Numayra EB IB (3150-3000 BC),[64] EB III (2900-2600)[65] Occupied for less than 200 years.[66] Nabatean, Rom. & Byz.[67]	ca. 2300 BC[68] 2550 BC[69] 2600 BC[70]
Feifa (also Fifa, Feifeh, or Fifah)	1. Gomorah 2. Admah	Walter E. Rast and R. Thomas Schaub[71] Mohammad Najjar of DOA	Discovered in 1973 Dec 1989- Jan 1990[72] 2001 second salvage season.[73]	Neolithic,[74] EB IA cemetery,[75] IAII fortress built over the EB cemetery.[76] Town site initially identified as EB but IA,[77]	Cemetery N/A, What was earlier considered by Rast and Schaub to be an EB town site was in fact an IA site.

---

[59] Rast, "Bronze Age Cities along the Dead Sea," 47; "Bab Edh-Dhraʿ (ABD)," 1:560; "Bab Edh-Dhraʿ and the Origin of the Sodom Saga," 194; Chesson and Schaub, "Life in the Earliest Walled Towns," 247.

[60] Schaub, "Bab Edh-Dhraʿ (OEANE)," 1:249.

[61] Rast and Schaub, *Bab Edh-Dhraʿ: Excavations in the Cemetery*, 36.

[62] http://expeditiondeadseaplain.org. Rast, "Bronze Age Cities along the Dead Sea," 47; Walter Rast, R. Thomas Schaub, and Meredith S. Chesson, eds., *Numayra: Excavations at the Early Bronze Age Townsite in Jordan, 1977-1983* (Winona Lake, Ind.: Eisenbrauns, Forthcoming); Rast and Schaub, *Bab Edh-Dhraʿ: Excavations at the Town Site (1975-1981)*, 12–15.

[63] Rast, Schaub, and Chesson, *Numayra: Excavations, 1977-1983*, forthcoming.

[64] Chesson and Schaub, "Life in the Earliest Walled Towns," 247.

[65] Walter E. Rast, "The 1975-1981 Excavations at Bab Edh-Dhraʿ," in *Bab Edh-Dhraʿ: Excavations at the Town Site (1975-1981): Part 1: Text*, ed. Walter E. Rast and R. Thomas Schaub, vol. 1, Reports of the Expedition to the Dead Sea Plain, Jordan 2 (Winona Lake, Ind.: Eisenbrauns, 2003), 1:1; "Settlement at Numeira," 42; Rast et al., "Preliminary Report of the 1979 Expedition," 43; Coogan, "Numeira 1981," 75–81.

[66] Rast, "Bab Edh-Dhraʿ and the Origin of the Sodom Saga," 194; Chesson and Schaub, "Life in the Earliest Walled Towns," 247.

[67] Schaub, "Southeast Dead Sea Plain," 63.

[68] Chesson and Schaub, "Death and Dying on the Dead Sea Plain," 258.

[69] "The latest calibrated radiocarbon date we have for Numayra is 2550 BC (the earliest being 2850 BC cal)." Meredith S. Chesson, "Personal Correspondence: Dates for the Terminal Destruction of an-Numayra," April 16, 2014, 1.

[70] Chesson and Schaub, "Life in the Earliest Walled Towns," 247.

[71] "Sadly the Rast and Schaub season at Feifa has not been published, it is one of the things we are working on as part of www.followthepotsproject.org." Personal correspondence with Morag Kersel, April 11, 2014.

[72] Rast and Schaub, *Bab Edh-Dhraʿ: Excavations at the Town Site (1975-1981)*, 15.

[73] http://expeditiondeadseaplain.org. Najjar spent 2 weeks and excavated about 50 tombs.

[74] MacDonald et al., "Southern Ghors and Northeast ʿArabah Archaeological Survey 1986," 405.

[75] Rast and Schaub, "Survey of the Southeastern Plain of the Dead Sea, 1973," 11–12, 17; "The 1975-1981 Excavations at Bab Edh-Dhraʿ," 1; MacDonald, "Southern Ghors and Northeast 'Arabah (OEANE)," 65.

[76] de Vries, "Archaeology in Jordan, 1991," 262; MacDonald, "Southern Ghors and Northeast 'Arabah (OEANE)," 65; MacDonald et al., "Southern Ghors and Northeast ʿArabah Archaeological Survey 1986," 408.

The Location of Sodom

Site	Identification	Excavators	Date	Periods	Destruction
				Nabatean, Rom, Byz.,[78] & Mamluk. Van Hattem's indication of EB III is mistaken.[79]	While Rast and Schaub stated that "The destruction dating probably to the end of the Early Bronze Settlement"[80] it actually dated to the IA.[81]
Khirbet Khanazir	1. Sodom 2. Zeboiim	Burton MacDonald and Nancy Lapp; Walter E. Rast and R. Thomas Schaub; Chesson, Meredith S.	Discovered in 1973 by MacDonald & identified as site 141 in the survey of the southern Ghor. Dec 1989- Jan 1990[82]	EB I cemetery,[83] EB IV cemetery with no domestic occupation.[84] IA[85], IA II[86], Rom.[87] Van Hattem's indication of EB III is mistaken.[88] The walls which Rast and Schaub identified in 1973[89] were in reality chanel houses marking EB IV shaft tombs.[90]	N/A cemetery
eṣ-Ṣafi	Zoar	Konstantinos D. Politis	1999 – Present (15 years)[91]	EB (3150 BC),[92] IA II, Late Rom., Byz., Umay.,	N/A

---

[77] MacDonald et al., "Southern Ghors and Northeast `Arabah Archaeological Survey 1986," 405; Rast and Schaub, "Survey of the Southeastern Plain of the Dead Sea, 1973," 17.

[78] Schaub, "Southeast Dead Sea Plain," 63; Rast and Schaub, "Survey of the Southeastern Plain of the Dead Sea, 1973," 11.

[79] Hattem, "Once Again," 88.

[80] Rast and Schaub, "Survey of the Southeastern Plain of the Dead Sea, 1973," 11.

[81] Meredith S. Chesson, "Personal Correspondence: Feifa Occupation," April 17, 2014, 1.

[82] Rast and Schaub, *Bab Edh-Dhra`: Excavations at the Town Site (1975-1981)*, 15.

[83] Rast, "The 1975-1981 Excavations at Bab Edh-Dhra`," 1.

[84] Chesson and Schaub, "Death and Dying on the Dead Sea Plain," 253; MacDonald, "EB IV Tombs at Khirbet Khanazir," 129–34; MacDonald et al., "Southern Ghors and Northeast `Arabah Archaeological Survey 1986," 406; Rast and Schaub, "Survey of the Southeastern Plain of the Dead Sea, 1973," 18.

[85] Rast and Schaub, "Survey of the Southeastern Plain of the Dead Sea, 1973," 18.

[86] Rast and Schaub, "Expedition to the Dead Sea Plain," 63; Rast and Schaub, "Survey of the Southeastern Plain of the Dead Sea, 1973," 17; MacDonald et al., "Southern Ghors and Northeast `Arabah Archaeological Survey 1986," 408.

[87] Rast and Schaub, "Survey of the Southeastern Plain of the Dead Sea, 1973," 18.

[88] Hattem, "Once Again," 88.

[89] Rast and Schaub, "Survey of the Southeastern Plain of the Dead Sea, 1973," 12–14.

[90] de Vries, "Archaeology in Jordan, 1991," 262; Rast, "Bab Edh-Dhra` (ABD)," 560; MacDonald et al., "Southern Ghors and Northeast `Arabah Archaeological Survey 1986," 406; Schaub, "Southeast Dead Sea Plain," 62.

[91] http://gr.linkedin.com/pub/konstantinos-d-politis/4b/99/1a9

| | | | | | Abb., and Mam.[93] Van Hattem's indication of EB III is mistaken.[94] | |

---

[92] The EB site consists of "cist tombs built of cobble stones with a large flat stone over the top." MacDonald et al., "Southern Ghors and Northeast `Arabah Archaeological Survey 1986," 405; Rast and Schaub, "Survey of the Southeastern Plain of the Dead Sea, 1973," 15–16.

[93] See *Fact 33*. Rast and Schaub, "Survey of the Southeastern Plain of the Dead Sea, 1973," 16.

[94] Hattem, "Once Again," 88.

The Location of Sodom

Chart 7: Timeline

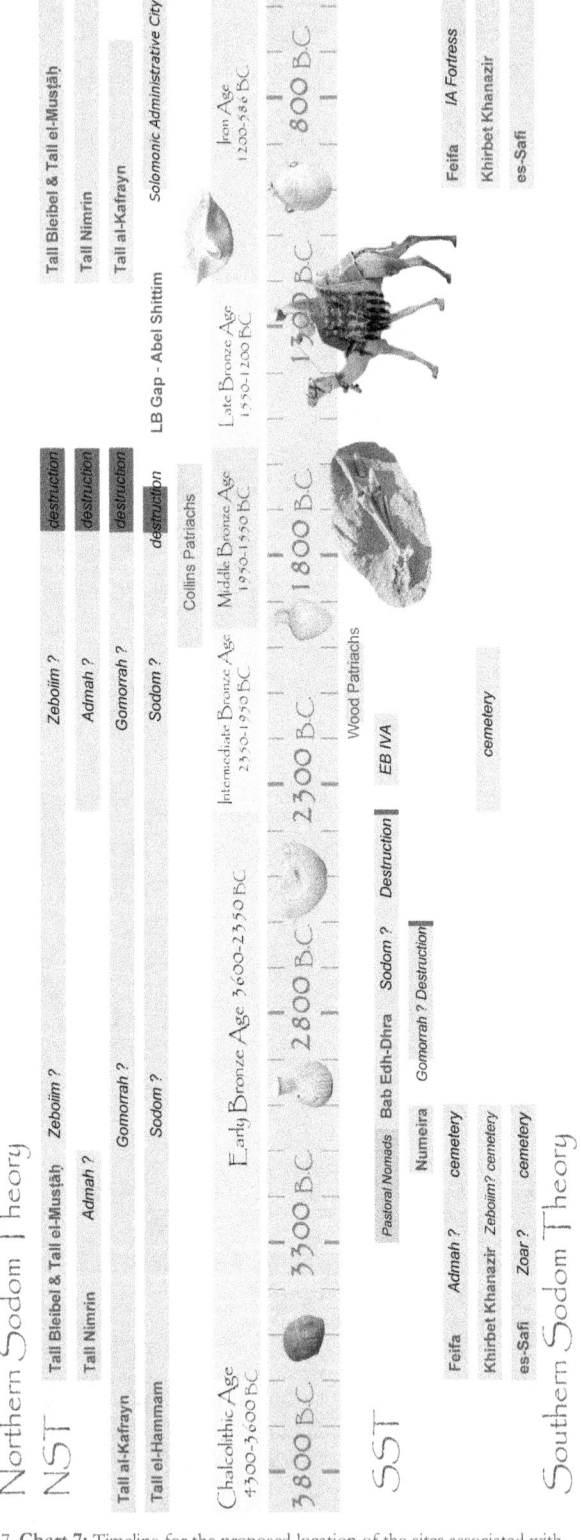

67. **Chart 7:** Timeline for the proposed location of the sites associated with the Northern and Southern Sodom theories.

68. **Timeline:** The period of the Patriarchs.
© David E. Graves

Glossary

Acropolis: (ἀκρόπολις; from ἄκρος [*akros*] "highest, topmost, outermost" and πόλις [*polis*] "city") Although technically this has referred to citadel in Athens which houses the Parhenon it can refer to any high elevation of a city which is easily fortified. This is usually where cities placed their temples and palaces.

Amphora(e): (ἀμφιφορεύς *amphiphoreus* from ἀμφί *amphi* "on both sides" or "around" + φέρειν *pherein* "to carry") Large storage jar with two handles and a pointed bottom; used for storing and transporting wine, oil, grapes, olive oil, olives, grain, fish, and other commodities.

Aqueduct: Water channel usually associated with high arches to traverse a ravine, though they can also run along the ground, as at Tall el-Ḥammâm.

Assemblage: A group of artifacts of different types found near to each other (stratum see Fig. 34).

Balk (baulk): (baulk) The vertical wall of a square left to preserve and read strata. This includes a one-meter strip of unexcavated earth left in place on the north and east sides between squares.

Body sherds: Unrecognizable pieces of broken pottery that cannot be used as diagnostic sherds.

Capital: The top decorative section of a column (or pilaster). In classical architecture there are three types: Doric, Ionic, and Corinthian.

Ceramic typology: The careful observation of changing pottery (ceramic) forms to determine the chronological dating sequence.

Chalcolithic: (χαλκός, *chalkos* "copper" + λίθος, *lithos*, stone). The first archaeological period to use copper.

Codex: (pl. *codices*; Lat. *caudex* "tree trunk", "book", or "notebook") A ancient bound manuscript (distinguished from a scroll) comprising a collection of single pages stitched together with a binding to form a book.

Commentary: A book that gives the author's opinion and background information about the meaning of the text of Scripture, book by book, chapter by chapter, or verse by verse.

Covenant: A legal contract between two parties. In the ancient Near East and the OT, it refers to binding parties through an intensified oath, sometimes ratified by a sacrifice (cf. Gen 15:9-11, 17-18). In the NT the term may carry the same meaning (e.g., new covenant) and signify an agreement, testament, or will.

Diagnostic sherds: Pieces of pottery, such as rims, handles, bases and painted body sherds, that identify the structure of the whole vessel.

Dolmen: (Breton language, "stone table"; also called *Menhir*). A prehistoric megalithic structure constructed of two large upright stones with a capstone placed across them. Corpses were then placed on top while the interior was primarily used for commemorative purposes (see Fig. 34, 35 and Map 9).

Field: The area of excavation on a tel composed of a unit of one or more squares.

Flint: A hard quartz stone used by primitive man as a tool for cutting.

Fulgurite: Glass created from sand by means of a lightning strike.

Graben: (Ger. "ditch" or v. "to dig"). A geology term indicating a rectangular ditch cut out of the Earth's crust that forms a dug-out depression. The Dead Sea region is often called the Dead Sea graben.

Hoard: A group of coins or other small artifacts discovered together (see Fig. 34).

Hyksos: (Ὑκσώς, Ὑξώς, Ηχῶς or Ὑκουσσώς *Hykussōs*, Egyptian *heqa khaseshet* "ruler(s) of the foreign countries") An ethnically mixed group of Western Asiatic Semitc people who overthrew the Egyptian Thirteenth Dynasty and formed the Fifteenth and Sixteenth Dynasties in Egypt (ca. 1674–1548 BC). The Hyksos are known for introducing new tools of warfare into Egypt including the composite bow and the horse-drawn chariot.

Klinker: (clinker) A piece of brick or pottery that is melted or burned under high temperature (see Fig. 47).

Krater: A large bowl used for mixing wine and food (see Fig. 29, 31).

Level: A surveyor term to indicate the height above sea level and used to designate a layer or stratum. It can also be used to indicate a locus.

Lisan: (Arabic for "tongue") The small peninsula on the eastern side of the Dead Sea which separates the North and the South basins (Josh 15:2).

Locus (pl. *loci*): The feature in an archaeological square, such as a wall, pit, or installation which is different from a previous feature. It can be as minute as the difference in soil or as large as a room.

Maximalists: Those who maximize (or prioritize) the biblical data with respect to the archaeological data and do not limit the historicity of the biblical accounts (See Introduction).

Minimalists: Those who minimize the biblical data in deference to the archaeological data and limit the historicity of biblical accounts (before the return from exile. See Introduction).

Monolith: (Lat. *monolithus*; μονόλιθος *monolithos* from μόνος *monos* "one" or "single" + λίθος *lithos* "stone") A large, single-cut stone.

Neolithic: (Gr. *neîos*, "new" +*lithos*, "stone"). The New Stone Age period (ca. 10,200-4,500/2,000 BC).

Obsidian: (Lat. *obsidianus* from *Obsianus lapis* "[stone] of Obsius") A hard dark volcanic glass formed from lava.

Palynology: (παλύνω *palunō* "strew, sprinkle") The analysis of particles that are strewn such as dust or pollen.

Patriarchs: (from πατριά *patria* "lineage, family"; πατηρ *patēr* "father" + ἄρχειν *archein* "to rule"; Heb. אבות *Avot* or *Abot*) The term refers to the three biblical patriarchs of the people of Israel: Abraham, Isaac, and Jacob.

Pentateuch: (πεντάτευχος *pentateuchos* "five scrolls") The first five books of the OT: Genesis, Exodus, Leviticus, Numbers and Deuteronomy.

Period: A time of occupation in the history of a site or stratum (i.e., Early Bronze Age, Iron Age, etc.). Sometimes it is used to refer to sub-periods or phases of sites (i.e., IIa or IVb).

Phase: A subdivision of a period or stratum of occupation. It is sometimes used as a temporary designation during excavation before the stratigraphy is clear.

Pilgrim flask: (ampullae). A small metal, glass, or ceramic vial shaped like a flattened canteen with one or two small handles on the side and a small spout. Used by pilgrims in antiquity to carry water or oil.

Probe square: An exploratory trench or square dug to determine the extent or nature of a locus for future excavation.

Qumran: An archaeological site located on a plateau north northwest of the Dead Sea that hosted a Jewish community from the Iron Age II through the end of the Second Temple Period (until the destruction by the Romans in AD 68). The Jewish community of the Second Temple period produced and preserved the Dead Sea Scrolls.

Sanhedrin: (Heb. סַנְהֶדְרִין *sanhedrîn* "[great] council"; Συνέδριον *synedrion* "assembly sitting together") A term designating the Jewish political assembly at Jerusalem that represented the highest magistracy of the country (Josephus *Ant.* 14.5.4). It was also an assembly of twenty to twenty-three men appointed in every city in the biblical land of Israel (*m. Sanh.* 1:1).

Sealed: A Locus that is free of contamination by another locus.

Septuagint: (abbr. LXX, Lat. *septuaginta* "The Seventy") The Koine Greek translation of the Hebrew textual tradition that included certain texts which were later included in the canonical Hebrew Bible (Old Testament) made in Alexandria, Egypt by Jewish scholars (ca. 280–150 BC).

Shaft tomb: A type of vertical underground burial chamber dug down into a deep rectangular burial structure. Such tombs were often built with a stone floor and lined with mudbrick, masonry, or wood.

Slip: The thin clay coating applied to pottery by dipping the pot into a thick clay liquid, then firing it.

Square: The basic area of excavation developed for precise documentation of the location of artifacs within a numbered grid system. The standard size is 5 meters x 5 meters, leaving a 1-meter unexcavated balk on the north and east sides (making 6 m x 6 m).

Stratification: The layers (strata) of a tel created by successive destructions. Consists of archaeological deposits identified as periods of occupation containing artifacts.

Stratum (s) (Lat. "a spread for a bed, quilt, or blanket"; pl. *strata*) A horizontal layer of soil containing artifacts and debris representing a particular time period and dated by using pottery and coins.

Talmud: (תַּלְמוּד talmūd "instruction, learning") The collection of rabbinic writings that form the authoritative body of Jewish tradition comprising Jewish civil and ceremonial law, including the Mishnah (abbr. *m.*). There are two versions of the Talmud: the Babylonian Talmud (abbr. *b.* which dates from the fifth cent. AD, but includes earlier material) and the earlier Palestinian or Jerusalem Talmud (abbr. *y.*).

Tel or Tell (Heb. תֵּל "mound or hill"; Arabic تل, tall used in Arabic countries) An unnatural mound created by the repeated destruction and rebuilding of ancient cities (see Fig. 12).

Threshold: The horizontal sill under a door made of stone or wood that provides support for the structure.

Trinitite: The glassy residue created when sand was exposed to the affects of the Trinity, New Mexico nuclear bomb test in 1945 (see Fig. 47).

Typology: The study and comparison of the various shapes of artifacts (i.e. pottery, glass, bone, flint, organic, etc.) for their classification.

Wadi: (Arabic *Wādī* "valley, ravine") A dried up waterbed or gully which only flows during the rainy season.

BIBLIOGRAPHY

Abelson, Meir, Yoseph Yechielei, Onn Crouvi, Gideon Baer, Daniel Wachs, Amos Bein, and Vladimir Shtivelman. "Evaluation of the Dead Sea Sinkholes." In *New Frontiers in Dead Sea Paleoenvironmental Research*, edited by Yehouda Enzel, Amotz Agnon, and Mordechai Stein, 241–53. Special Papers: Geological Society of America 401. Boulder, Colo.: Geological Society of America, 2006.

"About William M. Thomson." *Logos Bible Software*, January 16, 2014. https://www.logos.com/product/26753/the-land-and-the-book.

Agnes, Michael E. *Webster's New World College Dictionary*. 4th ed. Cleveland, Ohio: Webster's New World, 1999.

Aharoni, Yohanan. "The Land of Gerar." *IEJ* 6, no. 1 (1956): 26–32.

———. *The Land of the Bible: A Historical Geography*. Translated by Anson F. Rainey. 2nd ed. Louisville, Ky.: Westminster/Knox, 1981.

Albright, William F. "A Revision of Early Hebrew Chronology." *Journal of the Palestine Oriental Society* 1 (1921): 49–79.

———. "Shinar–Sangar and Its Monarch Amraphel." *The American Journal of Semitic Languages and Literatures* 40, no. 2 (1924): 125–33.

———. "The Archæological Results of an Expedition to Moab and the Dead Sea." *BASOR* 14 (1924): 2–12.

———. *The Archaeology of Palestine*. London, U.K.: Taylor & Francis, 1956.

———. "The Jordan Valley in the Bronze Age." *AASOR* 6 (1926): 13–74.

———. "The Site of Bethel and Its Identification." In *The Excavation of Bethel (1934-1960)*, edited by James Leon Kelso and William F. Albright, 1–3. AASOR 39. Cambridge, Mass.: ASOR, 1968.

Albright, William F., J. L. Kelso, and J. P. Thorley. "Early Bronze Age Pottery from Bab-ed-Dra in Moab." *BASOR* 95 (1944): 1–13.

Albright, William Foxwell. *The Archaeology of Palestine and the Bible*. The Richards Lectures Delivered at the University of Virginia. New York, N.Y.: Flavell, 1935.

Aling, Charles F. "Historical Synchronisms and the Date of the Exodus." *Artifax* 17, no. 2 (n.d.): 19.

Allen, Susan Heuck. *Finding the Walls of Troy: Frank Calvert and Heinrich Schliemann at Hisarlik*. Berkeley, Calf.: University of California Press, 1999.

Alliata, Eugenio, and Michele Piccirillo, eds. *The Madaba Map Centenary: Travelling Through the Byzantine Umayyad Period. Proceedings of the International Conference Held in Amman 7–9 April 1997*. Studium Biblicum Franciscannum Collectio Maior 40. Jerusalem: Studium Biblicum Franciscannum, 1999.

Al-Marashi, Ibrahim, and Sammy Salama. *Iraq's Armed Forces: An Analytical History*. Middle Eastern Military Studies. London; New York: Routledge, 2009.

Amit, Ora, and Amos Bein. "The Evolution of the Dead Sea Floating Asphalt Blocks: Simulations by Pyrolisis." *Journal of Petroleum Geology* 2, no. 4 (1980): 429–47.

———. "The Genesis of the Asphalt in the Dead Sea Area." *Journal of Geochemical Exploration* 11, no. 3 (1979): 211–25.

Anderson, Robert T. "Bethel (Place)." In *EDB*, edited by David Noel Freedman, Allen C. Myers, and Astrid B. Beck, 170. Grand Rapids, Mich.: Eerdmans, 2000.

"Archaeologists Excavate Massive Ancient Gateway in Jordan." *Popular Archeology*. Accessed May 7, 2014. http://popular-archaeology.com/issue/september-2012/article/archaeologists-excavate-massive-ancient-gateway-in-jordan.

Archer, Gleason L. *A Survey of Old Testament Introduction*. Rev Upd. Chicago, Ill.: Moody, 1996.

Archi, Alfonso. "Are 'The Cities of the Plain' Mentioned in the Ebla Tablets?: Cities Identified by Pettinato Are Nowhere near the Dead Sea." *BAR* 7, no. 6 (1981): 54–55.

———. "Ebla Texts." In *OEANE*, edited by Eric M. Meyers, 2:184–86. Oxford, U.K.: Oxford University Press, 1997.

———. "Further Concerning Ebla and the Bible." *BA* 44, no. 3 (1981): 145–54.

———. "The Archives of Ebla." In *Cuneiform Archives and Libraries*, edited by Klaas R. Veenhof, 72–86. Papers Read at the 30e Rencontre Assyriologique Internationale, Leiden, 4-8 July 1983. Leiden: Netherlands Institute for the Near East, 1986.

———. "The Epigraphic Evidence from Ebla and the Old Testament." *Biblica* 60, no. 4 (1979): 556–66.

———. "The Epigraphic Evidence from Ebla: A Summary." *BA* 43, no. 4 (1980): 200–203.

Armstrong, Patrick. *The English Parson-Naturalist: A Companionship Between Science and Religion*. Leominster: Gracewing, 2000.

Arnold, Bill T. *Encountering the Book of Genesis*. Grand Rapids, Mich.: Baker, 2003.

Astour, Michael C. "Political and Cosmic Symbolism in Genesis 14 and in Its Babylonian Sources." In *Biblical Motifs: Origins and Transformations*, edited by Alexander Altmann, 65–112. Philip W. Lown Institute of Advanced Judaic Studies, Brandeis University, Studies and Texts 3. Cambridge, Mass.: Harvard University Press, 1966.

———. "Siddim, Valley of (Place)." Edited by David Noel Freedman, Gary A. Herion, David F. Graf, and John David Pleins. *ABD*. New York, N.Y.: Doubleday, 1996.

———. "Zoar (Place)." Edited by David Noel Freedman, Gary A. Herion, David F. Graf, and John David Pleins. *ABD*. New York, N.Y.: Doubleday, 1996.

Avigad, Nachman. "Samaria (City)." In *NEAEHL*, edited by Ephraim Stern, Ayelet Levinson-Gilboa, and Joseph Aviram, 3:1300–1310. New York, N.Y.: MacMillan, 1993.

Avi-Yonah, Michael. *The Madaba Mosaic Map with Introduction and Commentary*. Jerusalem: Israel Exploration Society, 1954.

Avi-Yonah, Michael, and Ephraim Stern, eds. "Ai; Hai." In *EAEHL*. Upper Saddle River, N.J.: Prentice Hall, 1978.

———. , eds. "Beth-El." In *EAEHL*. Upper Saddle River, N.J.: Prentice Hall, 1978.

———. , eds. *Encyclopedia of Archaeological Excavations in the Holy Land*. 3rd ed. 4 vols. New York, N.Y.: Prentice Hall, 1996.

Bain, David Haward. *Bitter Waters: America's Forgotten Naval Mission to the Dead Sea*. New York: Overlook, 2011.

Baney, Ralph E. *Search for Sodom and Gomorrah*. 2nd ed. Kansas City, MO: CAM Press, 1962.

Bartov, Yuval, Mordechai Stein, Yoseph Enzel, Amotz Agnon, and Ze'ev Reches. "Lake Levels and Sequence Stratigraphy of Lake Lisan, the Late Pleistocene Precursor of the Dead Sea." *Quaternary Research* 57 (2002): 9–21.

Ben-Avraham, Zvi. "Rift Propagation along the Southern Dead Sea Rift (Gulf of Elat)." *Tectonophysics* 133 (1987): 193–200.

———. "Structural Framework of the Gulf of Elat (Aqaba), Northern Red Sea." *Journal of Geophysical Research* 90 (1985): 703–26.

Bender, Friedrich. *Geology of the Arabian Peninsula, Jordan*. U.S. Geolological Survey Professional Paper 560. Washington, D.C: United States Government Printing Office, 1975.

Berenbaum, Michael, and Fred Skolnik, eds. *EJ*. 2nd ed. 22 vols. New York, N.Y.: MacMillan, 2006.

Bienkowski, Piotr. *Jericho in the Late Bronze Age*. Ancient Near East. Warminster, Wiltshire: Aris & Phillips, 1986.

Bietak, Manfred. "The Setting of the Minoan Wall Paintings at Avaris." In *Aegean Wall Painting: A Tribute to Mark Cameron*, edited by Lyvia Morgan, 83–90. British School at Athens Studies 13. London, U.K.: British School at Athens, 2005.

Bietak, Manfred, and N. Marinatos. "The Minoan Paintings of Avaris." *Ägypten Und Levante* 5 (1995): 49–62.

Biggs, Robert D. "Ebla Texts." Edited by David Noel Freedman, Gary A. Herion, David F. Graf, and John David Pleins. *ABD*. New York, N.Y.: Doubleday, 1996.

———. "On Regional Cuneiform Handwritings in Third Millennium Mesopotamia." *Orientalia (NS)* 42 (1973): 39–46.

———. "The Ebla Tablets: An Interim Perspective." *BA* 43, no. 2 (1980): 76–86.

Billington, Clyde E. "Tall El-Hammam Is Not Sodom." *Artifax*, Spring 2012, 1–3.

Bimson, John J. "Archaeological Data and the Dating of the Patriarchs." In *Essays on the Patriarchal Narratives*, edited by Alan R. Millard and Donald J. Wiseman, 59–92. Downers Grove, Ill.: InterVarsity, 1980.

———. *Redating the Exodus and Conquest*. 2nd ed. JSOT Supplement Series 5. Sheffield, U.K.: Almond, 1981.

Birch, William F. "Sodom." *PEFSt*. 13 (1881): 101–2.

———. "Zeboim." *PEFSt*. 11, no. 1 (1879): 101–3.

———. "Zoar." *PEFSt*. 11, no. 1 (1879): 15–18, 99–101.

Blaiklock, Edward M., and R. K. Harrison, eds. *The New International Dictionary of Biblical Archaeology*. Grand Rapids, Mich.: Zondervan, 1983.

Blake, George Stanfield. *The Mineral Resources of Palestine and Transjordan*. Jerusalem: Azriel, 1930.

Blanckenhorn, Max. *Entstehung und Geschichte des Toten Meeres: Beitraeg zur Geologie Palaestinas*. Zeitschrift des deutschen Palästina-Vereins 19. Leipzig: Baedeker, 1896.

———. *Naturwissenschaftliche Studien Am Toten Meer Und Im Jordental*. Berlin: Friedländer & Sohn, 1912.

———. *Noch eimal Sodom und Gomorrha*. Zeitschrift des deutschen Palästina-Vereins 21. Leipzig: Baedeker, 1898.

Block, J. W. "Sodom and Gomorrah: A Volcanic Disaster." *Journal of Geological Education* 23 (1975): 74–77.

Bolen, Todd. "Arguments Against Locating Sodom at Tall El-Hammam." *Biblical Archaeology Society*, February 27, 2013. http://www.biblicalarchaeology.org/daily/biblical-sites-places/biblical-archaeology-sites/arguments-against-locating-sodom-at-tall-el-hammam/.

———. "Bab Edh-Dhra." *Pictorial Library of Bible Lands*, 2014. http://www.bibleplaces.com/babedhdhra.htm.

———. "Excavator Finds Evidence of Destruction at 'Sodom.'" *BiblePlaces*, December 19, 2011. http://blog.bibleplaces.com/2011/12/excavator-finds-evidence-of-destruction.html.

———. "Search for Sodom under Dead Sea." *BiblePlaces*, December 14, 2010. http://blog.bibleplaces.com/2010/12/search-for-sodom-under-dead-sea.html.

———. "Sodom Identified?" *BiblePlaces*, May 13, 2006. http://blog.bibleplaces.com/2006_05_01_archive.html.

———. "Video: Search for Sodom and Gomorrah." *BiblePlaces*, August 10, 2009. http://blog.bibleplaces.com/2009/08/video-search-for-sodom-and-gomorrah.html.

Bookman (Ken-Tor), Revital, Yoseph Enzel, Amotz Agnon, and Mordechai Stein. "Late Holocene Lake Levels of the Dead Sea." *Geological Society of America Bulletin* 116, no. 5–6 (2004): 555–71.

Bookman, Revital, Yuval Bartov, Yoseph Enzel, and Mordechai Stein. "Quaternary Lake Levels in the Dead Sea Basin: Two Centuries of Research." In *New Frontiers in Dead Sea Paleoenvironmental Research*, edited by Yehouda Enzel, Amotz Agnon, and Mordechai Stein, 155–70. Special Papers: Geological Society of America 401. Boulder, Colo.: Geological Society of America, 2006.

Bookman, Revital, Sagi Filin, Yoav Avni, Daniel Rosenfeld, and Shmuel Marco. "Possible Connection between Large Volcanic Eruptions and Level Rise Episodes in the Dead Sea Basin." *Quaternary Science Reviews* 89 (2014): 123–28.

Botterweck, G. Johannes, Helmer Ringgren, and Heinz-Josef Fabry, eds. *Theological Dictionary of the Old Testament*. Translated by Douglas W. Stott. 15 vols. Grand Rapids, Mich.: Eerdmans, 2003.

Bourke, Stephen J., Jaimie L. Lovell, Rachael Thyrza Sparks, Peta L. Seaton, and Lachlan D. Mairs. "A First Season of Renewed Excavation by the University of Sydney at Tulaylat Al-Ghassul." *ADAJ* 39 (1995): 31–63.

Bourke, Stephen J., Jaimie L. Lovell, Rachael Thyrza Sparks, Peta L. Seaton, Lachlan D. Mairs, and John Meadows. "A Second and Third Season of Renewed Excavation by the University of Sydney at Tulaylat Al-Ghassul (1995-1997)." *ADAJ* 2000, no. 44 (2000): 37–90.

Briggs, Charles A., Samuel R. Driver, and Francis Brown, eds. *A Hebrew and English Lexicon of the Old Testament with an Appendix Containing the Biblical Aramaic. Based on the Lexicon of William Gessenius as Translated by Edward Robinson*. Boston, Mass.: Houghton Milfflin, 1907.

———. *The Brown-Driver-Briggs Hebrew and English Lexicon: With an Appendix Containing Biblical Aramaic*. Oxford, U.K.: Clarendon, 1907.

———. "כָּבֵד." In *BDB*, 503, no 4673. Oxford, U.K.: Clarendon, 1997.

Bright, John. *A History of Israel*. 4th ed. Philadelphia, Pa.: Westminster/Knox, 2000.

Brodsky, Harold. "Bethel (Place)." Edited by David Noel Freedman, Gary A. Herion, David F. Graf, and John David Pleins. *ABD*. New York, N.Y.: Doubleday, 1996.

Bromiley, Geoffrey W., ed. *The International Standard Bible Encyclopedia*. Revised. 4 vols. Grand Rapids, Mich.: Eerdmans, 1995.

Brysbaert, Ann. *The Power of Technology in the Bronze Age Eastern Mediterranean: The Case of the Painted Plaster*. Monographs in Mediterranean Archaeology 12. London, U.K.: Equinox, 2008.

Burstein, Stanley Mayer. *The Babyloniaca of Berossus*. 2nd ed. Vol. 1. 5 vols. Sources from the Ancient Near East 1. Malibu: Undena Publications, 1978.

Bury, J. B. "The Provincial List of Verona." *JRS* 13 (1923): 127–51.

Bunch, Ted E., Malcolm A. LeCompte, A. Victor Adedeji, James H. Wittke, T. David Burleigh, Robert E. Hermes, Charles Mooney, et al. "A Tunguska Sized Airburst Destroyed Tall El-Hammam a Middle Bronze Age City in the Jordan Valley near the Dead Sea." *Scientific Reports* 11, no. 1 (September 20, 2021): 18632.

Butler, Trent C. *Joshua*. Vol. 7. 32 vols. WBC 7. Waco, Tex.: Word Books, 1983.

Callaway, Joseph A. "Ai." In *NEAEHL*, edited by Ephraim Stern, Ayelet Levinson-Gilboa, and Joseph Aviram, 1:39–45. New York, N.Y.: MacMillan, 1993.

———. "Ai (Place)." Edited by David Noel Freedman, Gary A. Herion, David F. Graf, and John David Pleins. *ABD*. New York, N.Y.: Doubleday, 1996.

Casson, Lionel. "The Administration of Byzantine and Early Arab Palestine." *Aegyptus* 32, no. 1 (1952): 54–60.

Chang-Ho, C. Ji, and Jong-Keun Lee. "The Survey in the Regions of ʿIrāq Al-Amīr and Wādī Al-Kafrayn." *ADAJ* 49 (2002): 179–96.

Chavalas, Mark W., and K. Lawson Younger, eds. *Mesopotamia and the Bible: Comparative Explorations*. Grand Rapids, Mich.: Baker Academic, 2002.

Chesson, Meredith S. "Libraries of the Dead: Early Bronze Age Charnel Houses and Social Identity at Urban Bab Edh-Dhraʿ, Jordan." *Journal of Anthropological Archaeology* 18 (1999): 137–64.

———. "Personal Correspondence: Dates for the Terminal Destruction of an-Numayra," April 16, 2014.

———. "Personal Correspondence: Feifa Occupation," April 17, 2014.

———. "Remembering and Forgetting in Early Bronze Age Mortuary Practices on the Southeastern Dead Sea Plain, Jordan." In *Performing Death: Social Analyses of Funerary Traditions in the Ancient Near East and Mediterranean*, edited by Nicola Laneri, 109–23. Oriental Institute Seminars 3. Chicago: The Oriental Institute of the University of Chicago, 2007.

Chesson, Meredith S., and Morag M. Kersel. "Tomato Season In The Ghor Es-Safi: A Lesson in Community Archaeology." *NEA* 76, no. 3 (2013): 159–65.

Chesson, Meredith S., and R. Thomas Schaub. "Death and Dying on the Dead Sea Plain: Fifa, Al- Khanazir and Bab Adh-Dhraʿ Cemeteries." In *Crossing Jordan: North American Contributions to the Archaeology of Jordan*, edited by Thomas Evan Levy, P. M. Michèle Daviau, Randall W. Younker, and May Shaer, 253–60. London, U.K.: Equinox, 2007.

———. "Life in the Earliest Walled Towns on the Dead Sea Plain: Numayra and Bab Edh-Dhraʿ." In *Crossing Jordan: North American Contributions to the Archaeology of Jordan*, edited by Thomas Evan Levy, P. M. Michèle Daviau, Randall W. Younker, and May Shaer, 245–52. London, U.K.: Equinox, 2007.

Chisholm, Hugh, ed. "E. H. Palmer." In *Encyclopædia Britannica Online*, 11th ed. Cambridge, U.K.: Cambridge University Press, 1911. http://www.britannica.com/EBchecked/topic/440173/E-H-Palmer.

Clamer, Christa. "The Hot Springs of Kallirrhoe and Baarou." In *The Madaba Map Centenary: Travelling Through the Byzantine Umayyad Period. Proceedings of the International Conference Held in Amman 7–9 April 1997*, edited by Michele Piccirillo and Eugenio Alliata, 221–25. Studium Biblicum Franciscannum Collectio Maior 40. Jerusalem: Studium Biblicum Franciscannum, 1999.

Clapp, Frederick G. "Geology and Bitumens of the Dead Sea Area, Palestine and TransJordan." *Bulletin of the American Association of Petroleum Geologists* 20, no. 7 (1936): 881–909.

———. "The Site of Sodom and Gomorrah: A Diversity of Views." *AJA* 40, no. 3 (1936): 323–44.

Clermont-Ganneau, Charles S. *Archaeological Researches in Palestine During the Years 1873 - 1874*. Translated by John MacFarlane. Vol. 2. 2 vols. London, U.K.: Palestine Exploration Fund, 1896.

———. "Gomorrah, Segor et Les Filles de Lot: Lettre à M. F. de Saulcy." *Revue Archéologique* 33 (1877): 193–98.

———. "Segor, Gomorrah, and Sodom." *PEFst.* 18, no. 2 (1886): 19–21.

Cline, Eric H. *From Eden to Exile: Unraveling Mysteries of the Bible*. Tampa, Fla.: National Geographic, 2007.

Cline, Eric H., and Assaf Yasur-Landau. "Aegeans in Israel: Minoan Frescoes at Tel Kabri." *BAR* 39, no. 4 (2013): 37–44, 64, 66.

Cline, Eric H., Assaf Yasur-Landau, and N. Goshen. "New Fragments of Aegean-Style Painted Plaster from Tel Kabri, Israel." *AJA* 15, no. 2 (2011): 245–61.

Cocks, Harry G. "The Discovery of Sodom, 1851." *Representations* 112 (Fall 2010): 1–27.

Cohen, S. "Ashteroth-Karnaim." Edited by G. A. Buttrick and Keith R. Crim. *IDB*. Nashville, Tenn.: Abingdon, 1962.

Cole, R. Alan. *Exodus*. Tyndale Old Testament Commentaries 2. Downers Grove, Ill.: IVP Academic, 2008.

Collins, Steven. "2005-2006 Season Summary." *Digging the Past: Voice of the Tall El-Hammam Excavation Project, Jordan*, 2006.

———. "A Chronology for the Cities of the Plain." *BRB* 2, no. 8 (2002): 1–9.

———. "A Response to Bryant G. Wood's Critique of Collins' Northern Sodom Theory." *BRB* 7, no. 7 (2007): 1–36.

———. "Explorations on the Eastern Jordan Disk." *BRB* 2, no. 18 (2002): 1–28.

———. "Forty Salient Points on the Geography of the Cities of the Kikkar." *BRB* 7, no. 1 (2007): 1–7.

———. "If You Thought You Knew the Location of Sodom and Gomorrah... Think Again." *BRB* 7, no. 4 (2007): 1–6.

———. *Let My People Go!: Using Historical Synchronisms to Identify the Pharaoh of the Exodus*. Albuquerque, N.M.: TSU Press, 2012.

———. "Reassessing the Term Hakikkar in Nehemiah as Bearing on the Location of the Cities of the Plain." *BRB* 7, no. 3 (2007): 1–4.

———. "Rethinking the Location of Zoar: An Exercise in Biblical Geography." *BRB* 4, no. 1 (2006): 1–5.

———. "Sodom and the Cities of the Plain." *Bible Dictionary*. Albuquerque, N.M.: TSU Press, 2013.

———. "Sodom: The Discovery of a Lost City." *BS* 20, no. 3 (2007): 70–77.

———. "Tall El-Hammam: A Key Witness to the Archaeology and History of the Southern Jordan Valley—Summary, Conclusions, and Recommendations from the 2006/2007 Excavation Season." In *Annual Meeting of the American Schools of Oriental Research: San Diego, CA*, 1–20. Albuquerque, N.M.: TSU Press, 2007.

———. "Tall El-Hammam and Biblical Sodom: A Match." *Digging the Past: Voice of the Tall El-Hammam Excavation Project, Jordan*, 2006.

———. "Tall El-Hammam Is Sodom: Billington's Heshbon Identification Suffers from Numerous Fatal Flaws." *Artifax* 27, no. 3 (Summer 2012): 16–18.

———. "Tall El-Hammam Is Still Sodom: Critical Data-Sets Cast Serious Doubt on E. H. Merrill's Chronological Analysis." *BRB* 13, no. 1 (2013): 1–31.

———. "Ten Reasons Why Sodom and Gomorrah Are Not Located in the Southeast Dead Sea Region." *BRB* 6, no. 1 (2006): 1–4.

———. "The Architecture of Sodom." *BRB* 2, no. 14 (2002): 1–9.

———. "The Geography of Sodom and Zoar: Reality Demolishes W. Schlegel's Attacks Against a Northern Sodom." *BRB* 13, no. 2 (2013): 1–14.

———. "The Geography of the Cities of the Plain." *BRB* 2, no. 1 (2002): 1–17.

———. *The Search for Sodom and Gomorrah*. Research & Discovery Series 2. Albuquerque, N.M.: TSU Press, 2008.

———. "Trowling Down: Tall El-Hammam News Letter," December 31, 2011.

———. "Using Historical Synchronisms to Identify the Pharaoh of the Exodus." *BRB* 5, no. 7 (2005): 1–70.

———. Where is Biblical Sodom? An interview with Dr. Steven Collins, Director of the Tall el-Hammam Excavation project, Jordan. Interview by Scott Stripling, 2006.

———. "Where Is Sodom? The Case for Tall El-Hammam." *BAR* 39, no. 2 (2013): 32–41, 70–71.

Collins, Steven, Gary A. Byers, and Michael C. Luddeni. "Tall El-Hammam Excavation Project, Season Activity Report, Season One: 2005/2006 Probe Excavation and Survey: Submitted to the Department of Antiquities of the Hashemite Kingdom of Jordan, Jan 22, 2006." *BRB* 6, no. 4 (2006): 1–13.

Collins, Steven, Gary A. Byers, Carroll M. Kobs, David E. Graves, Phillip J. Silvia, Khalid Tarawneh, and Khalid al Hawawrah. "Tall El-Hammam Season Ten, 2015: Excavation, Survey, Interpretations And Insights." *BRB* 15, no. 1 (2015): 1–37.

Collins, Steven, Gary A. Byers, Michael C. Luddeni, and John W. Moore. "Tall El-Hammam Excavation Project, Season Activity Report, Season Two: 2006/2007 Excavation and Survey: Submitted to the Department of Antiquities of the Hashemite Kingdom of Jordan, January 26, 2006." *BRB* 7, no. 9 (2007): 1–13.

Collins, Steven, Khalil Hamdan, and Gary A. Byers. "Tall El-Hammam: Preliminary Report on Four Seasons of Excavation (2006–2009)." *ADAJ* 53 (2009): 385–414.

———. "The Tall El-Hammam Excavation Project Season Activity Report: Season Four: 2009 Excavation, Exploration, & Survey." *BRB* 9, no. 1 (2009): 1–30.

Collins, Steven, Carroll M. Kobs, and Michael C. Luddeni. *An Introduction to Tall Al-Hammam with Seven Seasons (2005-2011) of Ceramics and Eight Seasons (2005-2012) of Artifacts*. Vol. 1. Winona Lake, Ind.: Eisenbrauns, 2015.

Collins, Steven, Carroll Kobs, and Phillip J. Silvia. *Tall El-Hammam Excavation Project Field Manual*. Albuquerque, N.M.: TSU Press, 2013.

Collins, Steven, and Latayne C. Scott. *Discovering the City of Sodom: The Fascinating, True Account of the Discovery of the Old Testament's Most Infamous City*. New York, N.Y.: Simon & Schuster, 2013.

Collins, Steven, Khalid Tarawneh, Gary A. Byers, and Carroll M. Kobs. "Tall El-Hammam Season Eight, 2013: Excavation, Survey, Interpretations and Insights." *BRB* 13, no. 2 (2013): 1–20.

Conder, Claude Reignier. *Heth and Moab*. London, U.K.: Bentley & Son, 1883.

———. "Lot's Wife." *PEQ* 17–18 (1885): 20.

———. *Tent Work in Palestine: A Record of Discovery and Adventure*. 2 vols. London, U.K.: Bentley & Son, 1879.

Conder, Claude Reignier, and Horatio H. Kitchener. *The Survey of Eastern Palestine: The Adwan Country*. Vol. 1. 7 vols. London, U.K.: Palestine Exploration Fund, 1881.

Coogan, Michael David. "Numeira 1981." *BASOR* 255 (Summer 1984): 75–81.

Coote, Robert B., and Keith W. Whitelam. *The Emergence of Early Israel in Historical Perspective*. Social World of Biblical Antiquity Series. Sheffield: Sheffield Phoenix, 2010.

Corpus Inscriptionum Semiticarum: Ab Academia Inscriptionum et Litterarum Humaniorum Conditum Atque Digestum. Vol. 2. 5 vols. Paris: Reipublicae Typographeo, 1881.

Craigie, Peter C. *The Book of Deuteronomy*. Edited by R. K. Harrison. NICOT 5. Grand Rapids, Mich.: Eerdmans, 1976.

Culver, Robert D. "Zoar." In *ZPEB*, edited by Merrill C. Tenney and Moisés Silva, Revised, Full-Color Edition., 5:1240. Grand Rapids, Mich.: Zondervan, 2009.

Currid, John D. *A Study Commentary on Exodus*. 2 vols. An Evangelical Press Study Commentary. Auburn, Mass.: Evangelical, 2000.

Dahood, Mitchell J. "Appendix." In *The Archives of Ebla: An Empire Inscribed in Clay*, edited by Giovanni Pettinato. Translation of Ebla: Un Impero Inciso Nell'Argilla. Garden City, N.Y.: Doubleday, 1981.

———. "Ebla, Ugarit and the Old Testament." In *Vetus Testamentum Supplements*, 29:81–112. Leiden: Brill, 1978.

———. "Ebla, Ugarit and the Old Testament." *BS* 8, no. 1–16 (1979).

———. "Ebla, Ugarit E l'Antico Testamento." *La Civiltà Cattolica* 129, no. 2 (1978): 328–40.

Dan, Yaron. "Palaestina Salutaris (Tertia) and Its Capital." *IEJ* 32, no. 2/3 (1982): 134–37.

Davies, John K. "The Reliability of the Oral Tradition." In *The Trojan War: Its Historicity and Context*, edited by Lin Foxhall and John Kenyon Davies, 87–110. Papers of the First Greenbank Colloquium, Liverpool, 1981. Bristol: Bristol Classical, 1984.

Davies, Philip R. *In Search of "Ancient Israel": A Study in Biblical Origins*. The Library of Hebrew Bible/OT Studies. London, U.K.: Continuum International, 2006.

———. *Memories of Ancient Israel: An Introduction to Biblical History--Ancient and Modern*. Louisville, Ky.: Westminster/Knox, 2008.

Davis, Thomas W. "Theory and Method in Biblical Archaeology." In *The Future of Biblical Archaeology: Reassessing Methodologies and Assumptions*, edited by James K. Hoffmeier and Alan R. Millard, 20–28. Grand Rapids, Mich.: Eerdmans, 2008.

de Velde, Chevalier Van. "M. De Saulcy's Discoveries." *The Literary Gazette: A Weekly Journal of Literature, Science, and the Fine Art* 1944 (April 22, 1854): 377–78.

Dever, William G. "The Current School of Revisionist and Their Nonhistories of Ancient Israel." In *What Did the Biblical Writers Know, and When Did They Know It?*, 23–52. Grand Rapids, Mich.: Eerdmans, 2001.

———. "The Western Cultural Tradition Is At Risk." *BAR* 32, no. 2 (2006): 26, 76.

———. *What Did the Biblical Writers Know, and When Did They Know It?* Grand Rapids, Mich.: Eerdmans, 2001.

Dever, William G., Ofer Bar-Yosef, Ephraim Stern, and James F. Strange. "Palestine, Archaeology of." Edited by David Noel Freedman, Gary A. Herion, David F. Graf, and John David Pleins. *ABD*. New York, N.Y.: Doubleday, 1996.

de Vries, Bert, ed. "Archaeology in Jordan, 1991." *AJA* 95, no. 2 (1991): 253–80.

———. , ed. "Archaeology in Jordan, 1992." *AJA* 96, no. 3 (1992): 503–42.

———. "Archaeology in Jordan, 1993." Edited by Pierre Bikai. *AJA* 97, no. 3 (1993): 457–520.

Dombrowski, Bruno W. W. "'Eblaite': The Earliest Known Dialect of Akkadian." *Zeitschrift Der Deutschen Morgenländischen Gesellschaft* 138 (1988): 211–35.

Donahue, Jack. "Geologic Reconstruction of Numeira." *BASOR* 255 (Summer 1984): 83–88.

Donner, Herbert. *The Mosaic Map of Madaba. An Introductory Guide*. Palaestina Antiqua 7. Kampen: Kok Pharos, 1992.

Dornemann, Rudolph H. "Preliminary Comments on the Pottery Traditions at Tell Nimrin, Illustrated from the 1989 Season of Excavations." *ADAJ* 34 (1990): 153–81.

Driessen, Jan. "The Proliferation of Minoan Palatial Architectural Style: (I) Crete." *Acta Archaeologica Louvanensia* 28–29 (1989 1990): 3–23.

Drinkard Jr., Joel F. "'AL PÉNÊ as 'East of.'" *Journal of Biblical Literature* 98 (1978): 285–86.

Driver, Samuel R. "Siddim, Vale of." In *DBib5*, edited by James Hastings and John A. Selbie, 4:512. New York, N.Y.: Scribner's Sons, 1911.

———. "Zoar." In *DBib5*, edited by James Hastings and John A. Selbie, 4:986. New York, N.Y.: Scribner's Sons, 1909.

Dumper, Michael R. T., and Bruce E. Stanley. *Cities of the Middle East and North Africa: A Historical Encyclopedia*. Santa Barbara, Calf.: ABC-CLIO, 2007.

Dyer, Charles H. "The Date of the Exodus Reexamined." *BSac* 140, no. 559 (1983): 225–43.

Easton, Mathew George. *Illustrated Bible Dictionary*. 3rd ed. Nashville, Tenn.: Nelson, 1897.

Egeria. *The Pilgrimage of Etheria*. Translated by M. L. McClure and C. L. Feltoe. London, U.K.: Society for Promoting Christian Knowledge, 1919.

Encyclopedia Miqra'it (Encyclopaedia Biblica). 8 vols. Jerusalem, 1976.

Eusebius, Pamphilus. *The Onomasticon of Eusebius Pamphili: Compared with the Version of Jerome and Annotated*. Edited by Noel C. Wolf. Translated by C. Umhau Wolf. Washington, D.C.: Catholic University of America Press, 1971.

Ewald, Georg Heinrich. *Geschichte Des Volkes Israel*. 2nd ed. Vol. 1. 8 vols. Göttingen: Dieterich, 1864.

———. *History of Israel: Introduction and Preliminary History*. Edited and translated by Russell Martineau. 2nd ed. Vol. 1. 8 vols. London, U.K.: Longmans, Green, & Company, 1869.

Fagan, Brian. *Archaeologists: Explorers of the Human Past*. Oxford, U.K.: Oxford University Press, 2003.

Falconer, Steven. "The Middle Bronze Age." In *Jordan: An Archaeological Reader*, edited by Russell B. Adams, 263–80. London, U.K.: Equinox, 2008.

Faulstich, E. W. *History, Harmony and the Hebrew Kings*. Spencer, Iowa: Chronology Books, 1986.

Feinman, Peter Douglas. "Canaanites, Catholics, and Chosen Peoples: William Foxwell Albright's Biblical Archaeology." *NEA* 75, no. 3 (2012): 148–60.

———. "Methodism and the Origins of Biblical Archaeology: The William Foxwell Albright Story." *AUSS* 47, no. 1 (2009): 61–72.

———. *William Foxwell Albright and the Origins of Biblical Archaeology*. Berrien Springs, Mich.: Andrews University Press, 2004.

Fensham, F. Charles. "Salt as a Curse in the Old Testament and the Ancient Near East." *BA* 25, no. 1 (February 1962): 48–50.

Fields, Weston W. *Sodom and Gomorrah: History and Motif in Biblical Narrative*. New York, N.Y.: Continuum International, 1997.

Finkelstein, Israel, and Amihai Mazar. *The Quest for the Historical Israel*. Edited by Brian B. Schmidt. Archaeology and Biblical Studies 17. Atlanta, Ga.: SBL, 2007.

Finkelstein, Israel, and Nadav Na'aman, eds. *From Nomadism to Monarchy: Archaeological and Historical Aspects of Early Israel*. Jerusalem: Israel Exploration Society, 1994.

Finkelstein, Israel, and Neil Asher Silberman. *The Bible Unearthed: Archaeology's New Vision of Ancient Israel*. New York, N.Y.: Touchstone, 2002.

Fischer, Peter M., ed. *Chronology of the Jordan Valley during the Middle and Late Bronze Ages: Pella, Tell Abu Al-Kharaz, and Tell Deir Alla*. Contributions to the Chronology of the Eastern Mediterranean 12. Vienna: Österreichische Akademie der Wissenschaften, 2006.

———. , ed. *Tell Abu Al-Kharaz in the Jordan Valley, Volume 2: The Middle and Late Bronze Ages*. Denkschriften Der Gesamtakademie, Band 39. Contributions to the Chronology of the Eastern Mediterranean 11. Vienna: Österreichische Akademie der Wissenschaften, 2006.

———. "The Southern Levant (Transjordan) during the Late Bronze Age." In *The Oxford Handbook of the Archaeology of the Levant: C. 8000-332 BCE*, edited by Margreet L. Steiner and Ann E. Killebrew, 561–76. Oxford Handbooks in Archaeology. Oxford, U.K.: Oxford University Press, 2013.

Fisher, Kevin, and William F. Wyatt. "Sodom and Gomorrah: The Cities of the Plain: Ash and Brimstone Remain." *Ark Discovery: Revealing God's Treasure*, 2013. http://www.arkdiscovery.com/sodom_&_gomorrah.htm.

Flanagan, James W., David W. McCreery, and Khair N. Yassine. "First Preliminary Report of the 1989 Tell Nimrin Project." *ADAJ* 34 (1990): 131–52.

———. "Preliminary Report of the 1990 Excavation at Tell Nimrin." *ADAJ* 36 (1992): 89–111.

———. "Tall Nimrin: Preliminary Report on the 1995 Excavation and Geological Survey." *ADAJ* 40 (1996): 271–92.

———. "Tall Nimrin: The Byzantine Gold Hoard from the 1993 Season." *ADAJ* 38 (1994): 245–65.

———. "Tell Nimrin: Preliminary Report on the 1993 Season." *ADAJ* 38 (1994): 205–44.

Fouts, David Mark. "A Defense of the Hyperbolic Interpretation of Large Numbers in the Old Testament." *JETS* 40 (1997): 377–87.

———. "The Demographics of Ancient Israel." *BRB* 7, no. 2 (2007): 1–10.

Franken, Hendricus J. "Deir 'Alla, Tell." In *OEANE*, edited by Eric M. Meyers, 2:137–38. Oxford, U.K.: Oxford University Press, 1997.

Freedman, David Noel. "The Real Story of the Ebla Tablets: Ebla and the Cities of the Plain." *BA* 41 (1978): 143–64.

———. "William Foxwell Albright: In Memoriam." *BASOR* 205, no. 1 (February 1972): 1+3–13.

Freedman, David Noel, Gary A. Herion, David F. Graf, and John David Pleins, eds. *The Anchor Yale Bible Dictionary*. 6 vols. New York, N.Y.: Doubleday, 1996.

Freedman, David Noel, and J. Lundbom. "דוֹד." In *TDOT*, edited by G. Johannes Botterweck, Helmer Ringgren, and Heinz-Josef Fabry, translated by Douglas W. Stott, Geoffrey W. Bromiley, David A. Green, and John T. Willis, 3:173–81. Grand Rapids, Mich.: Eerdmans, 2003.

Freedman, David Noel, Allen C. Myers, and Astrid B. Beck, eds. *Eerdmans Dictionary of the Bible*. Grand Rapids, Mich.: Eerdmans, 2000.

Free, Joseph P., and Howard F. Vos. *Archaeology and Bible History*. Grand Rapids, Mich.: Zondervan, 1992.

Freund, R., Z. Garfunkel, I. Zak, M. Goldberg, and T. Weissbrad. "The Shear along the Dead Sea Rift." *Philosophical Transactions of the Royal Society of London: Series A, Mathematical and Physical Sciences* 267 (1970): 107–30.

Frumkin, Amos. "The Holocene History of Dead Sea Levels." In *The Dead Sea: The Lake and Its Setting*, edited by Tina M. Niemi, Zvi Ben-Avraham, and Joel R. Gat, 237–48. Oxford Monographs on Geology and Geophysics 36. New York, N.Y.: Oxford University Press, USA, 1997.

Frumkin, Amos, and Yoel Elitzur. "Historic Dead Sea Level Fluctuations Calibrated with Geological and Archaeological Evidence." *Quaternary Research* 57 (2002): 334–42.

———. "The Rise and Fall of the Dead Sea." *BAR* 27, no. 6 (2001): 42–50.

Fuller, Thomas. *A Pisgah-Sight of Palestine and the Confines Thereof: With the History of the Old and New Testament Acted Thereon*. London, U.K.: John Williams, 1650.

Gardosh, Michael, Eliezer Kashai, Shalom Salhov, Haim Shulman, and Eli Tannenbaum. "Hydrocarbon Exploration in the Southern Dead Sea Area." In *The Dead Sea: The Lake and Its Setting*, edited by Zvi Ben-Avraham, Tina M. Niemi, and Joel R. Gat, 57–72. Oxford Monographs on Geology and Geophysics 36. New York, N.Y.: Oxford University Press, USA, 1997.

Garfunkel, Zvi. "Internal Structure of the Dead Sea Leaky Transform (Rift) in Relation to Plate Kinematics." *Tectonophysics* 80, no. 1–4 (1981): 81–108.

———. "The History and Formation of the Dead Sea Basin." In *The Dead Sea: The Lake and Its Setting*, edited by Tina M. Niemi, Zvi Ben-Avraham, and Joel R. Gat, 36–56. Oxford Monographs on Geology and Geophysics 36. New York, N.Y.: Oxford University Press, USA, 1997.

Gaster, Theodor Herzl, and James G. Frazer. *Myth, Legend, and Custom in the Old Testament: A Comparative Study with Chapters from Sir James G. Frazer's Folklore in the Old Testament*. New York, N.Y.: Harper & Row, 1975.

Geikie, J. Cunningham. *Hours with the Bible or The Scriputues in the Light of Modern Discovery and Knowledge: From Creation to the Patriarchs with Illustrations*. Vol. 1. 5 vols. New York, N.Y.: Pott, 1882.

———. *The Holy Land and the Bible: A Book of Scripture Illustrations Gathered in Palestine*. 2 vols. London, U.K.: Cassell & Company, 1887.

Geisler, Norman L. *Explaining Hermeneutics: A Commentary on the Chicago Statement on Biblical Hermeneutics*. ICBI Foundation Series. Oakland, Calf.: International Council on Biblical Inerrancy, 1983.

Geisler, Norman L., and Joseph M. Holden. *The Popular Handbook of Archaeology and the Bible*. Eugene, Oreg.: Harvest House, 2013.

Gelb, Ignace J. *Thoughts About Ibla: A Preliminary Evoluation*. Syro-Mesopotamian Studies 1. Malibu, Calf.: Undena, 1980.

Geraty, Lawrence T. "Dates for the Exodus I Have Known." In *Out of Egypt: Israel's Exodus Between Text and Memory, History and Imagination Conference*. University of California, San Diego, 2013. https://www.youtube.com/watch?v=6MM2ao1euTU.

Gertman, Isaac. "Changes in the Surface Level of the Dead Sea and in the Total Stability of the Dead Sea Water Column." *Israel Oceanographic & Limnological Research*, 2014. http://isramar.ocean.org.il/isramar2009/DeadSea/LongTerm.aspx.

Gertman, Isaac, and A. Hecht. "The Dead Sea Hydrography from 1992 to 2000." *Journal of Marine Systems* 35 (2002): 169–81.

Ginsberg, H. L. "A Prepostion of Interest to Historical Geographers." *BASOR* 122 (1951): 12–14.

Glueck, Nelson. *Explorations in Eastern Palestine II*. AASOR 15. New Haven, Conn.: ASOR, 1935.

———. *Explorations in Eastern Palestine IV. Part 1*. 4 vols. AASOR 25-28. New Haven, Conn.: ASOR, 1945.

———. *Rivers in the Desert: A History of the Negev*. New York, N.Y.: Farrar, Straus and Cudahy, 1959.

———. "Some Ancient Towns in the Plains of Moab." *BASOR* 91 (1943): 7–26.

———. *The Other Side of the Jordan*. New Haven, Conn.: ASOR, 1970.

Gnanaraj, D. "Fire from Heaven? Archeological Light on the Destruction of Sodom and Gomorrah (Genesis 19:23-28)." *New Life Review* 1 (2012): 1–12.

Goldingay, John E. "The Patriarchs in Scripture and History." In *Essays on the Patriarchal Narratives*, edited by Donald J. Wiseman and Alan R. Millard, 11–42. Winona Lake, Ind.: Eisenbrauns, 1983.

———. "The 'Salvation History' Perspective and the 'Wisdom' Perspective within the Context of Biblical Theology." *The Evangelical Quarterly* 51, no. 4 (1979): 194–207.

Goldman, Shalom. "The Holy Land Appropriated: The Careers of Selah Merrill, Nineteenth Century Christian Hebraist, Palestine Explorer, and U.S. Consul in Jerusalem." *American Jewish History* 85, no. 2 (June 1997): 151–72.

Gordon, Cyrus H. "Biblical Customs and the Nuzu Tablets." *BAR* 2 (1964): 21–33.

———. "Hebrew Origins in the Light of Recent Discovery." In *Biblical and Other Studies*, edited by Alexander Altmann, 3–14. Cambridge, Mass.: Harvard University Press, 1963.

———. *Introduction to Old Testament Times*. Ventnor, N.J.: Ventnor, 1953.

———. "The New Amarna Tablets." *Orientalia* 16 (1947): 1–21.

———. "The Patriarchal Narratives." *JNES* 13 (1954): 56–59.

———. *Ugaritic Textbook: Grammar, Texts in Transliteration, Cuneiform Selections, Glossary, Indices*. Analecta Orientalia 38. Rome: Pontifical Biblical Institute, 1998.

Gordon, Cyrus Herzl, Gary Rendsburg, and Nathan H. Winter, eds. *Eblaitica: Essays on the Ebla Archives and Eblaite Language*. Winona Lake, Ind.: Eisenbrauns, 1987.

Govier, Gordon. "Looking Back: Claims to New Sodom Location Are Salted with Controversy." *Christianity Today* 52, no. 4 (2008): 15–16.

———. "Searching for Sodom: Is It Time to Rewrite Old Testament Chronologies?" *ChristianityToday.com*, February 18, 2014. http://www.christianitytoday.com/ct/2014/february-web-only/searching-for-sodom.html.

Graf, David F. "Zoora Rises from the Grave: New Funerary Stelae from Palaestina Tertia." *JRA* 22 (2009): 752–58.

Graham, Peter. *A Topographical Dictionary of Palestine, or the Holy Land*. London, U.K.: J. Davey, 1836.

Graves, David E. *Key Facts for the Location of Sodom Student Edition: Navigating the Maze of Arguments*. Moncton, N.B.: Graves, 2014.

———. *Key Themes of the Old Testament: A Survey of Major Theological Themes*. Moncton, N.B.: Graves, 2013.

———. "My Journey to Locate the Genesis Pentapolis North of the Dead Sea." In *Kikkar Dialogues*, edited by Steven Collins, 2nd ed., 100–128. Research & Discovery Series 1. Albuquerque, N.M.: Trinity Southwest University Press, Forthcoming.

———. "Sodom And Salt in Their Ancient Near Eastern Cultural Context." *Near East Archaeological Society Bulletin* 61 (2016): 15–32.

Graves, David E., and D. Scott Stripling. "Identification of Tall El-Hammam on the Madaba Map." *BS* 20, no. 2 (2007): 35–45.

———. "Is Tall El-Hammam on the Madaba Map?" In *Near East Archaeological Society*, 1–20. San Diego: Near East Archaeological Society, 2007.

———. "Locating Tall El-Hammam on the Madaba Map." *BRB* 7, no. 6 (2007): 1–11.

Bibliography

———. "Re-Examination of the Location for the Ancient City of Livias." *Levant* 43, no. 2 (2011): 178–200.

Grimal, Nicolas. *A History of Ancient Egypt*. Oxford, U.K.: Wiley-Blackwell, 1994.

Grove, George. "Sodom." Edited by William Smith. *A Dictionary of the Bible*. Philadelphia, Pa.: Winston, 1884.

———. "The Salt Sea." Edited by William Smith. *A Dictionary of the Bible*. Philadelphia, Pa.: Winston, 1884.

———. "Zoar." Edited by William Smith. *A Dictionary of the Bible*. Philadelphia, Pa.: Winston, 1884.

Gunkel, Hermann. *Das Marchen Im Alten Testament*. Fourth. Religionsgeschichtliche Volksbücher. Tübingen: Mohr, 1917.

Haigh, Stuart K., and S. P. Gopal Madabhushi. "Dynamic Centrifuge Modelling of the Destruction of Sodom and Gomorrah." *Proceeding of the International Conference on Physical Modelling in Geotechnics*, 2002, 507–11.

Har-El, Menashe. "The Pride of the Jordan–The Jungle of the Jordan." *BA* 41 (1978): 64–75.

Harland, James Penrose. *Prehistoric Aigina. A History of the Island in the Bronze Age*. Paris: Librairie Ancienne Honore Champion, 1925.

———. "Sodom and Gomorrah Part II: The Destruction of the Cities of the Plain." *BA* 6, no. 3 (1943): 41–52.

———. "Sodom and Gomorrah Part I: The Location of the Cities of the Plain." *BA* 5, no. 2 (1942): 17–32.

Harlan, Jack R. "Natural Resources of the Southern Ghor." In *The Southeastern Dead Sea Plain Expedition: An Interim Report of the 1977 Season*, edited by R. Thomas Schaub and Walter E. Rast, 155–64. AASOR 46. Boston, Mass.: American Schools of Oriental Research, 1979.

Harris, Graham M., and Anthony P. Beardow. "The Destruction of Sodom and Gomorrah: A Geotechnical Perspective." *Quarterly Journal of Engineering Geology* 28 (1995): 349–62.

Harrison, R. K. *Introduction to the Old Testament*. Grand Rapids, Mich.: Eerdmans, 1969.

Harrison, R. K. "Shittim." Edited by Edward M. Blaiklock. *NIDBA*. Grand Rapids, Mich.: Zondervan, 1983.

Harris, R. Laird, Gleason L. Archer, Jr., and Bruce K. Waltke, eds. *Theological Wordbook of the Old Testament*. 2 vols. Chicago, Ill.: Moody, 1980.

———. , eds. "כִּכָּר." In *TWOT*, no. 1046c. Chicago, Ill.: Moody, 1980.

Hastings, James, and John A. Selbie, eds. *A Dictionary of the Bible*. Single Volume. New York, N.Y.: Scribner's Sons, 1909.

———. , eds. *A Dictionary of the Bible: Dealing with Its Language, Literature and Contents Including the Biblical Theology*. 5 vols. New York, N.Y.: Scribner's Sons, 1911.

Hattem, Willem C. van. "Once Again: Sodom and Gomorrah." *BA* 44, no. 2 (Spring 1981): 87–92.

Hawkins, Ralph K. "Propositions for Evangelical Acceptance of a Late-Date Exodus-Conquest: Biblical Data and the Royal Scarabs from Mt. Ebal." *JETS* 50, no. 1 (2007): 31–46.

Hendel, David. "Review of D. Neev and K.O. Emery, Destruction of Sodom, Gomorrah and Jericho: Geological, Climatological and Archaeological Backgrounds." *BAR* 23, no. 1 (1997): 70.

Hennessy, J. B. "Preliminary Report on a First Season of Excavations at Teleilat Ghassul." *Levant* 1, no. 1 (1969): 1–24.

Herbermann, Charles George, Condé Bénoist Pallen, and Edward Aloysius Pace, eds. *The Catholic Encyclopedia; An International Work of Reference on the Constitution, Doctrine, Discipline, and History of the Catholic Church*. 16 vols. New York, N.Y.: Appleton & Company, 1913.

Herzog, Ze'ev. "Deconstructing the Walls of Jericho." *Ha'aretz Magazine*, 1999, 1–9.

Hess, Richard S. *Joshua: An Introduction and Commentary*. Tyndale Old Testament Commentaries. Downers Grove, Ill.: InterVarsity, 1996.

Hill, Carol A. "Making Sense of the Numbers of Genesis." *Perspectives on Science and Christian Faith* 55, no. 4 (2003): 239–51.

Hindson, Ed, and Elmer L. Towns. *Illustrated Bible Survey: An Introduction*. Nashville, Tenn.: B&H, 2013.

Hitchcock, Louise A. "Minoan Architecture." In *The Oxford Handbook of the Bronze Age Aegean*, edited by Eric H. Cline, 189–99. Oxford, U.K.: Oxford University Press, 2012.

———. "Minoan Crete: Understanding the Minoan Palaces." *Athena Review* 3, no. 3 (2003): 27–35.

Hoerth, Alfred J. *Archaeology and the Old Testament*. Grand Rapids, Mich.: Baker, 1999.

Hoerth, Alfred, and John McRay. *Bible Archaeology: An Exploration of the History and Culture of Early Civilizations*. Grand Rapids, Mich.: Baker, 2006.

Hoffmeier, James K., ed. *The Archaeology of the Bible: Reassessing Methodologies and Assumptions*. Oxford, U.K.: Lion Hudson, 2008.

———. "The North Sinai Archaeological Project's Excavations at Tell El-Borg (Sinai): An Example of the 'New' Biblical Archaeology?" In *The Future of Biblical Archaeology: Reassessing Methodologies and Assumptions*, edited by James K. Hoffmeier and Alan R. Millard, 53–68. Grand Rapids, Mich.: Eerdmans, 2004.

———. "What Is the Biblical Date for the Exodus? A Response to Bryant Wood." *JETS* 50, no. 2 (2007): 225–47.

Hoffmeier, James Karl, and Alan R. Millard, eds. *The Future of Biblical Archaeology: Reassessing Methodologies and Assumptions*. The Proceedings of a Symposium, August 12-14, 2001 at Trinity International University. Grand Rapids, Mich.: Eerdmans, 2004.

Holladay, William L. *A Concise Hebrew and Aramaic Lexicon of the Old Testament*. Based upon the Lexical Work of Ludwig Koehler and Walter Baumgartner. Leiden: Brill, 2000.

Holland, Thomas A. "Jericho (Place)." Edited by David Noel Freedman, Gary A. Herion, David F. Graf, and John David Pleins. *ABD*. New York, N.Y.: Doubleday, 1996.

Horn, Cornelia B., and Robert R. Phenix Jr. *John Rufus: The Lives of Peter the Iberian, Theodosius of Jerusalem, and the Monk Romanus*. Atlanta, Ga.: SBL, 2008.

Howard, Jr., David M. "Sodom." Edited by Geoffrey W. Bromiley. *ISBE2*. Grand Rapids, Mich.: Eerdmans, 1995.

———. "Sodom and Gomorrah Revisited." *Journal of the Evangelical Theological Society* 27, no. 4 (1984): 385–400.

Irwin, Dorothy. *Mytharion: The Comparison of Tales from the Old Testament and the Ancient Near East*. Alter Orient Und Altes Testament 32. Neukirchen-Vluyn: Neukirchener Verlag, 1978.

Jacobs, Paul F. "Jericho." In *EDB*, edited by David Noel Freedman, Allen C. Myers, and Astrid B. Beck, 689–91. Grand Rapids, Mich.: Eerdmans, 2000.

Jagoda, Barry. "Leading Scholar of the Bible, David Noel Freedman, Dies at 85." *UCSanDiego News Center*, April 11, 2008. http://ucsdnews.ucsd.edu/archive/newsrel/general/04-08FreedmanObit.asp.

Jampoler, Andrew C. A. *Sailors in the Holy Land: The 1848 American Expedition to the Dead Sea and the Search for Sodom and Gomorrah*. Annapolis, Md.: Naval Institute, 2005.

J., D. A. "Obituary: Major-General Sir Charles William Wilson, K. C. B., K. C. M. G., F. R. S., Etc." *The Geographical Journal* 26, no. 6 (December 1905): 682–84.

Jones, Floyd Nolen. *Chronology of the Old Testament: A Return to the Basics*. Green Forest, Ark.: Master Books, 2004.

Josephus, Flavius. *Jewish Antiquities: Volume I, Book 1-3*. Translated by H. St. J. Thackeray. Vol. 5. 13 vols. LCL 242. Cambridge, Mass.: Harvard University Press, 1930.

———. *Jewish Antiquities: Volume VI, Books 14-15*. Translated by Ralph Marcus and Allen Wikgren. Vol. 10. 13 vols. LCL 489. Cambridge, Mass.: Harvard University Press, 1943.

———. *The Jewish War: Volume I, Books 1-2*. Translated by H. St. J. Thackeray. Vol. 2. 13 vols. LCL 203. Cambridge, Mass.: Harvard University Press, 1927.

———. *The Jewish War: Volume II, Books 3-4*. Translated by H. St. J. Thackeray. Vol. 3. 13 vols. LCL 487. Cambridge, Mass.: Harvard University Press, 1927.

———. *The Jewish War: Volume III, Books 5-7*. Translated by H. St. J. Thackeray. Vol. 4. 13 vols. LCL 210. Cambridge, Mass.: Harvard University Press, 1928.

———. *The Works of Josephus: Complete and Unabridged*. Translated by William Whiston. New Updated. Peabody, Mass.: Hendrickson, 1980.

Kafafi, Zeidan A., and Hugo Gajus Scheltema. "Megalithic Structures in Jordan." *Mediterranean Archaeology and Archaeometry* 5, no. 2 (2005): 5–22.

Kaiser, Jr., Walter C., and Duane Garrett, eds. *NIV Archaeological Study Bible: An Illustrated Walk Through Biblical History and Culture*. Grand Rapids, Mich.: Zondervan, 2006.

"Kay Prag Reports on Tall Iktanu and Tall El-Hammam 515-516," n.d.

Kazhdan, Alexander. "Arabia, Province of." In *The Oxford Dictionary of Byzantium*, edited by Alexander Kazhdan, 147. Oxford, U.K.: Oxford University Press, 1991.

———. , ed. *The Oxford Dictionary of Byzantium*. 3 vols. Oxford, U.K.: Oxford University Press, 1991.

Kempinski, Aharon, and Ronny Reich. *The Architecture of Ancient Israel: From the Prehistoric to the Persian Periods*. Jerusalem: Biblical Archaeology Society, 1992.

Kenyon, Kathleen M. *Amorites and Canaanites*. Schweich Lectures on Biblical Archaeology. Oxford, U.K.: Oxford University Press, 1967.

———. "Excavations in Jerusalem, 1965." *PEQ* 98, no. 1 (1966): 73–88.

Khouri, Rami G. *Antiquities of the Jordan Rift Valley*. Manchester, MI: Solipsist, 1988.

Kitchen, Kenneth A. *Ancient Orient and Old Testament*. Wheaton, Ill.: Tyndale, 1966.

———. *On the Reliability of the Old Testament*. Grand Rapids, Mich.: Eerdmans, 2003.

———. *The Bible in Its World*. Exeter, U.K.: Paternoster, 1977.

———. "The Patriarchal Age: Myth or History?" *BAR* 21, no. 2 (1995): 48–57, 89–95.

Kitchen, Kenneth A., and T. C. Mitchell. "Chronology of the Old Testament." Edited by I. Howard Marshall, A. R. Millard, J. I. Packer, and D. J. Wiseman. *NBD*. Downers Grove, Ill.: InterVarsity, 1996.

Kittel, Rudolf. *Biblia Hebraica*. 2 vols. Leipzig: Hinrichs, 1906.

Knopf, R. *Ausgewählte Märtyreracten: Martyrium Des Pionius*. Edited by G. Krüger. Sammlung Ausgewählter Kirchen- Und Dogmengeschichtlicher Quellenschriften 3. Tübingen: Mohr, 1913.

Koehler, Lidwig, Walter Baumgartner, B. Hartmann, and Johann J. Stamm, eds. *The Hebrew and Aramaic Lexicon of the Old Testament*. Translated by M. E. J. Richardson. 3rd ed. 5 vols. Leiden: Brill, 1994.

Koehl, Robert B. "The Chieftain Cup and a Minoan Rite of Passage." *JHS* 106 (1986): 99–110.

Koeppel, Robert, H. Senès, J. W. Murphy, and G. S. Mahan. *Teleilāt Ghassūl, II.: Compte Rendu Des Fouilles de l'Institut Biblique Pontifical, 1932-1936*. Scripta Pontificii Instituti Biblici 68. Archaeological Institute of America, 1940.

Kreiger, Barbara. *The Dead Sea: Myth, History, and Politics*. Hanover, N.H.: University Press of New England, 1988.

Kyle, Melvin Grove, and William F. Albright. "Results of the Archaeological Survey of the Ghor in Search for the Cities of the Plain." *BSac* 81 (1924): 276–91.

Labat, René. *Manuel D'épigraphie Akkadienne: Signes, Syllabaire, Idéogrammes*. 5th ed. Geuthner Manuels. Paris: Librairie orientaliste Paul Geuthner, 1976.

Lapp, Paul W. "Bab Edh-Dhra', Perizzites and Emim." In *Jerusalem Through the Ages: The Twenty-Fifth Archaeological Convention*, 1–25. Jerusalem: Israel Exploration Society, 1968.

———. "Bab Edh-Dhra' (RB 1966)." *RB* 73 (1966): 556–61.

———. "Bab Edh-Dhra' (RB 1968)." *RB* 75 (1968): 86–93, pls. 3–6a.

———. "Bab Edh-Dhra' Tomb A 76 and Early Bronze I in Palestine." *BASOR* 189 (1968): 12–41.

———. "Palestine in the Early Bronze Age." In *Near Eastern Archaeology in the Twentieth Century: Essays in Honor of Nelson Glueck*, edited by James A. Sanders, 101–31. Garden City, N.Y.: Doubleday, 1970.

———. "The Cemetery at Bab Edh-Dhra', Jordan." *Archaeology* 19, no. 2 (1966): 104–11.

———. *The Dhahr Mirzbaneh Tombs: Three Intermediate Bronze Age Cemeteries in Jordan*. Philadelphia, Pa.: American Schools of Oriental Research, 1966.

La Sor, William Sanford, David Allan Hubbard, Frederic William Bush, and Leslie C. Allen. *Old Testament Survey: The Message, Form, and Background of the Old Testament*. 2nd ed. Grand Rapids, Mich.: Eerdmans, 1996.

Latham, James E. *The Religious Symbolism of Salt*. Theologie Historique 64. Paris: Beauchesne, 1982.

Lawrence, T. E. *Seven Pillars of Wisdom*. Wordsworth Classics of World Literature. Ware, Hertfordshire: Wordsworth, 1997.

Lemche, Niels Peter. *The Israelites in History and Tradition*. Library of Ancient Israel. Louisville, Ky.: Westminster/Knox, 1998.

Lensky, N. G., Y. Dvorkin, Vladimir Lyakhovsky, I. Gertman, and Ittai Gavrieli. "Water, Salt, and Energy Balances of the Dead Sea." *Water Resources Research* 41, no. 12 (2005): 1–13.

Le Quien, Michel. *Oriens christianus in quatuor patriarchatus digestus, in quo exhibentur Ecclesiae patriarchae caeterique praesules totius Orientis*. 3 vols. Paris: Typographia Regia, 1740.

Lev, David. "Russia Decides to Search for Sodom and Gomorrah-in Jordan." *Arutz Sheva 7: Israel National News*, December 14, 2010. http://www.israelnationalnews.com/News/News.aspx/141132.

Lewis, Bernard. *Islam in History: Ideas, People, and Events in the Middle East*. Peru, Ill.: Open Court, 2013.

Lewis, Naphtali, Jonas C. Greenfield, and Yigael Yadin, eds. *The Documents from the Bar Kokhba Period in the Cave of Letters, Greek Papyri*. Judaean Desert Series 2. Jerusalem: Israel Exploration Society, 1989.

Livingston, David P. "Excavation Report for Khirbet Nisya." *BS* 12, no. 3 (1999): 95–96.

———. "Locating Biblical Ai Correctly." *Ancient Days*, 2003. http://davelivingston.com/ai15.htm.

———. "One Last Word on Bethel and Ai." *BAR* 15, no. 1 (1989): 11.

———. "The Location of Biblical Bethel and Ai Reconsidered." *Westminster Theological Journal* 33, no. 1 (1970): 20–44.

Longman III, Tremper. *Fictional Akkadian Autobiography: A Generic and Comparative Study*. Winona Lake, Ind.: Eisenbrauns, 1991.

"Lt. Claude R. Conder, R.E., 1848-1910." *Palestine Exploration Fund*, January 16, 2014. http://www.pef.org.uk/profiles/lt-claude-r-conder-re-1848-1910.

Lyakhovsky, Vladimir, Zvi Ben-Avraham, and Moshe Achmon. "The Origin of the Dead Sea Rift." *Tectonophysics* 240 (1994): 29–43.

Lynch, William Francis. *Narrative of the United States Expedition to the River Jordan and the Dead Sea*. Philadelphia, Pa.: P. G. Collins, 1849.

MacDonald, Burton. *East of the Jordan: Territories and Sites of the Hebrew Scriptures*. Edited by Victor H. Matthews. ASOR Books 6. Boston, Mass.: American Schools of Oriental Research, 2000.

———. "EB IV Tombs at Khirbet Khanazir: Types, Construction, and Relation to Other EB IV Tombs in Syria-Palestine." *Studies in the History and Archaeology of Jordan* 5 (1995): 129–34.

———. "Review of John R. Bartlett, Mapping Jordan through Two Millennia. Palestine Exploration Fund Annual 10. Leeds: Maney, 2008." *BASOR* 358 (2010): 82–84.

———. "Settlement Patterns Along the Southern Flank of Wadi Al-Hasa: Evidence from 'The Wadi Hasa Archaeological Survey.'" In *Studies in the History and Archaeology of Jordan*, edited by Muna Zaghloul, K. 'Amr, F. Zayadine, R. Nabeel, and N. R. Tawfiq, 4:73–76. SHAJ. Amman, Jordan: Department of Antiquities, 1992.

———. "Southern Ghors and Northeast 'Arabah (OEANE)." In *OEANE*, edited by Eric M. Meyers, 5:64–66. Oxford, U.K.: Oxford University Press, 1997.

MacDonald, Burton, Geoffrey A. Clark, Michael P. Neeley, Russel Adams, and Michael Gregory. "Southern Ghors and Northeast `Arabah Archaeological Survey 1986, Jordan: A Preliminary Report." *ADAJ* 31 (1987): 391–418.

Mallon, Alexis. "Biblica" 10 (1929): 94–98.

Mallon, Père Alexis. "Chronique Palestinienne: Voyage D'exploration Au Sud-Est de La Mer Morte." *Biblica* 5, no. 3–4 (1924): 413–55.

———. "Les Places Fortes Du Sud-Est de La Vallée Du Jourdain Au Temps d'Abraham." *Biblica* 13 (1932): 194–201.

Mallon, Père Alexis, Robert Koeppel, and René Neuville. *Teleilāt Ghassūl. I: Compte Rendu Des Fouilles de l'Institut Biblique Pontificale, 1929-1932*. Rome: Archaeological Institute of America, 1934.

Manetho. *History of Egypt and Other Works*. Translated by W. G. Waddell. Loeb Classical Library 350. Cambridge, Mass.: Harvard University Press, 1940.

Masom, Caroline, Pat Alexander, and Alan R. Millard, eds. *Picture Archive of the Bible*. Tring, Herts, UK: Lion, 1987.

Matthiae, Paolo. "A Letter to the Editor." *Biblical Archaeologist* 43 (1980): 134.

———. "Ebla Recovered." In *Ebla to Damascus: Art and Archaeology of Ancient Syria: An Exhibition from the Directorate-General of Antiquities and Museums, Syrian Arab Republic*, edited by Harvey Weiss, 134–39. Washington, D.C.: Smithsonian Institution Traveling Exhibition Service, 1985.

Mazar, Amihai. *Archaeology of the Land of the Bible: 10,000-586 B.C.E.* Vol. 1. The Anchor Yale Bible Reference Library. New Haven, Conn.: Yale University Press, 1992.

———. "Tel Beth-Shean: History and Archaeology." In *One God - One Cult - One Nation Archaeological and Biblical Perspectives*, edited by Reinhard Gregor Kratz and Hermann Spieckermann, 239–71. Beihefte Zur Zeitschrift Fur Die Alttestamentliche Wissenschaft 405. Berlin: De Gruyter, 2010.

———. "The Patriarchs, Exodus and Conquest Narratives in Light of Archaeology." In *The Quest for the Historical Israel*, edited by Israel Finkelstein and Brian B. Schmidt, 57–67. Archaeology and Biblical Studies 17. Atlanta, Ga.: SBL, 2007.

Mazar, Benjamin. *The World History of the Jewish People: Ancient Times: Patriarchs.* Vol. 2. 2 vols. London, U.K.: Rutger's University Press, 1970.

McCreery, David W. "The Paleoethnobotany of Bab Edh-Dhraʿ." In *Bab Edh-Dhraʿ: Excavations at the Town Site (1975-1981): Part 1: Text*, edited by Walter E. Rast and R. Thomas Schaub, 2:449–63. Reports of the Expedition to the Dead Sea Plain, Jordan. Winona Lake, Ind.: Eisenbrauns, 2003.

McGovern, Patrick E. "A Neutron Activation Analysis Study of Bronze Age-Mamluk Period Pottery From Tell Nimrin, Jordan." *Virtual Nimrin*, 1998. http://www.cwru.edu/affil/nimrin/data/geol/gpm_0001.pdf.

———. "Central Transjordan in the Late Bronze and Early Iron Ages: An Alternative Hypothesis of Socio-Economic Transformation and Collapse." In *Studies in the History and Archaeology of Jordan*, edited by Adnan Hadidi, 4:267–73. London, U.K.: Taylor & Francis, 1987.

McGovern, Patrick E., and Robin Brown. *The Late Bronze and Early Iron Ages of Central Transjordan, the Baqʿah Valley Project, 1977-1981*. Pittsburgh, Penn: University of Pennsylvania, Museum of Archaeology, 1986.

McRay, John. *Archaeology and the New Testament*. Grand Rapids, Mich.: Baker, 1991.

Ménage, V. L. "Review of Speros Vryonis, Jr., The Decline of Medieval Hellenism in Asia Minor and the Process of Islamization from the Eleventh through the Fifteenth Century, Berkeley, 1971." *Bulletin of the School of Oriental and African Studies* 36, no. 3 (1973): 659–61.

Merrill, Eugene H. "Fixed Dates in Patriarchal Chronology." *BSac* 137, no. 547 (1980): 241–51.

———. *Kingdom of Priests: A History of Old Testament Israel*. 2nd ed. Grand Rapids, Mich.: Baker Academic, 2008.

———. "Texts, Talls, and Old Testament Chronology: Tall El-Hammam as a Case Study." *Artifax* 27, no. 4 (2012): 20–21.

Merrill, Selah. *East of the Jordan: A Record of Travel and Observation in the Countries of Moab, Gilead, and Bashan*. London, U.K.: Darf, 1881.

———. "Modern Researches in Palestine." *Journal of the American Geographical Society of New York* 9 (1877): 109–25.

———. "Modern Researches in Palestine." *PEFSt.* 11, no. 1 (1879): 138–54.

Meyer, Eduard, and Bernhard Luther. *Die Israeliten und ihre Nachbarstämme: Alttestamentliche Untersuchungen*. Halle: Max Niemeyer, 1906.

Meyers, Eric M., ed. *The Oxford Encyclopedia of Archaeology in the Near East*. 5 vols. Oxford, U.K.: Oxford University Press, 1997.

Mickelsen, A. Berkeley. *Interpreting the Bible*. Grand Rapids, Mich.: Eerdmans, 1963.

BIBLIOGRAPHY

Millard, Alan R. "Methods of Studying the Patriarchal Narratives as Ancient Texts." In *Essays on the Patriarchal Narratives*, edited by Donald J. Wiseman and Alan R. Millard, 43–58. Winona Lake, Ind.: Eisenbrauns, 1983.

Miller, James Maxwell, and John Haralson Hayes. *A History of Ancient Israel and Judah*. Louisville, Ky.: Westminster/Knox, 1986.

Miller, J. Maxwell, and Gene M. Tucker. *The Book of Joshua*. The Cambridge Bible Commentary of the English Bible. Cambridge, Mass.: Cambridge University Press, 1974.

Mitchell, T. C. *Biblical Archaeology: Documents from the British Museum*. Cambridge, U.K.: Cambridge University Press, 1988.

———. "Gerar." Edited by I. Howard Marshall, Alan R. Millard, J. I. Packer, Donald J. Wiseman, and D. R. W. Wood. *NBD*. Downers Grove, Ill.: InterVarsity, 1996.

Montague, Edward P. *Narrative of the Late Expedition to the Dead Sea*. Philadelphia, Pa.: Carey & Hart, 1849.

Moore, John. "Dr. John Moore and Dr. Steven Collins Reflect on TeHEP's First Nine Years." *Update: Tall El-Hammam Excavation Project, The Official Newsletter of TeHEP*, April 11, 2014.

Morandi Bonacossi, Daniele, ed. *Urban and Natural Landscapes of an Ancient Syrian Capital: Settlement and Environment at Tell Mishrifeh/Qatna and in Central-Western Syria*. Proceedings of the International Conference held in Udine, 9-11 December 2004. collana Studi archeologici su Qatna. Udine: Forum Editrice, 2007.

Mouchy, Antoine de. *Christianae religionis institutionisque Domini Nostri Jesu-Christi et apostolicae traditionis*. Paris: Macaeum, 1562.

Mulder, M. J. "Sodom and Gomorrah." Edited by David Noel Freedman, Gary A. Herion, David F. Graf, and John David Pleins. *ABD*. New York, N.Y.: Doubleday, 1996.

———. "Sodom; Gomorrah." In *TDOT*, edited by G. Johannes Botterweck, Helmer Ringgren, and Heinz-Josef Fabry, translated by Douglas W. Stott, 10:152–65. Grand Rapids, Mich.: Eerdmans, 2003.

Musil, Alois. *Arabia Petraea: Moab*. Vol. 1. Wien: A. Hölder, 1907.

Na'aman, Nadav. "Bethel and Beth-Aven: The Location of the Early Israelite Sanctuaries." *Zion* 50 (1985): 15–25.

Neev, David, and Kenneth O. Emery. *The Dead Sea: Depositional Processes and Environments of Evaporites*. Ministry of Development: Geological Survey 41. Jerusalem: Geological Survey of Israel, 1967.

———. *The Destruction of Sodom, Gomorrah and Jericho: Geological, Climatological and Archaeological Backgrounds*. Oxford, U.K.: Oxford University Press, 1995.

Neev, David, and John K. Hall. *The Dead Sea Geophysical Survey 19 July-1 August 1974: Final Report No. 2*. Vol. 76. Geological Survey of Israel 6. Jerusalem: Marine Geology Division, 1976.

Negev, Avraham. "Jericho." In *AEHL*, 3rd ed. New York: Prentice Hall Press, 1996.

———. *The Archaeological Encyclopedia of the Holy Land*. 3rd ed. New York: Prentice Hall Press, 1996.

———. "Zoar." In *AEHL*, 3rd ed. New York: Prentice Hall Press, 1996.

Niemi, Tina M., and Zvi Ben-Avraham. "Active Tectonics in the Dead Sea Basin." In *The Dead Sea: The Lake and Its Setting*, edited by Zvi Ben-Avraham, Tina M. Niemi, and Joel R. Gat, 73–81. Oxford Monographs on Geology and Geophysics 36. New York, N.Y.: Oxford University Press, USA, 1997.

Niemi, Tina M., Zvi Ben-Avraham, and Joel R. Gat, eds. *The Dead Sea: The Lake and Its Setting*. Oxford Monographs on Geology and Geophysics 36. New York, N.Y.: Oxford University Press, USA, 1997.

Nigro, Lorenzo. "Tell Es-Sultan – A Pilot Project for Archaeology in Palestine." *The ASOR Blog*, 2014. http://asorblog.org/tell-es-sultan-a-pilot-project-for-archaeology-in-palestine/.

Nissenbaum, Arie. "Dead Sea asphalts—Historical Aspects." *Bulletin of the Association of Petrolum Geologists* 62, no. 5 (1978): 837–44.

Nissenbaum, Arie, and Z. Aizenshatat. "Geochemical Studies on Ozokerite From the Dead Sea Area." *Chemical Geology* 16 (1975): 121–27.

Nissenbaum, Arie, and M. Goldberg. "Asphalts, Heavy Oils, Ozocerite and Gases in the Dead Sea Basin." *Organic Geochemistry* 2, no. 3 (1975): 167–80.

Nixon, Brian. "Archaeological Evidence for Sodom: Recent Findings Shed Light on Discoveries of 'Biblical Proportions.'" *ASSIST News Service*, December 8, 2011.

———. "Sodom Found? The Quest For The Lost City Of Destruction -- Part 3." *ASSIST News Service*, June 16, 2009. http://www.assistnews.net/Stories/2009/s09060102.htm.

North, Robert. *Les Fouilles Dans La Region de Jericho*. Rome: Pibia, 1967.

Noth, Martin. *A History of Pentateuchal Traditions*. Upper Saddle River, N.J.: Prentice-Hall, 1972.

———. *The History of Israel*. New York, N.Y.: Harper, 1960.

Nötling, Fritz. "Das Todte Meer Und Der Untergang von Sodom Und Gomorraha." In *Deutsches Montagsblatt*, 27, 31, 33. Berlin: Rudolf Mosse, 1886.

Orni, Efraim, and Shaked Gilboa. "Dan." Edited by Fred Skolnik and Michael Berenbaum. *EJ*. New York, N.Y.: MacMillan, 2006.

Orr, James, and Melvin Grove Kyle, eds. *The International Standard Bible Encyclopedia*. 5 vols. Chicago, Ill.: Howard-Severance, 1915.

Ortiz, Steven M. "Hermeneutical and Methodological Comments on the History of the Conquest and Settlement: The Archaeological and Biblical Support for the 13th Century." In *Southwest Regional ETS Meetings*. Fort Worth, Tex., 2006.

Ortner, Donald J. "A Preliminary Report on the Human Remains from the Bab Edh-Dhra' Cemetery." In *The Southeastern Dead Sea Plain Expedition: An Interim Report of the 1977 Season*, edited by R. Thomas Schaub and Walter E. Rast, 119–32. AASOR 46. Boston, Mass.: American Schools of Oriental Research, 1979.

Ortner, Donald J, and Bruno Frohlich. *The Early Bronze Age I Tombs and Burials of Bâb Edh-Dhrâ', Jordan*. Reports of the Expedition to the Dead Sea Plain, Jordan 3. Lanham, MD: AltaMira, 2008.

Packer, J. I., Merrill C. Tenney, and William White, eds. *Illustrated Manners and Customs of the Bible*. Nashville, Tenn.: Nelson, 1997.

Palmer, Edward H. *The Desert of the Exodus: Journeys on Foot in the Wilderness of the Forty Years' of Wanderings Undertaken in Connexion with the Ordance Survey of Sinai and the Palestine Exploration Fund*. Vol. 1. 2 vols. Cambridge, U.K.: Deighton, Bell & Co., 1871.

Papadopoulos, Thanasis J. "The Hellenic Archaeology Project of the University of Ioannina in Jordan: A Preliminary Synthesis of the Excavation Results at Ghawr as-Sāfī and Tall Al-Kafrayn (2000-2004)." In *Studies in the History and Archaeology of Jordan*, edited by Fawwaz al-Khraysheh, 175–91. IX. Amman: Department of Antiquities, 2007.

Papadopoulos, Thanasis J., and Litsa Kontorli-Papadopoulos. "Preliminary Report of the Seasons 2005-2008 of Excavations by the University of Ioannina at Tall Kafrayn in the Jordan Valley." *ADAJ* 54 (2010): 283–310.

Pellegrino, Charles R. *Return to Sodom and Gomorrah: Bible Stories from Archaeologists*. New York, N.Y.: Avon Books, 1995.

Pettinato, Giovanni. "Ebla and the Bible." *BA* 43 (1980): 203–16.

———. "Gli archivi reali di Tell Mardikh-Ebla: riflessioni e prospettive." *Rivista Biblica Italiana* 25, no. 1 (1977): 225–43.

———. "Report on Ebla." In *Conference Paper*. St. Louis, Miss., 1976.

Pettinato, Giovanni, and A. Alberti. *Catalogo Dei Testi Cuneiformi Di Tell Mardikh-Ebla*. Materiali Epigrafici Di Ebla 1. Naples: Istituto Universitario Orientale di Napoli, 1979.

Pfeiffer, Charles F. "Exodus." In *The New International Dictionary of the Bible*, edited by Merrill C. Tenney and James D. Douglas, 333. Grand Rapids, Mich.: Zondervan, 1987.

Philip, Graham. "The Early Bronze Age I-III." In *Jordan: An Archaeological Reader*, edited by Russell B. Adams, 161–226. London, U.K.: Equinox, 2008.

Philo. *The Works of Philo Judaeus: The Contemporary of Josephus*. Translated by C. D. Yonge. 3 vols. Whitefish, Mont.: Kessinger, 2007.

Piccirillo, Michele, ed. "Ricerca Storico-Archeologica In Giordania 16 - 1996." *LASBF* 46 (1996): 391–424.

———. "The Roman Esbus-Livias Road." In *Mount Nebo: New Archaeological Excavations 1967-1997*, edited by Michele Piccirillo and Eugenio Alliata, 133–35. Studium Biblicum Franciscanum 27. Jerusalem: Franciscan, 1998.

Politis, Konstantinos D. "Biblical Zoar: The Looting of an Ancient Site." *Minerva* 5/6 (1994): 12–15.

———. "Death at the Dead Sea." *BAR* 38, no. 2 (2013): 42–54.

———. "Report to the Palestine Exploration Fund on the Surveys and Excavations at Zoara in the Ghor Es-Safi 2003-2004." *PEQ*, 2005.

———. *Sanctuary of Lot at Deir 'Ain 'Abata in Jordan Excavations 1988–2003*. Amman: Jordan Distribution Agency, 2012.

———. "The Lost Cities of Sodom and Gomorrah." In *The Seventy Great Mysteries of the Ancient World: Unlocking the Secrets of Past Civilizations*, edited by Brian M Fagan, 34–37. New York: Thames & Hudson, 2001.

———. "The Monastery of Aghios Lot at Deir 'Ain 'Abata in Jordan." In *Byzanz – Das Römerreich Im Mittelalter*, edited by Falko Daim and Jörg Drauschke, 1–23. 3. Mainz: Römisch-Germanischen Zentralmuseums, 2010.

———. "Where Lot's Daughters Seduced Their Father Excavations Reveal Commemorative Monastery." *BAR* 30, no. 1 (2004): 20–31, 64.

Politis, Konstantinos D., Amanda M. Kelly, Daniel Hull, and Rebecca Foote. "Survey and Excavations in the Ghawr as-Safi 2004." *ADAJ* 49 (2005): 313–26.

Politis, Konstantinos D., Adamantios Sampson, and Margaret O'Hea. "Ghawr As-Safi Survey and Excavations 2008-2009." *ADAJ* 53 (2009): 297–310.

Politis, Konstantinos D., Adamantios Sampson, Margaret O'Hea, and Georgios Papaioannou. "Survey and Excavations in the Ghawr as-Safi 2006–07." *ADAJ* 51 (2007): 199–210.

Pollock, Susan. *Ancient Mesopotamia: The Eden That Never Was*. Cambridge, Mass.: Cambridge University Press, 1999.

Power, E. "The Site of the Pentapolis: Part 1." *Biblica* 11 (1930): 23–62.

———. "The Site of the Pentapolis: Part 2." *Biblica* 12 (1930): 149–82.

Prag, Kay. "Iktanu, Tell." In *OEANE*, edited by Eric M. Meyers, 1:143–44. Oxford, U.K.: Oxford University Press, 1997.

———. "Preliminary Report on the Excavations at Tell Iktanu and Tall El-Hammam, Jordan 1990." *Levant* 23 (1991): 55–66.

———. "Preliminary Report on the Excavations at Tell Iktanu, Jordan, 1987." *Levant* 21 (1989): 33–45.

———. "Preliminary Report on the Excavations at Tell Iktanu, Jordan, 1989." *ADAJ* 34 (1990): 119–30.

———. "Tall El-Hammam as Livias, 8 Jan 2009," January 8, 2009.

———. "Tell Iktanu and Tell Al-Hammam. Excavations in Jordan." *Manchester Archaeological Bulletin* 7 (1992): 15–19.

———. "The Excavations at Tell Al-Hammam." *Syria* 70, no. 1–2 (1990): 271–73.

———. "The Excavations at Tell Iktanu 1989 and 1990." *Syria* 70 (1993): 269–73.

———. "The Intermediate Early Bronze-Middle Bronze Age: An Interpretation of the Evidence from Transjordan, Syria and Lebanon." *Levant* 6 (1974): 69–116.

———. "The Intermediate Early-Middle Bronze Age Sequences at Jericho and Tell Iktanu Reviewed." *BASOR* 264 (1986): 61–72.

Price, J. Randall. *The Stones Cry Out: What Archaeology Reveals About the Truth of the Bible*. Eugene, Oreg.: Harvest House, 1997.

Rabinowitz, Louis Isaac, and Stephen G. Wald. "Right and Left." *Jewish Virtual Library*. Accessed March 14, 2014. http://www.jewishvirtuallibrary.org/jsource/judaica/ejud_0002_0017_0_16755.html.

Rainey, Anson F. "Historical Geography." In *Benchmarks in Time and Culture: An Introduction to Palestinian Archaeology*, edited by Joel F Drinkard, Gerald L Mattingly, and J. Maxwell Callaway, Joseph A Miller, 353–68. ASOR/SBL Archaeology And Biblical Studies. Atlanta, Ga.: Scholars Press, 1988.

Ramm, Bernard. *Protestant Biblical Interpretation: A Textbook of Hermeneutics*. 3rd ed. Grand Rapids, Mich.: Baker Academic & Brazos, 1980.

Rast, Walter E. "Bab Edh-Dhra' (ABD)." Edited by David Noel Freedman, Gary A. Herion, David F. Graf, and John David Pleins. *ABD*. New York, N.Y.: Doubleday, 1996.

———. "Bab Edh-Dhra' and the Origin of the Sodom Saga." In *Archaeology and Biblical Interpretation: Essays in Memory of D. Glenn Rose*, edited by Leo G. Perdue, Lawrence E. Toombs, and Gary L. Johnson, 185–201. Atlanta, Ga.: Knox, 1987.

———. "Bronze Age Cities along the Dead Sea." *Archaeology* 40, no. 1 (1987): 42–49.

———. "Patterns of Settlement at Bab Edh-Dhra'." In *The Southeastern Dead Sea Plain Expedition: An Interim Report of the 1977 Season*, edited by R. Thomas Schaub and Walter E. Rast, 7–34. AASOR 46. Boston, Mass.: American Schools of Oriental Research, 1979.

———. "Settlement at Numeira." In *The Southeastern Dead Sea Plain Expedition: An Interim Report of the 1977 Season*, 35–44. AASOR 46. Cambridge: American Schools of Oriental Research, 1979.

———. "Sodom and Its Environs: Can Recent Archaeology Offer a Perspective?" *NEASB* 51 (2006): 19–26.

———. "The 1975-1981 Excavations at Bab Edh-Dhra'." In *Bab Edh-Dhra': Excavations at the Town Site (1975-1981): Part 1: Text*, edited by Walter E. Rast and R. Thomas Schaub, 1:1–17. Reports of the Expedition to the Dead Sea Plain, Jordan 2. Winona Lake, Ind.: Eisenbrauns, 2003.

———. "The Southeastern Dead Sea Valley Expedition, 1979." *BA* 43, no. 1 (1980): 60–61.

Rast, Walter E., and R. Thomas Schaub. "A Preliminary Report of Excavations at Bab Edh-Dhraʿ, 1975." In *Preliminary Excavation Reports: Bab Edh-Dhraʿ, Sardis, Meiron, Tell El-Hesi, Carthage (Punic)*, edited by David Noel Freedman, 1–32. AASOR 43. Chicago, Ill.: American Schools of Oriental Research, 1978.

———. , eds. *Bab Edh-Dhraʿ: Excavations at the Town Site (1975-1981): Part 1: Text*. Reports of the Expedition to the Dead Sea Plain, Jordan 2. Winona Lake, Ind.: Eisenbrauns, 2003.

———. , eds. *Bab Edh-Dhraʿ: Excavations in the Cemetery Directed by Paul W Lapp, 1965-1967*. Reports of the Expedition to the Dead Sea Plain, Jordan 1. Winona Lake, Ind.: Eisenbrauns, 1989.

———. "Expedition to the Dead Sea Plain." Accessed December 4, 2008. http://www.nd.edu/~edsp/.

———. "Expedition to the Southeastern Dead Sea Plain, Jordan, 1979." *American Schools of Oriental Research Newsletter*, no. 8 (1980): 12–17.

———. "Survey of the Southeastern Plain of the Dead Sea, 1973." *ADAJ* 19 (1974): 5–53, 175–85.

———. "The Dead Sea Expedition: Bab Edh-Dhraʿ and Numeira, May 24-July 10, 1981." *American Schools of Oriental Research Newsletter*, no. 4 (1982): 4–12.

Rast, Walter E., R. Thomas Schaub, David W. McCreery, Jack Donahue, and Mark A. McConaughy. "Preliminary Report of the 1979 Expedition to the Dead Sea Plain, Jordan." *BASOR* 240 (1980): 21–61.

Rast, Walter, R. Thomas Schaub, and Meredith S. Chesson, eds. *Numayra: Excavations at the Early Bronze Age Townsite in Jordan, 1977-1983*. Winona Lake, Ind.: Eisenbrauns, Forthcoming.

Rawashdeh, Saeb. "Ancient Ghor Safi Comes to Light with the Zoara Project." *Jordan Times*, July 3, 2017. http://www.jordantimes.com/news/local/ancient-ghor-safi-comes-light-zoara-project.

Ray Jr., Paul J. "The Duration of the Israelite Sojourn In Egypt." *BS* 17, no. 2 (2004): 33–45.

Redford, Donald B. *Egypt, Canaan, and Israel in Ancient Times*. Princeton, N.J.: Princeton University Press, 1993.

Regev, Johanna, Pierre de Miroschedji, Raphael Greenberg, Eliot Braun, Zvi Greenhut, and Elisabetta Boaretto. "Chronology of the Early Bronze Age in the Southern Levant: New Analysis for a High Chronology." *Radiocarbon* 3–4 (2012): 525–66.

Rendsburg, Gary A. "Ebla." In *Encyclopedia Judaica*, edited by Michael Berenbaum and Fred Skolnik, 2nd ed., 6:85–87. New York, N.Y.: MacMillan, 2007.

Roberts, Alexander, James Donaldson, Philip Schaff, and Henry Wace, eds. *Ante-Nicene Fathers*. New Ed. 10 vols. Peabody, Mass.: Hendrickson, 1994.

———. , eds. *Nicene and Post-Nicene Fathers, Series II*. 14 vols. Peabody, Mass.: Hendrickson, 1994.

Robinson, George L. "Jordan." In *Dictionary of the Bible, One Vol.*, edited by James Hastings and John A. Selbie, 493–94. New York, N.Y.: Scribner's Sons, 1909.

Rollin, Sue, and Jane Streetly. *Jordan*. 3rd ed. Blue Guide. London, U.K.: A & C Black, 2001.

Ross, Allen P. *The Table of Nations in Genesis*. Dallas, Tex.: Dallas Theological Seminary, 1976.

Running, Leona Glidden, and David Noel Freedman. *William Foxwell Albright: A Twentieth-Century Genius: A Biography of the Acknowledged Dean of Biblical Archaeologists*. Berrien Springs, Mich.: Andrews University Press, 1975.

Ryken, Leland, Jim Wilhoit, Tremper Longman, Colin Duriez, Douglas Penney, and Daniel G. Reid, eds. *Dictionary of Biblical Imagery*. Downers Grove, Ill.: InterVarsity, 1998.

Saldarini, Anthony D. "Babatha's Story." *BAR* 24, no. 2 (1998): 28–37, 72.

Saller, Sylvester J. "Iron Age Tombs at Nebo, Jordan." *LASBF* 16 (1966): 165–298.

———. *The Memorial of Moses on Mount Nebo I: The Text; II: The Plates*. 3 vols. Studium Biblicum Franciscanum Collection 1. Jerusalem: Studium Biblicum Franciscanum, 1941.

Saller, Sylvester J., and Bellarmino Bagatti. *The Town of Nebo (Khirbet El-Mekhayyat): With a Brief Survey of Other Ancient Christian Monuments in Transjordan*. Publications of the Studium Biblicum Franciscanum 7. Jerusalem: Franciscan, 1949.

Sarna, Nahum M. *Genesis: The Traditional Hebrew Text with the New JPS Translation*. JPS Torah Commentary. Philadelphia: Jewish Publication Society, 1989.

———. "The Patriarchs Genesis 12-36." In *Genesis: World of Myths and Patriarchs*, edited by Ada Feyerick, Cyrus Herzl Gordon, and Nahum M Sarna, 117–66. New York, N.Y.: New York University Press, 1996.

Saulcy, Félix de. "Lettre à M. Clermont-Ganneau Sur Les Ruines de Gomorrhe." *Revue Archéologique* 32 (1876): 303–12.

Saulcy, Louis Félicien J. Caignart de. *Narrative of a Journey Round the Dead Sea and in the Bible Lands in 1850 and 1851: Including an Account of the Discovery of the Sites of Sodom and Gomorrah*. Edited by Edward de Warren. 2 vols. London, U.K.: R. Bentley, 1853.

Schath, Kenneth, Steven Collins, and Hussein Aljarrah. "Excavation of an Undisturbed Demi-Dolmen and Insights from the Al-Hammam Megalithic Field, 2011 Season." *ADAJ* 55 (2011): 329–50.

Schatz, Werner. *Genesis 14: Eine Untersuchung*. Vol. 2. Europäische Hochschuleschriften 23. Bern: Herbert Lang, 1972.

Schaub, R. Thomas. "Bab Edh-Dhra' (NEAEHL)." In *NEAEHL*, edited by Ephraim Stern, Ayelet Levinson-Gilboa, and Joseph Aviram, 1:130–36. Jerusalem: The Israel Exploration Society, 1993.

———. "Bab Edh-Dhra' (OEANE)." In *OEANE*, edited by Eric M. Meyers, 1:248–51. Oxford, U.K.: Oxford University Press, 1997.

———. "In Memoriam: Walter Emil Rast 1930-2003." *BASOR* 332 (2003): 1–5.

———. "Southeast Dead Sea Plain." In *OEANE*, edited by Eric M. Meyers, 5:62–64. Oxford, U.K.: Oxford University Press, 1997.

Schaub, R. Thomas, and Walter E. Rast. "Preliminary Report of the 1981 Expedition to the Dead Sea Plain, Jordan." *BASOR*, no. 254 (1984): 35–60.

———. *The Southeastern Dead Sea Plain Expedition: An Interim Report of the 1977 Season*. AASOR 46. Boston, Mass.: American Schools of Oriental Research, 1979.

Schick, Robert. "Northern Jordan: What Might Have Been in the Madaba Mosaic Map." In *The Madaba Map Centenary: Travelling Through the Byzantine Umayyad Period. Proceedings of the International Conference Held in Amman 7–9 April 1997*, edited by Michele Piccirillo and Eugenio Alliata, 228–29. Studium Biblicum Franciscannum 40. Jerusalem: Studium Biblicum Franciscannum, 1999.

Schlegel, Bill. "Biblical Problems with Locating Sodom at Tall El-Hammam." *BiblePlaces*, January 4, 2012. http://blog.bibleplaces.com/2012/01/biblical-problems-with-locating-sodom.html.

Schultz, Samuel J., and Gary V. Smith. *Exploring the Old Testament*. Wheaton, Ill.: Crossway, 2001.

Schumacher, Gottlieb. *Across the Jordan: Being an Exploration and Survey of Part of Hauran and Jaulan*. London, U.K.: Watt, 1889.

Seters, John Van. *Abraham in History and Tradition*. New Haven, Conn.: Yale University Press, 1975.

———. "Review of John J. Bimson, Redating the Exodus and Conquest." *The Journal of Egyptian Archaeology* 70 (1984): 180–82.

Shahîd, Irfan. *Byzantium and the Arabs in the Sixth Century: Ecclesiastical History*. Washington, D.C.: Dumbarton Oaks, 1995.

Shanks, Hershel. "BAR Interviews Giovanni Pettinato: Original Ebla Epigrapher Attempts to Set the Record Straight." *BAR* 6, no. 5 (1980): 46–52.

———. "Ebla Evidence Evaporates." *BAR* 5, no. 6 (1979).

———. "The Sad Case of Tell Gezer." *BAR* 9, no. 4 (1983): 30–42.

Shanks, Hershel, Niels Peter Lemche, Thomas L. Thompson, William G. Dever, and P. Kyle McCarter Jr. "Face to Face: Biblical Minimalists Meet Their Challenge." *BAR* 23, no. 4 (1997): 26–42, 66.

Shea, William H. "Two Palestinian Segments from the Eblaite Geographical Atlas." In *Word of the Lord Shall Go Forth: Essays in Honor of David Noel Freedman in Celebration of His Sixtieth Birthday*, edited by Carol L. Meyers and M. O'Connor, 589–612. ASOR. Winona Lake, Ind.: Eisenbrauns, 1983.

Siculus, Diodorus. *Library of History: Books 19.66-20*. Translated by Russel M. Geer. Vol. 10. 12 vols. LCL 390. Cambridge, Mass.: Harvard University Press, 1954.

Silberman, Neil Asher. *Digging for God and Country: Exploration, Archaeology, and the Secret Struggle for the Holy Land, 1799-1917*. New York, N.Y.: Doubleday, 1990.

Silvia, Phillip J. *The Destruction of Sodom: What We Have Learned from Tall El-Hammam and Its Neighbors*. Albuquerque, N.M.: Trinity Southwest University Press, 2016.

———. "The Middle Bronze Age Civilization-Ending Destruction of the Middle Ghor." Ph.D. diss., Trinity Southwest University, 2015.

Silvia, Phillip J., and Steven Collins. "The Civilization-Ending 3.7KYrBP Kikkar Event: Archaeological Data, Sample Analyses, and Biblical Implications." In *Annual Meeting of the Near East Archaeological Society: Atlanta, Ga.*, 1–6. Albuquerque, N.M.: TSU Press, 2015.

Simons, Jan Jozef. *The Geographical and Topographical Texts of the Old Testament: A Concise Commentary in Xxxii Chapters*. Leiden: Brill, 1959.

Slemen, Tom, and Keith Andrews. *Jack the Ripper: British Intelligence Officer?* Liverpool: The Bluecoat Press, 2010.

Smith, Curtis. "Paleo-Botanical Report for Tall El-Hammam, 2014," May 22, 2014.

Solinus, Gaius Julius. *Collectanea rerum memorabilium*. Translated by Theodor Mommsen. Berlin: Weidmann, 1895.

Sollberger, Edmond. *Administrative Texts Chiefly Concerning Textiles (L. 2752)*. Archivi Reali de Ebla, Testi 8. Rome: Missione Archaeologica Italiana in Siria, 1986.

Sparks, Brad C. "Egyptian Text Parallels to the Exodus: The Egyptology Literature." In *Out of Egypt: Israel's Exodus Between Text and Memory, History and Imagination Conference*, edited by Thomas E. Levy. University of California, San Diego, 2013. https://www.youtube.com/watch?v=F-Aomm4O794.

Speier, Salomon. "On Hebrew `Ad Meaning 'At, By, near.'" *BASOR* 126 (1952): 27.

Sproul, R. C. *Explaining Inerrancy: A Commentary*. Oakland, CA: International Council on Biblical Inerrancy, 1980.

Sproul, R. C., and Norman L. Geisler. *Explaining Biblical Inerrancy: Official Commentary on the ICBI Statements*. Edited by Christopher T. Haun and Norman L. Geisler. Matthew, N.C.: Bastion, 2013.

Steinmann, Andrew E. "The Mysterious Numbers Of the Book of Judges." *JETS* 48 (2005): 491–500.

Stein, Mordechai. "The Sedimentary and Geochemical Record of Neogene-Quaternary Water Bodies in the Dead Sea Basin - Inferences for the Regional Paleoclimatic History." *Journal of Paleolimnology* 26, no. 3 (2001): 271–82.

Stern, Ephraim, Ayelet Levinson-Gilboa, and Joseph Aviram, eds. *The New Encyclopedia of Archaeological Excavations in the Holy Land*. 4 vols. New York, N.Y.: MacMillan, 1993.

Stiebing, Jr., William H. "When Civilization Collapsed: Death of the Bronze Age." *Archaeology Odyssey* 4, no. 5 (2001).

Strabo. *Geography: Books 10–12*. Translated by Horace Leonard Jones. Vol. 5. 8 vols. LCL 211. Cambridge, Mass.: Harvard University Press, 1928.

Strange, James F. "The Late Bronze Age." In *Jordan: An Archaeological Reader*, edited by Russell B. Adams, 281–310. London, U.K.: Equinox, 2008.

Stripling, D. Scott, Bryant G. Wood, Gary A. Byers, and Titus M. Kennedy. "Renewed Excavations at Khirbet El-Maqatir: Highlights of the 2009–2011 Seasons." In *Collected Studies of the Staff Office of Archaeology of Judea and Samaria*, Forthcoming. Judea and Samaria Publication 13. Jerusalem: Israel Antiquities Authority, 2014.

Swanson, James. *A Dictionary of Biblical Languages with Semantic Domains: Hebrew Old Testament*. Electronic Edition. Oak Harbor: Logos Research Systems, 1997.

Swenson, Astrid. "Sodom." In *Cities of God*, edited by David Gange and Michael Ledger-Lomas, 197–227. Cambridge, U.K.: Cambridge University Press, 2013.

Tacitus, Cornelius. *The Complete Works of Tacitus: The Annals. The History. The Life of Cnaeus Julius Agricola. Germany and Its Tribes. A Dialogue on Oratory*. Edited by Alfred John Church and William Jackson Brodribb. New York, N.Y.: Random House, 1942.

Taylor, Joan E. "The Dead Sea in Western Travellers' Accounts from the Byzantine to the Modern Period." *Bulletin of the Anglo-Israel Archaeological Society* 27 (2009): 9–29.

Taylor, John B. *Ezekiel: An Introduction and Commentary*. Tyndale Old Testament Commentaries. Downers Grove, Ill.: InterVarsity Press, 2009.

Tenney, Merrill C., and Moises Silva, eds. *The Zondervan Encyclopedia of the Bible: Revised Full-Color Edition*. Revised. 5 vols. Grand Rapids, Mich.: Zondervan, 2009.

Tertullian. *De Pallio: A Commentary*. Translated by Vincent Hunink. Amsterdam: Gieben, 2005.

Theodosius. "Topografia: The Topography of the Holy Land." In *Jerusalem Pilgrims Before the Crusades*, edited by John Wilkinson, 103–16. Oxford, U.K.: Aris & Phillips, 2002.

Thiele, Edwin Richard. *The Mysterious Numbers of the Hebrew Kings: A Reconstruction of the Chronology of the Kingdoms of Israel and Judah*. Revised. Grand Rapids, Mich.: Kregel Academic & Professional, 1994.

Thompson, Thomas L. *Early History of the Israelite People: From the Written & Archaeological Sources*. Leiden: Brill, 2000.

———. *The Historicity of the Patriarchal Narratives: The Quest for the Historical Abraham*. Valley Forge, PA: Trinity Press International, 2002.

Thomson, William M. *The Land and the Book: Lebanon, Damascus, and Beyond Jordan*. Vol. 3. 3 vols. New York, N.Y.: Harper & Brothers, 1886.

———. *The Land and the Book: Southern Palestine and Jerusalem*. Vol. 1. 3 vols. New York, N.Y.: Harper & Brothers, 1880.

BIBLIOGRAPHY

Torfstein, Adi, Ittai Gavrieli, and Mordechai Stein. "The Sources and Evolution of Sulfur in the Hypersaline Lake Lisan (paleo-Dead Sea)." *Earth and Planetary Science Letters* 236 (2005): 61–77.

Trifonov, Vladimir G. "The Bible and Geology: Destruction of Sodom and Gomorrah." In *Myth and Geology*, edited by L. Piccardi and W. Bruce Masse, 133–42. Geological Society Special Publication 273. London, U.K.: Geological Society, 2007.

Tristram, Henry Baker. *The Land of Israel: A Journal of Travels in Palestine with Reference to Its Physical History*. London, U.K.: Society for the Promoting Christian Knowledge, 1865.

———. *The Land of Moab: Travels and Discoveries on the East Side of the Dead Sea and the Jordan*. New York, N.Y.: Harper & Brothers, 1873.

Tubb, Jonathan N. "Sa'idryeh. Tell Es-." In *OEANE*, edited by Eric M. Meyers, 4:452–55. Oxford, U.K.: Oxford University Press, 1997.

Tuchman, Barbara Wertheim. *Bible and Sword: England and Palestine from the Bronze Age to Balfour*. London: Phoenix, 2001.

Udd, Kris J. "Bab Edh-Dhra', Numeira, and the Biblical Patriarchs: A Chronological Study." Ph.D. diss., Andrews University, 2011.

Ullendorff, Edward. *From the Bible to Enrico Cerulli: A Miscellany of Ethiopian and Semitic Papers*. Berlin: Franz Steiner, 1990.

VanGemeren, Willem A., ed. *New International Dictionary of Old Testament Theology and Exegesis*. Grand Rapids, Mich.: Zondervan, 1997.

Virolleaud, Charles. "Les Nouveaux Textes Alphabetiques de Ras-Shamra (XVIe Campagne, 1952)." *Syria* 30 (1953): 187–95.

Wade, G. W. "Siddim, Vale of." In *DBib1*, edited by James Hastings and John A. Selbie, 853. New York, N.Y.: Scribner's Sons, 1909.

Waltke, Bruce K., and Cathi J. Fredricks. *Genesis: A Commentary*. Grand Rapids, Mich.: Zondervan, 2001.

Walton, John H. *Chronological and Background Charts of the Old Testament*. Grand Rapids, Mich.: Zondervan, 1994.

Warner, S. M. "The Patriarchs and Extra-Biblical Sources." *JSOT* 2 (1977): 50–61.

Warren, Charles. "Jordan." In *DBib5*, edited by James Hastings and John A. Selbie, 2:756–67. New York, N.Y.: Scribner's Sons, 1899.

Waterhouse, S. D., and R. Ibach. "Heshbon 1973: The Topographical Survey." *AUSS* 13 (1975): 217–33.

Weinstein, James M. "A New Set of Radiocarbon Dates from the Town Site." In *Bab Edh-Dhra': Excavations at the Town Site: 1975-1981: Part 1 Text*, edited by Walter E. Rast and R. Thomas Schaub, 1:638–48. Reports of the Expedition to the Dead Sea Plain, Jordan 2. Winona Lake, Ind.: Eisenbrauns, 2003.

Wenham, Gordon J. *Genesis 1-15*. Edited by David Allan Hubbard and Glenn W. Barker. Vol. 1. 32 vols. Word Biblical Commentary. Dallas, Tex.: Word Books, 1987.

———. *Genesis 16-50*. Edited by David Allan Hubbard and Glenn W. Barker. Vol. 2. 32 vols. Word Biblical Commentary. Dallas, Tex.: Word Books, 1994.

Wilkes, John. "Changes to Roman Provincial Organization." In *The Cambridge Ancient History: The Crisis of Empires AD 193-337*, edited by Alan K. Bowman, Averil Cameron, and Peter Garnsey, 12:704–13. Cambridge, U.K.: Cambridge University Press, 2007.

Wilson, Charles W. "On the Site of Ai and the Position of the Altar Which Abram Built Between Bethel and Ai." *PEFSt*. 1, no. 4 (1869): 123–26.

Wilson, Clifford. "Ebla: Its Impact on Bible Records." *Institute for Creation Research: Acts & Facts. 6 (4)*, 1977. http://www.icr.org/article/92/.

Wilson, Clifford A. *Ebla Tablets: Secrets of a Forgotten City: Revelations of Tell Mardikh*. Third, Enlarged and Updated. San Diego, CA: Creation-Life, 1981.

———. *The Impact of Ebla on Bible Records: The Sensational Tell Mardikh*. Word of Truth, 1977.

Wiseman, Donald J. *1 and 2 Kings: An Introduction and Commentary*. Tyndale Old Testament Commentaries. Downers Grove, Ill.: IVP Academic, 2008.

Wolcott, Samuel. "The Site of Sodom." *BSac* 25, no. 97 (1868): 112–51.

Wood, Bryant G. "Bryant G. Wood, PhD. Biography." *Detroit Baptist Theological Seminary*, 2013. http://dbts.edu/pdf/rls/WoodBio.pdf.

———. "Excavations at Kh. El-Maqatir 1995–2000, 2009–2013: A Border Fortress in the Highlands of Canaan and a Proposed New Location for the Ai of Joshua 7-8." *The Bible and Interpretation*, 2014, 1–16.

———. "Have Sodom And Gomorrah Been Found?" *BS* 3, no. 3 (1974): 65–90.

———. "Khirbet El-Maqatir, 1995-1998." *IEJ* 50, no. 1–2 (2000): 123–30.

———. "Khirbet El-Maqatir, 1999." *IEJ* 50, no. 3–4 (2000): 249–54.

———. "Khirbet El-Maqatir, 2000." *IEJ* 51, no. 2 (2001): 246–52.

———. "Locating Sodom: A Critique of the Northern Proposal." *BS* 20, no. 3 (2007): 78–84.

———. "Sodom and Gomorrah: Is There Evidence for Their Destruction?" *Associates For Biblical Research*, May 6, 2008, 1–4.

———. "The Biblical Date for the Exodus Is 1446 BC: A Response to James Hoffmeier." *JETS* 50, no. 2 (2007): 249–58.

———. "The Discovery of the Sin Cities of Sodom and Gomorrah." *Bible and Spade* 12, no. 3 (1999): 67–80.

———. "The Rise and Fall of the 13th-Century Exodus-Conquest Theory." *JETS* 48, no. 3 (2005): 475–89.

———. "The Search for Joshua's Ai." In *Critical Issues in Early Israelite History*, edited by Richard S. Hess, Gerald A. Klingbeil, and Paul J. Ray Jr., 205–40. Bulletin for Biblical Research Supplement 3. Winona Lake, Ind.: Eisenbrauns, 2008.

———. "The Search for Joshua's Ai: Excavations at Kh. El-Maqatir." *BS* 12, no. 1 (1999): 21–32.

Wood, Bryant G., and D. Scott Stripling. *Joshua's Ai at Khirbet El-Maqatir: History of a Biblical Site*. Houston, Tex.: Houston Baptist University Press, 2014.

Wright, George Frederick. "Sodom." Edited by James Orr and Melvin Grove Kyle. *ISBE1*. Grand Rapids, Mich.: Eerdmans, 1915.

———. "Zoar." Edited by James Orr and Melvin Grove Kyle. *ISBE1*. Grand Rapids, Mich.: Eerdmans, 1915.

Wright, G. Ernest. *Biblical Archaeology*. Abridged. Philadelphia, Pa.: Westminster, 1960.

Wyllie, B. K. N. "The Geology of Jebel Usdum, Dead Sea." *Geological Magazine* 68, no. 8 (1931): 360–72.

Yamauchi, Edwin M. "Historic Homer: Did It Happen?" *BAR* 33, no. 2 (2007): 28–37, 76.

———. "Homer and Archaeology: Minimalists and Maximalists in Classical Context." In *The Future of Biblical Archaeology: Reassessing Methodologies and Assumptions*, edited by James K. Hoffmeier and Alan R. Millard, 69–90. Grand Rapids, Mich.: Eerdmans, 2008.

Yardeni, Ada, Jonas C. Greenfield, Yigael Yadin, and Baruch Levine, eds. *The Documents from the Bar Kokhba Period in the Cave of Letters: Hebrew, Aramaic and Nabatean-Aramaic Papyri*. Jerusalem: Israel Exploration Society, 2002.

Yassine, Khair, Moawiyah M. Ibrahim, and James A. Sauer. "The East Jordan Valley Survey 1975 (Part One)." In *The Archaeology of Jordan: Essays and Reports*, edited by Khair Yassine, 189–207. Amman: Department of Archaeology, University of Jordan, 1988.

———. "The East Jordan Valley Survey 1975 (Part Two)." In *The Archaeology of Jordan: Essays and Reports*, edited by Khair Yassine, 159–89. Amman: Department of Archaeology, University of Jordan, 1988.

Zak, I. "The Geology of Mt. Sedom." Ph.D. diss., Hebrew University of Jerusalem, 1967.

Zevit, Ziony. "The Biblical Archaeology versus Syro-Palestinian Archaeology Debate in Its American Institutional and Intellectual Contexts." In *The Future of Biblical Archaeology: Reassessing Methodologies and Assumptions*, edited by James Karl Hoffmeier and Alan R. Millard, 3–19. The Proceedings of a Symposium, August 12-14, 2001 at Trinity International University. Grand Rapids, Mich.: Eerdmans, 2004.

Zuhdi, Omar. "Dating the Exodus: A Study in Egyptian Chronology." *KMT: A Modern Journal of Ancient Egypt* 4, no. 2 (1993): 14–20, 22–27.

INDEX OF SUBJECTS

A

a priori 80, 164
Abbasid 107, 110, 130, 198
Abel-Shittim 35, 49, 66, 70, 72, 100, 101, 120, 177, 206
Abila 46, 51, 66
Abila, Bishop of 201
Abraham 28–30, 32, 34–35, 37, 57, 68, 71–74, 89, 91, 94–96, 100, 102–3, 105, 114, 119, 121, 146, 162–64, 179, 180, 203–4
Abu Al-Kharaz, Tell 135
Abu Hureira, Tel 31
acropolis 216
Admah 25, 34, 35, 39, 46, 56, 61, 63, 66, 67, 68, 70, 71, 75, 77, 89, 91, 104, 165, 174, 207, 211
Aegyptiaka 28
Ai 27, 32, 69, 74, 83, 94, 95, 96, 97, 98, 176, 181, 183
Ain Abata (Lot's Cave) 107, 109
Akkadian 38, 87, 98
Albright, William F. 53, 54, 55, 58, 66, 67, 68, 75, 77, 99, 106, 115, 116, 167, 172, 180, 199, 203, 204
Alexandria 41, 49
al-Ghassul, Tulaylat 59, 74, 159
al-Kafrayn, Tall 129, 130, 133, 134, 206
al-Qadi, Tel 32
Amalekites 34
Amenhoptep II 113
Amman 59, 135
Amorites 34, 74, 103, 150, 179, 203
Amos 25, 36
Anastasius 201
ancient Near East 29, 30, 93, 115, 116, 150, 177, 180
antiquity, quotes from 41, 42, 43, 49
aqueduct 216
Arabia 26, 43, 46, 47, 48, 49, 50, 53, 63, 159, 201
Archi, Alfonso 38, 105, 137, 138
Areopolis 36
Areopolis, Bishop of 50, 201
Arnon River 32, 36, 46, 104, 109, 157, 173, 208
ash 41, 43, 45, 107, 119, 141, 142, 145, 146, 151
Ash'-ari, Tel 33
Ashkelon 124
ash-Shaykh 'Īsā, Khirbet 107
Ashteroth-Karnaim 33
asphalt 42, 99, 104, 155, 156, 157, 158, 170
Associates for Biblical Research 27, 57, 83
Asterius Germanus 201
Athens 216
Azeimah 135

B

Baarou 32
Bab edh-Dhra 26–27, 35, 40, 53, 55, 56, 57, 58, 61, 66, 67, 68, 75, 76, 77, 83, 86, 89–91, 99, 100, 102, 104, 106–7, 110, 115–21, 124–28, 140–43, 145, 147–50, 154, 156, 160, 162–65, 168–74, 177–78, 180, 183, 203–4, 210
Babylonian 28, 87, 197
Bala 32, 46
balk 85
Bara, King 25
Barakat 134
Beitin 94
Bela 34, 38, 39
Beni-Hasan mural 115, 179, 204
Beth Haran 36
Bethel 32, 33, 72–73, 83, 94–98, 105, 165, 176, 181, 183
Bethramtha 51
Bible and Spade 27, 56, 210
Billington, Clyde 57, 135–36, 142, 163
Birch, William F. 71, 72, 88, 108, 109, 168, 173
bitumen 34, 42–43, 86–88, 98–99, 147, 154–56, 158, 170, 175
bitumen pits 34, 86–88, 98, 154, 156, 158, 170, 175
Bleibel, Tall 59, 60, 89, 129, 131, 134, 208
Bolen, Todd 57, 162
brimstone 35, 53, 66, 121, 140, 147
British Museum 110, 150
Bronze Age 181
burn 41, 85, 140
Byzantine 32, 36, 40, 49–51, 53–54, 62, 79, 91, 101, 104, 106–8, 110, 129–31, 133–34, 154, 167, 172, 173, 198, 201, 207

C

C-14 date 117–19, 178, 197, 210
Caesarea, Bishop of 46, 201
Callirhoe 32, 46
Canaan 29, 32, 94, 102, 114, 163, 181
Canaanites 29, 31–32, 46
Cappadocia 33
cave 50, 63, 72, 104, 106, 109, 110, 159
cemetery 55, 56, 107, 124–29, 145, 148, 150, 168–69, 181, 206, 211, 212
Cenozoic 160
ceramic typology 27
Chalcedon, Council of 202
Chalcolithic 60, 62, 74, 116, 121, 124–25, 133, 142, 177, 197, 199
Chaldaika 28
chariot 217
charnel houses 117, 126–27, 129, 148–50, 169
Chedorlaomer 33–34, 42, 74, 87–89, 98, 102–3, 172

Index of Subjects

Chesson, Meredith S. 56, 117, 119, 125, 127–29, 148–49, 178, 210–12
Chicago Statement on Biblical Inerrancy 90
Cities of the Plain 25–27, 31–32, 34–35, 37–41, 43–44, 50, 52–56, 60–66, 68–77, 83, 86–89, 96, 98–100, 103–4, 136–38, 140, 146–47, 154, 156, 160, 165–66, 172, 175, 180, 183, 203, 206, 207, 209
Clermont-Ganneau, Charles 65, 82, 167
Cline, Eric H. 80, 164
Cocks, H. G. 64
Codex Theodosianus 48
Conder, Claude Reignier 40, 71, 72, 73, 79, 168
Copenhagen School 27
covenant 102, 204
Crete 139, 184
Cyprion 201

D

Dan 26, 31, 34, 35, 48, 49, 82, 201
date 2350 BC 58, 91, 116–18, 120, 127, 147, 172, 177, 178, 180, 197, 199, 203, 206
dates 29, 38, 48, 68, 91, 112–19, 127, 145, 163, 174, 177, 178, 180, 197, 203, 204, 210
dates, fruit 161
de Saulcy, Louis Felix 64, 167
Dead Sea 25–26, 28, 32–36, 39–49, 52–58, 60–79, 87–90, 92, 95, 97–99, 102–8, 110, 116–19, 121, 125–29, 132, 138, 141, 143, 145–48, 150–78, 183–84, 209–13, 218
Dead Sea Scrolls 28
Deir 'Allā, Tall 97, 131, 135, 175
destruction 25, 35, 38, 40–44, 46, 57, 60, 68, 72–73, 77, 79, 84, 91, 93, 100, 104, 110, 115–20, 124, 127–30, 140–48, 150–51, 154, 160, 162, 165–66, 168, 169, 172, 174, 176–78, 180, 183, 203, 210, 212, 218
Deuteronomy 26, 35
dolmen 72, 146, 168
dunams 121

E

Early Bronze Age 40, 43, 56–58, 67, 68, 75, 77, 79, 81, 85, 88, 108, 110, 115, 117, 121, 124–29, 133–34, 138, 143–44, 163, 165, 173–74, 180, 199, 203, 206–13
Early Bronze I 55, 126–29, 134, 168, 197
Early Bronze IA 56, 116, 125, 127, 149
Early Bronze IB 116–19, 125, 127, 177, 197, 206, 211
Early Bronze II 116, 125–27, 129, 149, 168, 177, 197, 199, 210
Early Bronze III 38, 57, 67, 115–19, 125–27, 129, 131, 139, 140–41, 143, 148–49, 174, 177–78, 199, 203, 210–11
Early Bronze IV 56, 89, 108, 115–18, 125, 127, 129, 130, 133, 141, 173, 177–78, 199, 210, 212
earthquake 35, 42, 62, 64, 65, 98–99, 116, 119, 140, 142, 145–49, 155, 156, 170, 178

Ebla 114, 179
Ebla tablets 37–40, 56, 67, 104, 136–38, 174, 203
Edom 63, 109, 173
Edomite 32
Egeria 47, 48, 49, 50, 52, 201
Egypt 33, 44, 61, 83, 87, 94, 102, 105, 114–16, 124, 138, 165, 177, 179–80, 197, 203–4
Egyptian 28
Eilat 34
Ein Feshkha 64
Ektanu, Tall 66, 70–72, 101, 108
el Mazra'a 66
Elam 74, 87–88, 150
Elamite 33, 42, 87
Elassar 33
el-Dab'a, Tell 138
el-Hasa, Wadi 106, 107
el-Maqatir, Khirbet 27, 83, 94–95, 167
el-Maskhuta, Tell 83
el-Mḥeyyeṭ 36
el-Mushaqqar 108–9, 173, 209
el-Mustah, Tall 59, 60, 89, 129, 131, 134, 208
El-Paran 34
el-Qureiyeh, Khirbet 33
Emim 33, 76
En-Gedi 34, 46, 63–64, 67, 74, 103, 106, 150, 156, 157–58
En-Mishpat 34
Ephesus, Council of 50, 201
Ephraim 35, 199
Epiphanius the Monk 158
er-Rameh, Tall 36, 66, 70–71, 73, 108, 135, 206
es Sharab, Tall 88
esh Sha'ib, Tall 88
esh Shaghur, Tell 108, 173
es-Safi 36, 50, 53, 55–56, 62, 66, 68, 89, 105–10, 126–28, 172–73, 178, 212
eš-Šaġūr, Tell 108, 173
es-Saidiyeh, Tell 97, 175
Eš-Šari'ah, Wadi 31
et-Tawabin, Umm 106, 107
Eusebius 41, 46–47, 50–51, 74, 109, 201
Ewald, Georg H. 167
Ewald, Georg Heinrich 65
Exodus 69, 80, 87, 112–15, 179–80, 197, 203
Ezekiel 37, 86, 90–92, 172, 175

F

Feifa (Fifa) 55–56, 75, 88, 126, 128, 211, 212
figs 161
fire 25, 41–44, 46, 53, 64, 104, 117–19, 121, 140–41, 144, 147, 150, 169, 178, 206
flint 134
Freedman, David Noel 38–39, 56–57, 67, 76, 92, 115, 136–37, 180, 199, 203
frescos 138
Fulco, William J. 60, 166

G

fulgurite	151, 169, 216
Fuller, Thomas	63, 167
Galilee, Sea of	97, 98, 152, 175, 176
gap, Late Bronze	60, 92–93, 133–34, 207
gas	99, 147, 155
gate	66, 75, 109, 116, 127, 138, 142–44
Gaza	31, 61, 136
Gedi, Ein	171
Geikie, John Cunningham	73, 79, 96, 100, 103, 156, 158, 168
Geisler, Norman L.	28, 163, 199, 200, 203, 204
geography	58
Gerar	31, 61
Gezer	82
Ghamr, Wadi	65, 66
Ghor	65, 100, 105–7, 117, 126, 171–72, 212
Gibeon	82
Gilead	35
Gomorrah	25–27, 29, 31–40, 44–45, 52–57, 61–77, 79, 82–83, 87–100, 103–5, 109–10, 126, 136–37, 146–47, 150, 152–54, 158–59, 162–65, 169–76, 179–80, 206, 209–11
Govier, Gordon	57, 80
graben	157, 160, 171, 216
Graham, Peter	63, 167
Great Rift Valley	99, 148, 152, 154, 170
Greek	28
Grove, George	40, 65, 73, 168

H

Ham	33
Haran, Beth	72
Harland, James Penrose	32, 67, 100, 146, 167
Haror, Tel	31
Hattem, Willem C. van	57, 115, 180, 203, 211–13
Hazazon-Tamar	34, 103, 150
Hazor	82, 124, 136
Hebrew	28
Hebron	32, 34–35, 37, 74, 82, 89–91, 95, 100, 171, 181
Hellenism	106, 173, 198
hermeneutics	86, 87, 91, 183
Heshbon	109, 135–36, 163, 209
Hittites	33, 138, 203
Holden, Joseph M.	28, 163, 164, 203–4
Homer	81–83
Horites	34
Horonaim	36
human remains	60, 120, 145
Hyksos	114, 179, 203, 204, 216
hypostyle	138

I

Iktanu, Tall	59, 60, 92, 107–8, 133–34, 173, 206–7, 209
Intermediate Bronze	57, 197, 199, 203
Intermediate Bronze II	124, 199
Iraq	26, 53
Iron Age	28, 56, 60, 79, 82, 85, 91, 101, 107–9, 120–21, 125, 127–30, 133–35, 138, 149, 153, 172–73, 177, 197, 204, 206–12
Iron Age I	85, 120, 130, 133, 200, 208
Iron Age II	85, 128, 134, 206–8, 212
Isaiah	36, 105
Israel	28
Israelites	28, 29, 63, 87, 109, 120, 173, 177

J

Januarius	201
Jebel Usdum	42, 53, 63–66, 104, 158
Jeremiah	36, 86, 91, 92, 105, 172, 175
Jericho	32, 33, 35, 46, 48–49, 68, 71–73, 96, 98, 109, 124–26, 133, 135, 147, 176, 201
Jerome	162
Jerusalem	27, 32, 37, 42, 45, 50, 66– 69, 72, 74, 76, 82, 90–92, 94–95, 97, 124–26, 135–36, 156, 165, 175, 198
Jeshimoth, Beth	70, 72, 100, 206
Jordan	58, 106, 147, 173
Jordan River	32, 42, 44–45, 47, 50, 63, 82, 97, 152, 154, 157, 159, 174–75, 177
Jordan Valley	32, 36, 42, 45, 47, 50, 59, 65, 68, 77–79, 85, 88, 92–100, 103–4, 107, 129, 131–32, 134–36, 159–60, 165, 168–69, 171, 174–76, 183, 203
Josephus	32, 41–43, 62, 65–66, 68–69, 74, 114, 154–55, 160, 162, 165, 170
Joshua	28, 29, 37, 70, 83, 101
Judah	34, 35, 61

K

Kadesh	34, 103
Kadesh-Barnea	34
Kefrein, Tall	60, 66, 70, 72–73, 88, 101, 108, 134, 206
Kerak	55, 63, 162
Khanazir, Khirbet	55, 56, 75, 88–89, 110, 126, 129, 212
Kharbet-Esdoum	64
Khouri, Rami G.	59, 78, 79, 124, 129, 134, 208
kidnapping	139, 184
kikkār	32–33, 35–36, 53, 58, 60, 69, 71–73, 79, 92, 94, 96–100, 131–32, 134–35, 151, 159, 165, 175–76, 181
King's Highway	33, 135
klinker	151, 169
Kufrayn, Wadi	132

L

Lachish 136, 150, 169
Laish 31, 34
Lake Asphaltites 43, 71, 76, 154–55, 170
Lapp, Paul 55, 56–57, 76–77, 83, 115, 125–26, 128–29, 149, 177, 210, 212
Lasa 32
Lasha 31
Late Bronze age 60, 76, 83–85, 100, 101, 130–36, 159, 176–77, 197, 207
legend 30, 53, 61, 79
Letoius 201
lightning 41, 43–44, 140, 147, 151, 169, 216
Lisan 46, 53, 54, 74–75, 87–88, 98, 109, 147, 154, 156–57, 159, 163, 217
Livias 48, 49, 51, 52, 66, 101, 109, 167, 201
Livias, Bishop of 50, 201, 202
Livias, Priest of 50, 201
locus 82, 217, 218
Lot 25, 30, 32–34, 37, 42, 46, 49–50, 57, 63, 65, 68, 71, 72–74, 76, 89, 91–98, 100, 102–3, 105–7, 109–10, 114, 121, 158–59, 163–64, 176, 179, 180, 203
Lot's wife 35, 93, 158, 159
Luḥith 36
Luḥitu 36
Lynch, William F. 63, 158, 167

M

Madaba map 31, 51, 106–7, 154, 167, 173
Madaba Plains Project 81, 136
Madeba 33
Mahawuat, Wadi 157
Mallon, Père Alexis 74, 129, 168
Mamluk 106–7, 130, 198, 211
Mamre 34–35, 74, 100
Manasseh 35
Manetho 28
manuscript 28
Mardikh, Tell 37, 136, 174
Marduk 28
Masada 42, 64, 65, 157
Masoretic 39, 114
maximalist 27, 29, 30, 31
Mazar, Amahai 97, 115, 165, 180, 204
Mazra'a plain 143
Mazra'a, Bay of 109, 173
Mediterranean Sea 35, 102, 135
Megiddo 136
Merrill, Eugene 57, 163, 203
Merrill, Selah 26, 32, 40, 53, 55, 66, 68–69, 88, 97, 100, 105, 107–8, 154, 168, 173, 176, 206
Mezra'a 63
Middle Bronze Age 43, 57, 59, 60, 81, 85, 89, 106, 108–110, 114–15, 120, 124–25, 128–31, 133–34, 139–40, 144–45, 151, 153, 164, 169, 173, 176–77, 179, 180, 197, 199, 203, 205, 206–9
Middle Bronze I 57, 114–15, 133, 179–80, 197, 199, 203, 207, 209
Middle Bronze II 131
Middle Bronze IIA 115, 124, 180, 203
Middle Bronze IIB 120, 176
military 29, 36, 59, 68, 83–85, 92, 119, 125, 142, 150, 178, 199
minimalist 27–31, 61
Minoan 138–39, 183
Moab 33, 35–37, 46, 63, 69, 71–72, 100, 105, 109, 173
Moabite 32, 36, 105, 208
monastery 50, 110
mosaic 106
Mount Nebo 181
Mount of Sodom 42, 53, 159
Mt. Nebo 34–36, 49–50, 82, 98, 101, 108–9, 175–76
mudbrick 119, 124, 127, 130, 140–42, 144, 148
Mujib, Wadi 156
Mullins, Robert A. 164
Musonius 201–2
Mustah, Tall 134, 208
Mwais, Tall 135, 151, 169
myth 61, 82, 91

N

Nabatean 36, 106, 107, 211
Naphtali 35
narrative 25, 30, 37, 60, 72, 83, 86, 90–91, 148, 165, 166, 175
Near East Archaeological Society 163
Negev 35, 36, 50, 83, 102, 115, 179, 204
Neolithic 62, 116, 197, 199, 211, 217
Nicaea, Council of 46–48, 50, 63, 201
Nimrah, Beth 72
Nimrin, Tall 59, 60, 72–73, 79, 89, 129–34, 207–8
Nimrin, wadi 132
Nisya, Khirbet 83, 94
Northern Sodom Theory - NST 27, 32, 36, 40–41, 45, 47, 49, 53, 55, 58, 68, 74, 100, 103, 112, 162, 163, 171
Numeira 55–56, 58, 67–68, 75–77, 89, 110, 115–20, 124, 126–27, 140–41, 145, 149, 159, 164–65, 178, 180, 211
Nuzi 114, 179, 203–4

O

obsidian 151, 169
Ottoman 59, 84, 121, 130, 198
ozocerite 154, 156, 170

P

paiderastia 139, 184
Palæstina 47, 48, 201
Palæstina I 201–2
Palæstina III 48, 50, 201–2

Palæstina Prima	48	Roman	41–43, 46, 48, 51, 65, 79, 91, 101, 106–7, 109–10, 128–30, 134, 172, 198, 200, 207
Palæstina Secunda	48		
Paleolithic	115	roof	150, 169
Palestine	27–29, 36, 44, 46, 48–50, 63–64, 68–71, 73, 76, 104, 179, 199, 203, 206, 217	Russian	54

S

Palestine Exploration Fund (PEF)	69, 71, 73
Palmer, Edward Henry	40, 69, 168
Palynology	135, 217
Pancratius	201, 202
pastoral nomads	55, 116–17, 135
patriarch(s)	30, 57, 112–15, 121, 154, 179–81, 197, 203–4, 217
Paul, the apostle	55, 126
Pella	135
Pentapolis	25, 27, 32–37, 40–50, 53, 55, 58, 61–62, 64, 67–68, 74, 90, 96–99, 103–4, 108, 121, 136–37, 138, 146–47, 160, 167, 170, 174–79, 181, 183, 201
Pentateuch	217
Persian	28, 69, 115, 120, 130, 134, 180, 197, 200, 205
Petra	48–49
Petra, Bishop of	201
petroleum	147, 152, 155–57
Petrus	201
Pharaoh	113, 199
Philadelphia, Bishop of	201
Philistia	31
Phoenicia	31
pilgrimage	55, 110
Pilgrims	52
pillar of salt	35, 65, 92, 93, 103, 158
Pionius	44, 45
piriform juglet	142
Pisgah	35, 63, 72, 101
Pliny the Elder	155, 170
poetic	37, 90, 91, 92
Politis, Konstantinos D.	106–7, 110, 212
Pollen	135
Power, E.	27, 32–37, 40–42, 45, 47–49, 62, 74, 90, 103, 160, 168
Prag, Kay	59, 108, 129, 133, 159, 173, 206, 209
Price, J. Randall	163, 199–200, 203–4
promised land	35, 36, 100, 102

Q

Qarn al Qubish, Khirbet	109, 173, 209
Qasr et-Tuba	106–7
Qazone, Khirbet	125, 148, 168
Qumran	46, 63, 64, 110, 217

R

Rainey, Anson	97, 165
Rast, Walter E.	55–57, 61, 75–77, 83, 86, 89, 115–20, 125–43, 148–49, 163, 177–78, 180, 203, 210–13
Rephaim	33
rift	99, 160
Ritmeyer, Leen	124, 142, 165

Saghîr	72
Salt	63, 65–66, 73, 87–88, 93, 99, 102, 153
salt curse	93
Samaria	37, 89, 90, 91, 92
Schaub, R. Thomas	56–57, 61, 75–77, 83, 89–90, 107, 115–20, 125–29, 141, 143, 148, 163, 177–78, 180, 203, 210–13
Schlegel, Bill	57
Schliemann, Heinrich	82–83
Sebbeh, Wadi	157
Sedom, Mt.	157, 158, 159, 171
Segor	46–49, 65, 71, 106, 108–9, 173, 201–2
Seir	34, 74, 103
Septuagint	218
Serâbît el-Mushaqqar	35, 108–9, 173, 208–9
Severus	46–48, 63, 201
shaft tombs	125
Shaghûr, Tell	71–73
Shaveh-Kiriathaim	33
Shea, William H.	38, 56, 67, 104–5, 138
Sheik 'Issa, Khirbet	107
sherd	81, 85, 89, 101, 120–21, 129–31, 133–34, 142, 151, 177, 206, 209, 216
Shiloh	82
Shinar	33, 61, 150
Shittim	33, 35, 70, 72, 105
Siddim, Valley of	34, 42, 71, 74, 87–88, 98–99, 103, 170–72
Sidon	31, 32, 61
sink holes	34, 87–88, 155, 158, 170–71
skeleton	120, 142, 145
slime pits	42, 43, 87, 99, 155, 170
smoke	35, 41, 43–45, 74, 100, 171
So'ar	32, 35–36, 42, 108, 173
Sodom	57, 60, 137, 164, 166, 181
Sodom apple	44–45
Sodom, Bishop of	46–50, 201
Sodomites	44, 46, 49, 104
Solinus, Gaius Julius	45–46
Southern Sodom Theory - SST	27, 32–33, 36, 40, 42, 45, 47, 56–57, 62–63, 66–67, 72, 79, 97–98, 100, 102, 104, 112, 115, 162–63, 171, 174–76, 180, 203
Stoic	41
Strabo	42, 62, 139, 155, 157, 170, 184
submarine	54
Succoth	97–98, 135, 175, 176
sulphur	41–42, 68, 73, 99, 104, 140, 150, 169–70
Sumer	38, 197
Suweimeh	51, 66, 70, 72, 108, 206

T

Tabor, James D. 164
Tacitus 43, 62, 155, 170
Tahouneh 134
Tall el-Ḥammâm 26–27, 35, 37, 40, 53, 55, 57, 59–60, 62, 68, 70–73, 77–85, 91–92, 99–102, 104, 107–9, 120–21, 124–25, 129, 132, 134–36, 138–47, 151, 154, 159, 162–72, 174–77, 183–84, 204, 206, 216
Tamar 34
tar 87, 99, 155, 157, 170–71
Targum 32
temples 216
Tertullian 44
tesserae 51
Theodosius 108
Thomson, William M. 72, 168
tombs 55, 89, 108, 116–17, 125–29, 145–46, 149, 168, 211–13
Transjordan 35, 48, 74, 76, 98, 136, 159, 176
trinitite 60, 151, 169, 218
Trinity 151, 169
Trinity Southwest University 27, 163, 206
Tristram, Henry Baker 69, 168
Tulaylat al-Ghassul 135
Tutmose III 113

U

Ugaritic 40, 87, 98
Umayyad 91, 101, 107, 110, 130, 172, 198

V

Valley of Siddim 34, 69, 87, 88, 98, 99

vegetation 41, 93, 159
volcano 53, 142, 146, 148, 151, 169

W

wadi 218
Warren, Charles 167
Warren, Sir Charles 65
Wenham, Gordon J. 34, 35, 68, 87, 119, 178
wheat 41, 161
wilderness of Zin 34
Wilson, Charles W. 167
Wilson, Charles William 38, 40, 68, 69, 136
Wolcott, Samuel 25, 64–65, 73, 167
Wood, Bryant G. 83

X

x-ray 59, 84

Z

Zarethan 97, 175
Zarqa River 131
Zeboiim 25, 34–35, 39, 55–56, 61, 67, 75, 88–89, 91, 165, 208, 210, 212
Zoar 25, 31–38, 41, 43, 48–51, 53–54, 56, 62–75, 77, 89, 94, 98, 104–10, 140, 159, 165, 172–73, 176, 181, 201, 208–9, 212
Zoar, Bishop of 50, 201, 202
Zoora (Zoor) 46, 106, 110, 172, 173
Zouera-et-Tahtah, Khirbet 64
Zuweirah, Wadi 158

www.ingramcontent.com/pod-product-compliance
Lightning Source LLC
Chambersburg PA
CBHW082037230426
43670CB00016B/2692